DISCARD

KATANGA SECESSION

KATANGA
SECESSION

by Jules Gérard-Libois

TRANSLATED BY
REBECCA YOUNG

The University of Wisconsin Press

MADISON, MILWAUKEE, AND LONDON   1966

Published by

THE UNIVERSITY OF WISCONSIN PRESS

Madison, Milwaukee, and London

U.S.A.: Box 1379, Madison, Wisconsin 53701

U.K.: 26–28 Hallam Street, London, W.1

English translation copyright © 1966 by the
Regents of the University of Wisconsin

Originally published by

Centre de Recherche et d'Information Socio-Politiques (CRISP)

and Institute National d'Etudes Politiques (INEP), Leopoldville

Copyright © 1963 by Jules Gérard-Libois

Printed in the United States of America

by the North Central Publishing Company

St. Paul, Minnesota

Library of Congress Catalog Card Number 66-22851

Preface

"MAY God protect independent Katanga." With these words, the provincial Council of Ministers headed by Moise Tshombe concluded the declaration of July 11, 1960, by which Katanga proclaimed itself totally independent and requested Belgium to join with it "in a close economic community."

"We are ready to proclaim before the world that the Katanga secession is ended." In these terms, on January 14, 1963, the Council of Ministers headed by Tshombe announced from Kolwezi that it accepted reintegration of Katanga into the Republic of the Congo, in accordance with the Thant Plan of August, 1962.

From July 11, 1960, to January 14, 1963, for thirty months and three days there existed and functioned a Congolese province in secession, set up as a *de facto* state whose independence was officially recognized by no country. These thirty months of secession have, to this day, fed many impassioned polemics but little objective research or study.

Whence came this idea of independence for Katanga? Who sustained it and put flesh on its bones? How and by what powerful means could it be proclaimed, then attempted? What factors finally called a halt to the secession?

It is probably still too early to try to write the whole history of the secession. Useful accounts are still lacking. Sources currently available are often tendentious or incomplete, and vital elements of truth, if they find expression in the press or in declarations and reports of the authorities involved, appear only as allusions or sweeping assertions.

We should like to recount in more modest fashion here what happened in Katanga, aiming thereby to shed light on local and foreign influences on the secession.

This story is based on collections of public sources currently available as well as on oral accounts and unpublished documents, often of a confidential nature, which permit an understanding of the secession and its workings, particularly in matters involving military personnel and assistance or diplomatic action taken with regard to Tshombe's regime.

Some of the sources and documents used here have already been printed in works in the collection "Dossiers du C.R.I.S.P.": *Congo 1959, Congo 1960, Congo 1961, and Congo 1962.*

In order not to overburden the book with long quotations, the reader is referred at times to these works. In addition, a section of relevant or original documents is appended to each part of the book.

The history of the secession cannot be isolated from the process which led to it. The whole story of autonomist or secessionist tendencies among Katanga Europeans throughout the entire colonial period cannot be retraced here. However, it would seem useful to show what stages led to the creation in Katanga of a party whose program essentially demanded autonomy for the province. At the end of June, 1960, the party was in a position of strength, capable of proclaiming Katanga independent, if this solution seemed desirable and possible both to its leaders and to their powerful local supporters.

Contents

Preface   v

Introduction to the Social and Economic Context of Katanga   3

PART I: KATANGA POLITICS BEFORE INDEPENDENCE IN THE CONGO   7

1   Contending Groups and Forces   11

2   The Threat of Secession   31

PART II: KATANGA IN SECESSION   91

3   The Anti-Lumumba Common Front in Elisabethville and in Brussels   93

4   The Period of the Anti-Lumumbist and Anti-U.N. Front   119

5   Before the Trial of Strength in Katanga   185

6   The Trials of Strength in the Second Half of 1961   210

7   From Kitona to Leopoldville: The Adoula-Tshombe Talks   233

8   The Thant Plan for National Reconciliation   253

9   The Final Trial of Force   272

Concluding Observations   277

Appendix I: Documents for Part I   293

Appendix II: Documents for Part II   328

Index   347

MAPS

THE PROVINCE OF KATANGA   32
    June 30, 1960

ELECTORAL MAP OF KATANGA   64
    Elections of May, 1960

RAIL AND RIVER EXPORT ROUTES   117
    From Katanga

DIAGRAM

SOCIÉTÉ GÉNÉRALE IN KATANGA   320

TABLES

1	Population of Katanga before June 30, 1960	3
2	Legislative Elections — Chamber	65
3	Provincial Assembly Elections	66
4	Provincial Elections — Party Votes	67
5	The Katangan Budget	206
6	Percentage of Shares Held by CSK in Other Companies	317
7	UMHK Production	322
8	Principal Stockholders in the UMHK	323
9	Quotations of UMHK Shares on the Brussels Stock Market	324
10	Establishment of Institutions in June, 1960	325

KATANGA SECESSION

Introduction to the Social and Economic Context of Katanga

BEFORE June 30, 1960, Katanga represented, with its 1,654,000 inhabitants, 12.5 percent of the total population of the Congo, but owing to a greater than average rate of demographic increase, the province could rapidly surpass the population of Equateur or Orientale province; according to predictions made by A. Romaniuk in 1959, Katanga could in fact have 3.1 million inhabitants by 1980.

TABLE 1
Population of Katanga before June 30, 1960

District	Total population	Density per sq. Km.
Tanganika	442,716	3.3
Lualaba	271,676	3.1 (excluding Jadotville)
Haut-Lomami	483,223	3.0
Luapula-Mweru	217,972	2.6 (excluding Elisabethville)
Jadotville and Elisabethville	238,589	
Katanga	1,654,176	3.3

The European population of Katanga — 31,887 at the beginning of 1960 — amounted to 2.08 percent of the total provincial population, the highest percentage in the Congo. Although this ratio was comparable to that of Kenya or of Rhodesia, it must be noted that the social and professional composition of this population was markedly different in the two cases. In Katanga, the vast majority of Europeans held salaried positions in the public or private sectors or were self-employed outside the agricultural sector. Compared to the European population of neighboring territories under British influence, that of Katanga was distinguished by

3

its recent arrival[1] and by the existence of numerous Europeans who did not wish to settle permanently in Katanga; this helped to weaken the cohesiveness of the European community and its resistance to political evolution. It was, moreover, very clearly concentrated: 13,808 in Elisabethville and 11,480 in the district of Lualaba, including Jadotville, where the ratio of Europeans in the total population reached 8.08 percent and 3.36 percent, respectively, as against 0.83 percent, 0.82 percent, and 0.70 percent for the districts of Haut-Lomami, Luapula-Mweru, and Tanganika.

The percentage of the Katangan population living outside the traditional milieu as wage earners was 36.18 percent in 1959, the highest in the Congo. The province of Leopoldville, the next highest after Katanga, counted only 27.65 percent of its population outside the traditional milieu; Orientale province, 23.03 percent Equateur, 21.62 percent; Kivu, 19.03 percent; and Kasai, 12.04 percent. These figures clearly show that the degree of industrialization in Katanga was very high, compared to the other provinces or even in absolute terms. It must be noted, however, that the development of the industrial population was due in good part to immigrant labor from other provinces and from Kasai in particular. This fact helped to widen the gulf between the population living in the traditional milieu and that in the *centres extra-coutumiers* (CEC), composed of a mixture of ethnic groups, the most numerous of whom were foreigners to the province.[2]

The great mass of this wage-earning population had to deal with employers whose role encompassed not only the economic functions of society but all social and cultural functions as well, a situation characteristic of the mining regions of Central Africa. The relatively late emergence of political consciousness among the peoples of Katanga must be seen in relation to the particular characteristics of the urban and industrial environment.

At the time of independence, Katanga's agricultural production represented 10 percent of total Congolese production and was insufficient to feed the population. In contrast, Katanga's mining production (estimated

---

[1] 11,341 Europeans in 1947. Compared to other provinces in the Congo, this population appeared to be of fairly long standing.

[2] Translator's note: A *centre extra-coutumier* (CEC) was an urban administrative unit for Africans in which African "chiefs" were selected and closely supervised by the Belgian colonial administration. Urban CEC's correspond to *chefferies*, rural administrative units modeled on the same pattern.

at 11.8 billion Belgian francs)[3] represented 75 percent of Congolese mining production; the province was the sole producer in the Congo of copper (280,403 metric tons, 7,567 million Belgian francs), cobalt, (8,431 metric tons, or 1.7 billion Belgian francs), silver, germanium, platinum, palladium, radium, uranium, and raw zinc concentrates. Because copper represented more than 70 percent of Katanga's mining production, the economy of the province was very sensitive to fluctuations in the world market for this metal. Katanga produced 2,200 million kilowatt hours of electricity (exceeding local demand), had more than 500 kilometers of electrified railroad, 25,000 kilometers of roadbed (6,900 kilometers over "national routes"[4]), and was soon to be linked to Beira in Mozambique.

In the opinion of Professor Fernand Herman in the CRISP publication, *Courrier Africain* (March 4, 1960), the contribution of Katanga to the total resources of the Congo, on the basis of 1957 receipts, was on the order of 5.25 billion Belgian francs out of 11.2 billion, or close to 50 percent. The province's share in Congolese budgetary expenditures other than those of the colonial administration in Belgium and the *gouvernement général* staff in Leopoldville constituted some 20 percent of the total, or 1.24 billion Belgian francs.

[3] Translator's note: There are 50 Belgian francs to one U.S. dollar.
[4] Translator's note: Highways of *intérêt général* or "national routes" were major roads integrated into the national network of railways and roads and underwritten by the central budget.

Part I KATANGA POLITICS BEFORE INDEPENDENCE IN THE CONGO

December 1957–June 1960

THE MOVEMENT for Katangan autonomy is not a product of the years 1957–1960; before that time, however, it had been a monopoly of the Europeans, at least publicly.

In 1910, Katanga, already a special case because of the Comité Spécial du Katanga,[1] was set up under a Vice-Governor-General. This was the work of Colonial Minister Jules Renkin, who wanted to give Katanga "the greatest possible autonomy,"[2] making it in practice dependent on Brussels and not on Boma, first capital of the Congo.

In 1920, Msgr. Jean de Hemptinne, Apostolic Vicar of Katanga, and a group of magistrates and representatives of Katanga European society, suggested transfer of the *Gouvernement Général* from the Congo to Brussels. In this way, there would have been no intermediate links between the Minister of Colonies and the autonomous provinces.

In 1933, the stripping of legislative powers from provincial vice-governors, in favor of centralization under Leopoldville, Boma's successor as capital, provoked violent reactions in Katangan European circles. Their fury was exacerbated by a serious economic crisis in the Congo; the settlers accused Leopoldville of abandoning to a sad fate the "Katangans who had invested all they possessed in the country."[3]

On the occasion of these centralization measures, Jean Sépulchre[4] expressed himself in these terms in *L'Essor du Congo* of July 3, 1933, under the headline "A Demolition Enterprise": "If Leopold II were to

[1] See Appendix I, pp. 316–20.
[2] Declaration to Parliament, February 1, 1911.
[3] *L'Essor du Congo* (Elisabethville), June 25, 1931.
[4] Translator's note: Outspoken editor of the leading Elisabethville daily, *L'Essor du Congo*. After the Katanga secession was proclaimed, *L'Essor du Congo* became *L'Essor du Katanga*.

rise in his tomb, his genial brow would furrow deeply and he would say: 'My intuition did not play me false, alas! They have made a botch of my Congo!' " (" 'Mon intuition ne m'a pas trompé, hélas! Ils me l'ont bien cochonné mon Congo!' ")

Katangan opposition directed against centralization of power in Leopoldville (the symbol of public spending and administrative "megalomania") is linked logically with a strong tendency toward autonomy, or "home rule." To understand this aim, especially after 1954, one cannot underestimate the desire of the Europeans to preserve a certain type of traditional, paternal society. The political, social, and ideological influences, deriving at first from Belgium itself and subsequently from Congolese nationalists in Leopoldville, appeared as dangerous threats. The European was all the more sensitive to such threats, inasmuch as Katanga was, in his eyes, a country where he could settle down and live for a long time to come. In large measure, the whole of local European society reacted unfavorably to anything that might dilute the homogeneity of influences affecting African urban and traditional milieux. This reaction was especially sharp against the transplanting of Belgian parties and trade unions to Congolese soil and against liberal efforts to introduce new religious, ideological, and political currents to Africans.

CHAPTER 1 · *Contending*
Groups and Forces

THE BIRTH OF THE CONAKAT

LESS than two years before the Secretary-General of the United Nations came to Elisabethville in person to meet with Moise Kapenda Tshombe, chief of the Katanga secessionist state, the Conakat, the ethnopolitical group which on Congolese independence day was to hold a monopoly of political power in the copper province, was not yet in existence.

On October 4, 1958, there met for the first time in Elisabethville the group which became the Confédération des Associations Tribales du Katanga, the Conakat. On October 11, 1958, there was elected to the presidency of this group a clerk in the pensions office, Godefroid Munongo, brother of the paramount chief of the Bayeke in Bunkeya, where he himself had been born in 1925. Between the Conakat and the provincial authorities, the first official contact (said to be "very fruitful") took place on October 19, 1958, just exactly one week before the arrival in Elisabethville of the *groupe de travail*, or Working Group, of the Belgian Parliament. This group was to make recommendations on the political future of the Congo.

It is interesting to note that in Leopoldville on October 10, 1958, the Mouvement National Congolais (MNC) carried out its first official act, a motion addressed to the Belgian Minister of the Congo and bearing the signatures of Patrice Lumumba, Cyrille Adoula, Joseph Ileo, Arthur Pinzi, Gaston Diomi, Joseph Ngalula, and Alphonse Nguvulu, among others.

When the founders of the Conakat were asked their reasons for founding this ethnic grouping, they generally invoked the threat to life in the urban and mining centers of a growing ascendancy of immigrants to Katanga from Kasai: "[Our movement] was from the beginning a reac-

tion against the existing situation; it is the work of authentic Katangans
. . . it saw the light of day after the 1957 elections." [1]

We may note in this brief quotation an expression cherished by both
European settler and Conakat leader — "authentic Katangans" — and
the allusion to the 1957 elections.

The "authentic Katangans" were, in the minds of these leaders, all those
who belonged to so-called indigenous [2] ethnic groups, in contrast to
"strangers," [3] recent immigrants, drawn to Katanga by recruiters for the
Union Minière du Haut-Katanga (UMHK) or by the attraction of accelerated industrialization and urbanization in Katanga. Thus, the ethnic
groups considered Katangan (Lunda, Baluba of Katanga, Bayeke, Basanga, Tshokwe, Batabwa, Babemba) were opposed to "strangers," especially from Kasai, be they Lulua or Baluba. [4]

The ethnic distinction of "natives" from "strangers" was essentially
a socioeconomic (and not traditional) phenomenon localized in the cities
and mining centers. It is explained by the presence of important active
minorities, or even majorities, from Kasai in *centres extra-coutumiers* [5]
and by the fact that these "strangers" were drawn from elements socially

---

[1] Declaration of Tshombe in *Le Courrier d'Afrique* (Leopoldville), December 10,
1959.

[2] In fact, "natives, if we so call the inhabitants settled on Katanga territory for
at least two generations, are in the minority." — J. Sauvy, *Le Katanga, 50 ans
décisifs* (Paris: Connaissance de l'Afrique, 1961).

[3] Translator's note: "Strangers" is the term used throughout sub-Saharan Africa
for urban Africans drawn from areas at a substantial distance, outside the immediate hinterland of the city. In West Africa, "strangers" come from beyond the territorial boundaries.

[4] "Baluba and Balubaized, in the broadest sense, refer to a linguistic group
formed by the indigenous population of the Belgian Congo speaking the diverse
Luba dialects: people from the province of Congo Kasai, people from Katanga, and
people from the district of Maniema." — Edmond Verhulpen (ed.), *Baluba et
balubaisés du Katanga* (Anvers: Avenir Belge, 1936), p. 23.

Translator's note: In most Bantu languages, the prefix "mu" refers to an individual member of an ethnic group, "ba" to the group as a whole, and "ki" to the
language. Thus, a Muluba is a member of the Baluba ethnic group and speaks
Kiluba.

[5] Thirty-five percent of the male inhabitants of the *centre extra-coutumier* of
Elisabethville and 53 percent of the workers of Lubumbashi in 1956 were of Kasai
origin. — E. Toussaint, in *Comptes Rendus du Congrès Scientifique d'Elisabeth-
ville*, VI (August, 1950), 45. According to J. Denis in his study, "Élisabethville,
Matériaux Pour une Étude de la Population Africaine," the Baluba of Kasai repre-
sented 26.8 percent of the African population of Elisabethville and the Baluba
Shankadji, 18.1 percent against 6.3 percent Lunda and 4.25 percent Babemba. —
Bulletin du CEPSI, No. 34 (1956), p. 137.

and professionally in the ascendant, in both private and administrative sectors. The perception was not uniform; thus, Baluba of Katanga living in the cities felt close links to Baluba of Kasai by affinities at once ethnic and socioprofessional.

In the traditional milieux, ethnic coexistence nowhere degenerated into violent tensions. In the north and west, the Baluba had preserved a certain sense of unity, an inheritance from the Luba empire which was created about 1500 and survived more or less until 1885.[6] The feeling of community did not, however, call for a Luba nation, regrouping all elements of this ethnic group from east of Katanga to south of Kasai. In their relations with other ethnic groups, numerous in the rural regions of the north, the Baluba constituted a relatively homogeneous and active nucleus.

In the south, rich in deposits of copper and other minerals, the Lunda had preserved fairly strong customary structures and the tradition of the empire of the Mwata Yamvo which stretched to the Rhodesias and Angola. On these lands, the Tshokwe apparently lived in the tradition of the vanquished; conquered after a short victorious period of their own (1885–95), the Tshokwe were in fact awaiting a turn of events which might make another more favorable status possible.

Thus, the rallying platform proposed by the "authentic Katangans" was that of self-defense against the "strangers."[7] This defensive reflex became all the more vigorous in urban centers in 1958 and 1959 when unemployment grew severe,[8] especially among the unskilled workers, and when the colonial authorities began to urge the return of the unemployed to their regions of origin.[9] The "authentic Katangans" of the cities openly accused the authorities of favoritism toward Kasaians: "The native Katangans have good reason to wonder if the authorities did not accord permanent residence permits to the people from Kasai in our towns so

[6] Jason Sendwe, "Traditions et coutumes ancestrales des Baluba Shankadji," *Bulletin du CEPSI*, No. 24 (1954), pp. 116–17.

[7] In 1957 in Elisabethville, 53 percent of employed workers were "strangers," that is, they came from territories outside the province of Katanga. — *Affaires indigènes et main d'oeuvre*, 1957.

[8] The census figures on this subject are to be used with caution. Let us note, however, that at the end of November, 1958, out of a labor force of 45,800 people, the official figure was 7,099 registered unemployed persons in Elisabethville, to which no doubt should be added some 50 percent of this figure for unreported unemployment. Nearly 50 percent of the unemployed are unskilled workers.

[9] In 1958, the administration returned 758 men and their families to their original homes. The traditional authorities were reluctant to see the return of these "city-dwellers."

that the natives [of Kasai] can, because of their ever-increasing numbers, crush those from Katanga." [10] In a region where there was intimate cohesion between public authority and the group of employers who hold a quasi-monopoly on the employment market, the criticism was aimed both at the colonial administration and at the use made of the "social achievements" of Union Minière in recruitment, training, and housing for workers and their families.

Munongo's argument, in his letter to the governor, turned essentially on social factors, while Tshombe's declaration in *Courrier d'Afrique* made allusion to a political fact — the 1957 municipal elections in Leopoldville, Jadotville, and Elisabethville.

At the end of December, 1957, the first elections took place in the five Elisabethville communes. At this point, there existed only one African political party, the Union Congolaise, of Social Christian inspiration, still embryonic in organization and mass appeal. The electoral system adopted was that of single member districts. The tribal factor was undoubtedly operative in the four African communes and especially in favor of candidates whose ethnic group was the most tightly knit. This was not, however, the sole factor as is often said. Even in the absence of parties, a certain clandestine para-political life existed in the African communes, oriented against the settlers and the colonial administration. Of the four communal African burgomasters appointed [11] after the balloting, none was named on the basis of an "authentic Katangan" return. Three were

[10] Letter from the president of the Conakat, Godefroid Munongo, to Governor André Schoeller, February 13, 1959.

[11] Translator's note: Elections to the communal councils took place during 1957 in Leopoldville, Elisabethville, and Jadotville, and during 1958 in Coquilhatville, Stanleyville, Bukavu, and Luluabourg. The cities were divided into communes of 20,000 to 30,000 voters each, which elected communal councils from single member constituencies within each commune. In the 1959 communal elections, the voting system was changed to proportional representation so that candidates ran either on party slates or as individuals in the multimember constituency, the commune. Each elected council in turn nominated a communal burgomaster, usually from its own ranks. Although the colonial administration reserved the prerogative of rejecting the burgomaster nominations and appointing one of its own choice, in fact, the wishes of the communal councils on the selection of burgomasters were by and large respected.

In the competition for burgomaster posts, the parties sought to rally to their side the communal councilors who had run as individuals, on no party ticket. Frequently, the parties resorted to violence to win adherents on the communal councils, especially following the 1959 elections. See pp. 53–55.

The May, 1960, elections to the provincial assemblies and to the national Chamber of Representatives also were held under a system of proportional representation.

from Kasai; the fourth, appointed in Albert commune,[12] belonged to a Bakusu clan (Kivu) and owed his election to the role he played in a trade union organization active in behalf of African *evolués*.[13]

After these elections, the "authentic Katangans," like the Bangala of Leopoldville in regard to the Abako burgomasters,[14] accused the elected Kasaians of favoritism toward their compatriots. The political victory and the favorable social position of the "strangers," they attributed to the absence of an electoral cartel to unite Katangan ethnic groups.

The "strangers" themselves were indeed organized in such a way as to spread fear among the leaders of the underprivileged natives, thus providing the grounds for the indigenous ethnic confederation desired. A federation of Kasaians was established in 1955 under the name of the Association de Baluba-Central Kasai au Katanga,[15] then rechristened November 18, 1957, under the name Fegebaceka. This association was based upon a certain degree of linguistic-cultural unity and common behavior toward Katangan ethnic groups other than the Baluba from the north. The Fegebaceka was noteworthy not only for being composed of Kasaians, particularly active in the entourage of the burgomasters, but also for being openly in opposition to the values and groups within European society in Elisabethville (mission school, newspaper, and settler association in Katanga, UMHK social work, and especially the dispensaries). The Katangan *Sûreté*[16] also accused the Fegebaceka of being illegally in contact with African nationalists from Rhodesia and with the Abako.[17]

[12] Albert commune, 16,500 inhabitants; Kenia commune, 52,474; Ruashi, 15,000; and Katuba, 55,038; Elisabeth commune, the so-called European commune, numbered 22,600 inhabitants and the zone around Elisabethville, 6,455, for a total of 168,700.

[13] Antoine Rubbens, "La consultation populaire du 22 décembre 1957 à Elisabethville," *Problèmes sociaux congolais*, No. 42 (September, 1958), pp. 77–81. (Translator's note: *Evolué* throughout French-speaking Africa is the term employed for educated Africans who have left their traditional milieux.)

[14] Translator's note: The Abako, a Bakongo ethnic-political movement, had swept elections held at the same time in Leopoldville.

[15] Bylaws approved by the Haut-Katanga district commission, July 12, 1955.

[16] Translator's note: In the Congo, the police operated on three levels: the *Sûreté* for the colony as a whole with its headquarters in Leopoldville, the various provincial *Sûretés*, and the provincial police. By the same token, there were also the army for the entire colony — the *Force Publique*, which, after independence, became the *Armée Nationale Congolaise* (ANC) — as well as the provincial gendarmeries.

[17] Through a "Mouvement du Peuple," spawned on the fringes of Fegebaceka, and by means of a relegated (exiled) Kimbanguist, Emmanuel M'Bamba, Finance

As if by coincidence, the Conakat was born just at the moment when the most "hard-line" organization confronting it disappeared: on November 10, 1958, the Fegebaceka was dissolved. Investigations took place; arrests were made; President André Kadima was imprisoned and Baudouin Kayembe, secretary, was forbidden to reside in all but three of the twenty-two territories in Katanga. Thus, the group which caused most concern among the founders of the Conakat as well as among Europeans in Elisabethville was officially eliminated.

The identical reaction of these two groups toward the activities and dissolution of the Fegebaceka contributed in great part to strengthening the view that the Conakat had originated in the missions and in European right-wing, colonialist circles and that it was directed against the Kasai element, as being a group over politicized, if not "gangrenous," through contact with Leopoldville and allegedly dominant leftist [18] influences.

Thus, when we look into the motives of the Conakat's African founders, we must take into account the anti-Kasai reflex, realizing, however, that its true importance is not exclusively ethnic; it involves very broad factors of social competition, as well as of cultural and political opposition.

Likewise, probably the constitution of the Working Group on the political future of the Congo hastened the creation of a group like the Conakat, which could thus present itself to the representatives of the three Belgian parties as spokesman for "authentic Katangans." The provincial administration for its part tried to show that it indulged in no tribal favoritism; thus it helped to stimulate the creation of the Conakat.

Evariste Kimba, who was in May and June, 1960, deputy *chef de cabinet* [19] of the Belgian Minister resident in the Congo, W. J. Ganshof van der Meersch, then in the autumn of 1960 Katanga's Foreign Minister,

---

Minister in the Adoula government from June, 1962, to June, 1964. (Translator's note: The Kimbanguist movement, a separatist Bakongo church, had long been held subversive by the colonial administration, and persons active in the sect were relegated, or exiled, to distant parts of the Congo.)

[18] In the Belgian sense of the term: Liberal or Socialist, that is to say, anti-clerical, hostile to the monopoly of the Catholic missions.

It must always be remembered that Dr. Van Eeckhout, first official Conakat adviser, who was suggested by the provincial administration, belonged to the State University in Elisabethville.

[19] Translator's note: Under the Belgian (and later Congolese) parliamentary system, each minister has two staffs: that of the ministry itself composed of permanent civil servants and that of his own *Cabinet* which he personally selects to offer him political advice. Kimba was deputy-chief of the latter. *Cabinet* is also used in reference to the Council of Ministers.

has produced his version of the origins of the Conakat.[20] A Muluba from Katanga who rallied to the Conakat, Kimba underlined among the objectives of its founders — aside from the desire to avoid repetition of the electoral experience of December, 1957, and aside from the protest against "the fatal policy" of the administration and big business favoring the immigrants from other provinces — the wish "to demonstrate to the settlers that Katanga was not a desert before the arrival of the Europeans and that this province could not be made to serve (as some settlers had hoped, for reasons abundantly clear) as a region for massive European settlement." In texts and declarations of the Conakat leaders in 1958 and 1959, few traces of a similar underlying antisettler animus had been visible.

To the extent that, from the outset, African founders of the Conakat were in direct contact with Europeans — especially those who belonged to the urban settler circles (self-employed European residents) — the motives of the latter seem clear. In October, 1958, their concern was to show that Africans were not all fiercely antisettler, as were those of the Fegebaceka, all of whose activities jeopardized the social and political organizations of the white settlers. Their concern was equally to ensure that "authentic" Katanga expressed itself either in a single voice or in concordant voices before the parliamentary working group.

In case the "extremists" from Leopoldville should decisively influence the Belgian governmental declaration on the future of the Congo, anticipated for late 1958 or early 1959, the Elisabethville settler group felt it indispensable to give Katanga a "moderate" African spokesman. The moderate voice had to appear as the expression of a common front of all the local ethnic groups and in this way claim the role of sole party and negotiator to exert effective pressure on the colonial authority.[21]

[20] J. Gérard-Libois and Benoît Verhaegen, *Congo 1960* (Brussels: CRISP, 1961), I, 226.

[21] It may be noted that the Ucol spokesman in 1952 had a very poor opinion of the "authentic Katangans" on whom the Conakat was to be based in 1958 and 1959. They were considered especially incompetent, and, because of their lack of ability, the UMHK recruited "stranger" workers. It is also to be noted that, if the Ucol were in principle favorable to the development of independent professions among the Africans, its recommendations and reports to the Belgian authorities insisted above all on the necessity for review of the "current educational system of the natives [which] tends to focus on intellectual rather than professional training," in order to direct it toward the vocational training of masons, mechanics, carpenters, etc. — Ucol Memorandum, August, 1952.

THE SETTLERS ORGANIZE: UCOL AND UNION KATANGAISE

Who were these Europeans and what did they represent in Katanga? In the first place, among the direct sponsors of the Conakat were to be found the directors of the Ucol-Katanga (Union pour la Colonisation) and of the Rassemblement Katangaise. The Ucol was created in May, 1944, to promote European settlement.[22]

Katanga had, at the end of 1957, some 3,065 settlers while the five other provinces had a total of 6,550. Among the settlers in Katanga, 50 percent were of Belgian nationality (1,536); the other important national groups were Greeks (507), Italians (519), Britons (177), Portuguese (100), and French (63). Nearly a third of the settlers were members of professional associations: 923 belonged to the Ucol-Katanga and 52 to the Union des Planteurs et Agriculteurs du Katanga (Upak).[23] Consequently, in Fédacol, the federation linking provincial settler associations of the Congo and Ruanda-Urundi [after 1962, Rwanda, Burundi], the influence and importance of the Ucol-Katanga was considerable after 1950. According to its bylaws (Article 10), the General Council of the Fédacol could take no decision without the support of three quarters of its dues-paying members (a total of 2,595 in January, 1959). This meant that no action was possible without the accord of the Ucol-Katanga.

Among the leading activities of organized settler pressure groups must be cited — especially after 1952 — a vast campaign in favor of white settlement, with the slogan "one hundred thousand Belgian settlers within ten years or the Congo will no longer be Belgian."[24] Especially in Kivu

[22] The settler, in the sense in which it was understood in the Belgian Congo, was "any person who resided in the colony and exercised there, on his own, some sort of professional activity." Article 75, Decree of September 10, 1951. At the end of 1957, nearly 40 percent of the settlers in the Congo were traders; 27 percent were manufacturers and artisans; 20 percent farmers; 9 percent came from the liberal professions or had independent incomes.

Since 1923, there has existed an Association des Colons belges au Katanga which was joined in 1934 to the Fédération des Groupements et Associations du Katanga, a pressure group seeking to obtain aid for settlers from the colonial administration after the great economic depression.

[23] See on this subject: "La Fédération congolaise des classes moyennes (FÉDA-COL), organisation et action des colons au Congo," *Courrier Hebdomadaire du CRISP*, No. 25 (July 3, 1959). In interpreting these figures it must be noted that double affiliations were numerous.

[24] The view was favorably received at this stage by European opinion frightened in the climate of the cold war between East and West. It must be noted that the representative of the Comité Spécial du Katanga in Africa was skeptical about the Ucol scheme for white settlement of 600,000 hectares on the plateaus of the Kun-

and Katanga, the objective was to transform the colonial emphasis in these provinces from administration to settlement. O. Defawe, president of the Ucol-Katanga, attached his name along with that of Charles Bonte, spokesman for the Orientale settlers, to a "plan for European settlement" calling for the creation of blocs of 8,000 to 10,000 Europeans in regions of moderate climate, to the east and north of the Congo. These blocs would be "firmly in the hands of Europeans," and no indigenous labor would be employed. In his argument, Defawe explicitly declared on August 18, 1952, to Colonial Minister André Dequae: "Nothing in the past of the Congolese justifies any rights whatsoever to the whole of the country. They have never created anything — not a motor, not a wheelbarrow — nothing. We have lifted them out of cannibalism and slavery."

Aside from this theme of European settlement, the Ucol defended with particular fervor what it called decentralization, i.e., a re-establishment of vice-governors-general to head the provinces and a status of real autonomy for the provinces. In fact, the settlers essentially demanded a transfer of power from Belgium and from Leopoldville to the provinces, where their capacity for pressure was greater and where it could be exercised on most political issues, along with that of the rest of the local European establishment (missions, companies, administration).[25] Thus, the settlers demanded that "power be situated in the Congo and vested in the hands of a viceroy." This could have been the brother of the King, who would reside in the Congo and be responsible for coordinating action of royal commissioners or vice-governors-general, who would enjoy real power in the autonomous provinces.[26]

The Congolese society envisaged by the Ucol was, in the cities, a soci-

---

delungu, from whence the colonization movement would then spread out to the valley of the Lufira, designated, after irrigation, to become the granary of Katanga. — *Revue Nouvelle*, Brussels (October 15, 1950), p. 321.

[25] Very often, the settlers or the Katangan press favorable to their views claimed the sponsorship of Professor Arthur Doucy to defend their program, referring to his study, "Sociologie coloniale et réformes de structure," *Revue de l'Université de Bruxelles*, IX (1957), 212–29. In this study, he disputed "the possibility of applying a single policy to the entire Congo" and advocated a structural reform to replace *the colony* of the Congo by *several colonies*, responsible directly to Brussels and each having at its head a royal commissioner. If in fact this reform entailed the abandonment of the notion of Congolese territorial unity, Doucy's scheme also sought to maintain a unity of direction and of political responsibility in Brussels, which was not the case with the reforms desired by the settler colony. (Translator's note: Professor Doucy was Director of the Institut de Sociologie Solvay and a prominent member of the Belgian Socialist Party.)

[26] General Council of Fédacol, June, 1957.

ety with strictly balanced political organs, "securing parity of representation to Whites and Blacks."[27] The element of order in this society was
to be constituted by settlers and by self-employed groups both European
and African. The sociopolitical "strategy" of the settlers was to seek a
transfer of social tensions from the ethnic to the class level. This strategy
is expressed very well in the confidential note delivered by the settler representative to the Colonial Minister, March 3, 1955:

> It is necessary to organize a class of native *evolués*, who will declare them-
> selves in accord with the ideals and principles of our Western civilization
> and who will be, with equal "status," our equals in rights and duties; less
> numerous than the indigenous mass, but powerful and influential, they will
> be those allies indispensable for us in the indigenous communities. These
> middle classes will be the black *bourgeoisie* who are beginning to emerge
> everywhere, whom we must help to advance economically and to organize,
> and who, like all the *bourgeois* in the world, will be opposed to any upheaval
> in the system from within or from without.
> There will no longer be differences of race, but, as in the rest of the world,
> there will be only differences among the classes, these remaining open to all.

The black *bourgeoisie* in Elisabethville was represented in 1957 and
1958 by the leaders of the Association des Classes Moyennes Africaines
(Acmaf), among whom were Isaac Kalonji from Kasai and Moise
Tshombe of Lunda origin, a wholesale merchant.

On June 21, 1958, the Ucol reached an agreement with Isaac Kalonji
by which, "on the grounds that there existed in the Congo a common
interest among all self-employed, devoid of any racial discrimination,"
the Ucol and the Acmaf-Katanga decided to cooperate and to create
"offices in common between the existing associations." Based on this
agreement, Joseph Onckelinx and Jean Humblé said they were mandated
to speak in behalf of the African middle class at the *Commission du
Colonat*, or Settlers' Commission, at the meeting on July 11, 1958. The
legality of the agreement was disputed by Tshombe and by the Acmaf-
Brussels.

To what extent did the non-settler Europeans of Katanga — the employees in the private sector and the administrators — identify themselves
with the views of the Ucol? To what extent, in particular, did these groups
of Europeans share the Ucol's opposition to the introduction of trade
unionism, to activities of Belgian political parties, and the Ucol's scarcely

[27] Fédacol declaration, July, 1955.

disguised hostility to political direction by Brussels and to administrative direction by Leopoldville?

These questions were answered in the election of December, 1957; in Elisabethville and in Jadotville, candidates sponsored by the Ucol ran in European quarters against candidates claiming to represent Belgian political tendencies. Candidates endorsed by the Ucol won nearly all the seats. This success was due to the great number of votes cast by salaried employees, laborers, and public officials — to the choice of persons called upon to live in the Congo, rather than to votes cast by true settlers, the farmers who, residing for the most part in outlying areas (*"en zone annexe"*), were not included on the list of electors.[28]

The Ucol was thus permanently engaged in a campaign of pressure on the Belgian authorities in favor of European settlement and provincial autonomy. Strengthened by the electoral results of December, 1957, it used the threat of secession constantly as a means of pressure:

> Colonies have revolted against direction by the metropolitan power, when the latter did not concern itself with regional differences nor take into account the legitimate aspirations of the colonial peoples.
>
> The Belgians revolted in the last century because an administration which was too centralized disregarded their aspirations, their desires, their needs. . . . Wedged in between stabilized colonies, Katanga has a high rate of [European] immigration, which exerts an ideological and social influence upon it.
>
> Autonomist tendencies have appeared and discontent with the excessive centralization of the *Gouvernement Général* has increased. A policy which ignores the vested rights of the settlers, the most numerous and established in the Congo, would be dangerous and could have regrettable repercussions.[29]

In February, 1958, the political orientation of some Ucol leaders was clearly expressed. Clamorous demonstrations, in which the organizers tried to involve Africans, were organized against Colonial Minister Auguste Buisseret during his visit to Elisabethville. What did Buisseret symbolize in the eyes of the demonstrators? Was he simply the person responsible for a Congolese economic policy, a cause for complaint by certain

[28] Rubbens, "Consultation populaire du 22 décembre 1957 à Elisabethville," p. 79. It is probable that the rallying was strengthened by the fact that the top administration had put pressure on colonial officials not to stand for election. A number of voters tried to vote against "imported" (i.e., Belgian) trade union organizations and political parties.

[29] "Notre politique," by the Central Committee of Ucol, *Eurafrica* (Fédacol journal), No. 1 (September, 1957).

settlers, victims of the economic crisis?[30] Or the Liberal Minister who
founded the official university at Elisabethville and public schools throughout the Congo — actions vigorously criticized in the press and by conservative Catholic circles?[31] Or the Minister who was bitterly reproached
by European civil servants for proposing the integration of African and
European under a single civil service code and pay scale? Or was he
simply a symbol of a colonial mother country which understood nothing
about Katanga?

The response to these questions was unclear, both among Europeans,
who hoisted hostile signs ("Death! To the gallows!"), and among Africans, who defended "the liberator of the Congolese." This confusion
and ambiguity is important, for it was to create a stereotype of the contending forces, less perhaps on the basis of the existence of ties among
groups of a given bloc than on the basis of images of unity and opposition.

Thus emerged the pattern of cartels or at least of groupings and collu-
sions among, on the one hand, European settlers, "authentic Katangans,"
conservative and Catholic Europeans in both public and private sectors,
as well as in missionary circles; and, on the other hand, "unruly" African
elements from Kasai, Europeans of a secular anticlerical persuasion, and
black and white "progressives."

In February, 1958, the president of the political commission of the
Ucol, Achille Gavage, advocated the creation of a single party in Katanga,
open both to settlers and to employees in the public and private sectors.
In May, 1958, the Union Katangaise was born, becoming quite firmly
rooted in Elisabethville and, to a lesser degree, in Jadotville and Kolwezi.[32]

At the beginning, the party undeniably benefited from certain key
assets among European circles: the Ucol framework; the good will of the
daily newspaper *L'Essor du Congo*, which, while denying it had had any
role in founding the Union, considered its ideas "firmly related to those
which we hold" and promised friendly consideration of "the weighty
and intelligent words of its principal spokesman, A. Gavage";[33] appre-

[30] Translator's note: A 50 percent decline in world copper prices in 1957 had
produced a sharp recession on the Copperbelt.

[31] "Liberal" in the Belgian sense of the term, that is to say, a partisan of secular
education. From 1955 to 1958 there prevailed in Belgium a "school war" which
opposed the Socialist and Liberal "Left" to the Social Christian "Right"; this war
was also waged for a time in the Congo.

[32] Its membership numbering 550 dues-paying members (50 Belgian francs
apiece per year) in August, 1958; and 600 dues-paying members (300 Belgian
francs) in June, 1959, according to reliable estimates.

[33] *L'Essor du Congo* (Elisabethville), May 28, 1958.

ciable financial support, and so forth.[34] In contrast, the personality of Gavage, "a veritable prophet of his doctrine"[35] provoked misgivings in European federalist circles — misgivings that extended to the methods of the Union Katangaise. They feared that the demonstrations and activities of the Union would compromise among Africans the ideas he defended and would furnish a basis for strong resistance in Leopoldville and Brussels. To Kasaians, members of the Union Congolaise, and anti-settler Africans, the Union Katangaise immediately took on the image of an implacable enemy, incarnating the position of European extremists. The Fegebaceka demonstrations, the editorials in African newspapers like *Notre Opinion*, or the column reserved to the Union Congolaise in *Katanga* were all expressions of African opinion, violently hostile to the Union Katangaise, to its positions, or to views attributed to it by its adversaries.

The Union Katangaise program, published at the end of June, 1958, essentially stressed the division of the Congo into large autonomous regions, the federation of these territories with Belgium "as equal partners," as well as the encouragement of immigration from Belgium and other Western nations. We may note in this program a call for "the assignment of garrisons of troops from Belgium to all the large centers of Katanga."

According to Antoine Rubbens, certain publications of the Union Katangaise proposed to adjust the frontiers of Katanga to include the diamond fields of Kasai; they sought an active Belgian military presence to defend European centers against "foreign enemies or others"; they demanded the outlawing of labor unions and extolled the glory of the Rhodesian regime. Some leaders of the Union Katangaise, according to Rubbens, demanded that the Katanga-Rhodesia road be improved to facilitate commercial and military traffic.[36]

The Elisabethville political climate in August, 1958, was rather tense at the arrival of Léon Pétillon, former Governor-General of the Congo, called to be Minister for the Congo in a homogeneous Social Christian government which had just succeeded (although, it turned out, only temporarily) Achille Van Acker's Socialist and Liberal government. The Union Katangaise had, according to African sources, let it be understood

[34] By way of example, a gift of 50,000 Belgian francs by Mr. G[uillaume], president of the Comité Spécial du Katanga.

[35] As the *Sûreté* in Elisabethville said of him.

[36] "La confusion politique au Katanga," *Revue Nouvelle*, Brussels (October, 1958), pp. 308–13.

that Pétillon shared its point of view.[37] The Africans intended to convince the Minister of their hostility to the Union Katangaise and they expressed it by daubing crude slogans on the walls and putting up posters in Kenia commune on his arrival ("Down with federalism!" "Down with the Union Katangaise!")

On August 21, the Minister made public a declaration which must have bitterly disappointed the Union Katangaise, even if it did not close all doors for the future: "There is no question at the moment of promoting any federal system whatsoever, nor of extensive autonomy for the provinces, nor, above all, of any modification or alteration of the policy which, in accordance with the unanimously expressed desire [of the Africans], looks toward the establishment of a Belgo-Congolese community."

This idea was confirmed, and renewed with increased vigor, on September 1, 1958, in the opening speech to the *Conseil de Province:*

It is beyond doubt that the only formula which, at the present time and for long years to come, is suitable for this country is the unitary formula. We have created the Congo and we have every reason to be proud of it. We have given it highly centralized institutions, which conform to the spirit of our race and which have inevitably engendered over the long run among the inhabitants, who were at one time ignorant of each other's existence, the concept of a nation and the budding of a kind of nationalism.

In this context of a provisional setback for European settlers,[38] the only realistic way to relaunch the views of the Union Katangaise was to have Africans assimilate them and take up their defense.

These events came — we must recall — on the eve of the creation of the Conakat.

CONAKAT 1959 AND THE BALUBAKAT CARTEL

At the beginning of its existence, the Conakat took scarcely any definite political positions, contenting itself with affirming — as on December 21, 1958, on the occasion of a welcoming demonstration at Leopold II

[37] In July, 1958, the Union Katangaise published in *L'Essor du Congo* an open letter to Léon Pétillon, assuring him of its confidence and reminding him that he had already declared himself a partisan of a federation of larger territories in the Congo. On the eve of Pétillon's arrival, the Union Katangaise published its program and a facsimile of the Minister's letter of acknowledgement in response to the congratulations tendered to him by the Union Katangaise on his nomination. On August 19, a Union Katangaise delegation was received by Pétillon at Elisabethville.

[38] A setback which was celebrated by the Africans, who organized a big parade to mark the occasion.

Stadium in honor of Vice-Governor-General André Schoeller — that it intended to help "safeguard the interests of all Katangans," including those in rural areas, and that it acted legally and favored the peaceful coexistence of Europeans and Africans. It did not participate directly in campaigns launched by the settler community, such as one aimed to be a massive protest against replacement of Léon Pétillon ("technician" Minister with royal backing) by Maurice Van Hemelrijck (Social Christian Senator, president of Boerenbond, a farm association, and former Minister of Education) at the Ministry of the Belgian Congo and Ruanda-Urundi.[39]

At this stage, the Conakat included the several ethnic associations of so-called native Katangans and, from February 5, 1959, attached even the Association of the Baluba, founded in 1957 by Jason Sendwe (a Muluba from Katanga) to promote Baluba unity.[40] Sendwe was a member of the Protestant Council of the Congo. Among the Conakat member associations were the following:

Group of Mutual Associations of the Lunda Empire (Gassomel)
Association of the Baluba (Balubakat)
Association of the Basonge
Federation of Tribes of Haut-Katanga (Fetrikat)
Association of the Bena Marunga
Association of Bahemba Peoples (Allibakat)
Association of the Minungu.

The Belgian governmental declaration of January 13, 1959, was greeted with strong misgivings in traditional Lunda and Bayeke circles,[41] particularly with respect to the introduction of universal suffrage at the territorial level. From that point forward, the Conakat became progressively more involved in the publication of political programs strongly

[39] These demonstrations did not spread to African quarters. The Union Katangaise demanded the retention of Pétillon by telegram to Prime Minister Gaston Eyskens on November 4, 1958. The African mass remained totally indifferent.

[40] Sendwe specified, on this occasion, that membership in the Conakat could not deprive his organization of autonomy in leadership and action. This was theoretically the legal situation of all member associations of the Conakat. At the beginning, membership was confined to associations. Later, the Conakat did recruit individual members, but its central committee sought to remain a cartel representative of ethnic associations.

[41] See on this subject the declarations of the Mwata Yamvo in *Congo 1959* (2nd ed.; Brussels: CRISP, 1961), p. 84, and those of his son Mbako Ditende in the presence of the Belgian minister at Sandoa in June, 1959: "We do not understand the haste of many to have independence."

inspired by the views of the Ucol and the Union Katangaise and in direct cooperation with the leaders of these organizations.

On May 26, 1959, under the presidency of Godefroid Munongo,[42] the Conakat opted for a Katanga, "autonomous and federated," headed by "authentic Katangans or men of good will who have given proof of their devotion to the cause of Katanga." There would be a federal Congo in the future only if each autonomous state secured a part proportionate to its economic importance. In the same proclamation, the Conakat denied to anyone else the "right to represent Katanga." In a text which was supposed to be conciliatory and was published in Kolwezi by the *Phare du Katanga*, July 3, 1959, the Conakat stated that it should be understood that the party would "henceforward fight assumption of any power whatsoever in this province by a non-Katangan." This claim to a monopoly of representation in Katanga was strengthened, among the Conakat leaders, after June, 1959, when the "Union Katangaise of Elisabethville and its current or future sections" were officially admitted to the Conakat by the central committee.[43] "The Conakat can therefore now say that it represents the interests of Africans and Europeans in Katanga," the central committee declared on July 13, 1959, after the admission of the Union Katangaise.

On July 11, 1959, in view of the elections scheduled for the end of the year at the communal and territorial level, the Conakat decided "to adopt a name appropriate to its political activity. . . . It has thus been suggested that the political association, directed and controlled by the Conakat, take the following name: The Rassemblement Katangais, political party of the Conakat." This title was rarely used but it is interesting to note that in mid-1959, less than a year before the independence of the Congo, the Conakat accepted the affiliation of a European political group such as the Union Katangaise and recognized in it, within the framework of a political campaign, a monopoly for recruitment of members and solicitation of support among European circles. At this moment, the Conakat broadened its program to appeal outside the urban areas, particularly with plans for rural development, fully "respecting the vested rights of traditional authorities."

[42] In May, Munongo made it known — after receiving a warning and reprimand from the colonial administration — that his duties as territorial agent would no longer permit him to preside over the Conakat. In the second half of the year, Tshombe succeeded him; in December, 1959, Munongo became a member of the board of directors of Inga, the proposed dam complex in the Lower Congo, development of which has now been indefinitely postponed.

[43] In fact, the fusion had existed since March, 1959.

In October, November, and December, 1959, links between the leaders of the Union Katangaise and the Conakat were strengthened, the former furnishing "technical and material aid" to President Tshombe, as a member association, with help garnered directly from European circles. The influential role of the Union Katangaise was particularly great at this time when the Conakat lost the participation of the important Association of Baluba of Katanga (Balubakat) and when the first electoral contest took place since the creation of parties or ethnic groups functioning as parties.

The Balubakat resulted from the regrouping of a series of Baluba associations from several large chiefdoms represented in Elisabethville (for example, Mutombo, Mukulu, Kabongo). The bylaws were drafted January 17, 1957, and appeared January 26 in the *Etoile Nyota*. They were accepted by the colonial authorities on June 14, 1957, all the more readily because they set as goals of the association the promotion of mutual aid among the Baluba as well as harmony between them and their "civilizers." The formal inauguration took place, according to Sendwe, on July 27, 1957.

The first president elected was Jason Sendwe and the two losing candidates, Evariste Kimba and Bonaventure Makonga, rallied in the end to the Conakat.[44] In 1958, Sendwe visited Belgium as a medical assistant at the World's Fair, and was not involved in the Fegebaceka incidents nor in the actual genesis of the Conakat. He and his friends joined the Conakat despite the leading roles played in it by Kimba and Makonga (the latter expelled from the Balubakat on April 23, 1958). However, they became cool toward the Conakat from the spring of 1959 onward, because of its relations with the Union Katangaise and of its violently anti-Kasai positions, which were not easily acceptable to men of Luba ethnic groups maintaining some solidarity with the Baluba of Kasai. Attempts at reconciliation took place, but they failed; the Conakat refused to accept the conditions posed, namely, denunciation of the accord reached with Union Katangaise and the revision of its attitude toward "stranger" workers, especially those from Kasai.

As it drew away, the Balubakat rejected all the more clearly the Conakat theses (in particular, separatism); it felt that the settler community

---

[44] See the biographies in Appendix I, pp. 294–95. Evariste Kimba had already tried to organize the Baluba — since 1952, according to Bonaventure Makonga — but the latter accused him of badly managing the funds and the association was dissolved. Makonga himself was at odds with Rémy Mwamba, the Balubakat vice-president, and he led a grouping called "Balubakat pro-Conakat" with limited influence.

and the Conakat wished to use this proposal, at least as a means of pressure, to eliminate the Baluba of Kasai from the political and social scene in Katanga.

Vice-Governor-General Schoeller, at least, was persuaded that the threat was not illusory. While acting as Governor-General *ad interim* in Leopoldville, and influenced in part by the situation in the Bas-Congo, he wrote in August, 1959, a report to the Colonial Minister which advocated concessions in the direction of federalism for the Congo:

> We must, of course, do all we can to end up with a strong federal power. In opting for this system, we must also assure serious guarantees to minorities. I am thinking notably of the very large Kasai minority in Katanga (about 38 percent of the population and 50 percent in some centers).
>
> This group fears, and not without reason, a federalist regime; in the background, "authentic Katangans" have expressed many times their intention of treating them as "strangers." The opposition would come from these important minorities of Katanga and Leopoldville rather than from other provinces.[45]

Having morally, then formally, broken with the Conakat,[46] was the Balubakat going to be involved in politics? Sendwe hesitated for some time; then, taking account of the urgency (communal elections), he joined the campaign, in some cases under the Balubakat label, in others under that of the Parti Progressiste Katangais (PPK), alone or in cartel with two other associations, the Atcar and the Fédéka.

Atcar was the Association Sociale et Culturelle des Tshokwe du Congo, de l'Angola et de la Rhodésie, which, led by Ambroise Muhunga, had its headquarters in Elisabethville and local branches in Jadotville, Kolwezi, Dilolo, and Sandoa. These Tshokwe — people from Angola who had entered the Congo through southeast Kasai and southwest Katanga — were traditionally hostile to the Lunda, who with the Bayeke dominated the Conakat.

In mid-September, 1959, the Atcar rallied to the Balubakat appeal of September 14, 1959, opting openly for the "defense of the principle of a Unitary Congo, and for the granting of independence or autonomy to the Congo with the shortest possible delay."[47]

The Fédéka (Fédération des Associations des Ressortissants de la Province du Kasai) was an organization of rather recent vintage whose

---

[45] *Congo 1959*, p. 144.

[46] The rupture dates formally from November 10, 1959.

[47] *L'Echo du Katanga* (Elisabethville), September 16, 1959.

objective was to unite Kasaians (Baluba, Lulua, or Basonge) after the dissolution of Fegebaceka in November, 1958. At this point, the colonial authorities "wanted to have it known that they bore no particular animosity toward the people from Kasai in general and the Baluba in particular. Consequently, they have decided to encourage the creation of a new association or federation . . . which will very probably be called Fédéka." [48] It is possible that such was the motivation of the administration at the time of the founding of the Fédéka on December 1, 1958. Among the Kasaians who took the initiative, the motivation was different; the dissolution of the Fegebaceka and the creation of the Conakat were perceived as direct threats and they considered it necessary to band together without delay. [49] Thus, the Fédéka was created in Elisabethville. Its vice-president, Isaac Kalonji, was provincial president of the Acmaf. At the same time, in Jadotville, an intellectual circle of Kasaians was also organized, including, in particular, Victor Lundula, future general of the *Armée Nationale Congolaise* (ANC).

The Fédéka did not accept individual members but brought together existing tribal and cultural associations as did the Fédéka organizations in Bukavu and in Leopoldville. "The Fédéka is a fragment of the Congo, trying to unite with other Congolese groups in the march toward Congolese unity; it deals with all problems of interest to its members, even Congolese political problems." It showed itself relatively little in its first six months, but its leaders — and especially Isaac Kalonji — played an important, although discreet, role in joining the forces of the Fédéka and the Balubakat. This was accomplished during the communal elections and immediately thereafter; but, meanwhile, the Fédéka had felt the impact of the bloody tribal struggles in Luluabourg. From this moment forward, a number of Lulua turned to the Conakat, while the Baluba of Kasai took their place in the Fédéka, in the Mouvement National Congolais (MNC), or in both groups at once. [50]

[48] *Rapport périodique de l'Administration de la Sûreté*, 4th quarter (1958), Bureau du Katanga.

[49] Other Kasaians from Elisabethville refused, however — even until the end of 1959 — to again join an ethnic-political association, feeling that it was necessary to free André Kadima from prison and to obtain authorization to relaunch the Fegebaceka. These Kasaians disapproved of the creation of the Fédéka. Kadima, in 1960, presided over the Fédération Générale du Congo (FGC), party belonging to the Abako-PSA-MNC/Kalonji Cartel.

[50] In September, 1959, the MNC in Katanga publicly approved the Balubakat appeal of September 14.

At the beginning of December, 1959, "the Parti Progressiste Katangais and the Balubakat, its parent" [51] declared themselves "in favor of unity for the Congo and against separatism," rallied to the Belgian ministerial declarations of October, 1959, and presented a program "taking into account the transition period that the Congo must necessarily pass through before acceding to its total independence" — a program which reserved to Belgium for an undetermined period, the following matters: currency, international security, foreign trade, and higher education.

From these three confederations and groupings, the Balubakat Cartel took form at the beginning of January, 1960. [52]

[51] Note sent to the Minister of the Congo on December 1, 1959, in Elisabethville by the PPK and signed by Rémy Mwamba, *président*, and Jason Sendwe, *président-général*.

[52] According to its founders, the Cartel was created on November 1, 1959, but only announced after the elections. Later, in April, 1960, the Parti de l'Unité Basonge and the Association des Kanioka joined.

CHAPTER 2 · *The Threat of Secession*
(December 1959—June 1960)

THE ROYAL VISIT AND COMMUNAL ELECTIONS:
TOWARD A *COUP D'ÉTAT?*

IN December, 1959, elections by universal suffrage took place for communal councils and territorial councils. The balloting constituted —
according to the Belgian plan — an essential step in the final designation
of members of the provincial councils. These elections were boycotted in
Leopoldville province by the Abako-PSA-MNC/Kalonji-Parti du Peuple
Cartel, but in Katanga, electoral participation was very high (81.7
percent).

In the Belgian press at the time, especially in Catholic, Liberal, and
neutral newspapers, news was focused favorably upon the Conakat, whose
friendly views regarding union with Belgium were reported with great
satisfaction. At the same time, these newspapers denounced the extremism of the Abako Cartel, which they contrasted to the "moderation" of
the Parti National du Progrès (PNP) or of the Conakat. Thus, while the
position of the Conakat was far from being the dominant one in Elisabethville, the dispatches from the Belga-Congo news service described the
electoral climate in the following terms:

It can be said that the city votes under the banner of independent Katanga.
Saturday, the different parties held public meetings, but the Conakat was
the most active in the various communes, where it organized parades with
cars and trucks.

Conakat President Moise Tshombe made a speech in which he tried to trace
the political future of Katanga. His principal points were:

A sovereign Katanga accepts the idea of federal unity under certain minimal conditions. Tshombe officially reserves a place for the traditional chiefs
whose roles remain fundamental in the present structure, which can only
evolve by degrees if it is to escape the convulsions and extremism which have
taken place in many countries recently advanced to independence. Tshombe

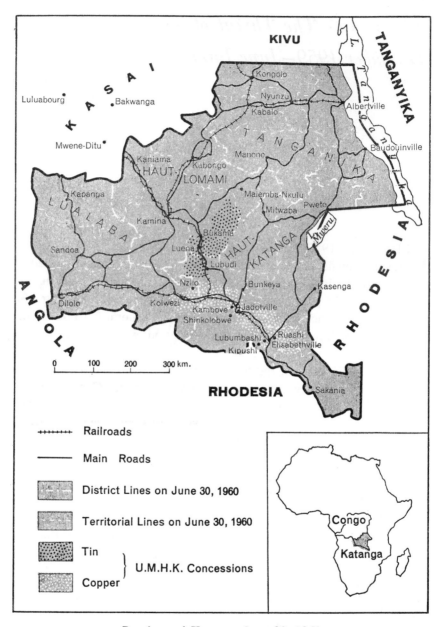

Province of Katanga, June 30, 1960

added: "Whether a federal Congo with a Katangan state is possible or not, Katanga will, in any case, seek a community with Belgium." [1]

The official results, available in January, 1960, scarcely permitted any clear-cut lesson to be learned concerning the relative strength of the Conakat and the parties of the Balubakat Cartel: 82.44 percent of the votes were cast for electoral lists, for individuals, or for traditional candidates, without explicit reference to existing Katangan parties. As parties, the Conakat received 10.82 percent of the votes and the Balubakat 3.89 percent.[2]

In a note sent to Minister Raymond Scheyven at the beginning of January, 1960, the Conakat said it had carried 427 seats out of 484. To get this result, it added to the 84 seats won under the Conakat label the 7 places of Lulua-Frères, 191 seats filled by traditional candidates, and finally 144 places which went to local or independent candidates. In the communes of Elisabethville and Jadotville, the Conakat was in the minority.

The Balubakat obtained 30 seats in its own name. It was very much opposed to this electoral arithmetic, remarking, "The two large Katangan parties, both based upon important ethnic groups in the province, obviously have followers in the traditional milieu." The Balubakat added in its communiqué, "Not having benefited from the same support and facilities that the Conakat had had during the electoral campaign, the Balubakat could not offer slates outside the large centers." The importance of other parties was even smaller: the Union Congolaise, for instance, obtained only six seats with 2,812 votes.

[1] Agence Belga-Congo, reprinted in *Le Soir* (Brussels), December 22, 1959.

[2] The slates of the Mouvement Solidaire Muluba (MSM) and of MNC/Kalonji, which were primarily aimed at the Baluba of Kasai, received 4,610 votes as against 9,982 for the Balubakat.

In Elisabethville, the balance of forces was as follows, before cartelization of the seats between the Balubakat and its allies:

Albert commune		*Kenia commune*	
Conakat	5 seats	Conakat	9 seats
Balubakat	4 seats	Balubakat	6 seats
Fédéka	3 seats	Fédéka	5 seats
(out of total of 17 seats)		(out of total of 27 seats)	
Ruashi commune		*Katuba commune*	
Conakat	5 seats	Conakat	6 seats
Balubakat	3 seats	Balubakat	8 seats
Fédéka	2 seats	(out of total of 27 seats)	
(out of total of 15 seats)			

Almost simultaneously with publication of the electoral results, and in particular of analyses giving the Conakat as the dominant group, the King of the Belgians arrived in Elisabethville, coming "to find out for himself the overall aspirations of the people," on the eve of the political "Round Table" which would give the Congo "institutions adapted to local traditions and preferences and responding to the needs of the country."[3]

Belgian journalist Pierre Davister, who was there, wrote on January 2, 1960, in *Pourquoi Pas?*:

> We are rushing headlong toward an amalgam of federated States of which Katanga would like to be the pole of attraction, and also the pole of loyalty to Belgium. All the elements are there: keeping good Belgian cement in the federal structure, with the Crown as a label of quality. . . . Kivu is already prepared to come to "attention" and take orders from Katanga.

According to Davister's account, "Katanga, as it appeared to the King . . . is a Katanga bent on immediately becoming an Independent State and on confronting Belgium with the *fait accompli*, if necessary."[4] There would be agreement in Katanga on a project for convening of a Katangan national assembly within sixty days, which would draft a constitution and establish means for union with Belgium. Other regions of the Congo could enter into confederation with Katanga, under certain conditions, one of which would be union with Belgium.

Who inspired this idea and scheme? Davister did not hesitate to say that it was Europeans who "very capably maneuvered in the wings to instill the notion among the Africans." Why did the Conakat rally to the idea? The same newsman wrote that the Conakat was going to support "the Katanga *coup d'état* with its authority as a single party; in return, the Katangan government would be entirely African and the Conakat would call all the shots."

This journalist's account has often been cited as proof of the first serious secessionist attempt in Katanga. No other public source exists which reveals to what extent this attempt was prepared and what forces were genuinely associated with it.[5] For this attempt to be serious, that is to

[3] Message from King Baudouin, December 17, 1959.

[4] Pierre Davister, *Katanga, enjeu du monde* (Brussels: Ed. Europe-Afrique, 1960), pp. 51–57.

[5] The project was mentioned by Jean-Baptiste Kibwe on July 31, 1960, in Brussels. — *La Libre Belgique* (Brussels), August 1, 1960.

say, for it to succeed locally, it needed support from the administration, from the *Sûreté*, from business, and from the *Force Publique* behind the initiatives of the Conakat and the settlers. Nothing indicates with any assurance that such support was acquired in December, 1959, from all these quarters.

What happened in Katanga was probably more modest. In early December (December 2, to be exact), the Belgian Minister for the Congo received a delegation from the Union Katangaise which gave him a memorandum relating to the "new institutions." It took up the themes of autonomy for the provincial entities, of federalism, and of the Belgo-Congolese community. The Minister expressed reservations about the plan. The delegates gave him to understand that the Belgian governmental view "would rapidly provoke in Katanga a hardening of opinion, already widespread among Congolese and Europeans both, that the moment had really come for Katanga to try every peaceful means that could lead it to an existence of its own." The Minister was "skeptical as to the possibilities for the existence of a truly Katangan state." [6]

Following this interview, the Union Katangaise circulated a manifesto to all post boxes in Katanga. The manifesto contained a questionnaire on which the addressees were supposed to indicate whether they were for or against "the proclamation of an independent Katanga, if the formula of a completely federal Congolese state is not accepted." [7]

The plan was to make a constituent assembly out of the future Katangan provincial assembly foreseen for March, 1960, of which 60 percent of the members were to be designated by the communal electors and the territorial electoral winners, 10 percent by the administration, and 30 percent co-opted by the members themselves. This assembly was to study, then adopt, a Katangan constitution and set up the first government of the state of Katanga, which would negotiate with Belgium and the "other Congolese states" on forms of association or federation.

The Union Katangaise asked those who received the manifesto-referendum to return the answers before December 31, which could have lent some credibility to the view that a *coup d'état* was planned for that date, especially since the Abako had announced this same date as marking

---

[6] *Le Katanga devra-t-il prendre sa propre indépendance?* manifesto of the Union Katangaise, December, 1959, Elisabethville.

[7] The Union Katangaise guaranteed utmost discretion and agreed to destroy all the answers, after establishing their statistics from them.

the end of the colonial regime in the Lower Congo, and transition to the Republique du Kongo Central.

At the bottom of the Union Katangaise campaign and of the Katangan reaction in the beginning of December, there was — besides the permanent factors — the impression that Brussels was responsive only to the demands of the "extremists" and more particularly to those of the Abako-PSA-MNC Cartel. That explains why *L'Echo du Katanga*, generally reserved toward the extremists of the Union Katangaise, wrote in its issue of December 3–4:

> In order to ingratiate himself with one faction, [Auguste] de Schrijver killed the confidence that Katanga could have had in the rigid and firm application of a coherent program destined to lead the Congo rapidly to independence in peace, order, and confidence, the conditions *sine qua non* of prosperity for all its inhabitants. Katanga is henceforward resolved to lead the way in becoming an independent entity.
>
> It will permit no one to interrupt its march toward progress which it considers indispensable: the installation of a free, democratic, and independent Katanga. It will establish relations of friendship and sincere cooperation with neighboring territories and with Belgium, dealing as equals with each and every one. From today on, it rejects the bureaucratic oligarchy of Leopoldville which, for decades, slowed its progress and tried to make all decisions which concerned only Katanga. Let the ministers and government do what they may, Katanga will not abandon its chosen path.

It is probable that, at the end of December, on the basis of the first electoral results and in taking account of the royal visit, some Europeans thought it opportune to announce solemnly the independence of Katanga to be achieved after the constitution of provincial assemblies and before that of a central government or parliament.

In fact, this boiled down to demonstrating, on the eve of the Round Table, that Katanga — the province which clamored with the most vehemence about its attachment to Belgium — demanded a regime with internal autonomy, within a federal, or rather confederal, Congo and within a Belgo-Congolese community.

On December 24, 1959, the Balubakat asked the King to interpose in "the work of destruction now in progress, that aims to dismantle the immense country created at the price of so much effort by [his] predecessors." It is interesting to note also the reaction of the Abako Cartel meeting in Kisantu, to which the Conakat and the Balubakat sent observers. The Cartel, on December 27, 1959, called for a federal regime with real autonomy for its members and to this end demanded the constitution of a Union of Republics of Central Africa (URAC). Nonetheless, the Cartel rejected in its fourth resolution "all separatist designs, which might threaten the integrity and unity of the national territory in its present geographic contours" (aiming at the ideas of the Conakat, among others, and the activities of the settlers who "try subtly to lead the Congolese after having set them one against the other").[8]

In Katanga itself, the beginning of January, 1960, was marked by a continuing spate of rumors and proclamations of intentions regarding the independence of Katanga: "The wishes of Katanga are firmer than ever: Katangan independence first, a pre-condition for any negotiations. Thus, Katanga in saving itself will save the whole Congo."[9]

CONAKAT AT THE BELGO-CONGOLESE CONFERENCES

THE POLITICAL ROUND TABLE AND THE FRAMEWORK OF THE STATE

At the beginning of January, 1960, two problems in particular preoccupied the parties and groups in Katanga: representation and participation in the Belgo-Congolese Round Table on the one hand; the choice of burgomasters for the communes on the other.

Contrary to allegations at the time, no accord was struck before the Round Table between the Conakat and the Cartel on the division of communal burgomaster posts. In the urban centers, the Cartel, through Fédéka president Isaac Kalonji, succeeded in rallying a certain number of elected individuals on whom the Conakat had once counted to build a majority. On his January 10 return from Brussels, Tshombe received a triumphal welcome from his followers. In contrast, his political position was less than brilliant. On January 12, Albert commune in Elisabethville designated Balubakat leader Jason Sendwe as its burgomaster candidate.

Several scuffles arose out of the Sendwe nomination, with tensions increasing shortly after the return, likewise triumphal, of Sendwe. The house of Kalonji, Fédéka leader, was stoned by Conakat partisans. Atcar president, Ambroise Muhunga, was pummeled at the commune. The gendarmery had to intervene, a curfew was imposed on the whole city, and meetings of more than five persons were banned. Later, a Conakat headquarters was stoned and the police used tear gas to disperse the crowd.

At this moment, Vice-Governor-General Schoeller intervened. He postponed meetings of the other communal councils and then called the

---

[8] *Congo 1959*, p. 267. Note that the Balubakat signed the resolution.

[9] A view which was never adopted in practice by the Conakat. — *L'Echo du Katanga* (Elisabethville), January 5, 1960.

two leaders to propose that they suspend any decision until their return from the Round Table. This compromise was accepted and the leaders set off for Brussels, after each had made very moderate declarations.

In regard to representation of Congolese groups at the Round Table, the difficulties were great for the "hosts." Confronted with contradictory demands, they had no valid criteria at their disposal to test the credentials of those demanding representation.[10] Out of forty-four Congolese delegates, Katanga had at different times seven or eight, of which two were identified with the Conakat, one with the Balubakat, two were pro-Conakat traditional chiefs, one was from the Union Congolaise, and one from the Fédération Générale du Congo, a member of the Abako Cartel. The Baluba of Kasai in Katanga were not represented by Fédéka, but at certain times, Albert Kalonji had a representative of MNC/Kalonji from Elisabethville, a Muluba from Kasai, seated.[11]

In relation to its population, Katanga had a representation greater than the average. The conference ruling of January 22, 1960, to recognize the principle of a vote by delegation,[12] also favored Katanga, since at the time of the vote the conference president recognized eleven votes of which three were from Katanga (one Conakat, one Balubakat, and one Union Congolaise), or 27 percent for an individual representation of 16 percent of the conference and for a population of 11 percent of the Congo.

The Conakat was nevertheless not at all satisfied with this representation: it had been denied the monopoly, or the quasi monopoly, of Katangan representation and its delegation was reduced to 4.5 percent of the whole group, even though in terms of voting rights it represented 9 percent and, through its traditional chiefs, substantially influenced that important so-called traditional delegation of ten members. On January 20, the very day of the opening of the Conference in Brussels, Joseph Onckelinx described to the executive committee of the Conakat in Elisa-

---

[10] In the elections of December, 1.3 million out of 1.8 million Congolese voters chose candidates running as independents on no party ticket. In addition, the Abako-PSA-MNC/Kalonji Cartel had boycotted the elections; the results of the whole election were available only very late and interpretation proved very difficult.

[11] Jean-Claude Yumba (MNC/Lumumba alternate) was likewise a Katangan.

[12] A delegation had one vote, whatever the numerical importance of the delegation (Article 17 of the standing orders). This decision was taken to limit the influence of the Abako Cartel which included 11 delegates and found itself thus reduced to one vote during the balloting. The scheme worked, however, in favor of Cartel views in many cases where the opposition was concentrated in four delegations with 25 members (the PNP, the Conakat, traditional chiefs, and the Alliance Rurale Progressiste).

bethville "the deplorable and unhappy situation of Katanga as to the division of seats at the Round Table."[13]

Evariste Kimba bitterly regretted this situation in turn and said he had decided, during the course of the committee meeting, that Tshombe would not go to Belgium if steps were not taken in favor of Conakat, that Conakat should therefore have stayed away from the Round Table. But Tshombe, continued Kimba, was absolutely determined to go to Belgium, despite the opposition of the members. . . . Tshombe made it known to the committee members that their decision to withdraw from the Round Table would be respected in Belgium if the Minister remained intransigent in the division of conference seats. It is thus that the committee let the President leave in complete confidence that he would respect the wishes of the masses. However, concluded Kimba, one wonders why Tshombe remained in Belgium, after the press had announced the division of seats was definitive. A deathly silence fell over the hall: Let us wait and see, responded all the members.[14]

At this point, the Conakat was inclined to play its role as a confederalist party strongly favorable to the Belgo-Congolese community. "What will we do after the Round Table if we do not obtain satisfaction?" asked a member of the Conakat *comité*, or executive committee, on January 20. "Will we have a *coup d'état* or will we accept a unitary regime for the whole Congo?"

The members present opted for the first solution: we must offer a demonstration of strength rather than remain docile: nothing ventured nothing gained; those who struggle, survive. It is better to try a *coup d'état* and fail than to stand with your arms folded and to accept like women a regime which can bring nothing to Katanga. Sékou Touré seized power; it is not impossible that we can do the same. Let us therefore prepare our masses, declared all the members.[15]

At the outset in Brussels, the Conakat was in a position of weakness within the "Common Front" of Congolese parties in relation to the nationalist parties such as the Abako, the Parti Solidaire Africain (PSA), the two MNC's, the Parti du Peuple, and the Centre de Regroupement Africain (Cerea), which saw in the Conakat an instrument of the European settlers. The "moderate" parties such as the Balubakat and the Union Mongo, both advised by representatives of the Institut de Sociologie Solvay, were also hostile to the "separatist" views of the Conakat. The only

---

[13] Minutes, *comité restreint* (executive committee) of the Conakat, drawn up by the secretary-general of the Conakat, Justin Meli.

[14] Minutes, *comité restreint* of the Conakat, January 20, 1960.

[15] *Ibid.*

means for the Conakat to break out of its isolation was to seek alliances, less on the basis of federalism than on that of opposition to the so-called extreme nationalists,[16] in becoming the hard core of a so-called moderate front (PNP, Alliance Rurale Progressive, traditional chiefs) and in presenting itself as "the pivot of the future Congo," the pole around which the federal Congo would be constructed in peace and order and in community with Belgium. At the very beginning there were Conakat attempts to join with the Abako Cartel to impose a federalist line,[17] but the Abako Cartel quickly discouraged them, since these efforts might set up obstacles in the way of other alliances more useful for the Abako, in the direction of the nationalist parties or of new parties still uncommitted.

The debate over the "state structures" appeared beforehand as the most dangerous pitfall for the Round Table, in respect to cohesion of African delegations. In fact, the confrontation was relatively moderate.

The Abako Cartel had opted at Kisantu (December 24 to 27) for a federal structure, judged "the most suitable in an independent Congo, to save its much desired national unity." The Kisantu scheme gave to the federation solid legislative and executive organs[18] and conferred on the center a field of competence large enough to ensure that centrifugal factors did not empty the federation of its substance and condemn it to impotence.

On January 25, Abako Cartel president Joseph Kasavubu decided on his own, and without informing his colleagues, to withdraw from the Conference if it were not turned into a constituent assembly and if it did not immediately grant the Congo a provisional government. The other parties to the Round Table — including those from the Cartel — tended to interpret this act of Kasavubu's as an indication of a Bakongo secessionist desire;[19] in order to fight it, they were more careful to strengthen

---

[16] Constituted on the eve of the opening of the Round Table, the Congolese Common Front did not include a Conakat delegate at its initial session, but the Conakat did participate later. From Elisabethville, Europeans sent telegrams to the Conakat delegates to denounce what they called "the Common Front trap."

[17] Jean-Baptiste Kibwe attended certain closed meetings with the Abako Cartel, but this led to nothing.

[18] Notably a lower chamber elected by universal suffrage.

[19] At this moment rumors circulated in Brussels, according to which France maintained what it called its right of pre-emption over the Congo, dating from 1883. These rumors were confirmed on February 26, 1960, by Maurice Couve de Murville, the French Foreign Minister. (Translator's note: By this treaty France had a theoretical right to claim the Congo in the event that Belgium terminated its colonial rule.)

the centripetal or unitarist factors than to give in to the federalists. This reaction made all the parties more sensitive to separatist threats, real or imaginary, than to the risks of unitarism and inevitably played against the Conakat position.

On the Belgian side — both Minister de Schrijver in his speech of January 27 and Senator H. Rolin in his working questionnaire [20] submitted to the commission on state structures — care was taken to defuse the bomb which could be set off by a confrontation between unitarists and federalists (or confederalists) about structures of the future independent state.

Unanimity was easily reached over the idea of political and economic unity for the Congo within its then current frontiers,[21] over the creation of a second House to represent the provinces equally, and over provincial representation at the central governmental level. Debate over terms was avoided and a procedure was chosen which normally would have satisfied the two parties; central institutions and their powers were defined; next, provincial governments and assemblies were accepted (with a law on provincial institutions); provincial powers were defined; matters of mixed jurisdiction were enumerated; a procedure for arbitration in case of jurisdictional conflicts was provided. The whole was drafted in rather general terms, while underlining clearly that the regime installed would last only until ratification of the Congolese constitution, which would be the work of the constituent assembly.

Opposition between federalists and unitarists nevertheless emerged, but on specific points — when it was necessary to agree on matters to be reserved to the central government or on mixed matters calling into question both the powers of the central authorities and those of the provinces.

Thus, on February 10, Tshombe demanded that "the resources of each province be properly its own." At the commission on state structures, the Conakat recommended a means of financing the central government by voluntary contributions from the provinces and suggested primary power be reserved to the provinces in mining matters. The Cona-

[20] See *Congo 1960*, pp. 35–36.

[21] The limits and the number of provinces were not questioned at the Round Table. This issue was left in the hands of the future constituent assembly. On January 18, 1960, Tshombe had announced that he would defend "gladly the view of attaching Kabinda [in Kasai] to the future State of Katanga." — *L'Echo du Katanga* (Elisabethville), January 18, 1960. "Gavage's heart's desire" (in the words of a member of the Conakat central committee, January 20, 1960).

kat would likewise have wished that in the higher Chamber each province would have an equal number of seats and that the constitution would be ratified by each province.

Some compromises were, in the course of events, rather easily found, at least in the formulation. The mining problem, which interested the Conakat leader, was the occasion of more passionate debate, first in commission, then in plenary session. Finally, a sort of *quid pro quo* permitted the realization of an accord within the Common Front: the ports (such as Matadi) and the great hydroelectric complexes (Inga) would fall within the province of the central authorities (and this could appear as a concession from the Bakongo). Similarly, legislation relating to the exploitation of mineral deposits was vested in the central authority, which undertook to assure to the provinces a fair share in the revenues collected. The central government would also guarantee to any expropriated companies an equitable prior reimbursement and would permit the provinces to exercise the right to allocate concessions under certain constitutional rules.[22]

In the discussion about the structure of the state on February 11, a significant incident occurred between the Conakat and Lumumba, who took issue directly with the Conakat's Belgian advisers and left the session in protest. The MNC leader arraigned the "very mysterious influences at work in this conference and the lobbying by certain European counselors who serve the interests of financial groups and foreign powers, instead of the Congo."

In the same debate, Ileo declared:

Those who call for important provincial powers run certain risks for the country. In effect, by putting such important powers at the disposal of the provinces, some of these will without doubt eventually conclude that they could survive by themselves. From that point, must it not be feared that they would be tempted to secede? Well, the conference certainly has no intention of preparing the collapse of the Congo.

An analysis of positions and votes expressed at the conference reveals clearly that the line of cleavage was not so much between Congolese

---

[22] This point is essential for the Conakat and the companies in Katanga, in so far as the UMHK concession would expire in 1990 which — in an enterprise of this nature — is relatively soon and this already exercised an influence over its planning. (Translator's note: The concessionary companies (*pouvoirs concédants*), the CSK, the Comité National de Kivu, and the CFL, had each been granted authority to administer and sell lands classified as belonging to the public domain in parts of the eastern Congo.)

federalists and unitarists as it was between the so-called moderate traditionalist groups on the one hand and the so-called extremist nationalists on the other.[23]

If only the non-unanimous votes on political questions are counted, the following tendencies may be noted:

1. The Conakat voted 14 times out of 14 in the same fashion as the traditional chiefs and the Parti National du Progrès (PNP); it also voted 12 times with the Alliance Rurale du Kivu.
2. The Conakat voted 7 times with the Balubakat Cartel.
3. The Conakat voted 1 time with the Abako Cartel, the MNC/Lumumba, and the Cerea.
4. The Balubakat Cartel voted 7 times with the Abako Cartel, the MNC/Lumumba, and the Cerea.

Among these votes, some are strongly indicative of certain tendencies. Thus, the Conakat wished that:

1. The lower Chamber would not be entirely elected by universal suffrage.
2. The Senate would include at least three members per province chosen by the traditional chiefs from among their own ranks.
3. The constitution of the Congo could not be promulgated without ratification by all the provincial councils, which meant each province would have an effective right of veto over the constitution.
4. The King of the Belgians would act as chief of an independent Congolese state, until the ratification of the constitution which the future constituent assembly would draft.[24]
5. Belgians resident in the Congo would be voters and eligible for office as of May, 1960.[25]

[23] Analyzing the rivalry at the commission on structures, Kibwe himself declared: "Two tendencies were manifested: the one in the minority which was greedy for total power on June 30 without a care for the real future of the country. Another, in the majority, aware of the interests of the country, accepted independence but without burning the bridges between Belgium and the Congo. We have made it known to the responsible people in Belgium that, if the latter, under the pretext of not wanting to be criticized as colonialists, abdicated before the active minority, we in Katanga would reserve for ourselves the right not to follow this path and to claim an independence in accordance with our policy and past conduct." — *L'Essor du Congo* (Elisabethville), February 8, 1960.

[24] There was no actual vote, but each delegation expressed its opinion on the question very clearly on February 15. Note that the three Katangan parties represented, as well as five other Congolese groups, backed the formula which was rejected by the Abako Cartel, the MNC/Lumumba, and the Cerea.

[25] On February 2, 1959, in the program delivered to Van Hemelrijck, the Conakat explained that, in its opinion, these rights must be accorded to "stable residents"

6. Provincial councilors would not be elected by universal suffrage in May, 1960, but would be chosen, indirectly, by those elected in the communal and territorial elections of December, 1959.[26]
7. The legal provisions governing eligibility for elective office would remain such that Patrice Lumumba would be disqualified by his court record.

In the course of the Round Table conference, the Conakat, in addition, took the following positions:

Nature of the Round Table

Tshombe was the spokesman for the Common Front on January 22, 1960, in demanding the moral and political commitment of the Belgian government to give executive force to the resolutions which would be passed at the Round Table.

Date of independence

After having agreed on the date of June 1, 1960, as had all the parties of the Common Front, Jean-Baptiste Kibwe recommended in the session of January 27 that this date must not be imposed as a matter of dogma; this position — as well as that of the PNP — led the Common Front to accept the date of June 30 as the date for independence.

Terms of independence

The Conakat spokesman declared on January 30 that the fixing of a timetable was necessary in order to know under what conditions the Congo would wholly exercise all the sovereign powers, for example, in the realm of national defense and foreign affairs. On February 10, Tshombe proposed, "to avoid the danger of a dictatorship," that Belgium retain control of finances and foreign affairs until the constitution of the young state was approved. But he nonetheless specified in what followed that his suggestion ought not to imply, in its spirit, a limitation on the powers of an independent Congo. The Conakat, in addition, wanted the Round Table to place economic and financial questions on its agenda.

When the conference ended, Tshombe was among the most enthu-

---

of the Congo and that in case they were refused to Belgians, under the pretext that they were "aliens," it would be necessary to consider also as "aliens" deprived of these rights "all those coming from Congolese areas outside Katanga."

[26] This would have excluded the nationalist parties that had urged voters to abstain in December and would have halted all development of parties such as the MNC and the Cerea, which did not yet have roots in rural areas.

siastic Congolese spokesmen, happy with the results obtained and interpreting the resolutions adopted as proof "that it had put an end to the excessive centralization under which the Congo suffered; that the Round Table conference had gone so far as to recognize in the former provinces all the powers of a political entity: legislative assemblies, governments proceeding from these assemblies, and autonomous administration and finance." Thanks to this fundamental reform, he added, the independent Congo of tomorrow would escape the collapse which had threatened it.

If the resolutions of the conference are compared with the Conakat programs and declarations of leaders and supporters,[27] Tshombe's optimism is surprising. On February 20, Kibwe told the Amis de Présence Africaine in Brussels that at no time had there been a serious question of proclaiming independence for Katanga; that was, he said, simply a means for pressure on the Belgian authorities and the other Congolese unitarists in order to bend the resolutions in a federalist direction.

Whatever the interpretation may be, it must be noted that the Conakat said it was very satisfied with the results of the Round Table. Gavage himself declared over Radio Ufac: "On the big issues: structure, mining regulations, finances, Katanga had won out." [28] Bonaventure Makonga, representing the pro-Conakat wing of the Balubakat, reconstituted on March 28, 1960, still maintained that the federalist views of the Conakat had triumphed in Brussels.[29]

THE POLITICAL COMMISSION AND THE PROVISIONAL LOI FONDAMENTALE

Following the conference, two transitional bodies were established: the one in Brussels — the political commission — worked with the Colonial Minister, assisting him in the elaboration of laws, decrees, and regulations as well as in draft-plans for conventions or treaties, resulting from commitments made at the Round Table (Resolution 12 of the Round Table); the other, in Leopoldville — the *Collège Exécutif Général* — was to assume the administrative powers of the *Gouvernement Général*. In addition, a provincial *Collège Exécutif* was provided for in each of the six provinces, to exercise the administrative powers of the

---

[27] "We shall return to Katanga with complete federalism, if not with independence." — Kibwe in *L'Essor du Congo* (Elisabethville), January 28, 1960.

"The Congolese Federal State, in the same fashion as all the federated states will be placed under royal authority, which will make the Belgo-Congolese Community concrete." — Tshombe in *L'Echo du Katanga* (Elisabethville), January 18, 1960.

[28] *L'Echo du Katanga* (Elisabethville), February 16, 1960.

[29] *L'Echo du Katanga* (Elisabethville), April 12, 1960.

governor. Each province had the right to designate five delegates: one for the political commission, one for the *Collège Exécutif Général* and three for the provincial *Collège* in question.

The most politicized groups — the Abako, the MNC/Lumumba, the Cerea, the MNC/Kalonji — directed their interests toward Leopoldville and the *Collège Exécutif Général*, which constituted the first concrete step in the change of regime, even if the six Congolese members sat with the Governor-General of the colony and if the latter continued to hold a position which was legally dominant at voting time.[30] In contrast, the Conakat chose the political commission which sat in Brussels and which could play a relatively important role in preparing the provisional constitution, executing the Round Table resolutions that defined the powers to be conferred on the provinces. Besides, the Conakat held one of the three Congolese posts on the provincial *Collège Exécutif* in Elisabethville. This choice was to crop up again at election time when the principal Conakat leaders were found on the provincial lists, leaving to less well-known representatives the national seats in Leopoldville.

THE ECONOMIC CONFERENCE AND THE STATUS OF THE COMITÉ SPÉCIAL DU KATANGA

In January and February, 1960, economic, financial, and social problems had been left off the agenda of the Round Table, despite the wishes of the Conakat, but it was decided to hold a special conference on these questions before independence.

Political leaders such as Kasavubu and Lumumba had reservations about the wisdom of the conference. By the end of April and beginning of May, 1960, the electoral campaign and the tasks of organizing parties had become all-absorbing so that the majority of leaders renounced their participation. Tshombe in contrast played an active role at the conference[31] and on the sidelines. Sendwe was also present for several days.

The two important Katangan delegations — the Conakat and the Cartel — published on this occasion declarations both optimistic and reassuring for private groups and for Belgians working in Katanga. Said Sendwe, "We must take into account the aspiration of the masses toward a better standard of living by progressive improvements . . . a political policy favoring investments. We shall guarantee foreign investments."[32] And

[30] Article 5 of Law of March 8, 1960, creating the *Collèges Exécutifs*.
[31] He was officially its vice-president.
[32] Sendwe declaration, Document 24, Economic Round Table.

Tshombe declared, "To assure a harmonious transfer of power . . . Conakat is committed to maintain the fundamental laws and decrees existing on June 30, 1960, and to make sure that the modifications which will be made thereafter will not in any way adversely affect the pursuit of economic progress."

The key problem for Katanga at the conference was to settle the distribution of the investment portfolios of the Congo, whose sum total was estimated on December 31, 1959, to be between 34.9 and 37.3 billion Belgian francs,[33] and at the same time the fate in store for the Comité Spécial du Katanga.

For the investments, Tshombe recommended from the outset the following position: they ought to be distributed by province and they would constitute the inalienable base-assets for the provincial development funds to be created.[34] What would be the portion of each province? The Tshombe text is not clear, but it could legitimately be thought that he wished to assure to each province a part proportional to its original contribution to the assets of the Congo, which would inevitably give a very substantial share to Katanga. "We want a relationship between development and people, a share on the basis of the contribution to the development and to the needs created by it."[35] This Conakat position was rejected by the other delegations.

On the question of the Comité Spécial du Katanga (CSK), a Katangan Common Front emerged and drew up a declaration which was read at the second commission of the conference on May 10, 1960.[36] The CSK affair was of primary importance for private groups in Katanga and especially for the Union Minière du Haut-Katanga (UMHK). The affair is complex, and in the press, it was sometimes brought out as an argument in the polemics aiming to prove that the Katanga secession was premeditated by the Belgian government or by financial groups with a dominant position in South Katanga and Northern Rhodesia.

The Comité Spécial du Katanga was set up on June 19, 1900, by convention between the Congo Free State (Leopold II) and a chartered company, the Compagnie du Katanga, to which had been awarded on April 15, 1891, some fifteen million hectares outright, with exclusive rights of

---

[33] According to whether, for the estimate, the book value or current trading price was used.

[34] Document 17, Economic Round Table.

[35] *Ibid.*

[36] Document 105, Economic Round Table, May 10, 1960.

mining, prospecting, and exploitation for ninety-nine years, plus, for a duration of twenty years, options on deposits uncovered on the thirty million hectares in the state domains.

The CSK — a committee of six persons, four designated by the colony and two by the Compagnie du Katanga — exercised the rights of the state and of the Compagnie over these immense domains in Katanga; and the profits were divided two thirds to the Congo and one third to the private company.

The CSK enjoyed the following rights:

1. Management of a domain belonging to the two partners.
2. Management of an investment portfolio which belonged to them.
3. Organization and management of quarries, forests, and waterfalls.
4. Right to award mining concessions and to collect royalties.

The management of the CSK was, in fact, exercised along a line fixed, or at the very least accepted, by the representatives of the private sector,[37] that is to say by the Compagnie du Katanga, a holding company controlled by the Société Générale de Belgique, through the Compagnie du Congo pour le Commerce et l'Industrie (CCCI). The CSK was at this time the principal stockholder in the Union Minière du Haut-Katanga, world's foremost producer of cobalt and third largest producer of copper, with 248,000 voting shares in the extraordinary general assembly of May 25, 1960, out of a total of 414,000 shares. The leading stockholders to follow were Tanganyika Concessions, Ltd., with 134,016 shares, and the Société Générale itself with 31,584 shares.

Until 1960, the Société Générale controlled the UMHK through its own shares and with the benevolent cooperation of the CSK; and through its interests in the CSK, the Compagnie du Katanga, and the CCCI, the Société Générale influenced the whole Katangan economy.

What would happen to this system if suddenly, in place of the colony, there sat at the CSK four representatives of an independent Congo inclined to apply different economic rules and management practices? No doubt there would have been a noticeable effect on companies subsidiary to the Société Générale in Katanga and on companies having like interests.[38] One can easily imagine that the problem did not escape the

[37] For more detail on the companies, financial groups, and their interrelationships, see *Morphologie des Groupes Financiers* (Brussels: CRISP, 1962), pp. 150–63. See also Appendix I.

[38] Note that the UMHK paid 40 percent of its returns to Tanganyika Concessions Ltd. and 60 percent to the CSK. The president and an administrator from Tan-

notice of the Belgian and British directors of the UMHK.

To avoid the threat of a breakdown of economic powers and controls, the groups involved could theoretically hope for or support various solutions, or combinations thereof:

1. To put in Leopoldville "moderate" directors who would accept for their representatives on CSK a position in the colonial tradition, that is to say the exercise of power along the path fixed by the private partner.

2. To dissolve the CSK, detaching the shares of the private partner from government influence over the whole. One third of the CSK investment portfolio (see Table 6) would revert to the private partner, the Compagnie du Katanga, together with the rights accruing to the latter; in this case, on the basis of the experience of May 25, 1960, the number of Union Minière shares exclusive of those of the Congo government was 248,403 out of a total of 414,000, and the risk of seizure by the state would be averted.[39]

3. To maintain the CSK but to see that the two thirds belonging to the colony would be split half for the Congo and half for Katanga; in this case — provided that the Katangan representatives were "malleable" — the CSK would remain unchanged, at least in the management policy for its investments.

4. To dissolve the CSK while taking care that the province of Katanga would take one third, the Compagnie du Katanga another third, and the Congo the last third. In this case, the directors of the UMHK would be assured of a continuity, without being subject to any Congolese authority, even Katangan.

The CSK was dissolved June 27, 1960, after a favorable resolution by the economic conference. How did it come about? What was the attitude of the Katangans in general, and of the Conakat in particular?

---

ganyika Concessions sat on the UMHK board, while one of the two vice-governors and two directors of the Société Générale, who were also vice-president and delegate-administrator of the UMHK, were found as well on the board of Tanganyika Concessions.

[39] Note that this formula theoretically meant a change in respective positions, in the sense that the "private" majority now depended on the support of Tanganyika Concessions. The *Financial Times* (London) deduced from this that Tanganyika Concessions "could accordingly divert a very great proportion of copper from Katanga by the Benguela railway." — Cited in *Le Soir* (Brussels), June 16, 1960.

If we look at the analyses and documents from the sessions, the process was as follows:

The question of "concessionary powers" was not examined by the mixed preparatory commission (the De Voghel commission) and it was in fact raised by the Congolese in plenary session, more especially in regard to the Comité National du Kivu (CNKi) for whose revision a desire had already been expressed in the *Conseil de Législation*.[40]

Monday and Tuesday, May 9 and 10, the second commission of the conference took up the debate on these problems. According to the minutes, "the Congolese delegates are unanimous in wishing to terminate the concessionary powers of the CSK, the CNKi, and the Compagnie des Chemins de Fer du Congo Supérieur aux Grands Lacs Africains (CFL)," [41] arguing that the right to concede public land is a prerogative of sovereignty which must be exercised by the Congolese government. The delegates disagreed over whether these agencies should be maintained in the exercise of all the prerogatives other than the concessionary powers and transformed into centers for stimulating economic development in the provinces involved, or whether they should be dissolved entirely, by Belgian decree, before June 30, 1960.[42]

At this point, the Katangan delegations made a common declaration,[43] signed by the Balubakat Cartel, the Union Congolaise, the Conakat, Chief Kasongo Nyembo, the Acmaf of Katanga, and the Katangan representative on the political commission, Jean-Baptiste Kibwe. The Katangans demanded that the CSK portfolio be split into three equal parts (one for Katanga, one for the Congolese state, and one for the Compagnie du Katanga.) They felt that it was up to Katanga to "adapt the statutes of the CSK to the new situation . . . the CSK will administer the lands of the province; it will retain all personnel without distinction with all their rights."

Thus, the proposal most favorable to private interests was presented by

[40] Document 80, Economic Round Table, May 7, 1960.

[41] Document 133, Economic Round Table, May 11, 1960.

[42] This last formula was born of a Belgian suggestion presented as follows: It would be perhaps injurious to the international credit of the Congo and to the confidence of private investors to begin its independent life by abolishing the concessionary powers; the Congolese then could wish that the Belgian government would do it before June 30, but the minister would do so only if the Congolese authorized him to negotiate at the same time the eventual indemnity of the parties involved. — Document 133, Economic Round Table, May 11, 1960.

[43] Document 105, Economic Round Table.

a common Katangan front including the Balubakat Cartel. Neither Sendwe nor Tshombe were signers of the motion but it was never repudiated; on the contrary, the advisers of all the Katangan groups made it authentic by stressing its values to those it was meant to satisfy.

How can this move be explained on the part of the Balubakat? At a time when elections were getting under way, the Balubakat could not a priori reject a formula which assured an income and important revenues to Katanga and it willingly associated itself with an initiative which could pull the teeth from the slogan, "Katanga, milk cow for the whole Congo." [44]

Besides — the argument was often employed in Balubakat circles — the formula had value as a test: if the Conakat continued after the adoption of such a formula to defend a secessionist position, this would be proof that it did not have solely in view the well-being of local peoples, but that it was trying a political adventure, under pressure from separatist elements. [45]

In any case, the existence of this document clearly established that support for division of the portfolio into three equal parts did not come solely from the Conakat and that on an issue such as this there was unanimous Katangan reaction. [46]

The Katangan declaration was not accepted without reservations by other delegations, especially the MNC/Lumumba, the PNP, and the PSA. The final resolution, No. 10, alluded to the respective rights, on the one hand, of the Congolese authorities — "the State and the provinces" — and on the other, of private interests, but it concealed many reservations. The Belgian legal view was in fact that the division of the portfolio was to operate by simple reversion of assets and delegation of controlling rights to the parties that had constituted the CSK, namely the Compagnie du Katanga and the Congo as a state.

The final resolution was far from satisfactory to the Conakat. Its spokes-

[44] Slogan used by the Katangan settlers for a long time; see, for example, *L'Essor du Congo* (Elisabethville), June 25, 1931.

[45] On May 31, 1960, the Balubakat Cartel maintained that after independence, Katanga would dispose "on its own of 55 percent of its resources." — *L'Echo du Katanga* (Elisabethville), May 31, 1960.

[46] It is probably on the basis of such experiences that Arthur Doucy thought he could record at the beginning of 1957 that an embryonic national consciousness had emerged in Katanga. He saw it as a sociological phenomenon to be taken into consideration by the lawmaker. — "Sociologie coloniale et réformes de structures au Congo Belge," *Revue de l'Université de Bruxelles*, No. 2–3, 1957, p. 229.

man was disturbed because no representative of the Conakat was to sit on the economic commission which would prepare the concluding conventions,[47] and it feared its suggestions would be discarded. "Under' these conditions," Joseph Yav said, "we ought to note our most formal reservations even on the principle of the dissolution of CSK. . . . We feel that Conakat cannot be bound at all because the Commission could prepare, establish, propose or decide!"

After the economic conference, a Belgo-Congolese working group was charged with drafting terms for the division of the CSK assets. The African delegates insisted that a company for development and investment be constituted in Katanga, with financial participation of the Campagnie du Katanga, which would give something in consideration for what it collected in mining royalties, and, if possible, from those of Tanganyika Concessions, Ltd., as well. In regard to the two thirds of the assets not belonging to the Compagnie du Katanga, this working group recommended a division into halves between the Congo and the province of Katanga, the latter providing compensation for that small part of the domain of the CSK stretching into Kasai province.

By decree, the CSK was liquidated on June 27, 1960, three days before the accession of the Congo to independence. A convention was signed between the Congo and the Compagnie du Katanga on June 24, 1960,[48] but no formula had been formally decided upon for the division of the CSK assets between the Congolese state and Katanga province.

The convention by itself was sufficient to assure a majority for the private interests in the UMHK. In supposing even that the Congolese state would have two thirds of the portfolio reserved to it, it would then control only 23.8 percent of the voting shares; that would be enough to give it a strong voting influence, as the most important individual stockholder, but nevertheless it would be in the minority, faced with a coalition of Tanganyika Concessions, Ltd., the Compagnie du Katanga, and the Société Générale.

[47] Neither the Abako, nor the PSA, nor the Cerea, nor the MNC/Kalonji were represented on this commission, whose role was minimal.

[48] The division of the CSK portfolio was carried out to the extent of returning to the Compagnie du Katanga its share. Thus, the number of non-voting shares of the CSK in the UMHK was reduced from 315,675 on June 20, 1960, to 210,450, while the balance sheet for the Compagnie du Katanga on December 30, 1960, showed a gain of 105,225 non-voting shares in the UMHK in comparison with the situation of the first half of 1960.

TOWARD A CONAKAT PROVINCIAL GOVERNMENT IN KATANGA

Disorder and Violence in Katanga

During the Round Table conference, it was thought in Elisabethville that the designation of burgomasters would not provoke any disturbance and that calm would prevail in the absence of the political leaders.

On January 31, 1960, Jadotville saw the first outbreaks. The origin of the trouble must be sought in the fact that the Conakat did not succeed in having Charles Mutaka, future president of the Katangan Assembly, nominated as burgomaster of Kinkula commune. The winner was Victor Lundula, the future ANC general, from Kasai.[49] The Conakat, in the minority, abstained from voting at the nomination of *échevins* [deputies to the burgomaster in the Belgian system] and representatives on the *Conseil de Ville*. On January 16, the traditional chiefs and the Conakat leaders addressed a letter of protest to the Vice-Governor-General of Katanga and sent copies to the Minister of Colonies and to the Governor-General. The Conakat argued that the Katangan people had voted in a calm and orderly fashion to prove its good will toward the government and its attachment to the Royal Family and to the King. The signers asserted that the administration imposed solutions contrary to the desires of the Katangan people in naming "strangers" burgomasters, and demanded revision of these decisions. In this letter, the parties involved declared that no merchandise could be sold by businessmen who were not card-carrying members of the Conakat; they forbade all businessmen who were not native Katangans from making purchases outside Jadotville; if the nomination of burgomasters were maintained by the administration, the signers of the letter would not recognize their authority.

Following the burgomaster designation, the Conakat had tried to provoke demonstrations when the new burgomaster took his oath of office. Conakat reinforcements arrived in Jadotville from Kambove on January 29.[50] The demonstrations did not take place. It was only on the following Sunday, January 31, about six o'clock in the evening, that a riot broke out inside Kinkula commune. These disturbances lasted only one night, and, by daybreak, calm had been restored. There were at least four killed, of whom three were mutilated, and twenty-six wounded. It

---

[49] Lundula was nominated by 14 votes out of 17 voting. A "stranger," he had been in Katanga 25 years, his wife was Katangan, and he had seven children "born in Katanga." — *L'Echo du Katanga* (Elisabethville), February 5, 1960.

[50] *L'Echo du Katanga* (Elisabethville), February 2, 1960.

was clear that the rivalry between the Conakat and the Balubakat Cartel played a large part in these riots.

At the end of the political Round Table in Brussels, on February 19, Katangan parties and traditional chiefs announced that an agreement had been reached among them, and the Elisabethville press thought it could reveal its terms: for the posts of burgomaster, Lundula would be confirmed in Kinkula/Jadotville, whereas in Elisabethville, two Conakat candidates, one Balubakat, and one Atcar candidate would be burgomasters of the four African communes. In fact, "the war of the burgomasters" was waged in Elisabethville during March, April, and May, and the Brussels convention was not applied.

At the beginning of March, tension mounted in Elisabethville, and on March 12, on the eve of his departure for Leopoldville, Rémy Mwamba, Katangan representative on the *Collège Exécutif Général*, launched an appeal for calm denouncing the "sterile quarrels" and the "crisis of authority" which "for some time [have provoked] veritable unrest in the cities of Kolwezi, Jadotville, and Elisabethville."

The very day of this call for calm riots erupted in these three cities, and grew worse the following day. Lumumba had arrived in Elisabethville and, on this occasion, provocative leaflets were disseminated: some denounced Patrice Lumumba as an agent of the Soviets; others alleged that the Conakat was dissolved. The incidents were bloody, the assaults savage.[51] Officially, there were seven killed, more than a hundred seriously hurt, and numerous houses burned or damaged. Hundreds of Africans were arrested and many were held for trial.

The commission of inquiry, set up by the *Collège Exécutif Général*, was paralyzed. The Conakat — which considered itself the victim of the incidents — refused to cooperate, questioning the impartiality of some commission members, but in particular rejecting the competence of Leopoldville to investigate an internal Katangan problem.[52]

---

[51] It seems that, in many cases, Baluba from Kasai and Baluba in Elisabethville clashed in bloody fashion.

[52] There was a mixed Cartel-Conakat meeting to try to make peace. — *L'Echo du Katanga* (Elisabethville), March 28, 1960. An appeal for calm was launched on March 21 by Vice-Governor-General Schoeller, on the occasion of the installation of the provincial *Collège Exécutif*, which included Godefroid Munongo (Conakat), and Gabriel Kitenge (Union Congolaise) and Paul Muhona (Tshokwe Catholic trade unionist). Note that the Conakat had a delegate on the political commission in Brussels and one on the *Collège Exécutif* in Elisabethville. The Cartel, in contrast, had only one representative on the *Collège Exécutif Général* in Leopoldville and was not associated with provincial leadership. This fact had

After these incidents, during the course of March, April, and May, reprisals took place against Kasai peoples in the interior, where they were in the minority. At Albertville, a nearly anarchic situation developed and at Lake Tshangalele, a serious incident set the chiefs against Baluba fishermen, who had to leave the region.[53]

ACTIVITIES OF THE TWO MNC WINGS IN KATANGA

In April and May, 1960, the activities of the MNC/Lumumba in Katanga were increased, especially after May 4, under the leadership of its executive committee director, Dominique Tshiteya. The activities of the MNC/Kalonji also intensified after the visit of its president to Katanga on April 18.[54] These two parties from outside Katanga incontestably exercised an attraction on young members of the Balubakat Cartel; Cartel leaders, subject to pressures from the ranks, refused to choose between Lumumba and Kalonji. "Kalonji is my brother; Lumumba is my political friend; I like them both." This game of informal alliances, concurrent with the intense electoral rivalry between the Cartel parties, the two MNC's, and other minor groups was pursued until the election. The partisans of the Cartel, favorable to the MNC/Lumumba, reproached the MNC/Kalonji for its Baluba tribalist character[55] and its federalist views, which in Katanga might raise very difficult problems for immigrants, from Kasai or elsewhere. In contrast, a number of Baluba were sensitive to the ethnic community with Kalonji and watched with apprehension the rallying of the Lulua in Kasai to Lumumba. On May 9, Sendwe still gave his word that he had not made an alliance with the MNC/Lumumba.

THE DECLARATIONS OF SIR ROY WELENSKY

On March 2, 1960, the *Daily Express* in London reported a declaration made by Sir Roy Welensky, Prime Minister of the Federation of Rhodesia

---

ill effects, since it gave the Balubakat all the more feeling of being left out, to the advantage of its rivals.

[53] *L'Echo du Katanga* (Elisabethville), April 27, 1960.

[54] After the Round Table, Elisabethville received visits from all the candidates for political leadership in the Congo: Lumumba, Albert Kalonji, Kasavubu, Jean Bolikango, and Ileo. In the case of Kasavubu, the Conakat tried to capitalize on the Abako leader's success with the crowds; he held his meeting in front of the railway station between Sendwe and Tshombe and stayed at the home of the Balubakat Cartel president.

[55] The partisans of Albert Kalonji were grouped in the MNC/Kalonji and in the Mouvement Solidaire Muluba. The MNC leader from Kasai also had supporters in Isaac Kalonji's Fédéka and in the Fédération Générale du Congo led by André Kadima and Henri Kasongo.

and Nyasaland, to its local correspondent: Persons from Katanga, he said, had given him to understand that the Rhodesias must "hold out the hand of friendship to Katanga with a view to a closer association." The journalist continued: "If Katanga decided to become one of the states of the Federation, its mining wealth could be joined to the copper, coal, and hydraulic energy of Northern and Southern Rhodesia. Central Africa would be even stronger and, therefore, closer to freedom." [56]

Who were the Katangan persons alluded to by Sir Roy? No name was cited. *The Times* (London) published a dispatch from its correspondent in Salisbury (March 3, 1960): "The initiative," he wrote, "has been taken by intermediaries whose identity the federal Prime Minister is not prepared to divulge." Brussels made representation to Selwyn Lloyd about this affair, considered as an unjustifiable Rhodesian interference in Congolese affairs. The British felt, according to Reuters, that the proposal for attaching Katanga to the Rhodesias could "only emanate from elements which were white, or of a color which would lose their power or their prestige once the Congo became independent."

Two days later, Agence France-Presse ascribed to Sir Roy the following: The contact with him had been established, not by a government or by official personalities, but by "private groups." "Such initiatives," added Sir Roy, "must come from the masses."

On March 10, the press published a denial from the UMHK management: Its agents, the UMHK declared, had made no approach to the Federation. On the contrary, the interviewer — journalist R. MacColl — made the following personal declaration: "Certain financial interests have doubtless inspired these moves. . . . It seems to me that, when there is a lot of money at stake and, in Katanga, it is a question of fantastic sums, it is obvious that certain interests would prefer in this uncertain world to gather around Sir Roy rather than to be put at the mercy of an African Republic." [57]

According to MacColl, the move had been inspired by mining groups,

[56] On February 26, 1960, furthermore, Couve de Murville had made it known to the Belgian ambassador that Paris had not renounced its right of pre-emption or priority right of acquisition over the Congo, conferred on it by the Ferry-Leopold II accord of 1883. This initiative took place at the behest of Abbé Youlou. The declaration by Sir Roy Welensky and the French position had served to provoke a unanimous wave of protest in the Congo.

[57] Agence France-Presse dispatch in *L'Echo du Katanga* (Elisabethville), March 10, 1960.

but who in fact had made it? The *Daily Express* let it be understood that the approaches had not been made by representatives of the 30,000 Europeans in the province, nor by the powerful Union Minière, but by Moise Tshombe, the Conakat leader.

"Moise Tshombe," wrote the author of the article, "burst out laughing at the idea that an African from the Congo, whoever it be, could find Sir Roy's paternalism to his taste in the current state of affairs." But the author underlined the final words and invited his readers to note them well: "I think," he concluded, "that if Moise Tshombe joined battle with Patrice Lumumba and Kasavubu, it would be prudent for him to consider an association with Sir Roy Welensky's Copperbelt, as an independent commercial partner."[58]

"The British interests (in London, to be precise) in Katanga mining companies are considerable and influential: mining industries of the Haut-Katanga and of the Copperbelt hold complementary points of view on economics and development. Meetings are said to have taken place on a high level in London several months ago, touching off the move toward Sir Roy. It is clear then what the source of this affair is."[59]

Suppositions, hypotheses, personal opinions have been expressed about the Rhodesian declaration. We do not know what really happened, except that a European group from Katanga and from Rhodesia must have discussed at the end of 1959 — and the first half of 1960 — questions of common interest, posed by the accession of the Congo to independence, and must have examined several hypotheses for the future of the Republic of the Congo with their ramifications for Katanga and the Copperbelt.

On the African side as well, contacts were made: thus the Conakat leaders of whom Tshombe was one held summit talks with United National Independence Party (UNIP) leaders, including Sikota Wina and Sipalo Munukumawa, and an agreement in principle was reached by virtue of which the Congolese gave their full support to UNIP, and the Rhodesian Africans in the Congo supported the Conakat.[60] A Rhodesian newspaper even cited a declaration attributed to a Katangan leader: "One of the Conakat projects is to unify the province of Katanga with Northern Rhodesia, under the authority of a single Black government, after Africans

[58] Agence France-Presse dispatch, March 11, 1960, circulated by the *Bulletin Interafricain Belga.*

[59] *L'Echo du Katanga* (Elisabethville), March 5, 1960.

[60] In Elisabethville, there were 7.13 percent classed as "Rhodesians." — *Bulletin du CEPSI*, No. 34 (1956), p. 167.

of the Congo and of Northern Rhodesia have their independence." [61]
Whatever these dealings were, they were in line neither with the declarations of Sir Roy Welensky nor with his hopes and ambitions.

It must be noted that, at this point, no one in Katanga admitted to having made overtures to the Prime Minister of the Federation: neither the UMHK; nor the settlers who published denials, nor the Conakat, which was "shocked at the rumors according to which certain persons extolled the idea of an eventual union of Katanga and the Federation. . . . [The Conakat would] fight vigorously against partisans of such an idea if they exist in Katanga, for the Conakat well knows how incompatible with its whole outlook and its dignity this idea is." [62] Tshombe said personally on March 7 that "never would Katanga join in a union or federation other than one with the provinces of the Congo and Belgium." [63]

On the Belgian side, there were protests against the schemes ascribed to Sir Roy, but above all their bases were minimized: "Katanga would not dream of seceding; there exists moreover no popular movement in this direction," said an unofficial declaration of the Belgian government on March 3, 1960. "No Katangan party manifests the slightest inclination toward secession; there is truly no basis in the allegation that a journalist attributed — wrongly, I hope — to the Prime Minister of the Federation," declared Vice-Governor-General Schoeller on March 4, 1960.

Even those who had, in December, 1959, and January, 1960, supported the idea of independence for Katanga were shocked at the thought of a federation with Rhodesia. For example, *L'Echo du Katanga* had once "by force of circumstances and in the face of monumental errors committed by our leaders" defended the idea of a reconstruction of the Congo, with an independent Katanga as a starting point. Yet it felt that now "things were settled at the Round Table," there could no longer be a question of following any other policy in Katanga than that decided in Brussels by its representatives.

Likewise, it was at this point more than at any other that both the

[61] "Conakat Moves into N.R.," *Northern News* (Ndola, Northern Rhodesia), May 25, 1960.

[62] March 5, 1960.

[63] Appeal to the Rhodesias always constituted, according to M. Ganshof van der Meersch, formerly the Minister charged with general affairs in Africa, "a project which possessed, especially for the Babemba, a veritable fascination." — *Fin de la Souveraineté belge au Congo* (Brussels: Institut Royal des Relations Internationales, 1963), p. 567.

Belgian and Congolese press adopted unitarist positions. Thus, *La Libre Belgique* of March 3, 1960, wrote:

> The Congo forms a balanced economic entity. To upset this balance would unquestionably be to plunge the Congo Central Basin, little favored by nature anyway, into profound misery and to retard, if not preclude forever, its chances for expansion. The Congo, as it exists, has a great future before it.
>
> Indeed, Katanga would find some immediate advantages in joining the Rhodesian Federation: it could devote its great resources to its own development, abandoning the other provinces of the Congo to their sad fate. But it would lose as well the chance to open vast outlets in these provinces for the industry it wishes to create.

WILDCAT STRIKES IN ELISABETHVILLE

On May 2, no bus circulated in Elisabethville, African personnel of Transports Communs du Katanga (TCK) having abandoned their work. The same day, the Compagnie du Chemin de fer du Bas-Congo au Katanga (BCK) rail workers met to draw up their list of demands, and, several days earlier, the personnel of the Banque du Congo Belge (BCB) had gone out on strike for an hour as a warning.

Thus developed a wave of wildcat or spontaneous strikes, launched by Africans without prior agreement by the unions and without respecting legal procedure; these had already begun in March and April in the banks. In fact, the unrest had been noticeable for some time, especially among teachers and Congolese sanitary personnel. The movement[64] caught on rapidly despite the interventions of the *Force Publique* and the police; despite the appeals and threats of sanctions voiced by the Vice-Governor-General and by the members of the provincial *Collège Exécutif*; despite the prohibitions on gatherings promulgated from May 5 on; despite the common declaration of labor unions and employers[65] and the appeals of political leaders.

In European circles, it was insinuated that the strikes were not so spontaneous as was alleged, and certain unions, political groups,[66] and

[64] The BCK (Elisabethville and Jadotville), Banque du Congo Belge, copper and zinc plants, Brasseries du Katanga, and a series of commercial firms.

[65] Joint declaration of the Association des Enterprises de la Province du Katanga and three labor unions of European origin (UTC, FGTK, and CGSLC). See *L'Echo du Katanga* (Elisabethville), May 7, 1960.

[66] Especially the MNC/Lumumba whose vice-president in Katanga, Roger Kabulo, was also president of the Union professionnelle des Cheminots congolais (Uproco). The Union had launched an appeal to go back to work, on May 6, and denied the accusations with regard to Kabulo. "The masses hardly listen

above all the "rabble-rousers" from Kasai were accused of being the perpetrators of the strike, the union agitators, and the guilty parties in the bloody incidents in Lubudi.

"There is no doubt that the strikes have political origins and are the doing of Congolese belonging to parties foreign to the province, surrounded by advisers who are strangers to the Congo. The majority of the Congolese who wish to work speak bluntly of Communism," wrote the anonymous correspondent of *La Cité*, the Belgian Catholic trade-union paper, on this subject on May 15, 1960.

In this atmosphere of suspicion toward the "stranger" agitators, the Balubakat Cartel — especially Sendwe — made many antistrike declarations:

> The evil Belgians must not be heeded or followed; we must not give them pretexts for sabotaging our elections. . . . Each at his post. . . . I call on all Baluba and members of the Cartel to show an example of discipline.[67]

> I have set in motion an inquiry into the strikes. Let measures be taken against the leaders.[68]

> Happily, my call has been heard and people have returned to work nearly everywhere. I thank the Katangan people, and especially the workers of Elisabethville. If they have let themselves be taken in by demagogic propaganda, they have seen that they were outside the law. They have sinned out of ignorance.[69]

Europeans themselves kept the main services running; numerous arrests took place among workers who tried to stop the resumption of work. The *Force Publique* paraded in Elisabethville on May 8 and in Jadotville on May 11,[70] after which its headquarters paid homage to the *Force Publique*, which "despite the wildcat strikes . . . maintained order everywhere," and whose parades, "while the strikes were in full swing, had stirred the enthusiasm and the confidence of the Katangan people."

EUROPEANS AND THE PARTIES

Before and during the political Round Table, the Conakat leaned heavily on Gavage's party, the Union Katangaise, which theoretically

---

to us and answer us that before they go back to work, we must tell them if they will have a raise, how much and when?" — *L'Echo du Katanga* (Elisabethville), May 7, 1960.

[67] *L'Echo du Katanga* (Elisabethville), May 7, 1960.

[68] Sendwe Report to *Collège Exécutif Général*, May 8, 1960.

[69] Sendwe in *L'Echo du Katanga* (Elisabethville), May 13, 1960.

[70] Officially, "on the occasion of the commemoration of the German surrender

constituted the European section affiliated to Tshombe's party. By this means, the Conakat received technical and material assistance. The party advisers themselves undertook, in many cases, to solicit local businesses, the funds being transmitted through them to the Conakat leaders. This procedure obviously strengthened the capacity of the advisers to influence the party.

Consequently, when Tshombe left the Round Table, interim Conakat president Bonaventure Makonga pressed Joseph Onckelinx, Georges Thyssens, and Hector Vanderbeken — the three Europeans present at the meeting of the executive committee of January 20, 1960 — to furnish the party "five million [Belgian francs] or more, not only to send additional delegates to the Round Table, but also to intensify our propaganda within Katanga."[71]

In Katanga, the Conakat thus benefited from the support of the European settlers. The local Union Minière directors all were inclined in favor of Tshombe, while in Brussels the UMHK accorded funds to the two large Katangan parties, by different channels, at least until May, 1960. The coefficient of uncertainty in political forecasts can explain the UMHK's position in Brussels.

After the Round Table, the situation evolved still further. The Congolese delegations had, by a majority of 7 to 4, rejected the right to vote and eligibility for office for Europeans in the Congo, pending preparation of a law on nationality. By this stroke European political organizations, and even mixed Belgo-Congolese parties, no longer had any justification. At the beginning of May, the Ucol declared that it renounced all intervention in political matters to return to the defense of its professional interests;[72] several days before, the Union Katangaise had announced its dissolution.

Under the headline "Calonne, Gavage, and Humblé must understand," *L'Echo du Katanga* had severely criticized European leaders of the Ucol and the Union Katangaise, denouncing "the disastrous role they play, in striving, against everyone's advice, to encourage the belief that they are

---

and of the arrival of General Janssens." — *L'Echo du Katanga* (Elisabethville), May 7, 1960.

[71] Minutes, *comité restreint* of the Conakat, January 20, 1960, p. 3. "Makonga was asking these five million francs until the end of the session," note the minutes. The same Makonga said at this meeting that the presence of Europeans "doesn't bother us at all."

[72] *Katanga*, May 4, 1960.

really the three big wheels of the Conakat." *L'Echo du Katanga* let it be understood that their activities often ran "counter to the opinions of the real party leaders."

No longer able to sit at the Round Table in Brussels, "our remaining role then is to act as informal advisers to our Katangan friends; which is what we are doing," Gavage declared on February 16, 1960, over Radio Ufac. Having no opportunity for acting as a European party or a mixed party, settler leaders could only dissolve the Union Katangaise in order to play an advisory role to the Conakat. This is what some of them, namely, Thyssens and Onckelinx, aided by local lawyers B—— and S——, tried to do.[73] Thus, the Cartel was being advised on the spot by several "individuals" or by its Brussels office, created with the aid of Arthur Doucy, director of the Institut de Sociologie Solvay. By the same token, the Conakat benefited more and more openly from the aid of the European community in Katanga, which saw in it "the party of order, of tradition, of understanding between Black and White," in contrast to the parties which had certain ties with the two nationalist wings of the MNC and with the "stranger" population of the *centres extra-coutumiers*.[74]

In Katanga, the European role in politics was a matter of public notoriety, and divergences among Europeans were reflected in conflicting African groups: "I think," declared Vice-Governor-General Schoeller on March 21, 1960, "that nowhere in the Congo are Europeans so closely involved in the activities of Congolese political parties. I do not at all doubt the sincerity of their intentions, but I fear that they are traveling the wrong path, that they serve neither their own cause, nor that of the parties they support."

This situation of material dependence on European advisers was bitterly resented at certain times by the Conakat leaders.

They tried accordingly to depend no longer on advisers who doubled as fund-raisers, but sought European contributions directly: "We willingly accept gifts by check, which may be addressed to the Conakat secretariat," declared a Conakat communiqué on March 8, 1960.[75]

---

[73] In contrast, Humblé withdrew from political life in April, 1960, and Gavage's role was diminished after the dissolution of the Union Katangaise.

[74] Recall that at the Round Table, opposition manifested itself less between confederalists and unitarists than between "extremists" and "moderates." The deliberately reassuring conservative votes of the Conakat sat especially well with the European majority in Katanga.

[75] The fact that they received European gifts was generally admitted. The president of the Union Congolaise, Gabriel Kitenge, declared in Katanga on Febru-

On March 10, Tshombe was even more explicit, in a declaration to his political friends: "The President [Tshombe] answered that he no longer intended to be for sale to the settlers. These gentlemen have collected much money in Conakat's name. They have made themselves the keepers of our money and some of them have traveled at Conakat expense and we do not even know the amount involved. In short, the financial situation is in the hands of the settlers; the break must be clear and even brusque." [76]

At this point, Tshombe sought a way to tone down the most conspicuous ties with the settlers, which had won him bitter criticism from the Congolese at the Round Table and which provided fuel for the most vigorous anti-Conakat campaigns in Katanga. He looked for funds elsewhere than in the pockets of the bourgeois merchants of Elisabethville. He consulted advisers other than those he had known locally (for example, A. A. J. Van Bilsen, the Abako adviser, was summoned to Elisabethville on March 30, and again in June, 1960), while remaining very close to the permanent secretary of the Ucol, Georges Thyssens.

The announced rupture with the settlers took place only to a certain degree and operated parallel to a strengthening of relations with the large industrial complex of Katanga.

THE ELECTIONS OF MAY, 1960

At stake in the elections of May, 1960, were, in Katanga, 16 national seats in the lower Chamber and 60 provincial seats. The Conakat carried 8 seats out of 16 in the Chamber and 25 out of 60 in the province; the Cartel parties won 7 in the Chamber and 23 in the province.

Electoral results gave the Conakat a certain measure of victory. By winning half the Katanga seats in the Chamber and 25 out of 60 in the provincial assembly, it stood as the leading party in the province and a candidate for the absolute majority if it could win over a few adherents, who had campaigned as individuals rather than on party tickets.

These results must, however, be examined from another perspective, that of the measure of influence of each political group. Here the indications are less conclusive for the Conakat. If the votes are added according to the slates that obtained seats, the Conakat received 104,871 votes and

---

ary 24, 1960: "You can certainly accept financial aid from Europeans if this is given without conditions."

[76] Minutes, *comité restreint* of the Conakat, March 10, 1960. The argument for a brusque rupture was rejected by certain important members who felt that an understanding reached between the settlers and the enemies of Conakat "must be enough to bury the Conakat alive."

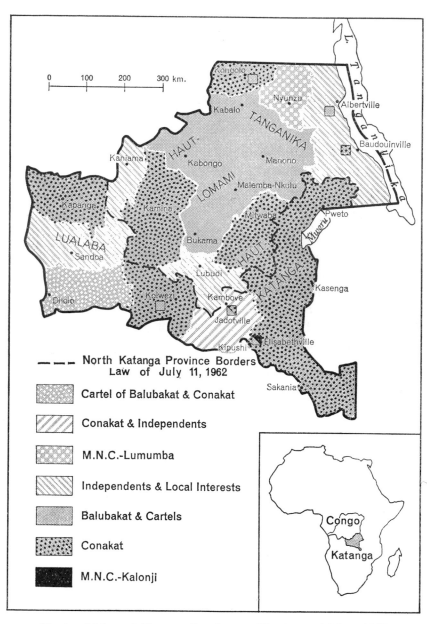

0   100   200   300 km.

Kongolo

Nyunzu

Kabalo

Albertville

TANGANIKA

HAUT-

Baudouinville

Kahiama

Kabongo

Manono

LOMAMI

Malemba-Nkulu

Kapanga

Kamina

Mitwaba

Pweto

LUALABA

Bukama

Sandoa

HAUT

Lubudi

KATANGA

Kasenga

Dilolo

Kolwezi

Kambove

Jadotville

Kipushi   Elisabethville

Sakania

— — — North Katanga Province Borders
Law of July 11, 1962

Cartel of Balubakat & Conakat

Conakat & Independents

M.N.C.-Lumumba

Independents & Local Interests

Balubakat & Cartels

Conakat

M.N.C.-Kalonji

Congo

Katanga

Electoral Map of Katanga Province — Elections of May, 1960

TABLE 2
Legislative Elections — Chamber

	Conakat	Balubakat Cartel	Individual
Elisabethville-Jadotville	1	1	
Tanganika	1	2	1
Lualaba	2	1	
Haut-Lomami	1	3	
Haut-Katanga	3	—	—
Total	8	7	1

32.07 percent for its eight seats in the Chamber; the Cartel, 80,434 votes and 24.60 percent for its six seats; Atcar, 29,657 votes and 9.07 percent for one seat (or 110,091 votes and 33.67 percent of the votes for slates of the Balubakat Cartel parties).[77]

In order to comprehend this phenomenon, it must be understood that the elections took place under a system of proportional representation within the *circonscriptions* or electoral districts and without electoral alliances. This system favored party slates at the expense of individuals running on their own, local candidates, or groups insufficiently disciplined to run on a single ticket.

In Katanga, for the provincial elections, there were 167 tickets competing for the 60 seats, of which 24 tickets were controlled by the Conakat, 16 by the Balubakat, and 12 by the MNC/Lumumba. This led to a considerable dispersion of the vote and a neutralization of a great number of votes cast for individuals. That explains why in the Chamber in Leopoldville, the Conakat could win 50 percent of the seats with 32.07 percent of the votes, and the Cartel 43.75 percent of the seats with 33.67 percent of the votes.

In the provincial balloting, the Conakat benefited more from the system than the Cartel, which could not always avoid having several of its own slates in the same *circonscription*, nor could it always form a single list with anti-Conakat political groups, such as MNC/Lumumba, MNC/Kalonji, and the Fédération Générale du Congo (FGC). This led to a loss of votes.

On the whole, the Conakat seats were acquired at less cost than those of the Cartel. For the entire province, with the exception of the territory

[77] Translator's note: Although a member of the Cartel, Atcar ran under its own label in Tshokwe areas, accounting for its separate election total.

TABLE 3
Provincial Assembly Elections

	Conakat	MNC/L	Union Congolais	Cartel Balubakat	Cartel Baluba MNC/L	Cartel Katangais	Atcar	MNC/L	Interlocal	Individuals
Elisabethville	3	1				2				
Jadotville	1			2						
District of										
Tanganika	*3*		*1*	*6*	*1*			*1*	*2*	*2*
Albertville			1		1					1
Baudouinville	1								2	1
Manono				3						
Kabalo				2						
Nyunzu								1		
Kongolo	2			1						
District of										
Lualaba	*6*			*1*			*2*		*3*	
Dilolo	2						2			
Kolwezi	2			1						
Lubudi									1	
Kapanga	2									
Sandoa									2	
District of										
Haut-Lomami	*3*			*9*					*1*	
Kamina	3									
Kabongo				3						
Kaniama									1	
Bukama				3						
Malemba-Nkulu				3						
District of										
Haut-Katanga	*9*									*1*
Kipushi	2									
Sakania	1									
Pweto	2									
Kasenga	2									
Mitwaba	1									
Kambove	1									1
Total	25	1	1	18	1	2	2	1	6	3

Cartel Parties = 23

of Malemba-Nkulu, the Conakat obtained twenty-five seats with 94,438 votes and the Cartel parties nineteen seats with 94,863 votes. Let us remember that, for the Chamber in Leopoldville, each Conakat seat was acquired with 13,109 votes and each Cartel seat with 15,728 votes — a situation resulting from an extraordinary distribution of votes.

TABLE 4
Provincial Elections — Party Votes

District	Conakat and Conakat trad. authorities			Cartel parties		
	Seats	Total votes	Votes per Seat	Seats	Total votes	Votes per seat
Elisabethville	3	8,617	2,873	2	8,610	4,035
Jadotville	1	4,970	4,970	2	8,079	4,040
Tanganika	3	11,342	3,781	6	26,898	4,483
Haut-Katanga	9	23,323	2,592	—	—	—
Lualaba	6	28,716	4,786	3	23,991	7,997
Haut-Lomami less Malemba-Nkulu*	3	17,470	5,624	6	27,285	4,548
Katanga	25	94,438	3,778	19	94,863	4,992

*At Malemba-Nkulu, the Cartel's was the only slate and won three seats without elections.

Thus, in Elisabethville, the Conakat elected three deputies to the provincial assembly with 8,617 out of 27,387 valid votes, but the anti-Conakat parties (the MNC/Kalonji, the Cartel, the FGC, and the Union Congolaise) also elected three but with 16,313 votes.[78] In the national legislative elections for Elisabethville-Jadotville where only three slates were competing, the Conakat received 14,684 votes and one seat; the Cartel, 23,112 and one seat as well; and the FGC, 2,369 votes.

Likewise in Kipushi, the Conakat won two seats with 3,324 votes, but its adversaries — the Cartel, MNC-FGC, MNC-Fédéka-Basonge — which ran on separate slates elected no one although they received, respectively, 822, 922, and 907 votes or a total of 2,651 votes.

The Cartel, which had counted on an electoral victory, contested the results of the balloting and introduced twenty-one appeals in Elisabethville-Jadotville. The complaints were serious: electoral rolls were irregular and incomplete, with Rhodesians included and Baluba or Kasaians miss-

[78] In Elizabethville, for the sixth seat, the tally was the Conakat 2,872; the Cartel 2,870.

ing; ballot boxes containing votes favorable to the Cartel had disappeared before the counting; territorial administrators had overtly aided the Conakat in its campaign;[79] violence was exercised against the partisans of the Cartel.[80] All these appeals were rejected.

THE CONSTITUTION OF THE KATANGAN GOVERNMENT

The provisional *Loi Fondamentale* had provided for the election of the president of the provincial government by an absolute majority of the provincial Assembly and that of the members of the government on one ballot (Article 123); a formula which ended necessarily in proportional representation of all *tendances*. In principle, such a procedure should permit the government to be constituted in orderly fashion, without the violent confrontation of groups aiming at complete take-over.

But such was not to be the outcome in Katanga. The Conakat immediately worked out alliances and recruited individuals with a view to ensuring an absolute majority; the Cartel, disappointed in the election results, feared in addition a *coup d'état* from the Conakat and a proclamation of Katangan independence before central institutions could be set up.[81] After the proclamation of the electoral results, the Cartel was even further disillusioned.

The MNC/Kalonji, at the end of April, had given "the order to all voters who are members of our party, and to all our sympathisers to vote for a single deputy, Jason Sendwe, in the electoral *circonscription* of Elisabethville-Jadotville," and recommended a vote in favor of provincial candidates of the Cartel where the MNC/Kalonji offered no slate itself. But, at the end of May, it began to demur from the Balubakat and its Cartel allies; MNC/Kalonji sought to constitute an autonomous "group"

[79] By advising the Conakat to avoid splinter tickets or by according preferential treatment to propagandists and later to witnesses for the Conakat. The Cartel also accused one provincial commissioner in this regard.

[80] In Kamina where the Muluba chief Kasongo Nyembo rallied to the Conakat: on May 22, pro-Cartel Kasaians were attacked and there were six deaths (one of which was a decapitated child). Following these incidents, many Kasaians emigrated from Katanga.

[81] In Kolwezi, on April 21, 1960, Tshombe had again promised to his supporters "the constitution of an independent Katanga that we wish to precede the establishment of the Congolese federal state." *L'Echo du Katanga* (Elisabethville), April 22, 1960. Van Bilsen, the Abako adviser who was consulted by the Conakat, wrote that: "Already in the month of March, 1960, Tshombe showed me before the *comité* of his party that he himself and his friends intended to proclaim independence for Katanga, before the transfer of power." — A. A. J. Van Bilsen, *L'Indépendance du Congo* (Brussels: Casterman, 1962), p. 209.

in the provincial Assembly, including in this group at least one Muluba from Kasai, a local MNC/Kalonji leader, elected on the Cartel list in Kolwezi.[82]

Later, on May 28, an agreement was nevertheless concluded between the Katangan leaders of MNC/Kalonji (Pierre Missakabo and Cléophas Mukeba) and those of the Cartel (Sendwe, Isaac Kalonji, and Mayele) by virtue of which the provincial seat won by MNC/Kalonji was "assigned" to the Cartel. The Cartel agreed to reach an understanding with MNC/Kalonji over the question of seats in the provincial government and the Cartel solemnly declared "it had no agreement of any sort with a political party at the provincial or national level." [83]

On May 30, Albert Kalonji himself came to Elisabethville; he wanted to assure himself that the Katangan parties would support him personally if he tried to become the first premier designate in the central government. He then concluded a covert agreement with the Conakat, with so much the fewer scruples since the Cartel had played Lumumba's game, and Lumumba in turn had allied himself with the Lulua of the Kasai. The Conakat would support Kalonji in Leopoldville; the MNC/Kalonji would back the Conakat at the provincial level and would get a ministerial post for Cléophas Mukeba; the Conakat agreed to protect "the goods and persons of the Baluba of the Kasai" in Katanga.[84] From that moment on, observers noted a certain relaxation of tension among the Kasaians in Elisabethville.

The Albert Kalonji–Conakat accord, from the point of view of electoral arithmetic, had relatively little importance (it was a question of one or two seats). But in the activities of Tshombe in June and July, 1960, the momentary alliance with the Kasai partisans of Albert Kalonji is a fact of considerable importance, in that it substantially reduced the threat of disturbances in the cities and in that it reassured European companies which employed a large number of Kasaians, notably among their skilled workers.

Meanwhile, the Cartel and the Conakat competed in a race for the

[82] *L'Echo du Katanga* (Elisabethville), May 27, 1960.

[83] The Cartel was then accused by the Conakat of being linked with the MNC/Lumumba and of having made commitments to it on the national level. On May 28, MNC/Lumumba made an offer of direct cooperation to the Cartel.

[84] On May 27, the Conakat had already published a communiqué directed to the "strangers," "formally guaranteeing security for themselves, their families, and their belongings."

majority. Each recruited allies as rapidly as possible, to find 30 votes, the number necessary to elect the president of the provincial government.

In this race, the Conakat held several major advantages, financial and otherwise. Successful candidates who had run as individuals (local notables and chiefs) and who had at first rallied to the Cartel, later published denials, alleging they had acted under duress. Such was the case of paramount Chief Tumbwe of Albertville and that of Chief Mukulu Mutombo of Kaniama. With the more or less certain rallying of three Batabwa from the Baudouinville region, of Chiefs Tumbwe and Mutombo, of Tshombe's brother elected from Sandoa, of Charles Mutaka elected in Kambove, of one traditional member from Lubudi and of one from MNC/Kalonji, the Conakat could quickly announce that it controlled a majority of the provincial Assembly.

Each party accused the other of using force or corruption in rallying adherents. Whatever the methods, the Conakat acquired those elected on individual tickets and traditional representatives whereas the Cartel could count only 22 votes in the Assembly against 38 for the Conakat. This swelling of the Conakat forces, including elements on which the Balubakat had counted, aggravated the bitterness of the Cartel leaders and reinforced the impression that the European administrative and private support which Tshombe enjoyed were such that henceforth their only possible effective protection would have to come from "outside," that is, from the future Congolese central authorities and, while awaiting their establishment, from Brussels.

It is in this atmosphere that, for the first time, on June 1, 1960, the provincial Assembly of Katanga met.

On the eve of the meeting, Vice-Governor-General Schoeller, who feared "a sabotage attempt" against the establishment of institutions, demanded that Leopoldville prepare an executive order with the force of law, amending the law on governmental structures. This law required, in Articles 110 and 114 of the *Loi Fondamentale*, the presence of two thirds of all members of the provincial Assembly to elect members of the provincial government, to coopt Assembly members, and to select senators for the upper chamber in Leopoldville. The abstention of more than one third of the provincial Assembly members could therefore paralyze the establishment of provincial governments. The Cartel had at the outset 22 members out of 60.

Vice-Governor-General Schoeller thought he had "serious proof" that the Cartel would try "to render impossible the procedure for the election of coopted members, members of the government and senators. . . . If at 3 o'clock session June 1 required quorum not present, signifying important abstention, [aforementioned] ordinance must be issued immediately; if not, ordinance must in any case be ready on first telephone appeal." [85] The Governor-General in Leopoldville informed Brussels of Schoeller's plan the very same day, since the requested modification implied a Belgian law and not a simple ordinance. "It seems to be difficult to have it in time. . . . I will intervene from here with [Rémy] Mwamba," [86] concluded the Governor-General.

At the first provincial Assembly session, Hubert Banza declared, for the Cartel, that he had entered appeals against the results of the elections and that his group had decided not to participate in the drawing of lots for the provisional president nor to take their seats in the Assembly as long as they did not know the results of the appeals.

The provision of the *Loi Fondamentale* did not stop the name of the provisional president of the Assembly from being drawn by lot. The procedure was not blocked by the withdrawal of the 22 Cartel members, but the Vice-Governor-General drew the conclusion that the attitude of the Cartel would paralyze the Assembly at the moment when the provincial government was to be constituted, Assembly members to be coopted, and senators to the upper chamber in Leopoldville to be elected. He asked the Control Commission to call in the Cartel leaders and to explain to them the outcome of their electoral appeals. On June 2, the Cartel withdrew at the moment when the provincial Assembly, ahead of its timetable by three days, was to coopt nine provincial Assembly members, and the 32 remaining could only declare their impotence to proceed further with the coopting process.

That day, Vice-Governor-General Schoeller called to the attention of Colonial Minister Auguste de Schrijver in Brussels that it appeared that the Cartel would now refuse to admit "election results as well as decisions of Control Commission which do not conform to its desires. Tactic adopted," said Schoeller in his telex message, "to consist almost certainly in abstaining sessions provincial Assembly June 5 and 11. Consequently," continued Schoeller, "quorum of ⅔ members will not be attained and establishment of institutions will be rendered impossible in Ka-

---

[85] Telex addressed to Brussels. Most of the quotations which follow and which relate to the activities of the Vice-Governor-General are of the same origin.

[86] Member of the *Collège Exécutif Général* in Leopoldville and Balubakat leader.

tanga. . . . To emerge from impasse, only means is to amend immediately law on structures by providing that if ⅔ quorum not attained, Assembly meets again next day and can then make laws if half members present." Schoeller also affirmed he would "make all possible efforts, but it seems question of concerted plan under advice of Europeans of left tendency STOP. Cite Mme. Perin sent especially by Solvay Brussels." Schoeller ended his telex: "Have charged *Sûreté* to collect precise information on acts these persons STOP. Energetic move on your part with Doucy desirable STOP."

On June 4, an attempted conciliation under the auspices of the provincial *Collège Exécutif* failed, for the Cartel did not accept the rejection of its appeals and contested the results of the elections. The rejection of its appeals seemed, moreover, to have taken place, in cases of disputes involving the interior, without special on-the-spot examination; on the Belgian side, the major preoccupation was not to upset the established timetable and not to be forced into new elections.

Again on June 5, the quorum of two thirds was not attained and, on Tshombe's suggestion, the 37 members addressed a telegram to the Minister of the Congo in Brussels in order to accelerate the change in the quorum rule. "Establishment of institutions in Katanga delayed by deliberate plan of sabotage," telexed Schoeller to Leopoldville. "Situation will be serious in Katanga if amendment not promulgated immediately."

June 6 and 7, confusion was total.

The political commission with the Minister of the Congo in Brussels rejected the idea of an amendment to the quorum rule of two-thirds, and Kasavubu and Pierre Nyangwile, members of the *Collège Exécutif Général* visiting in Brussels, were of the same opinion. The view hostile to the amendment was based on the following argument: the elections were fraudulent, or at least the results were contested; the Conakat was prepared to constitute a government that it would dominate and was ready to proclaim independence (the precise date cited was June 13); the amendment would play into the hands of the secessionists since it would permit them to set up a Conakat government while central institutions were still far from being established; it would be better to dispatch a commission of inquiry to Katanga, as the majority of the political commission had recommended.

In contrast, the provincial *Collège Exécutif* of Katanga, which had no Cartel representative, publicly declared that the electoral results were not to be discussed and therewith rejected even the idea of a commission of inquiry. It threatened not "to continue to carry out its responsibilities" if the Belgian Parliament did not correct immediately "the obvious loophole" in the matter of the quorum. The Vice-Governor-General was convinced — although he had no proof [87] — that, without the activities of European advisers, the results of the elections would not have posed serious problems, and complained in Brussels that a member of the *Collège Exécutif Général*, Rémy Mwamba, was on the spot in Elisabethville "to give the Cartel a boost." [88]

European circles favorable to the Conakat were very active in Elisabethville and their activities bordered on provocation. Thus, false rumors were launched over Radio Ufac [89] by Beckers and Fréart, of the Union Minière; they served to harden the Cartel in its position. In any case, the Cartel hoped that a control commission presided over by Kasavubu would come to resolve the electoral palaver. The Conakat leaders, on their part, were exasperated. Tshombe lodged a complaint against Mme. Perin-Hockers, Cartel adviser, and called for the expulsion of "advisers who have come from Belgium" at the very moment when, from Brussels, friends of the Cartel strongly recommended negotiation and moderation, suggesting a face to face meeting between Tshombe and Sendwe in the presence of the Minister of the Congo in Brussels. Mme. Perin-Hockers' residence was searched. [90]

Despite the opinion of the political commission, the Minister of the Congo proposed the amendment June 7. [91] Minister Ganshof van der Meersch, whose deputy *chef de cabinet* was Evariste Kimba, a pro-Conakat Muluba, insisted on proceeding with extreme urgency and felt it necessary, after the rejection of the Cartel appeals, to proclaim officially that the electoral results were definitive.

[87] The grievances of the Cartel on the subject of electoral fraud were expressed in Katanga, when the advisers, of whom Schoeller complained, were still in Belgium.

[88] See p. 71; it is Henri Cornélis, Governor-General, who intervened with Mwamba in regard to this affair.

[89] Ufac was the Union des Fraternelles des Anciens Combattants, a veterans' organization which, in Elisabethville, had among its principals a leading personality from the Union Minière, A. Sohier.

[90] On June 7, Professor Doucy wired Sendwe, Valentin Ilunga, and Isaac Kalonji: "Indispensable you reach understanding now. Let me advise you to undertake negotiations with other Katanga party. Consider Katanga future linked to serious conversations with other political party. . . . Insist that moderation reign in discussions. Understanding indispensable." On June 8, the Cartel was present at the Assembly session.

[91] Belgian Parliamentary Document, No· 544,1.

To appease the anxieties of the Cartel over the composition of the Katangan government, Vice-Governor-General Schoeller, in the name of the provincial *Collège Exécutif*, gave a radio speech on June 6 in which he declared "the party which accepts the results of the elections is quite ready to assure to the other party the broadest share in the government." He insisted nonetheless that because the Control Commission had "conscientiously examined the appeals of the Cartel, no one would any longer have the right to question the electoral results."

On June 8, in the morning session, a new development: the Cartel was participating in the session. The partisans of the amendment saw in this attendance proof that the first move toward an amendment in Brussels was sufficient to put the brakes on the attempt at obstruction. On the other hand, one can imagine that the Cartel, convinced of the secessionist intentions of the Conakat, decided to support any policy which would permit the establishment of central institutions, and especially the senate.[92] Prosper Mwamba Ilunga explained that the Cartel would continue to contest the validity of the Katangan government, declaring however, "Today we are prepared to let the Conakat form the government."

The Assembly coopted nine members — five Conakat and four from the Cartel — and fixed the number of senators from *milieux coutumiers*, or traditional sectors, at four, and ten as the number of provincial minististers in addition to the President. At the moment of the vote for the officers of the Assembly, contrary to forecasts and to promises, the Conakat used its majority and gave the presidency and the two vice-presidential posts to the Conakat, in the persons of Charles Mutaka-wa-Dilomba, Mathias Nzimbe, and Jean-Marie Mpweto, respectively.

In Brussels, the committee of the lower Chamber was reticent on the subject of amendments. It called for a formal promise from the Conakat,

[92] To be sure, it must be noted that the Cartel voted each time the balloting permitted the establishment of central institutions, except on June 2 and 5 when it refused to coopt the nine Assembly members, a condition *sine qua non* for the nomination of senators. This confirms the interpretation offered by Ganshof van der Meersch according to which the Cartel Assembly members boycotted the provincial institutions so that central organs would first be set up which could "impose a solution to conform to their desires." — *Fin de la souveraineté belge au Congo*, p. 574. (Translator's note: The elected members of the Katangan Assembly were required by the *Loi Fondamentale* to coopt an additional nine members. Once the Assembly membership was thus complete, the Assembly could proceed to elect its own officers, Katanga's senators to sit in Leopoldville, and members of the Katangan Council of Ministers. See pp. 325–27.)

guaranteeing that ministers and senators would be chosen by proportional representation. The Belgian Chamber had heard echoes of the rumors according to which Tshombe planned to proclaim independence for Katanga on June 13 and several members refused to provide him with a short cut to this end.[93]

This story of the Conakat plot for June 13, responded Elisabethville, was "invented out of whole cloth," and, according to these authorities, this in itself was additional proof of the work of agitation and incitement from irresponsible Cartel advisers. Tshombe lodged a complaint in court against the accusations of collusion with Rhodesia. On June 9, the Vice-Governor-General thought he could promise that proportional representation would prevail, unless the Cartel were not at the session.[94] On their side, Kibwe, Munongo, and Tshombe, in a telex to the Minister of the Congo, affirmed that "the Conakat program included in no way Katanga's secession nor an accord of any sort with Rhodesia." In addition they declared, "Our most sincere desire is to bring about government of national union with minority." The confusion, therefore, remained very great.

Saturday, June 11, the news that an independent Conakat government would be constituted on June 13 was confirmed, and it was believed in addition that in case of unilateral distribution of ministerial posts one wing of the Cartel would opt for a separate government. From these facts, some drew the conclusion that the plan attributed to the Conakat was not "invented out of whole cloth" as had been said in high quarters three days earlier. Others, on the contrary, felt that the obstruction of the Cartel created a veritable ferment within the Conakat and that without the amendment the Conakat might take dangerous initiatives. It is by this basic argument that pressure was put on the Belgian government and Parliament.

[93] "An agreement was to have been reached in this vein in Brussels between Jean-Baptiste Kibwe for the Conakat and Joseph Kasavubu, Abako president, to bring into being a federal Congolese state and to halt formation of a central government headed by Patrice Lumumba," wrote Ganshof van der Meersch in *Fin de la Souveraineté belge au Congo*, p. 567. It is a question here of a novel hypothesis which is not supported, it would seem, by any recognizable source. The author does not hold to it at any rate.

[94] Given the manner of voting, this promise is scarcely more than a statement of fact. It is surprising, moreover, that Belgian members of parliament had demanded such a promise when the law had prescribed the vote by proportional representation. The only question posed was to know what would happen in case of the absence of the Cartel at the moment of the vote.

Elsewhere, it was noted that without the amendment, illegal governments could be constituted while a legitimate government could not, because of the procedural obstacles. This could be a paradoxical situation, felt Schoeller and Ganshof both.

On Sunday, June 12, the Cartel was again at the session. Putting an end to the confusion, the Minister of the Congo gave out a statement confirming the impossibility of constituting homogeneous provincial governments. In the course of the June 12 session, the Assembly elected ten nontraditional senators according to proportional representation, but the Cartel won only three out of ten, which in their eyes augured very ill for the system proposed for the composition of the government.

Next on the agenda came the nomination of the president of the provincial government.

The Cartel felt that it had to insist on another sequence for the elections: election of traditional senators, election of ten members of government, and only then election of the president of the government. The law provided for three entire days between nomination of candidates and the election of "traditional" senators, while the vote on the presidency was to precede that of the provincial ministers.

"The Cartel is in no hurry to constitute the provincial government," declared Prosper Mwamba Ilunga in announcing the withdrawal of the Cartel members.

The Conakat spokesman flared up: "If in 48 hours the amendment has not arrived here, we shall take everything into our own hands. We shall put the question before international jurisdiction; we shall enter discussions even with the Confederation of Northern Rhodesia [*sic!*], officially, and not secretly."[95]

Kibwe's declaration, strongly applauded, was followed by Tshombe's: "If two days from now the law has not been changed, we shall take responsibility into our own hands. We shall make an appeal to the United Nations and I know that our rights will be protected. . . . It will be sad for us, Katangans, who would like to have our friendship with Belgium, to be forced at the last minute to be obliged to become enemies of Belgium."

Godefroid Munongo expressed threats in the same vein as Kibwe and Tshombe. Vice-Governor-General Schoeller, at this moment, tried both to

---

[95] Abstract of the Proceedings, Katangan Assembly, June 12, 1960. "These were empty threats provoked by indignation," declared Kibwe on June 13, to Vice-Governor-General Schoeller.

accelerate the procedure concerning amendments relative to the quorum and to calm the Cartel and the Conakat.

To Brussels, he promised by telex to intervene himself "with the majority leaders to advise strongly that even in case of Cartel's absence, they include members of this party in government. It could only be question of spontaneous gesture for which majority would gain all credit. Inconceivable to want to impose that as an obligation. Solemnly affirm to you that if this time again, Parliament does not understand situation, price to pay for its default very high."

The Vice-Governor-General also launched an appeal over the radio on June 13; he invoked the law to guarantee to the Cartel proportional representation in the provincial government. He publicly declared that he understood the anger of those who demanded the amendment immediately and "conceded" that the delay in the Belgian parliamentary procedure was "irritating." He condemned the declarations of Tshombe and Kibwe concerning the forty-eight hour ultimatum to Belgium and the appeals to the U.N. and to the Federation of Rhodesia and Nyasaland.

Also on June 13 Kibwe, a member of the political commission, addressed to Colonial Minister de Schrijver and Resident Minister Ganshof a telex in which he said that his presence was indispensable in Elisabethville to avoid an uprising of the population, "Katangan government not having been formed because of the Cartel maneuver." He continued, "Insist amendment you have put before Parliament pass immediately in 48 hours STOP. Useless to wish to push Katanga to take extreme positions for neither Belgium, nor rest of Congo would profit from secession of Katanga STOP."

The same day, Vice-Governor-General Schoeller announced in Brussels that he had gotten the Conakat leaders to maintain calm among their partisans while awaiting the amendment if they were given firm guarantees that this amendment would be voted by the Belgian parliament. For Schoeller felt that the "regrettable words pronounced by Kibwe at end session June 12, 1960, and provoked by default Belgian quarters must not be taken literally and constitute extremely maladroit attempt to overcome hesitations in promulgating indispensable text. If amendment adopted, I most formally guarantee that even if Cartel abstains, at least four candidates of this party will be elected to the government."[96] This

---

[96] Unsatisfactory formula, the Cartel is said to have declared to Schoeller the same evening, claiming *equality*, "either Assembly presidency or Katangan presidency," and soliciting arbitration by the Belgian government to this end.

promise furnished the decisive argument to the Colonial Minister before the parliamentary committees.

Tuesday, June 14, the situation had deteriorated.

The *Force Publique* headquarters in Elisabethville heard in the morning of a Conakat scheme according to which Tshombe would announce independence on that very day. The speech was drafted and ready to be broadcast. A high officer had himself seized the text in the office of the local daily newspaper.

At eleven o'clock, the provincial *Collège Exécutif* decided to apply Plan "Troubles" and at noon the "state of exception" was proclaimed, to the anger of the Conakat leaders who felt these measures uncalled for. Schoeller read over the radio a proclamation of the provincial *Collège Exécutif*, which was not countersigned, however, by the Conakat representative Munongo.[97] These decisions made an impression in Brussels where governmental circles saw in them additional proof of the urgent need to vote the amendment.

The text of the proclamation of independence was to appear in the newspaper *L'Essor du Congo*, dated June 15: the provincial Assembly was to declare "independence for Katanga within its present geographical frontiers," to launch an appeal to King Baudouin "so that he would respect the pledges undertaken by the Crown of Belgium," to Belgium, and to the U.N., asking the latter to defend "the oppressed minorities, Katanga in a unitary Congolese state being on the way to becoming a minority whose wishes would be neglected."

The project was provisionally to bring into being an independent Katanga while respecting "the essentials of the provisional constitution," that is, of the *Loi Fondamentale* of May 19, 1960, on the structures of the Congo: that meant also that Katanga would send its deputies and senators to Leopoldville[98] to prepare the definitive constitution for the Congo which must in fact be the result of "prior agreements between equally sovereign nations" and bring about a state with federal structures, in default of which "Katanga would reassume its entire freedom."

The "state of exception," proclaimed for the whole province, was

---

[97] On June 6, Schoeller had announced over the radio that, on his own suggestion, Munongo of the Conakat would no longer sit on the *Collège Exécutif*, whose only Congolese members would be Gabriel Kitenge and Paul Muhona.

[98] It is interesting to note that on June 14, Tshombe submitted to Lumumba, then Premier-designate, the conditions under which his party would participate in the central government: the Conakat demanded for itself the portfolios of Defense and Economic Affairs.

based officially on two facts: a certainty, namely, that the Conakat wanted to decree Katanga independent in the provincial Assembly session of June 14 at 6 P.M., and a threat of the Cartel to constitute "within the framework of a United Congo" a government of Northeast Katanga, which would begin to function some time after June 30, if a homogeneous Conakat government were established.

The authorities decided to let the provincial Assembly meet but special precautions were taken: crowds around the building were dispersed; the Assembly could proceed only to votes provided for, and if any other intervention were attempted the room would be cleared by the forces of order.[99]

Schoeller drew from the situation the following moral: "Only means to avoid this dramatic outcome is broadcast this morning by Belgian government of formal assurances that amendment to structures law would be passed in shortest possible time."

At 6:20 P.M., the Assembly met, the Cartel being present. The Assembly president announced that the amendment on the quorum had been adopted by the committee of the lower Chamber in Brussels: "He invites the Assembly members from the Cartel to see in this measure only the good of the country. He points out to them that in abstaining, they would commit an error, for they would find themselves facing a government of a single party. If the Cartel participates effectively in the balloting, and if it votes intelligently, it can obtain four ministerial posts."

The Belgian Chamber scheduled the public debate at 2:00 P.M., and adopted the articles at 5 P.M., while the Belgian Senate committee met the same day at 4:30 P.M.[100]

The designation of four "traditional" senators went off normally; two affiliated to each group were elected. What followed in the session was less serene.

The Assembly president having proposed to proceed to the election of the provincial government chief, Prosper Mwamba Ilunga took the floor in the name of the Cartel. His party, he said, rejected the electoral results, because the colonial administration had directed and controlled the voting to the benefit of the Conakat. The Cartel would remain within legal limits; it would not oppose the constitution of a government by the Cona-

[99] "The Belgian authorities had threatened to arrest Tshombe, Kibwe, and Munongo, when they had wished to proclaim independence before June 30 for Katanga," asserted Evariste Kimba in *La Libre Belgique* (Brussels), August 5, 1960.

[100] This committee adopted the bill by 22 votes to three abstentions.

kat but would challenge its validity: "there will be no trouble, even if an entirely Conakat government is installed." For Mwamba Ilunga, what divided the Cartel from the Conakat was that the first was "for unity and integrity of the Congo"; the second for "the total independence of Katanga on June 30, then attachment to the Rhodesias."

When the Assembly president interrupted the orator, the Cartel members again left the session.

On October 15, 1960, when he had become chief of state of Katanga, Tshombe gave his own interpretation to the event:

> In the month of June, 1960, Katangans of courage drafted a long study establishing the historical and legal rights of Katanga to its independence but adding that until the vote on the definitive constitution for the Congo, Katanga would submit to the *Loi Fondamentale* of May 19. The purpose of this study was essentially to draw attention to the provisional character of the *Loi Fondamentale*, in order to stop Lumumba, whose intentions we are aware of, from transforming the provisional into the definitive and from taking advantage of the situation.
>
> The study was to have been submitted to a vote of the Katanga provincial Assembly during the final days of June. . . . The Belgian administration . . . occupied the halls of the Assembly with *gendarmes* armed to the teeth.
>
> Barely a few inches away from me, these *gendarmes* had orders to arrest me and the members of my government as soon as I said the first words of this speech.[101]

At Leopoldville, where he was a national deputy and Balubakat president, Sendwe protested against the amendment bill which he interpreted as the road toward a homogeneous Conakat government.[102] He accused the Europeans of inciting the Conakat to separatism and lined up in solidarity with Lumumba, but nevertheless advised his party members to take their seats and to negotiate the demands for four ministries and one committee chairmanship.

On June 15, Vice-Governor-General Schoeller declared, "The state of exception provokes great irritation among one segment of the Conakat leadership," and, in another telex, said: "Have again had discussion with Cartel delegates STOP. They told me their decision to abstain from any

---

[101] Tshombe's speech on October 15, 1960, on the occasion of the departure of the Belgian technical mission from Elisabethville, Secrétariat d'Etat à l'Information, Service de Presse, Katanga, No. 1.

[102] Vice-Governor-General Schoeller "repeated for the hundredth time" to him that if the Cartel were in the session at the vote it was "certain to obtain at least four seats in the government."

session having as object election of government STOP. They added that they counted on central government to reopen the whole matter after June 30 STOP. All appeals to reason by [Paul] Muhona and myself were in vain."

At this point, the Vice-Governor-General had "high hopes" that the Conakat rank and file would follow their leaders and would elect, "whatever the state of affairs," four Cartel representatives as members of the government.

The same day, Minister de Schrijver announced the vote for the amendment of Articles 110 and 114: in the Belgian lower Chamber, 98 votes for, 5 against, and 66 abstentions; in the Belgian Senate, 66 votes for and 33 abstentions. The new text which went into effect after June 16, provided that "if after two consecutive meetings of the [provincial] Assembly, the presence of at least two-thirds of its members has not been obtained, the Assembly may duly proceed, provided a majority of its members are present."

At the time of the vote, the Belgian Parliament and the Minister of the Congo thought, on the faith of the promises transmitted by Elisabethville, that even in case of the absence of the Cartel at the session, proportional representation would be applied in constituting the Katangan government.

June 16 was the decisive day. The assembly was scheduled the same day for 10 A.M., 3 P.M. and 8 P.M. If the Cartel abstained at the first two sessions, it was therefore at the 8 P.M. session that the vote would take place by simple majority. This group of three meetings in a single day, which scarcely seemed to correspond to the spirit of the amendment voted by the Belgian Parliament, was decided upon, it was said in Elisabethville, to calm the Katangan people and to permit the rapid departure for Leopoldville of the Conakat leaders who were mandated to negotiate on setting up the central government.

On the morning of June 16, the Belgian authorities were optimistic. The Cartel would perhaps participate in the meetings; the Conakat maintained its promise to have four Cartel members elected, and Tshombe renounced "explosive declarations forever." [103] Minister de Schrijver on his side strongly emphasized that the rule on proportional representation

[103] Schoeller telex of the morning of June 16, 1960. In *L'Essor du Congo* of June 16, Tshombe declared: "From now until June 30, a *Loi Fondamentale* exists. We intend to respect it and to remain within the limits of legality. But no one can force us, after this date, to follow the other parties."

was "extremely desirable," even in the event of the absence of one of the parties.

A first session of the Assembly took place at 10 A.M., with 42 of the 69 members present; the quorum was not attained. The Assembly president advised the Assembly "to leave the Cartel two or three seats" if it were not present by the third session. The Conakat confirmed its agreements with Vice-Governor-General Schoeller who believed, moreover, that the Cartel would attend the following session. At 3 P.M., the second session convened with 42 attending. Godefroid Munongo "thought that for the good of Katanga and for the peace of our regions, we must reserve three seats in the government for the members of the Cartel." Schoeller "hoped that the Conakat, despite negative and provocative attitude of minority which considerably irritated traditional chiefs, would carry out its stated intentions this evening." At 8 P.M., the third session was held with 42 present, but the majority of two-thirds was no longer required according to the letter of the amendment. The Assembly president pleaded again for Cartel representation ("two or three members").

No one at this point spoke any longer of the four Cartel seats promised to De Schrijver on June 13 and 14, and no one seemed in fact to be preparing for the election of Cartel members. Without preparation of the vote and with 143 candidates for ten government posts, the chances for election of Cartel candidates were practically nil.

At the vote, four candidates received 30 votes out of 41 and five others were elected with a total of eleven votes. Two candidates were elected with a single vote. A second ballot was necessary to elect a tenth minister. He was Cléophas Mukeba, of MNC/Kalonji, named by thirty-one votes out of sixty-nine members, of which forty-two were present.

On June 30, Congo independence day, the government of Katanga was composed as follows:[104]

Moise Tshombe: 37 votes, Lunda, Conakat — President
Godefroid Munongo: 10 votes, Muyeke, Conakat — Interior
Jean-Baptiste Kibwe: 7 votes, Mutabwa, Conakat — Finance
Sylvestre Kilonda: 7 votes, Muhemba, Conakat — Agriculture
Joseph Kiwele: 6 votes, Mutabwa, Conakat — National Education
Evariste Kimba: 3 votes, Muluba, Conakat — Commerce and Industry
Paul Muhona: 3 votes, Tshokwe, individual — Labor and Social Matters
Salomon Tshizand: 3 votes, Lunda, individual — Economic Affairs
Valentin Ilunga: 1 vote, Muluba, Conakat — Justice

[104] After modifications of detail in the attributions and titles of the portfolios.

Alphonse Kiela: 1 vote, Mutabwa, Conakat — Communications

Cléophas Mukeba: 31 votes, Muluba-Kasai, MNC/Kalonji — Public Health

Tshombe and Kibwe, blaming an important colleague, guilty of a "last minute maneuver," expressed their regrets to Vice-Governor-General Schoeller for their failure to elect Cartel members.[105] "They did not succeed in imposing voting discipline," said the Vice-Governor-General, who considered that "new laborious negotiations were necessary to try to correct unhappy composition, namely by resignation of members obtaining only one vote."

The Belgian ministers apparently argued in the same vein, for certain members of Parliament who voted for the amendment on the basis of the Conakat promises reacted quite vigorously. Since the Conakat leaders were in Leopoldville, negotiations were removed there, but tentatively and without concrete results.

On June 21, the Cartel had announced, through Agence Belga, the composition of its "provincial government of a coalition of Baluba-Tshokwe and their allies, formed in Elisabethville since June 16, 1960," and associated with the MNC/Lumumba coalition in Leopoldville. The Cartel tried in particular to attain the post of Commissioner of State in Katanga, a position provided for by the provisional *Loi Fondamentale* (Articles 190 and following). Named for three years, the commissioner was to be the representative of the central government in the province.

On June 23, Lumumba made known the composition of the first Congolese government.[106]

SECESSION ATTEMPTS ON THE EVE
OF CONGOLESE INDEPENDENCE

"We are not separatists and we want to prove it by showing that we agree with the principle of participating in the central government."[107]

Tshombe's declaration of June 16 alluded to the telegram by which the Conakat leader — without considering the position of the Cartel of National Union constituted by the "moderates" of which he was theoreti-

[105] On the Belgian side, this explanation was discarded after inquiry. Schoeller telexed on June 17: "The unlucky result of the vote seems due simply to lack of maturity, to indiscipline and to personal ambition."

[106] There is, in Appendix I, a timetable for the establishment of provincial institutions, comparing the legal calendar originally established with the timetable as it worked out in practice in Katanga and Leopoldville (Table 10, pp. 325–27).

[107] *L'Essor du Congo* (Elisabethville), June 16, 1960.

cally a member — had already on June 14 made an overture to Patrice Lumumba, Premier designate named by Minister Ganshof. Lumumba the next day made a counterproposal: Economic Affairs would go to the Conakat as well as a vice-presidency of the lower Chamber in Leopoldville.

After the constitution of the Katangan provincial government on June 16, Tshombe returned to Leopoldville; on June 17 at 5 P.M., Lumumba learned that his mission as Premier-designate had been terminated.[108] The Conakat promised to cooperate with Kasavubu,[109] who announced on June 18 his proposed government, including Conakat ministers for Economic Affairs and Defense, with a federalist (from Abako) at the Ministry of the Interior and Jason Sendwe as Commissioner of State for Katanga.

On June 21, at the moment of the decisive vote on the officers of the lower Chamber, pro- and anti-Lumumba blocs confronted each other. The Conakat rallied to the anti-Lumumba Cartel d'Union Nationale, and there was no longer any question of Lumumba's offering it a vice-presidency.

However, for a brief instant it appeared that a settlement had been reached between the MNC leader and Tshombe. On June 23, two members of the Conakat were included in the Lumumba government: Joseph Yav at Economic Affairs, and Albert Nyembo as Secretary of State for Defense. At the time of the vote of confidence on June 24, all was less clear. A single vote from the Conakat went to the government and the next day, Tshombe made a sharp public declaration on the composition of the government. He had, he said, learned "with amazement" that Lumumba had himself taken the Defense portfolio when this, according to agreement, should have been assumed collectively by the Full Council of Ministers.[110] Interior went to a unitarist from the MNC/Lumumba and not a federalist from Abako and "besides, the idea of naming Sendwe Commissioner of State for Katanga had never been entertained."[111]

[108] In his plan for the government at the time, Lumumba put the Conakat in the post of Foreign Affairs. No name was mentioned and it is certain that no agreement was reached on this matter.

[109] But, according to Minister Ganshof who consulted them, Tshombe and Kibwe "were not a priori hostile to Lumumba." — *Fin de la souveraineté belge au Congo*, p. 237.

[110] This conception had also been presented to the chambers by Lumumba himself.

[111] Belga-Congo (Leopoldville), June 24, 1960. Recall that Kasavubu had envisaged the same functions for Sendwe on June 18.

Moreover, European circles were very conscious that Yav's responsibilities were sharply reduced by the existence of an MNC/Lumumba minister, Alois Kabangi, at Economic Coordination, where he would be assisted by Alphonse Nguvulu, of the *Parti du Peuple*, as Secretary of State for Economic Coordination, and by the existence of a Minister for Mines, Edmund Rudahindwa (Reko), and a Minister of Lands, Alexandre Mahamba (MNC/Lumumba).

Under these conditions, Tshombe felt his agreement was "null and void." Katangan Assembly President Charles Mutaka threatened secession if Sendwe became Commissioner of State,[112] considering this designation as a provocation inasmuch as the Balubakat leader was president of the autonomous government of Northeast Katanga whose creation the Cartel had announced. Meanwhile, the Cartel published victory communiqués,[113] because its leaders had obtained important national responsibilities. Sendwe and Isaac Kalonji were presented as Commissioners of State for Katanga and Kasai; Rémy Mwamba, Minister of Justice; Jacques Masangu, Vice-President of the Senate.

It is in this context that the so-called Scheerlinck affair took place.

On June 25, the Belgian authorities in Elisabethville learned of a plan for the proclamation of independence for Katanga which was to take place before June 30, on June 28, to be exact. A former agent of the Belgian *Sûreté* in Katanga, François Scheerlinck, had been cabled to come from Brussels by Tshombe himself on June 21, the day on which Kasavubu failed to form a government and on which it became clear that Lumumba would be the first chief of government. Scheerlinck arrived in Elisabethville on June 23. On June 25, at noon, the public prosecutor's office and the *Sûreté* searched his hotel, seized a personal notebook, but left Scheerlinck himself at liberty until 6 P.M., or ten hours after the authorities had been alerted. He was then questioned.

It was learned that Scheerlinck had been in daily contact with Tshombe and paramount Chief Antoine Mwenda Munongo during the political Round Table, that he had proffered advice to the Conakat delegates at the economic Round Table, and was very busy in the interim with the Conakat party members in training in Belgium. It was also learned that on June 24, Scheerlinck had discussed at length with Tshombe and the Katangan ministers the Conakat scheme to proclaim independence on June 28.

[112] *L'Essor du Congo* (Elisabethville), June 25, 1960.
[113] *L'Echo du Katanga* (Elisabethville), June 25, 1960.

On June 25, he had received from Tshombe, as "President of the Council of Ministers of the State of Katanga," and from Godefroid Munongo a letter accrediting him as a special ambassador for the state of Katanga. A Sabena air ticket detailed his itinerary: Elisabethville, Brussels, then eventually New York, Washington, and return, with a Conakat delegate.

The letter was worded as follows:

I have the honor of informing you that with the approval of the Council of Ministers of the State of Katanga, I name you Special Ambassador, charged with a mission on behalf of the Government of Katanga.

You will receive under separate cover from my office documents of accreditation, as well as all the necessary instructions for the execution of the missions which will be entrusted to you on behalf of the Government of the State of Katanga.

The proclamation officially investing you with the function of Ambassador will be made June 30, 1960, immediately after the transfer of power from Belgium to the legally constituted government of the State of Katanga.

Names cited in the seized notebook and the contacts of the Belgian agent during the war with the English, American, and South African intelligence services provoked uneasiness; was it necessary to look for international ramifications to this plot, in the direction of Rhodesia, South Africa, or Western capitals? Scheerlinck said he acted only with the Conakat leaders: his meeting with Sir F., ex-Chief Secretary of Northern Rhodesia, in Elisabethville on his arrival was purely by chance and his wartime contacts had long been severed. Of course, the scheme projected contacts with friendly countries and with influential authorities, but they were not implicated in the affair.

When questioned, Tshombe denied any participation in the plot. Munongo's reaction was sharper. He attacked the Balubakat's European advisers and even the mission chief of the Colonial Minister who had got wind of the affair and who, according to Munongo, deserved arrest and expulsion more than Scheerlinck.

How was the June 28 operation to be accomplished? Scheerlinck himself declared in the course of questioning:[114]

Separation [of Katanga] would be effected by a proclamation of the provincial government asking recognition for the independence of Katanga from Belgium and the United States.

[114] Cited in Ganshof van der Meersch, *Fin de la Souveraineté belge au Congo*, pp. 580 and 588.

Recognition was also to be sought in the countries bordering the Congo, and in England and Portugal. Simultaneously, an appeal would be made to the U.N. For the Katangan provincial government, it would be a race against the clock.

In fact, Conakat leaders were persuaded, according to their special ambassador, that "among the authorities responsible until June 30, no one would take the initiative to stop them."

"The affair had serious roots," wrote Ganshof van der Meersch. "It was a response to a widespread state of mind in Katanga and revealed elements of an emerging organization which other information confirmed."[115] Scheerlinck was in touch with Georges Thyssens, the Conakat adviser, and it seemed that it was here, in European and African circles where Thyssens was active, that the "serious roots" of the operation could be found.

The motive alleged for the plot was the "Lumumba-Communism" danger. At this point Belgian authorities in Elisabethville noted "agitation among the Conakat leaders, fanned by European advisers." The same influence was exerted on the traditional chiefs with some effect.

After it was explained to them that their chances of success were nil, the Conakat leaders, on June 26, "on their honor formally undertook" not to have recourse to secession, on condition that their representative Scheerlinck not be arrested in Leopoldville nor in Brussels.[116]

In Leopoldville, the new Congolese authorities and the Belgian authorities were apprised of the affair. No one minimized its seriousness. General Janssens was asked to prepare measures to avoid secession and to organize a show of force at the Rhodesian frontier; the expulsion of pro-Conakat European activists from Katanga was considered in some quarters. A new interrogation of Scheerlinck took place on his arrival in Leopoldville, the evening of June 26. He underwent questioning all night long until June 27 at 5 A.M., but without bringing anything new to light.

In Katanga, the idea of expelling European "ultras" appeared inopportune. It was thought better to profit from the critical situation in which the Conakat leaders were placed to re-open negotiations on the composition of the provincial government and to encourage the ministers to appeal

[115] *Ibid.*, p. 582.
[116] When Tshombe was arrested in Coquilhatville, he wrote to Kasavubu: "This man Scheerlinck was expelled from Katanga because the government and I myself judged him an individual with little to recommend him." This version hardly corresponds to reality.

to the competent *chefs de cabinet* rather than to irresponsible and inept advisers. In Leopoldville, the same tactic was suggested to the minister on June 26.

Meanwhile in Elisabethville, Minister Ganshof and Minister of the Interior Christophe Gbenye (MNC/Lumumba) on June 28 contacted the Conakat leaders. Despite violent criticism by Munongo who accused the Belgians "of imposing an artificial unity [on the Congo] in order to favor the big companies," an agreement seemed to be taking shape on the cession of three or four Katangan ministerial portfolios to the Cartel. The Katangan ministers who would give up their offices were to receive substantial compensation (administrative assignments or diplomatic posts).

When Ganshof and Gbenye left Elisabethville, on the eve of June 30, a certain amount of optimism prevailed. The Cartel could undoubtedly enter the provincial government and obtain four ministerial posts; the Conakat had promised to abandon its plots against Congolese unity, and there was no longer any question of a government of Northeast Katanga.[117]

Thus a secession attempt had failed. Its foreign ramifications were denied by those involved, but there appeared too many traces of intelligence services to ascribe them to pure coincidence. At this point, Vice-Governor-General Schoeller called it a "suicide project" for the Conakat because the Belgian authorities could not have avoided intervening against secession on the eve of independence. It seems that Tshombe had given way to the extremists in this affair for he was himself in a weak position. The "ultras," above all Europeans, circulated criminal accusations about him under the pretext that he was guilty of collusion with Patrice Lumumba in having accepted in principle participation in his government.

A final try for secession would have taken place again on June 29;[118] copies of a declaration of independence for Katanga were taken to the Assembly[119] by a European settler and were distributed to the members. The consular corps was specially invited to this session.

[117] According to Ganshof, the agreement in principle provided that the Conakat would give up four ministerial portfolios and that the resigning ministers had a guarantee from Lumumba that they would be named to "equivalent" functions in 'he purview of the central government. This was confirmed on July 12 by Tshombe in the provincial Assembly. He went to Leopoldville at the beginning of July, especially to define with Gizenga what these "similar posts" would be, to provide for the Katangan provincial ministers who would relinquish their positions to the Cartel members. Minutes, Katangan Assembly, July 12, 1960.

[118] Ganshof van der Meersch, *Fin de la Souveraineté belge au Congo*, p. 585.

[119] In the Assembly there were a number of elected members from the Cartel, led by Prosper Mwamba Ilunga, among the 53 present.

Tshombe and Mutaka were informed of the move by Vice-Governor-General Schoeller and, disapproving an enterprise of which they knew nothing, they collected the distributed documents. The initiative came, it was said, from Munongo. A detachment of the gendarmery was dispatched to be near the Assembly buildings.

The Assembly contented itself with accepting credentials of the new members; with choosing a provisional secretary-general; with raising their salaries to 300,000 francs in place of the legal maximum of 100,000 francs; with noting the fact that the ministers intended to grant themselves 500,000 francs and the president 650,000 francs a year.[120] The proclamation was not read. The last secession attempt before June 30, 1960, had aborted.[121]

[120] Minutes, Katangan Assembly, June 29, 1960, p. 3.

[121] "The impatience of the Conakat leaders to proclaim Katanga's independence during the course of the last few days of Belgian sovereignty derived from the fear that they would not be in a position to do it, once the Congo had become independent." — Ganshof van der Meersch, *Fin de la Souveraineté belge au Congo*, p. 572.

Part II KATANGA IN SECESSION

July 11, 1960–January 14, 1963

CHAPTER 3 · *The Anti-Lumumba Common Front in Elisabethville and in Brussels (July 11-September 5, 1960)*

IMMEDIATELY after the proclamation of Congolese independence, relations between the Katangan provincial authority and the central government were already showing strain.

The Conakat dominated the group in power in Elisabethville: Cartel representatives were excluded while the Conakat had had its key leaders elected — Tshombe as President, Jean-Baptiste Kibwe and Godefroid Munongo as the Ministers of Finance and Interior. In contrast, in the central government, the Conakat's position was singularly weaker than Tshombe had anticipated at the time when he had set his conditions for participation in the Lumumba government.

The European population of Katanga felt a certain bitterness at the accession of Lumumba as Prime Minister, a bitterness reinforced by the speech that the MNC leader had delivered on June 30, 1960, in the presence of the King of the Belgians.[1]

Certain Conakat circles, which had been involved in the Scheerlinck affair at the end of June, 1960, held a grudge against the Belgian government as well as against the central Congolese government. Experience had proved that Leopoldville would accept no drift of the provinces toward secession and that Belgian authorities had played Leopoldville's game in what were judged to be decisive circumstances. Besides, the designation of Jason Sendwe, president of the Balubakat, as Commissioner of State for Katanga was interpreted both as a Leopoldville option in favor of the Cartel, and as an attempt to reassert central power at the expense of

[1] Text in *Congo 1960* (Brussels: CRISP, 1961), pp. 323–25.

93

the real autonomy conferred on the provinces by the provisional *Loi Fondamentale*.

In its reaction of opposition to Congolese central authority, the Conakat also had allies among the Africans:

1. Several Katangan traditional chiefs had undergone since mid-June in Leopoldville a disillusioning experience with parliamentary politics. Out of their element in the legislative maneuverings, and without roots in the capital, they publicly avowed their hopes for an early return to their traditional milieu and they scarcely hid their nostalgia for some real power to exercise within their ethnic group, according to custom.
2. The Muluba leader from Kasai, Albert Kalonji, excluded from the Lumumba government, was himself embarked on the creation of an autonomous Baluba province in South Kasai[2] and in an administrative boycott by Baluba civil servants in Leopoldville. This action broadened the ethnic basis of opposition in Katanga to the central authorities by bringing in the particularly active Kasai Baluba townsmen.

Meanwhile, in Katanga itself, the Cartel never ceased to alert its rank and file about the threat of secession, and Atcar president Ambroise Muhunga warned the Conakat against any attempt at federation with the Rhodesias, for, he said, "even Belgium to whom we owe deepest gratitude" would come to the aid of the defenders of unity.[3]

Taking stock of his strengths and weaknesses, Tshombe went to Leopoldville to negotiate with the central authorities over the immediate problems: the CSK affair, compensation for the Katangan ministers who would resign to permit the election of Cartel members, additional funds for the struggle against unemployment and the financing of new institutions.[4]

During Tshombe's stay in Leopoldville, a new development was to occur that would radically change the situation of the central authorities: the rebellion on July 4 to 6 of soldiers and African non-commissioned officers in the *Force Publique* against white officers in Leopoldville and in the Bas-Congo.[5]

[2] *Ibid.*, p. 220. The Belgian and Congolese authorities had decided to maintain the state of exception in Kasai beyond June 30.

[3] *L'Echo du Katanga* (Elisabethville), July 7, 1960.

[4] Abstract of the Proceedings, Katangan Assembly, July 12, 1960, declaration of Tshombe.

[5] *Congo 1960*, pp. 371–517.

BELGIAN MILITARY INTERVENTION AND THE
PROCLAMATION OF INDEPENDENCE

The first disorders in Katanga occurred at a time when tensions gave signs of easing in Leopoldville, on July 8 — after the special meeting of the Council of Ministers, which took steps for the immediate Africanization of the officer corps and which named Victor Lundula, who was born in Kasai and was burgomaster of Jadotville, as Commander-in-Chief of the *Armée Nationale Congolaise* (ANC); Colonel Joseph Mobutu as Chief of Staff; and the Belgian, Colonel Henniquiau, as chief adviser to the ANC.

The first incidents took place in Kongolo on July 8, at 5 P.M. African elements in the *Force Publique*, fearing an attack by white officers,[6] became restless and threatened their European officers. On July 9, at Kabalo, Congolese civilians tried to stop the departure of a train evacuating 250 Europeans.[7]

The incidents, relatively minor by themselves, had a serious influence on Belgian government decisions of July 9. Because of the news of one victim at Kongolo, the departure of numerous Europeans from Katanga to Rhodesia, and unconfirmed rumors about a Rhodesian army intervention in the direction of Elisabethville, a special meeting of the Council of Ministers was held on the morning of July 9 in Brussels.[8] It was decided to send reinforcements of Belgian "paracommandos" to Kamina, to organize an airlift via Sabena for the evacuation of refugees, and to send ministerial emissaries to Lumumba in order to discuss with him the possibility of using Belgian forces for the maintenance of order and for the protection of persons.

Despite the appeals for calm on July 8 and 9 by the Katangan authorities, armed bodies of European volunteers organized, especially in Jadotville. In spite of the proclamation of the non-commissioned officers of the *Force Publique* to the civilian population ("We are here to protect you"), the number of departures of Europeans to Rhodesia grew during July 9. In the camps of the *Force Publique*, despite the appeal of Colonel Henniquiau to the white officers to try to organize at once the election of

[6] Account of a white officer, in *Congo 1960*, p. 413.

[7] Agence Belga, dispatch of July 9, 1960.

[8] This, although, on the previous evening, the ministers had adjourned under the impression of a *détente* in Leopoldville, without scheduling a meeting for July 9. At this moment, rumors concerning an eventual secession began to circulate at the headquarters of the First Group of the *Force Publique* and even in Kamina, where it was learned "Katanga is going to separate from the state," on July 8.

Congolese officers and of Belgian "advisers," [9] no measure of Africanization was applied. On the contrary, rumors circulated according to which
the soldiers were going to be attacked: "automatically, soldiers followed
the agitators and set off the mutiny," explained *L'Essor du Congo*.[10]

On July 9 at 10:30 P.M., elements from Camp Massart mutinied. There
were seven victims, five of them civilians killed [11] at a railway crossing
by a group of soldiers armed with a sub-machine gun. Once shooting
began, Europeans gathered in groups for self-defense, and two thousand
persons collected in the Collège St. François de Sales, transformed into a
stronghold for the purpose.

During the night of July 9, Belgian military intervention in the Congo
was decided upon, essentially under pressure of events in Elisabethville.
The question was debated among authorities in Elisabethville, the Belgian
ambassador in Leopoldville, and the Belgian government in Brussels.

From Elisabethville, the demand for intervention was urgently pressed
by European spokesmen, in particular by former Vice-Governor-General
Schoeller [12] who, acting in full accord with Colonel Matterne of the
local *Force Publique* headquarters general staff, was in communication
with the Ministry of Defense in Brussels, four times during the course of
the night.

Likewise, Tshombe, who had returned by special plane to Elisabethville, called for intervention of troops from Belgium, but wanted to call
on the Rhodesians at the same time.

From Brussels, the order to occupy Elisabethville was sent to the base
at Kamina in the middle of the night by the Ministers of Defense and of
Foreign Affairs. It was withdrawn, a first time on the insistence of the
Belgian ambassador in Leopoldville, who feared the consequences for
relations between the two countries and for the security of the Belgians
in the five other provinces, above all in Luluabourg where mutiny had
also broken out and where the position of the refugees was most precarious. The Ambassador opposed at that time an intervention which was
not requested by the Congolese government, that is to say one which
was in violation of Article 6 of the Treaty of Belgo-Congolese friendship.

[9] Appeal of July 8, 1960, in *Congo 1960*, p. 406.
[10] Issue of July 12, 1960.
[11] Among them the Italian consul.
[12] Report by Vice-Governor-General Schoeller in *Congo 1960*, Annexes et
Bibliographies, pp. 66–68.

Orders and counterorders were issued three times,[13] including once — a counterorder — to planes which had taken off from the Kamina base.

Finally, on Sunday, July 10 at 6:20 A.M., two Belgian companies, under Commandant Guy Weber, took off from the airfield at Luano. At 9:40 A.M., Agence Belga reported that Camp Massart had been occupied by Belgian forces without firing a shot. About 11 A.M., however, according to the minutes of the meeting of the Katangan Council of Ministers on July 10, 1960, "the mutineers (200 approximately) encircled by para-commandos, are not willing to lay down their arms."

Several hours after the Belgian military intervention, Tshombe met with his ministers. He described the situation in Leopoldville as "the most complete chaos." He said that there was, in his opinion, no means of settling the financial situation from Leopoldville. The news about the disorders in Katanga remained disquieting:

After all this, the question arises: how can the situation be saved? By the declaration of an independent state. What are the means? Agreement with the military authorities; agreement with the military authorities of foreign countries.[14]

The same day, July 10, Tshombe sent out an appeal for aid from British and Rhodesian police forces. In Brussels, rumors circulated about a proclamation of independence in Katanga,[15] and on July 10 and 11, the Minister of Foreign Affairs, Pierre Wigny, sent a note to the representatives of the United States, Great Britain,[16] France, the Netherlands, West Germany, and Luxembourg setting forth the Belgian view concerning "maneuvers in Katanga to set up the province as an independent state and to have it recognized by foreign powers."[17] Wigny opposed the move, to avoid the risk of imperiling the lives of Europeans in the other prov-

[13] According to *L'Essor du Congo* (Elisabethville), July 12, 1960, Commandant Weber claimed on July 12 in Elisabethville that "false orders," delivered in a voice "imitating high" Belgian "authorities," had been given to airplanes en route to Luano by "secret transmitters belonging, it seems, to the Soviet embassy in Leopoldville." The truth is simpler.

[14] Minutes, Council of Ministers, Katanga, July 10, 1960, in *Moniteur Katangais.*

[15] An Agence France-Presse dispatch from London had echoed it on July 10, implying that the decision would be taken only after "the situation was stabilized."

[16] "In the circumstances of the case, it would not be possible for troops to be sent in at the request of an authority other than the lawfully constituted central Government." Prime Minister Harold MacMillan, House of Commons Debates (Hansard), Vol. 626, col. 981, July 11, 1960.

[17] *Congo 1960*, p. 721.

inces. In the long run, the Congo without Katanga would not be viable and "would become a prey for Communism," and it is "doubtful if Katanga alone can resist aggression or subversion from outside its borders."

"Prudence and temporization," suggested Wigny to Tshombe, promising him that the Belgian forces would remain in Elisabethville "so long as necessary."[18]

These directives reached the Belgian consulate in Elisabethville, which, according to Evariste Kimba, "dissuaded us to the end from proclaiming independence, warning us that Belgium would not recognize it."[19] On the morning of July 11, a "state of exception" was proclaimed in Katanga. On this matter, Tshombe explained in the Assembly: "The powers for the maintenance of order have passed into the hands of the military authorities, under the direction of Commandant Weber who coordinates the action of the *Force Publique*, the gendarmery, the police and the Belgian forces."[20] The Belgian commander became in fact the adviser of President Tshombe, with the title "Commissioner Extraordinary for the maintenance of order in Katanga."[21]

The maintenance of order appeared at this time as the first requirement for the Katangan government which, according to Tshombe, wished "to profit from the occasion [of chaos reigning in Leopoldville] to proclaim independence for Katanga."[22] Without the restoration of order, the economic and administrative machine would be paralyzed by the massive exodus of Europeans and the new state could not count on its normal resources. Jadotville — emptied of its European population — was given over to pillage (July 11), despite the courageous interventions of the burgomaster Victor Lundula. At Shinkolobwe, riots broke out on July 10 in the evening and the order was given to Europeans to evacuate Kolwezi.

Without waiting any longer, on the evening of July 11, Tshombe proclaimed the total independence of Katanga, economically bound, he hoped, to Belgium, which would guarantee the re-establishment of order

[18] And that was the essential factor at that moment for the Katangan authorities.

[19] *La Libre Belgique* (Brussels), August 5, 1960, report of press conference in Brussels.

[20] Abstract of the proceedings, Katangan Assembly, July 12, 1960.

[21] Title cited in *Arrêté*, No. 11/275 of August 14, 1961, conferring the Katangan military cross on "Lieutenant Colonel Weber," in *Moniteur Katangais*, No. 18, September 1, 1961.

[22] Remarks of Tshombe on the departure of the Belgian Technical Mission, October, 15, 1960.

and public safety[23] and furnish its "technical, financial and military support."

Locally, in Katanga, Wigny's instructions to be prudent and to temporize were hardly applied by the military at all. Although official Belgian policy explanations linked the military intervention to protection of European lives and to possible evacuation of refugees who were stranded or threatened, the military presence was used in fact in Katanga immediately to re-establish economic and administrative activity.[24] Commandant Weber, especially, publicly expressed attitudes clearly hostile to the central government. He termed General Victor Lundula, whose attitude at Jadotville and at Shinkolobwe[25] had saved European lives, the "so-called Commanding General of the *Force Publique*"[26] and "neutralized" him. He claimed to have proof of the existence of a "subversive war" in which Leopoldville and Moscow were in league. On July 13, he rendered homage to Godefroid Munongo, who, according to him, "had permitted order to be maintained in Katanga,"[27] by halting the landing on the evening of July 12 of the airplane transporting the Chief of State Kasavubu and Prime Minister Lumumba. General Charles P. Cumont, head of the Belgian Chiefs of Staff (COCEM), adopted a similar attitude, declaring on July 13 in Elisabethville that the Belgian forces present are "at the disposition of Tshombe to protect the persons and the goods of all, Whites and Congolese," that refugees, including women, were to return to the towns, and that the Belgian Major Crèvecoeur was "the new commander of the Katangan Army."[28]

Simultaneously, military operations took place in other centers. Jadotville was reoccupied July 12. There was an armed parade through Kolwezi on July 13; disarmament of the *Force Publique* on July 12 at Kamina; parachuting of 140 men on the morning of July 13 in Kabalo, where a white officer of the *Force Publique* maintained that he "had his men well in hand";[29] and an ultimatum delivered on July 14 to Kongolo, where pillaging had taken place after the departure of Europeans.

[23] Proclamation, July 11, 1960. Complete text in Appendix II, pp. 328–29.

[24] Appeals to go back to work broadcast every half hour on July 11, 1960.

[25] Where he arrived on July 11, at noon, having been "delayed by numerous paracommando checks" and there liberated three Europeans. — Account of a priest in *Congo 1960*, p. 431.

[26] *L'Essor du Congo* (Elisabethville), July 12, 1960.

[27] *Ibid.*, July 14, 1960.

[28] *Congo 1960*, p. 722.

[29] *Ibid.*, p. 435.

In Brussels, meanwhile, the attitude of the government and of Parliament toward Katanga remained cautious. Wigny refused "to play the loser" and to sacrifice the last chance for an accord with Leopoldville. Socialist Senator Henri Rolin rejected the idea of recognizing Katanga, and he was supported at this juncture by his Social Christian colleague De Smet.[30] Nonetheless, the Council of Ministers on July 12 was divided; a group of Social Christian and Liberal ministers leaned toward open support for Katanga (involved particularly were Van der Schueren, Vanden Boeynants, and Vanaudenhove). The Belgian position was to evolve rapidly.

On July 11, a Belgian airplane, transporting a pacification mission of the *Armée Nationale Congolaise* led by Adjutant Justin Kokolo,[31] arrived at 11:05 A.M. above the Elisabethville airport which was occupied by Belgian soldiers. An order was first given from the ground for the plane to turn back, then finally authorization to land was granted on condition that the soldiers would not make contact with their colleagues in Elisabethville.

This delegation — on its return — stopped in Luluabourg where Kasavubu and Lumumba had just approved conditional maintenance of Belgian forces in Kasai.[32] Kokolo was a Mukongo in whom the Chief of State had full confidence. The report of what had happened enraged Kasavubu, and the accord concluded with the Belgian consul at Luluabourg was immediately denounced.

Kasavubu and Lumumba themselves tried to reach Elisabethville. The trip was not unplanned. It had been decided upon July 9 and 10. An Agence Belga dispatch confirmed that Tshombe was forewarned of it.[33] The Belgian airplane arrived above the airport at 9:30 P.M. Munongo, from the control tower, forbade the landing on Katangan territory. Subsequently landing at Kamina, Kasavubu and Lumumba were, according to the latter, threatened by Belgian soldiers and insulted by refugees.

[30] "The recognition of a provincial government would be tantamount to intervention," declared Senator Rolin. "The Tshombe government is not qualified to make such a decision," asserted De Smet. — Abstract of the Proceedings, Belgian Senate, July 12, 1960.

[31] Named on July 8 by the Congolese government to be commander of Camp Leopold.

[32] See the exchange of letters between Lumumba and the Belgian consul in *Congo 1960*, pp. 446–47.

[33] Tshombe announced that three of his ministers would go to greet Lumumba. The ministers of Katanga, after a short discussion, would request that Lumumba immediately leave Katanga." — Agence Belga, July 10, 1960.

On their return to Luluabourg, Lumumba demanded immediate fulfillment of an ultimatum addressed from Kamina to the Belgian forces (immediate withdrawal into the bases). The telegram to the U.N. of July 12, sent by Kasavubu and Lumumba with the aim of obtaining military aid, invoked as its essential argument the role of the Belgian forces in Katanga: "We accuse Belgian government of having carefully prepared Katanga secession with end to retain hold on our country."

Thus, the Katanga secession accelerated the deterioration of Belgo-Congolese relations — within the Congo, as the denunciation of the Luluabourg agreement indicated, and on the diplomatic level where Belgian action, interpreted as aggression, provided a reason for requesting U.N. military aid.

On July 14, still basing their position on the events in Katanga (secession, prohibition on landing of the Lumumba-Kasavubu airplane, and nomination of Commandant Weber as Katanga commander), the Chief of State and the Congolese Prime Minister broke diplomatic relations with Belgium and addressed a request to Premier Khrushchev, to maintain a close watch on developments in the Congo.

This rupture of diplomatic relations rapidly changed the position of the Belgian government. From the moment that the chances for an understanding with Leopoldville were reduced to nought, at least as long as Lumumba was in power, the tendency to favor support for the "Katanga experiment" was strengthened in Belgium. The conservative Catholic, Liberal, and neutral (*Le Soir*) press were inclined more and more in favor of Katangan positions, and pressure groups of former colonials and refugees called vigorously for aid to Tshombe.

BELGIAN ASSISTANCE TO THE KATANGAN STATE

By July 14, 1960, two events strongly influenced the Belgian governmental attitude toward Katanga. The decision to break diplomatic relations between Leopoldville and Brussels, formally announced by Kasavubu and Lumumba, built up pressures in favor of direct Belgian aid to secessionist Katanga. Belgian interests in Katanga were substantial, and local authorities, very hostile to Lumumba and to the decisions taken by Leopoldville, had opted for military and technical aid from Europeans. On the other hand, the first resolution of the U.N. Security Council requested Belgium to withdraw its troops from the Congo and anticipated military assistance for the Congolese central government, which would eventually make it possible for the Congolese army to fulfill the missions assigned to it by the government.[34] This precluded in the long run the founding of a Katangan state relying solely on the Belgian military presence and inspired caution regarding prospects, international or domestic, for secession.

On the spot — we have seen — the Belgian military authorities immediately embarked on a policy which fully suited the secessionist officials, deliberately violating the instructions which came from the central Congolese authorities and the sections of the provisional *Loi Fondamentale* concerning the respective powers of the provinces and of Leopoldville. The Belgian forces set out to restore order and to disarm and expel hostile elements of the *Force Publique*; to re-establish economic activity immediately by organizing the return of the European refugees; to have propaganda, food supply, and public health entrusted to Commandant Weber's operation; to accept responsibilities with political implications in the Katangan leadership, including the designation of a new Belgian chief of the "Katangan army."

These functions were crucial for the Katangan state, for, at this point, maintenance of "order" was the first requirement of Europeans, both in the private[35] and public sectors of Katanga. The Belgian military presence, as Weber conceived it, constituted a provisional guarantee sufficient for interested Europeans to risk working in the young independent Katanga. For Katanga, order meant access to immense resources — the certainty of being the refuge par excellence for foreign exchange and technicians; the chance of appearing to Western opinion as the oasis of peace which warranted aid and assistance.

THE ESTABLISHMENT OF MECHANISMS FOR ASSISTANCE AND THE BELGIAN ROLE

The attitude of the military in Katanga — not disavowed by the Minister of Defense and vigorously supported by the industrial and financial groups most involved in Katanga — was not sufficient to guarantee the survival of Katanga, without speedy reinforcement from the Belgian government. This reinforcement was extended July 15.

On that date Belgian forces were authorized by Belgian Defense Minister Arthur Gilson "to occupy all the important centers in Katanga, in particular Kolwezi and the rail depots of Sakania and Dilolo,"[36] although this step was not made necessary by any threat to the safety of Europeans.

[34] *Congo 1960*, p. 552.

[35] On July 14, 1960, Commandant Weber gave to the Union Minière every guarantee for the security of its installations. The management of the UMHK had sent a mission to Rhodesia to recall its agents, immediately after the Belgian intervention.

[36] Essential for the export of copper, without passing over the "national route"

On July 16, the Belgian government acknowledged "the fact that the government of Katanga has proclaimed its independence, that order reigns there, and that economic activity is continuing." It also acknowledged that "the government of Katanga asks the cooperation of Belgian technicians. The support of our cooperation is assured to Katanga, as to all other regions of the Congo where security and order prevail." [37]

The same day in Elisabethville, the Belgian consul addressed an "order to all agents and Belgian administrators of Katanga . . . to continue work as usual"; otherwise their attitude would be considered, the provincial secretary declared, as a "grave dereliction of duty."

On July 12, Colonel Champion, chief of Belgian forces in Katanga, had, according to the press, "been delegated the authority to mobilize on the spot all Belgians from 25 to 45 years of age needed in restoring the Katangan economy." [38] The same day, Harold d'Aspremont Lynden, deputy *chef de cabinet* of the Belgian Prime Minister, arrived in Elisabethville. He was on a special mission to study the need for extending aid to Katanga and to advise Tshombe to defer plans for an immediate trip to Belgium. [39] From D'Aspremont Lynden's visit the Belgian Technical Mission (MISTEBEL) was born on July 20. It was the first nucleus for technical assistance to Katanga.

On July 21, the King endorsed this policy. Referring to "whole ethnic groups at the head of which are honest and worthy men . . . who call upon us to aid them in building their independence," the sovereign concluded that it was the duty of Belgians to respond favorably. From this moment on, it was the Belgian Technical Mission which constituted the real command post for Katanga and which dealt with all the problems of implementation.

Head of the Belgian Technical Mission was D'Aspremont Lynden, on the basis of a mandate given by Prime Minister Gaston Eyskens to his former deputy *chef de cabinet* "to coordinate Belgian action in Katanga." He attended meetings of the Tshombe government. He gave direct instructions to Belgians in the public sector; he advised private parties

---

via Elisabethville–Port-Francqui–Matadi. Out of 23 Belgian interventions taking place by July 18, ten were in Katanga.

[37] Declaration of Prime Minister Gaston Eyskens.

[38] *L'Essor du Congo* and *L'Echo du Katanga* (Elisabethville), July 17, 1960.

[39] On October 15, 1960, Tshombe confirmed that he had received, several hours before seeing D'Aspremont-Lynden, "the visit of a completely official delegate of the Belgian government who came to promise us in very vague terms a certain amount of aid." — Secrétariat d'Etat à l'Information, Service de Presse, Katanga, No. 1, October 18, 1960.

faced with delicate legal situations. He met with military chiefs and he arranged with Brussels questions of technical and financial assistance. In addition, according to Eyskens and to D'Aspremont Lynden himself, his activities were based on a "broad delegation of powers" which made him "the interpreter of the will of the government."

The leaders of the Belgian Technical Mission had the status of Belgian mission chiefs; among them were: a former colleague of Vice-Governor-General Schoeller;[40] a Brussels police officer responsible for organizing the Katanga *Sûreté*; a professor from the University of Liège, René Clémens, adviser on legal problems, administrative reorganization, and "native policy."[41] Formally, Commandant Weber was also part of the Belgian Technical Mission. In addition, R. Rothschild, a ranking Belgian diplomat, was in Elisabethville from July 18 on, to carry out more specifically diplomatic and political missions; however, he reported directly to the Ministry of Foreign Affairs in Brussels.

Through the activities of the Belgian Technical Mission, together with the military, Belgium was directly committed to following Tshombe's

[40] Schoeller had, according to Tshombe's version, "left Katanga in total disagreement with my government over the policy which he still opposes." He served for a while as a contact of sorts between the Belgian Technical Mission and the Ministry of African Affairs. He is now a Grand Marshal of the Belgian Court.

[41] The channels through which Clémens operated in Katanga after 1955 were the Institut de Sociologie of the University of Liège and the Fondation de l'Université de Liège pour les recherches scientifiques au Congo Belge et au Ruanda-Urundi (Fulréac) which set up a center for development in Katuba (Elisabethville), with a welfare office, youth work-camp, and so forth, and an experimental center for the development of *paysannats* [rural settlement schemes] in Mangombo, a Katangan *chefferie* 85 kilometers from Elisabethville. Financially, these enterprises were funded under the budget of the colony, the budget of the Administration de la main-d'oeuvre indigène (AIMO), or from the Centre d'étude des problèmes sociaux indigènes (CEPSI).

The CEPSI was founded in Elisabethville on January 30, 1946, under the initiative of Jules Cousin (Union Minière), and gathered together the most representative names from European society in Katanga. The center benefited by subsidies from the *Office Central du Travail au Katanga* (OCTK) as well as from the CSK, the UMHK and other companies. In 1956, on its fiftieth anniversary, the Union Minière gave to this specifically Katangan center a donation of more than 200 million Belgian francs. The CEPSI delegated studies to Fulréac on problems of relieving congestion in the large cities. See, on this subject, *Problèmes sociaux congolais*, CEPSI, No. 42 (September, 1958), pp. 146–53. Note that Clémens appeared in Katanga as a partisan of traditionalist views. At the moment of the secession, with several of his researchers, he played an active role in favor of Tshombe, including direct action among the population. He is, in addition, the author of the Constitution of Katanga.

course. It was through this mission that it became most closely involved in the political choices of Katanga.

In certain Belgian circles, especially among Socialists, a current of hostility to the mission was manifest toward the end of July; its leaders were judged to be men of the extreme right, bent on installing a "fascist" regime in Katanga. At bottom, nevertheless, Europeans were in accord on support for Tshombe and even more on the need to maintain the Belgian military presence, to keep the *casques bleus* [U.N. troops] out of Katanga and to give persons in the technical assistance program meaningful professional guarantees.

At the end of July, the Belgian apparatus for staffing and for assistance could be described in the following manner:

1. The whole of the private sector cooperated with Tshombe, particularly by the payment of duties and taxes as well as by the maintenance of vital economic activity.
2. The Belgian government granted its financial, technical, and material aid via the Belgian Technical Mission (D'Aspremont Lynden), and endorsed instructions to Belgians in the public sector to continue their work.
3. The Belgian army furnished in the person of Commandant Weber [42] a special adviser to Tshombe for all problems involving the maintenance of order, an expert to build a gendarmery for the Katangan government, and a Belgian force whose deployment guaranteed order where the local authorities wanted it and contained by its very presence Katangan opposition tendencies to the new regime.
4. Consular relations were established directly between Brussels and Elisabethville (Crener) as well as paradiplomatic contacts (Rothschild), despite the rupture in official relations between the government of the Republic of the Congo and Belgium.

Besides, Belgians occupied posts as *chefs de cabinet* or as advisers to Katangan ministers. Certain of these had the confidence of Brussels; others recognized no tie of double loyalty. Among the "independent"

[42] According to the Belgian Minister of Defense, Commandant Weber acted in Katanga in the framework of the "state of exception." The Colonial Charter ("in default of the unratified Congolese constitution") provided that a Belgian authority should in this case take command of the troops and take charge of co-ordinating the maintenance of order under these circumstances. Reply to a parliamentary question, September 10, 1960.

advisers of note, Georges Thyssens [43] was included in the entourage of Tshombe, and Tignée [44] at the side of Godefroid Munongo.

The question arises as to when and in what direction this apparatus tried to channel the policies of President Tshombe, either in matters of internal Katangan politics or in "external" relations, namely, toward the Republic of the Congo, toward foreign capitals, and toward the U.N. Also, one may ask, at a moment when Belgian aid was a determinant factor in the existence of Katanga in secession, what the nature of relations was between Brussels and Elisabethville.

Officially, Belgium did not recognize the state of Katanga, either in law or in fact. In practice, under the cover of technical, civil, and military assistance, the Belgian government was led to act, directly or indirectly, in ways which implied an absolute preference for the Katangan authorities and at the very least a refusal on essential points to recognize the legitimacy of the central authorities.[45] The Belgian government was committed to an independent Katanga: by the people it requested, or ordered, to remain; by the financing of technical assistance; by its military presence and staff assistance; by the activities of political advisers, covered by Belgian "mission chiefs." However, this aid did not fully satisfy either Katangan authorities [46] or local European circles, who demanded legal recognition or at least *de facto* recognition in the politico-legal sense of the term.

It is not easy to describe the policy carried out by Belgian representatives in Katanga and in Brussels. There existed many channels through which influence was exercised and these did not always operate in the same direction, even when the sources of influence belonged to the Eyskens government.

In so far as possible, some essential aspects of the problem will be outlined, where Belgian action was relatively coherent or where one of the Belgian tendencies was dominant.

[43] See Appendix I, p. 299.

[44] Tignée was, before June 30, 1960, deputy *chef de centre* of the European commune in Elisabethville, then administrator in Baudouinville. He was on the U.N. priority list of Belgians to be expelled, August 4, 1960.

[45] For example, after the revocation of the Tshombe government and the proclamation of the "state of exception" in Katanga by the central government, supported by the Congolese Chamber of Representatives, July 15, 1960.

[46] "The Belgian government must recognize independent Katanga," declared Kibwe in Brussels on July 31. — *La Libre Belgique* (Brussels), August 1, 1960.

COMPOSITION OF THE KATANGAN GOVERNMENT

"The most urgent question is that of broadening the government, to restore confidence by the introduction of representatives of the Cartel," declared Tshombe on July 12 in the Assembly. On July 14, he added that "the Conakat agrees to reserve four ministries to the Cartel or even more," and on July 15 he claimed he was offering the Cartel "five ministerial portfolios, of which one was the vice-presidency." On July 24, Weber even spoke of "seven ministers from the Cartel." On July 13, Tshombe had tried to contact Sendwe through local collaborators of the Institut de Sociologie of the Université Libre de Bruxelles to encourage him to return to Elisabethville.

Tshombe's object was to gain new adherents to the cause of an independent Katanga. The proclamation of independence had been made by Tshombe with the agreement of several ministers. The Conakat and its allies[47] rallied to the proclamation in the Katangan Assembly (on July 14 and 17). But in contrast, Prosper Mwamba Ilunga declared: "In the name of the Cartel, we protest against the solemn proclamation of the independent State of Katanga." This stand was important not only for Katanga itself but also for the Belgian government and political groups in Belgium. Without the support of the Cartel for Tshombe, the Socialist group in the Belgian Senate[48] could not declare itself in favor of the Tshombe decision. Moreover, the position of Katanga and its defenders at the U.N. and before world opinion would be singularly weakened if there continued to be opposition from a group whose numerical importance was substantial as measured in the elections of May, 1960, and whose ethnic roots in Katanga were well known.

On the Belgian government side, the most fervent wish was that the Cartel would rally to the Tshombe government, in some sort of Katangan common front. The Belgian press had a tendency to anticipate this support. "The provincial Assembly of Katanga approves the secession," proclaimed headlines of *La Libre Belgique* on July 15, which, citing the Associated Press, asserted that Sendwe had accepted the vice-presidency of the Katangan government. On its part, *La Dernière Heure*, Brussels' Liberal daily, published an interview with Tshombe on July 19 confirming that the operation had succeeded and that four ministers of the Cartel had been designated.

[47] On July 17, approval was given by the 22 members present (out of sixty-nine). — Abstract of the Proceedings, Katangan Assembly, July 17, 1960.

[48] Rolin declaration of July 12, 1960, in *Congo 1960*, p. 721.

Despite recommendations from Brussels, all the attempts in July by Tshombe and by the Belgian Technical Mission to bring in the Cartel failed. Sendwe, Isaac Kalonji, and Ambroise Muhunga took a position against the secession in Leopoldville and the announced accord never took place.[49] On July 27 in the provincial Assembly, Mwamba Ilunga called for the immediate liberation of "all the members of the Cartel presently imprisoned for political reasons."

In fact, despite the Belgian military presence, popular opposition showed itself. Various public statements clearly reflected it: "Certain evil-intentioned individuals spread rumors that we want to cede power to the Europeans";[50] "[There is] intensive and permanent circulation of lie-mongering tracts in the various Congolese communes . . .";[51] "Congolese personnel are at the service of the government of Katanga. If they do not approve its decisions or dispute them, they will be immediately fired and expelled from the territory of Katanga";[52] "I learn with consternation that the majority of my compatriots treat me as a hireling."[53] On August 21, arrests of a hundred Baluba in Katanga took place along the route to the airport; a rumor announcing the return of Sendwe had circulated in Baluba circles.

Attempts at agreement with the Cartel were seriously hampered by several events in Katanga: the expulsion of General Lundula; the Belgian attack with air support against the *Force Publique* camp of Nzilo at Kolwezi (officially, 13 dead, 200 Congolese prisoners); disarmament and return to other provinces of *Force Publique* members who did not rally to the secession;[54] arrest of opposition Assembly members by Munongo's police under the charge of "subversive plotting and incitement of the masses"; nomination of pro-Conakat Baluba administrators in Baluba zones; creation of a Katangan flag and prohibition on display of the flag of the republic. In addition, neither Tshombe nor the Belgian Technical

[49] A couple did rally to Tshombe; one example was Jacques Masangu, vice-president of the senate in Leopoldville, who, after he was elected as a Balubakat candidate, endorsed Tshombe on July 15, 1960. Several times the lists of minister-candidates from the Cartel were delivered to Tshombe. — Rémy Mwamba declaration, Abstract of the Proceedings, Katangan Assembly, July 27, 1960.

[50] Radio declaration by Tshombe, July 13, 1960.

[51] Radio declaration by Munongo, July 15, 1960.

[52] Jean-Baptiste Kibwe in *L'Echo du Katanga* (Elisabethville), July 20, 1960.

[53] Text of Masangu in *L'Echo du Katanga* (Elisabethville), July 21, 1960.

[54] "If police and soldiers from other provinces of the Congo have left Katanga, it is at their own request. . . . They have declared they either wanted to be dismissed or demobilized, or to continue their career elsewhere." — Munongo declaration, August 3, 1960 in *Congo 1960*, p. 73.

Mission sought the help at this time of Belgians capable of mediating with the Balubakat, despite reports reaching Brussels at the end of July on the weakness of the Tshombe government.[55] The Europeans on the spot were as a whole very hostile to the Cartel, especially from the beginning of June, 1960, and readily identified Sendwe partisans as Lumumbists, who in their minds were identical with Communists.

In his effort to rally support, Tshombe had to be content with individuals "crossing the aisle," notably, Gabriel Kitenge, founder of the Union Congolaise, already elected senator by the Conakat votes in June, 1960. As for the traditional chiefs, support came from those from whom it had been expected, with the exception of Boniface Kabongo, Muluba chief from the Kabongo chieftaincy.[56] He had supported the Cartel before independence, but signed the appeal of the chiefs on July 16 in Elisabethville, to approve "without reservation" Katangan independence.[57]

RELATIONS BETWEEN KATANGA AND OTHER REGIONS OF THE CONGO

"This independence is total," declared Tshombe on July 11, when he proclaimed independence for Katanga. But he said nevertheless he had decided "to receive with open arms, all those from other regions of the Congo who have decided to work with us within the same ideal of order, fraternity, and progress."

This declaration raised — without resolving — the major controversy which was to develop in Belgian circles both in Katanga and Belgium on the objectives of the secession:

1. Would this lead Katanga to a real and definitive independence, including independence within the realm of foreign affairs?
2. Would an independent Katanga try as soon as possible to confederate the neighboring border regions in a new political entity, covering, for example, Katanga, Kivu, Kasai (as a whole or at least the south), Rwanda, and Burundi?
3. Was independence to be, on the contrary, only provisional and tactical (a means to escape the influence of Leopoldville as long as the central authorities were Lumumbists), while awaiting a more favorable con-

---

[55] The position of Tshombe was extremely precarious and entirely dependent on the Belgian military presence, an observer especially dispatched from Brussels concluded.

[56] This paramount chief was assassinated on October 28, 1960, at Kaloko.

[57] "We chiefs have been discredited in Leo, while here, we are treated as chiefs worthy of the name." — Chief Antoine Mwenda Munongo, Abstract of the Proceedings, Katangan Assembly, July 27, 1960.

juncture in Leopoldville; was it not more worthwhile merely to support all provincial attempts at secession or semisecession, without creating a new political grouping, if the future lay in the construction of a confederal or federal Congo within the present confines of the Republic?

The most "Katangan" wing of Belgian political and economic groups opted for definitive independence, supporting at the same time confederal relations with Kivu and, if possible, with Kasai.[58]

Other Belgians — such as Foreign Minister Wigny, faced with African accusations at the U.N. — stressed extenuating circumstances which had influenced the Katangan decision of July 11, thus letting the future of the secession hang in doubt.

Since the arrival of D'Aspremont Lynden and Rothschild in Elisabethville, emphasis in Katangan quarters had been placed on the possibilities of reconfederating the Congo, "To create a confederal Congo," said Tshombe on July 18, in a formula more precise than "a confederation of free states in Africa" which he had used the day before. This idea of a Congolese confederation was also taken up on July 25 in Tshombe's appeal for a Round Table, addressed to Kasavubu, Ileo, and their colleagues.[59]

From the moment when Tshombe employed the term confederal Congo, political support from the Belgian government became freer; on July 26, Wigny himself recommended encouragement for "[any] rallying of the other provinces of the Congo to Katanga . . . of course with discretion." [60]

Tshombe's declarations in fact allowed the Belgian position to be presented in new terms to "moderate" Congolese and international opinion. The argument was put in this fashion: the Katangan affair is less a secession than "a constitutional crisis" to be resolved by the establishment of a confederal or federal regime; Belgian aid does not aim to break up the Congo but to reconstruct it on a basis to be defined by the Congolese

[58] The idea of a confederation of Katanga, Kivu, Rwanda, and Burundi had, in the past, been defended by European settlers, but had no roots among Africans. But on July 18, 1960, *La Libre Belgique* (Brussels) noted a "very interesting rapprochement with Katanga," especially in Ruanda, Kivu, and Kasai ("under the auspices of the good Kalonji," asserted the conservative Catholic newspaper). Tshombe confided a similar account to *La Dernière Heure* (Brussels), July 18, 1960. On July 18, 1960, *La Libre Belgique* even published a dispatch, attributing to a member of the Belgian consulate in Elisabethville an appeal to the refugees, inviting them to return to their homes on the pretext that "Katanga, Kivu, and Kasai are no longer part of the Republic of the Congo."

[59] *Congo 1960*, p. 740.

[60] Telex to D'Aspremont Lynden, July 26, 1960. See *Congo 1960*, pp. 744–45.

themselves and the recognition of such a provisional state is hardly necessary since it is oriented toward a Congolese confederation.

This interpretation was not accepted in Katanga by the *ultras* and Europeans who wanted to obtain recognition from Belgium and from friendly countries and who sought without further ado to set up all the agencies and attributes of a state, including an army, diplomatic corps, currency, and foreign trade.

The point of agreement among all Belgians active in Elisabethville, was the recognition — on the hypothesis of a Congolese confederation — of the need for building it from a Katangan base and making Katanga the core and pole for the future grouping.[61] This agreement did not settle the question of whether or not it was necessary to achieve the confederation by a simultaneous adhesion of former Congolese provinces or whether one should seek at every propitious moment the rallying to Katanga of a province, or of a piece of a province, even if this process led to the division of the Congo into two or several blocks rather than a confederation within the given geographic framework of June 30, 1960.

This question was scarcely raised in July–August, 1960, for at that time, the instructions from Brussels were to weaken the Lumumbist central power by provoking conflict or secession at the level of ethnic groups or of provinces,[62] everywhere possible; by aiding the more or less organized opposition in Leopoldville; by acting through remaining local networks or operating out of Brazzaville and Elisabethville; by withdrawing, even at the beginning of September, certain Belgians still in the service of the central government who were engaged in work particularly harmful for the security of Katanga.[63]

In any case, Article 1 of the Katangan constitution, dating from August 8, 1960 (of which Professor René Clémens is the author), merely noted the fact that "the state of Katanga adheres to the principle of association

[61] "The pivot of the future Congo is Katanga," appeared as a headline in *L'Echo du Katanga* (Elisabethville), January 12, 1960.

[62] For example, the affair of the Baluba and "the Mining State" of South Kasai, see *Congo 1960*, pp. 798–811. Also, feelers were extended to the Bakongo and the provincial government in Kivu; support was given for the activities of the Bangala youth and of Jean Bolikango in Equateur. *Congo 1960*, pp. 658–704.

[63] It followed a brief but violent Katangan reaction, at the moment of the ANC attack against South Kasai. Belgian planes, they said, had transported Lumumbist troups. It was Belgian money which had permitted soldiers to be paid, and, in addition, they said, two Belgian officers had accompanied the Lumumbists. At this moment, the brother of President Tshombe, advised by the *ultras*, called for the expulsion of D'Aspremont Lynden and of the consul, Crener.

with other regions of the former Belgian Congo, provided that they are organized politically in respect for law and order and that Katanga will open negotiations to constitute with them a confederation founded on the equality of partners." [64]

DEFENSE OF THE FRONTIERS AND WITHDRAWAL OF BELGIAN TROOPS

At the end of July, 1960, two closely related fears began to dominate Elisabethville: Would the Belgian troops be forced to withdraw by the arrival of U.N. troops? Would the end of the Belgian military presence lead to a return in force of the ANC moving down from Kivu or South Kasai against Katanga, under the command of the central Congolese authorities?

On July 18, Eyskens had adopted the view that the U.N. did not have to intervene in Katanga nor above all "to meddle in the internal affairs of a country." [65] Belgian efforts tended from then on to delay as long as possible the arrival of U.N. troops. The Katangan government, on its side, radically opposed any U.N. intervention in Katanga, threatened to use "all the means at the disposition of the State" to keep out the U.N. forces which, it said, could not fail "to bring in their baggage the emissaries of Lumumba." [66] Meanwhile, in Leopoldville, relations between the U.N. and the central Congolese authorities were deteriorating; Leopoldville was not taking well the fact that the U.N. had not as yet set foot in Katanga. [67] In the question of the withdrawal of the Belgian troops and the arrival of the *casques bleus*, Katanga profited from an unlooked-for respite.

On August 2, the U.N. had announced that the first contingents were scheduled to arrive in Elisabethville August 6. The day before, Ralph Bunche, representing the Secretary-General, was to arrive on mission in Katanga. Bunche got the impression in Elisabethville that the new gendarmery and the "traditional" warriors would be capable of touching off serious incidents, with which the U.N. could not cope within the framework of the first mandates formulated by the Security Council. His recommendation was "to stop the Katanga operations" [68] and Dag Ham-

---

[64] Text of the Constitution of Katanga in *Congo 1960*, pp. 755–61.

[65] This last view was presented by Dag Hammarskjöld to the Security Council on July 21. Wigny remarked that the U.N. "should not, by any improvised measures, add new burdens to the already crushing task of the U.N.," Agence Belga, August 3, 1960.

[66] Appeal of Munongo, *L'Essor du Katanga* (Elisabethville), August 3, 1960.

[67] *Congo 1960*, p. 615.

[68] Bunche report, *Congo 1960*, p. 618, and U.N. Document, Security Council,

marskjöld followed his counsel. Lumumba and Antoine Gizenga were deeply irritated and made sharply critical statements against the U.N. Belgian authorities in Katanga, for their part, were greatly surprised. On August 9, the Security Council requested the Belgian government "to withdraw immediately its troops from the province of Katanga, under speedy modalities determined by the Secretary-General," reaffirming that the U.N. in the Congo would not attempt to influence "the outcome of any internal conflict, constitutional or otherwise." [69]

Back in Katanga, the Europeans threatened to go on strike or leave the territory if the *casques bleus* arrived;[70] while the Belgian Technical Mission addressed warnings to Belgian employees: those who quit their posts will be "dismissed automatically." [71] According to Hammarskjöld, "opposition to the United Nations is raised [in Katanga] in the shadow of the continued presence of Belgian troops." [72] Wigny pledged that Belgian troops in Katanga would not resist the U.N., nor would the officers seconded to the Katangan gendarmery.[73]

After the vote of the Security Council, Brussels strongly advised Tshombe to reject the notion of the U.N. presence in Katanga no longer, but to require guarantees of noninterference. The Katangan president formulated nine demands[74] which, according to him, were agreed on during the course of his discussion on August 12 with Hammarskjold. At this point, the replacement of Belgian forces by the U.N. began, the last Belgian contingents having to leave Katanga by August 31 at the latest. Belgian troops were also to evacuate their base at Kamina, to make

---

S/4417, para. 9, August 6, 1960. According to the Belgian journalist Pierre Davister there were 700 new recruits in Elisabethville, for the most part former unemployed. — *Katanga, enjeu du monde*, p. 126.

[69] U.N. Document, Security Council, S/4426, August 9, 1960.

[70] Positions of the Assekat, the Upak, the Ucol. On July 24, during the course of a meeting presided over by D'Aspremont Lynden, the *chefs de service* in the administration expressed their firm intention of leaving the territory in case of the withdrawal of Belgian troops, and this was, in large measure, the point of view of Europeans working in the major private firms. The Afac demanded a special premium for white administrators and a priority for reabsorption into the Belgian civil service.

[71] Security Council, Minutes, August 8, 1960.

[72] *Ibid.* This agreement undertaken by Wigny showed for the first time to the Katangans that the officers furnished within the framework of technical assistance could be bound by decisions in Brussels.

[73] *Congo 1960*, pp. 751–52. Note especially the sixth point, relating to the reorganization of a Katangan gendarmery and the taking of Belgian arms at Kamina by Katanga.

[74] Fewer than were hoped for by Tshombe's advisers.

way for the U.N. forces. This decision ran counter to Belgian and Katangan wishes but Belgium's Atlantic allies advised her to renounce the
base.

During the entire month of August, a veritable race against the clock
took place with the objective, for Tshombe and his advisers, of building
a more or less efficient Katangan gendarmery before the eventual withdrawal of the Belgian troops. To meet this objective, the commander of
the new gendarmery, Major Crèvecoeur, called for former officers of the
Force Publique who had left the Congo after the July troubles or who
were in Katanga. The Belgian Technical Mission also obtained from
Brussels a detachment of the Belgian gendarmery to Elisabethville as
technical assistance, and regular officers of the Belgian army[75] passed
directly into the service of Major Crèvecoeur.

For arming the new force, whose numbers in 1960 were originally
fixed at 1,500 volunteers from sixteen to twenty-one years of age recruited
from "safe" ethnic groups,[76] Major Crèvecoeur had available arms of the
Force Publique which had been stored in Kamina, and matériel recaptured
by Belgian troops in the course of their interventions at different points
in the Congo. In addition, almost all the aircraft of the *Force Publique*
had been transferred to Kamina, then requisitioned by Katanga. Thus,
Elisabethville had at its disposal nine de Havilland-Doves, one Piper
L-18 C for observation, the personal four-motored plane which had belonged to the Governor-General of the Congo, one or two S-55 helicopters; also, the Katangan authorities had some Harvards and two
Douglasses from the pilot-training school at Kamina.[77] In addition, deliveries of arms were made by Sabena DC-7's at the beginning of September, 1960, and it is probable that, despite Wigny's formal orders on
August 25 to the commander of Belgian metropolitan forces, not all of
their equipment left Katanga when the troops were evacuated at the end
of August, 1960.

Direct aid in addition was furnished for the defense of Katanga by
corps of European volunteers, locally constituted by settlers but advised
by white officers (for example, Kaniama). Furthermore, Elisabethville
benefited from useful assistance in the form of military and political

---

[75] *Arrêté* of the Chief of State, No. 221/111 of August 6, 1960, in *Moniteur
Katangais*, No. 2, August 15, 1960. Ministerial *Arrêté*, No. 221/112 of August 6,
1960, in the same number of *Moniteur Katangais*.

[76] Radio statement, August 3, 1960.

[77] According to Wim Dannau, in *Pourquoi Pas?* (Brussels), September 29, 1961,
pp. 142–43.

information, transmitted hour by hour over the *Sûreté* network still at the disposal of the Belgians, in Brazzaville and in certain provinces.

In spite of everything, at the end of August and in early September, 1960, the Katangan territory was threatened on two fronts: first at the border of South Kasai; then to the north in the direction of Kongolo, where the ANC had begun an advance into regions with anti-Tshombe populations. At this point, Brussels stepped up its direct military aid in men and arms and persuaded its Atlantic allies to put strong pressure on the U.N. to halt the invasion of Katanga by Lumumbist forces. This dual threat was averted in September following the *coup d'état* of Colonel Mobutu.

POLITICAL AND ADMINISTRATIVE STRUCTURE

The proclamation of independence signified for its authors the creation of a real Katangan state and the tranformation of the provincial apparatus into a complete state apparatus, including the attributes of external and internal sovereignty.

As for the functioning of the state itself, several steps and essential acts may be cited. The mining enterprises, the chartered companies, and the *Office Spécial d'Imposition de Brussels* (the tax bureau) acknowledged the fact that "since the proclamation of independence, on July 11, 1960, Katanga has become the collector of taxes and mining royalties and of all obligations due the state." [78] For the Union Minière, this amounted to 2,096 million Belgian francs (1961) and 1,485 million Belgian francs (1962), and for the Comité Spécial du Katanga some 431 million Belgian francs between June 30, 1960, and March 31, 1962, paid to the Katangan authorities on sums received from the companies figuring in the CSK portfolio. The Katangan state replaced the former Belgian Congo in relations with the parastatal [79] organizations in matters regarding pensions, savings accounts, family allowances, financial credits to the middle classes,

[78] Rule frequently recalled in the *Moniteur Katangais* (among others, Ordinance-law No. 334/250 of December 23, 1960, on the obligations toward the state, in *Moniteur Katangais*, No. 1, January 1, 1961).
"I arrived in Belgium and I met with the UMHK and several important persons and we came to an agreement that in the future the dividends would be paid to Katanga," Kibwe further explained. Minutes, Katangan Council of Ministers, December 27, 1960. From the monetary point of view Katanga was, in 1960, the refuge of Congolese foreign exchange.

[79] Translator's note: Parastatal organizations are autonomous public corporations or agencies set up in the Congo to carry out certain welfare services or to perform certain economic functions, such as transport, management of public lands, power, and water supply.

construction of African townships, and so forth.[80] Control over foreign exchange and foreign trade went to Elisabethville; pending creation of a Katangan currency, transfers were prohibited from the Central Bank of the Belgian Congo and Ruanda-Urundi to other branches in the Congo or in Brussels. There was frequent use — on the basis of the *Arrêté* No. 111/104 of July 27 (mobilization of Katanga) — of the right to requisition buildings and personnel of essential financial and economic agencies.[81] Extraordinary budgets were adopted by ordinance-laws, and so forth.

In Katanga, the problems of collecting taxes were relatively simple. The export duties were established at the point of shipment and were owed primarily by the important mining companies, whose production represented 84 percent of the total exports of Katanga. Personal income taxes were traditionally collected by the province for the colony, and personal property taxes on distributed dividends were collected in Brussels by the *Office Spécial d'Imposition* and credited to Katanga.

Assured of duties and fiscal receipts as long as mining activities and transportation of the output could be maintained,[82] the Katangan state had at its disposal important revenues since it no longer remitted any funds to Leopoldville. These revenues constituted the ideal means of providing for the operations of the state. Except in the case of Belgian technical assistance, the state was cast in the role of client or employer in regard to those who provided its supplies (including military provisions) and its daily management. This tendency toward financial independence was made even more concrete by the creation of a National Bank of Katanga, capitalized at 100 million francs, of which 60 percent was subscribed by the state and 40 percent by public issue. The director of the bank, named with powers retroactive to August 8, 1960, by an *arrêté* of January 26, 1961, was a Belgian, André Van Roey, who had been an

[80] Ordinance No. 334/114 of September 12, 1960, confirming the *de facto* situation created by the secession, in *Moniteur Katangais* (1960), p. 42.

[81] For example, Savings Bank by *Arrêté*, No. 111/174 of October 10, 1960 in *Moniteur Katangais* (1960), p. 81, and Comité Spécial du Katanga by *Arrêté*, No. 454/17 of January 19, 1961, in *Moniteur Katangais*.

[82] Normally three principal routes for transportation of their products existed: one, called the "national route," from Elisabethville to Matadi via Port-Francqui and Leopoldville (by rail and then by water); the railroad from Elisabethville to Lobito through Angola, controlled financially by Tanganyika Concessions, Ltd.; and the railroad from Elisabethville to Beira (on the Indian Ocean in Mozambique) through the Rhodesias. Katanga in secession used the last two routes and depended very largely on this means made possible by the Rhodesias and Angola for export of its minerals as well as for civilian and military supplies.

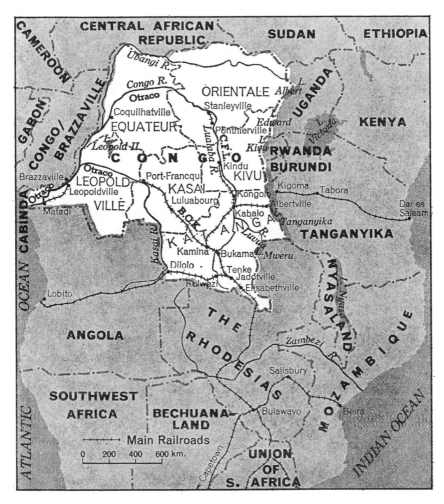

Rail and River Export Routes from Katanga

DISTANCES FROM ELISABETHVILLE: kms.

I)	Elisabethville to Matadi, via Port-Francqui:	2,770
	Elisabethville to Matadi, via Stanleyville:	4,004
	Elisabethville to Lobito (rail):	2,110
	Elisabethville to Beira (rail):	2,614
II)	Elisabethville to Port-Francqui (rail):	1,580
	Port-Francqui to Leopoldville (river):	825
	Leopoldville to Matadi (rail):	365
III)	Elisabethville to Stanleyville:	1,922
	Stanleyville to Matadi:	2,082

executive on the staff of the Central Bank of the Belgian Congo and Ruanda-Urundi in its Elisabethville headquarters. For preparing the issue of Katangan currency, the bank also had the help of currency experts from the Belgian Institut.

As regards political institutions, Katanga departed from the provisional *Loi Fondamentale* in its constitution of August 8. This constitution gave to Katanga the status of a sovereign state. It instituted — besides an elected Assembly — a Council of traditional chiefs, thus embodying the inclination of the Conakat to depend on the traditional authorities and have the President delegate to them, within the framework of a pact of allegiance, authority over their own administration, army, and justice. The Katangan constitution instituted a quasi-presidential regime, the "chief of state" having the power to name the ministers, whereas the *Loi Fondamentale* of May, 1960, had only provided for ministers elected by the Assembly.

Among the administrative and political sectors where Belgian assistance played a decisive role, intelligence services must also be mentioned. There existed in Katanga an internal *Sûreté* reporting to Munongo, a military *Sûreté*, and an external intelligence service. An attempt to coordinate all three under the President was made in October, 1960, with the creation of the *Service de la Centralisation et de la Coordination du Renseignement* (SCCR) with eight Europeans on its central staff and an external network of its own.

CHAPTER 4 · *The Period of the Anti-Lumumbist and Anti-U.N. Front (September 5, 1960-April 1961)*

IN the preceding chapter, attention was focused on the means of Belgian intervention and activity in Katanga, from the morning of July 10. These interventions, in fact, made possible the existence of the state of Katanga in July and August, 1960, decisive months for the establishment of the apparatus of secession.

At the beginning of September, the situation was profoundly changed. Since August 20, the leaders in Katanga had lived in the expectation of an invasion by the Armée Nationale Congolaise (ANC) and were disillusioned by the progressive withdrawal of the Belgian forces[1] and by the arrival of the U.N. force. They were disappointed as well by the total diplomatic isolation of Katanga and by the broad pro-Lumumbist African coalition.[2] For several weeks, the rebellion gained territory in the north along precisely the normal path of ANC penetration from Kivu to Katanga.

The beginning of September was to be a decisive period from the point of view of the future of the Katanga secession. On September 5, President Kasavubu dismissed Lumumba from office, thus consummating the break between the Chief of State and the Congolese Prime Minister. At this moment, the temptation was strong for the Belgian government to profit from the constitution of a "moderate" central government, presided over by Ileo, so that it would no longer bank everything on Katanga, and would be able to operate from Leopoldville, without necessarily cutting itself off from Elisabethville. In other words, the Katangan

[1] "Kamina is being evacuated, but without excessive haste," *La Libre Belgique* (Brussels), August 24, 1960.
[2] A coalition no doubt superficial and fragile rather than profound and tightly knit, as would be revealed in late August and early September, 1960.

119

monopoly over Belgium's African policy was called into question by those who had never considered the secession as permanent, but regarded it more simply as a tactical maneuver temporarily imposed by events, while awaiting the opportunity to rebuild a federal or confederal Congo of non-Lumumbist leanings.

Count d'Aspremont Lynden, head of the Belgian Technical Mission, was promoted to the post of Minister of African Affairs in the reshuffled Eyskens cabinet,[3] which, to a certain extent, compensated for the temptation of Brussels to give priority to Leopoldville.

The military operation of the ANC against Bakwanga and South Kasai in late August and early September degenerated into massacres of civilian populations, with military leaders no longer obeying any authority, and in the U.N., it provoked even among the Afro-Asian nations — as is shown by the reported proceedings of the Consultative Committee — a reaction unfavorable to the central government in Leopoldville. The Baluba leaders of the Mining State from this point forward benefited from technical assistance provided by the Belgians and by Katanga. Thus, for the first time, a scheme for the confederal reconstruction of the Congo based upon Katanga began to materialize.[4]

The total withdrawal of Belgian armed forces deprived Katanga of direct protection against a military invasion from the ANC. When the attack directly threatened Kongolo, an acceleration of direct military aid began in the form of arms supplies[5] and recruitment of officers coming directly from Belgium, as well as in the military training of Katangans in Belgium.

THE FIRST ATTEMPTS AT RAPPROCHEMENT BETWEEN LEOPOLDVILLE AND ELISABETHVILLE

The designation by Kasavubu, on September 5, of Joseph Ileo, a federalist of moderate tendencies, as Prime Minister of the central gov-

---

[3] This choice was warmly welcomed in Elisabethville by Tshombe, who paid homage from the start to "the master-builder" who continued to aid Katanga "in the high offices which he held."

[4] At the end of August, in his instructions to Elisabethville, Wigny again recommended a prudent attitude on the subject of aid to South Kasai, given the fact that Kalonji's secessionist government could not invoke a legitimacy dating from June 30, 1960. In August, a convention was concluded between Katanga and the Mining State.

[5] For example, the delivery made on September 7 involving seven to nine tons of arms. At this point, the Belgian authorities also sought to aid Tshombe in maintaining his freedom of movement by air, while the U.N. in the Congo had decided to blockade the air fields in Leopoldville as well as in Elisabethville (local measures by the Belgian consul, Crener; steps at the U.N. in New York by Walter Loridan.)

ernment, aroused varying reactions in Elisabethville. There was rejoicing at first because the political elimination of Lumumba was anticipated and probably the withdrawal of the ANC from the northern borders of Kivu as well. An attempt was made to exploit the event to Tshombe's glory by attributing to him the initial and principal position as an anti-Lumumbist. Tshombe called for a meeting of anti-Lumumbist leaders, and there were hopes for common action. Simultaneously, the attitude of the Belgian government, whose assistance remained vital for Katanga, was cause for worry. Was Belgium to deal with the Ileo government and keep its distance from Tshombe? Was financial and technical assistance for Leopoldville to have priority over that for Katanga? Would the return of the moderates to power at the center revive "unitarist" tendencies and weaken the confederalists?

R. Rothschild, head of the Belgian Technical Mission in Katanga after D'Aspremont Lynden became a minister, strongly advised Tshombe to make overtures in the direction of Ileo and Kasavubu and to make clear that Katanga would cooperate financially within the framework of a confederal Congo.[6] This position was fought by private advisers and by the "hard" wing of the Katangan government which wished to temporize and refused to sacrifice anything of Katanga's independence, at a moment when the political situation remained blurred in Leopoldville.

The same Rothschild simultaneously maintained that the political reconstruction of the Congo should take place from an Elisabethville base, that events had "strengthened" in an exceptional fashion Tshombe's leadership as defender of the political reconstruction of the former Belgian Congo on a confederal basis. "Seen from Elisabethville," he added, "it would be extremely unfortunate if the Belgian government made a premature declaration of assistance to the rest of the Congo. It is necessary that a priority, at least for the time being, be maintained in favor of Katanga."

The view was, therefore: rapprochement between Tshombe and the anti-Lumumbist leaders in Leopoldville, with a view toward future recon-

---

[6] Tshombe repeated this theme over the Elisabethville radio but the text, telexed to Brussels on September 6, does not seem to have been retransmitted to Brazzaville for Ileo (see pp. 333–35). This problem of financial solidarity has often been raised by Belgian authorities, for example, by D'Aspremont Lynden at the end of September, 1960. Concretely, that would have meant according to working papers, for an agreement to be freely concluded that Katanga would not consume its total receipts for its own needs. Such advice was not welcome in Elisabethville, in government circles, and among Europeans selling the supplies and services the Katangan authorities could order from them.

struction of the Congo on a confederal basis, Elisabethville would be assured the role of fulcrum and Tshombe that of a leader.[7]

Tshombe tried to establish contact, but he refused the offer which was made to him on September 10 by the Premier designate to enter the central government as Vice-Prime Minister.[8] Perhaps he had no confidence in Ileo's chances for success since Ileo had not yet faced the Parliament, where Lumumba counted on broad support. More probably, he did not feel that the crisis could be resolved by a simple change of government. He pleaded the opposite view, namely, that the path to follow was to abandon the provisional *Loi Fondamentale* as too unitarist and, at a Round Table of Congolese leaders, to decide upon a new confederal structure consolidating the essential powers that secession had secured for the former province. On this level, Tshombe did not have full confidence because Ileo, a federalist at the Brussels political Round Table, was likewise a stalwart antisecessionist; on September 10, 1960, he had announced his intention of "leading Tshombe back to the fold." "Without spilling a single drop of blood," he added, but the sense of his words was clear.

At Brazzaville, the emissaries of Tshombe — Evariste Kimba and Joseph Yav — were received by Ileo, who had a plan for a Katanga solution: two Conakat and two Balubakat ministers in the central government; in Katanga, six Conakat ministers and the presidency for Tshombe's party, and four ministers as well as the vice-presidency for the Cartel; recognition of the central authority by Elisabethville but a provisional status for Katanga based on the *status quo*, pending a Round Table on state structures. These discussions failed since the Katangans had instructions not to enter a central government before a new political structure was set up. On September 11, under pressure from "hard" elements in Elisabethville, who exploited the fact that Ileo had never effectively ousted Lumumba, Tshombe himself declared that his objective was still to secure "total independence of Katanga in the political domain."[9]

Several days later, on September 17, discussions resumed, but at this point, Colonel Mobutu had "neutralized" the politicians and was ready-

---

[7] "It is important for the West to give important stature to Tshombe," telex of September 8, 1960, from Belgian Technical Mission.

[8] Ileo proposed four portfolios for Katanga: two for the Conakat and two for the Balubakat.

[9] On September 12, the Belgian advisers let it be understood that Tshombe had confided to them that he had made this declaration "only for bargaining purposes."

ing his College of Commissioners. Meanwhile, on September 16, despite advice to the contrary from Brussels, Elisabethville appointed Evariste Kimba to the newly created Ministry of Foreign Affairs.[10] Nothing new came of the discussions in Brazzaville, except that Katanga tried to condition everything on a Round Table concerning state structures which would be held in "a neutral city" among a small number of "true leaders," dealing with each other "on an equal footing."[11]

Differences were not confined to the timing and procedure to adopt in solving the crisis. In Leopoldville, Kasavubu and Ileo were alarmed by the bloody incidents in North Katanga and asked Tshombe to accept a peace-making mission that the Balubakat leader Jason Sendwe would undertake in the troubled regions. In Brussels, the idea won support because the Sendwe mission was seen as a chance to loosen Lumumba's hold over the Balubakat. In Elisabethville, however, the Katangan authorities and Belgian advisers turned down the proposal. They had, they said, no confidence in Sendwe and, besides, the decision had already been made to set the forces of order[12] to work suppressing the "rebellion" in the north. One of the major complaints in Elisabethville was that "those people in Leopoldville don't know what they want." On September 29, 1960, Munongo came to the conclusion that Katanga must refuse confederation and held out for total independence. This position was confirmed by Evariste Kimba according to reports of Agence France-Presse. Tshombe was more subtle; on September 27, 1960, he argued that Katanga was struggling to have its independence recognized but it could negotiate with a "reasonable" government in Leopoldville.

RIOTS IN NORTH AND CENTRAL KATANGA

"According to news from Manono . . . , Europeans have been ordered to evacuate their homes in the suburbs and to gather in the center of town. Bands of Baluba are said to have taken a threatening position." This Reuters dispatch on August 11, 1960, is perhaps the first to take note of the mass movements which threatened in the Baluba regions.[13]

[10] On October 7, a Secretary of State for Defense would be named, Joseph Yav.

[11] Telegram from Tshombe addressed to Ileo, September 18, 1960, in *Congo 1960*, p. 965.

[12] The cease-fire brought about under the auspices of the U.N. in the Congo between the ANC and the Katangan gendarmery temporarily removed the threat of "external" activities in North Katanga.

[13] "Urban" incidents took place on August 15 in Jadotville (with several dead and wounded), on August 21 in Elisabethville (a hundred Baluba were arrested), and in Albertville on August 23.

According to reliable observers, the movement of noncooperation with Tshombe authorities was deeply rooted; it put pressure on the local chiefs against any rallying to the authorities in Elisabethville and caught up the "youth" especially.

In late August, Tshombe still minimized the gravity of the situation:

The troubles in the north are due exclusively to the activities of Baluba followers of Kitawala (Watch Tower) along the river. These people are fanatics who recognize no authority except that of God. The Belgians put the most frenzied members in camps. In June, all these people were released and they fanned out into the region preaching anarchy. There is nothing else to do except to pick them up again, put them back in camps, and all will be finished.[14]

In fact, at this moment, operations of the gendarmery were being mounted against the Baluba by Belgian officers and noncommissioned officers transferred from the former *Force Publique* or *Cométro* (troops from Belgium) to Major Crèvecoeur's gendarmery.

At the beginning of September, several of these operations had dramatic consequences for the Katangan forces. Thus, in the region of Malemba-Nkulu, on September 5, a patrol ran into an ambush; there were ten killed, one of whom was a Belgian captain and another a Belgian adjutant.[15] The survivors were disarmed by the U.N. force which thus could assure their protection. The affair ended in "reprisals" by Dove aircraft. The reprisals were, according to the Belgian Technical Mission, "unfortunately inevitable."

From this moment forward, news about the incidents became clearly more pessimistic in publications favorable to the authorities in Elisabethville: "The whole Baluba countryside is mobilized, it seems, for a sort of holy war. *Pirogues* [dugouts] filled with armed youth descend the river. The attackers are drugged with hemp, but they appear to follow very clear tactical orders, attacking convoys from the rear, and then closing

[14] Tshombe declaration to *La Libre Belgique* (Brussels), August 30, 1960. At this point, Pierre Davister published in *Pourquoi Pas?* (Brussels), August 26, 1960, a report on Manono which put the question very strongly, under the headline, "And if that North up there moves . . . ?".

[15] See Christian Lanciney, *Les Héros sont affreux* (Brussels: Charles Dessart, 1962), p. 10. The author is Christian Souris, a former territorial officer who accompanied the Malemba-Nkulu expedition, then was attached to the Katangan information office. The story of this operation was recounted in *La Libre Belgique* (Brussels), September 12, 1960.

in on those in front, trying most of all to kill the drivers of the vehicles. Some fear that these mobs will be directed into the south."[16]

The tales of battles, ambushes, reprisals — cruel and bloody — assumed an increasing gravity well reflected in Belgian newspaper headlines:

"Twenty-four Europeans encircled at Manono," September 16, 1960.

"Incidents in Manono have to date killed 70 Baluba," September 16, 1960.

"Eight hundred drugged and fanatic Baluba attack the gendarmery in Manono," September 17, 1960.

"Protest from the United Nations to Tshombe on repression at Luena," September 22, 1960.

"Massacres and tortures. Mitwaba encircled," October 11, 1960.

"Assassination of Chief Kabongo and several of his deputies," October 29, 1960.

"Irish patrol ambushed: 8 dead, 1 missing," November 12, 1960.

"Violent attack of Baluba rebels against mining center of Luena," December 3, 1960.

"The Besieged of Luena: in constant anguish," December 13, 1960.

To combat the Baluba rebellion, Tshombe resorted to the recruitment, in Katanga and abroad, of mercenaries specializing in guerrilla warfare. A mission was sent to Belgium on September 18. It was empowered to take on 180 officers and noncommissioned officers, while on September 22, another mission (Thyssens) was sent to Paris and London, likewise to recruit mercenaries.[17]

Two Belgian journalists at the time furnished useful information on the rebellion and on the repression in the north — J. K. [van der Dussen] of *La Libre Belgique* and Pierre Davister of *Pourquoi Pas?* to whom we owe these two passages:[18]

"In Indochina and in Korea, it was war," I was told by an *affreux*. "Here, it is mutual carnage. Our units lose few men but we no longer count the loyal villagers assassinated by the rebel raids. As for the rebels, sure, we make them pay a terrible price for it.

The repression cannot be carried through in its current form, which is too slow, too sporadic, too defensive to be truly effective. Other means are necessary: reconnaissance planes, a more ample officer corps with more stuff to it,

[16] J. K. [Jean de Kestergat van der Dussen], *La Libre Belgique* (Brussels), September 12, 1960.

[17] These organizational problems of the Katangan forces are dealt with later, pp. 155–69.

[18] For further discussion of the situation and the operations in north and central Katanga, see *Congo 1960*, pp. 774–79.

tactics better adapted to the guerrilla war waged by the rebels. We dream. Warriors have been recruited among the loyal tribes in the rebel regions. Armed, transported, transformed into gendarmes, these warriors provide precious aid to the mobile groups." [19]

For anyone trying to draw up a balance sheet of the situation in December, 1960, and to evaluate the extent of the regions unsubdued, some conclusions are strongly evident: since September, the greater part of the territories "of the north" have fallen — without a struggle, what is more — into rebel hands. Such is the case, for example, with almost all the district of Tanganika, where it is no longer possible to venture without danger. The extent of various regions which remain loyal is, moreover, impossible to establish. In Kabalo, a small core of the administration is counted on. That is all. The territory of Albertville is practically reduced to a north-south band about 40 kilometers wide which borders the road to Baudouinville. Weighty compensation: the territory of Baudouinville is almost completely spared. . . .

In December, 1960, the number of rebels killed since the beginning of "reprisal" operations of the Katangan army in North Katanga was evaluated at about 7,000. We know what figures of this kind mean in Africa. Generally, it is necessary to multiply by two, by three, by ten or even more, if the result obtained is not to be far short of the truth.

At Elisabethville, they do not hide the fact that the Katangan gendarmery had to use "strong means" to clean out certain rebel nests. Entire villages were razed and automatic weapons literally mowed down entire ranks of "youths" who — it must be agreed — marched idiotically to their death.[20]

In the struggle against the rebellion, Elisabethville authorities counted first on the gendarmery. They tried as well — but without great success — to win over the population to Elisabethville by operations of a psychological nature, by attempts to involve local traditional authorities, by pacification missions, and so forth. At the end of December, 1960, Elisabethville let it be understood that the end of the troubles was imminent. Negotiations were going to take place on the spot, according to Katangan sources, with representatives of the Balubakat in the presence of Indonesian observers from the U.N. Nothing happened to confirm this hypothesis. It seems, in fact, there were discussions with some of the Balubakat Assembly members, imprisoned by Munongo's police. These prisoners were said to be ready to cooperate on condition that five Balubakat ministers were named. But at the decisive moment, it was thought in Elisabethville that once liberated these representatives would go north to join the struggle against Tshombe.

[19] *La Libre Belgique* (Brussels), December 17 and 18, 1960.
[20] Davister, *Katanga, enjeu du monde,* pp. 249–54.

Thus, a not insignificant part of Katangan territory escaped the authority of the Tshombe government by October–November, 1960. Tshombe, in fact, limited his aims to holding important centers in troubled regions, to safeguarding the means of communication, and to stopping Prosper Mwamba Ilunga and the Balubakat from using Manono,[21] or any other center of any importance, as a capital for the Lualaba provincial "government," constituted in Stanleyville in late October and early November, 1960, with the support of Gizenga.

Nevertheless, confronted with worsening disorder in October, the Elisabethville authorities on October 17, 1960, at last acknowledged fairly extensive zones (Kabalo, Manono, Malemba-Nkulu, Luena, Bukama), where the maintenance of order would be essentially in the hands of the U.N. forces. The presence of armed persons other than the forces of order would be forbidden in the designated localities; these areas as well as the industrial installations would be the object of U.N. protection against raids by armed bands or pillaging. For the other zones, the gendarmery agreed only to adopt a defensive posture.[22]

In September, the same U.N. plan had been rejected by Elisabethville; it would result, it was said, in challenging the sovereignty of Katanga over a part of its territory.

RELATIONS OF KATANGA WITH BELGIUM AND THE U.N.

In July and August, the dependence of the Katangan authorities on the Belgian military presence and on Belgian assistance was such that public criticism toward Brussels was muted and remained strictly verbal. The Katangans did accuse the Belgians of playing into the hands of the unitarists before June, 1960. True, they also demanded recognition of their "State" by Belgium or hoped for a sterner attitude of the Belgian government toward the U.N. and Lumumba. But all this was no different from the arguments employed in the right-wing newspapers in Belgium toward the persons responsible for Congolese policy. At this point, *ultra* views were relatively neutralized and strong pressure was put on Tshombe by the Belgian Technical Mission "to make him avoid the multiple mistakes which irresponsible elements advised him to make." [23]

In September, the climate deteriorated and distrust was expressed on the Katangan side. Belgium, they said, played a double game, in the sense

[21] Manono was taken by the ANC in January, 1961, under orders from Stanleyville.

[22] Text of the agreement in *Congo 1960*, p. 794.

[23] Telex from the Belgian Technical Mission to Brussels, September 3, 1960.

that she put her money on the moderates in Leopoldville, rather than on an independent Katanga. On September 28, Belgium advanced 500 million Belgian francs to the Central Bank of the Congo[24] and, on top of everything, decided at the end of September that "Katanga must itself finance military deliveries and operations." Moreover, the political pressures exerted on Tshombe to accept an accord with Ileo and later with the commissioners drew bitter comment in Elisabethville.[25] Meanwhile, the overtures of Pierre Wigny to the Belgian allies to get the Kasavubu delegation recognized at the U.N.[26] provoked protests from Kimba and Tshombe,[27] who went so far as to threaten "to abandon the constant solicitude that it [the Tshombe government] had maintained for Belgian interests since independence." This allusion was made following a declaration of Henri Kambola, member of the Conakat Central Committee before June 30, 1960, threatening UMHK (among others) with nationalization.

In this atmosphere, on October 12, 1960, the Belgian Technical Mission, with Rothschild, left Elisabethville at the request of the Katangan authorities. By common consent, they agreed to avoid allowing the dissolution to be interpreted as a sign of tension and misunderstanding between Brussels and Elisabethville. Tshombe, nevertheless, profited by the occasion to list at length "Belgian mistakes" and to regret the "equivocal conditions" under which the Belgian Technical Mission worked.[28] He repeated his threat to break the Belgian monopoly over technical assist-

---

[24] From August 14 to 24, Belgo-Congolese discussions took place in Geneva on the liquidation of the Central Bank of the Belgian Congo and Ruanda-Urundi and on the creation of a National Bank of the Congo. Elisabethville protested against this meeting to which the Katangans were not invited. By the same token, Elisabethville protested against "the blockage in the National Bank of Belgium of 200 million francs accruing from exports from Katanga before July 11."

[25] On September 7, Jean-Baptiste Kibwe accused the Belgian Technical Mission of having inspired the declaration of solidarity made the day before by Tshombe. — *La Libre Belgique* (Brussels), September 8, 1960.

[26] In opposition to that of Lumumba. This question had fairly serious repercussions when the issues were taken up again at Brazzaville with the College of Commissioners.

[27] "Diplomatic activities entered upon by the Belgian government against recognition of the Katangan State are interpreted by my government as an unfriendly act consequences of which could be very serious." — Letter from Tshombe to Eyskens, October 9, 1960.

[28] From the end of July, 1960, a governmental observer had reported to Brussels the feeling that the Katangan ministers had been irritated by the activities of the Belgian Technical Mission which was giving them the impression that the Belgians had thus created an agency parallel to the government.

ance and industrial exploitation in Katanga[29] and again demanded recognition of Katanga by Brussels.

The Belgian Technical Mission was replaced by the Technical Assistance Bureau under the direction of Professor R. Clémens, while political and consular agents Vanden Bloock and Crener, respectively, remained, in direct contact with Wigny.

In retrospect, the dissolution of the Belgian Technical Mission appears, in Katanga, as an index of the desire to depend less on Belgian personalities of "double loyalty"[30] and to deal with problems of assistance, supply, and recruitment in accordance with criteria set exclusively by President Tshombe and his personal advisers. In Brussels, it was a question of retrenching somewhat on involvement in Katanga by abandoning, without immediate risk of losing influence, a Belgian governmental responsibility too direct and too visible in the management of the secessionist state.[31] It was at this moment that Belgium was looking for a way to reestablish itself in Leopoldville and that the U.N., through its Secretary-General, was denouncing the risks of the "Belgian factor" in Katanga. The desire to identify itself no longer with direct management in Katanga was expressed in a telex from Wigny on October 6, 1960, in which he showed the desire to limit Belgian representation in Elisabethville to the consulate general. The hoped-for disengagement could not be put into practice because the change in the method of assistance was not made apparent. Clémens worked in the same pattern and according to the same procedures as had the Belgian Technical Mission.

In practice, the official Belgian policy was characterized from this moment forward by what must be called, quite objectively, a double game, although the end was one and the same. On the one hand, through Brazzaville, material and political support was to be given to the Leopoldville College of Commissioners and to Colonel Mobutu.[32] On the

[29] Secrétariat d'Etat à l'Information, Service de Presse, Katanga, No. 1, October 18, 1960.

[30] This expression was aimed at Belgian representatives on missions in Katanga whose position was such that they could not, in spite of local pressure and their own personal political inclinations, ignore Belgian instructions.

[31] Wigny hoped that the dissolution would have taken place before the debate on the Congo in the U.N. to obviate reference to the Belgian Technical Mission as an argument against Belgium.

[32] Translator's note: After his *coup d'état* of September 14, 1960, Colonel Mobutu appointed a College of Commissioners to act as a provincial government pending restoration of the constitutional processes. The commissioners served from September, 1960, until February, 1961.

other hand, in Elisabethville, technical assistance and the cooperation
of the private industrial sector continued to furnish Tshombe with the
means of maintaining a separate state. An effort was made to reconcile
certain inherent contradictions in this double game. In keeping with its
general mode of action in the Congo, Brussels, guided especially by the
Minister for African Affairs (*Minaf*), tried to lay the groundwork for a
de facto alliance between Leopoldville, Elisabethville, and, if possible,
Bakwanga. A common position on the institutional structures for the
Congo was out of the question — the alliance was to be based on a simple
defensive response against both Lumumbism and the policies of the
U.N. in the Congo.

Lumumbism at this juncture was still incarnated by Lumumba, who
had at his disposal a virtual majority in a Parliament which had been
sent packing by the Chief of State. It was later embodied in the *de facto*
authorities that were first set up in October and November, 1960, in
Stanleyville, and later, at the end of December, in Bukavu under the control of Gizenga and of his ministers, especially Marcel Bisukiro and
Anicet Kashamura.

Were relations with the U.N. at this point so bad that it was possible to
build an alliance based on the common opposition of the Leopoldville
commissioners and Tshombe's government to the international organization?

For Katanga, tensions had eased following the arrival of the U.N.
troops on August 12.[33] The arrival of the U.N. forces did not set off any
of the catastrophes which were feared: not the massive departure of
Europeans, nor the arrival of Lumumbist emissaries, nor U.N. meddling
in Katanga's internal affairs. On September 8, at 9 o'clock in the morning, brief but violent tensions flared when the U.N. decided to forbid use
of the airfields the day after the Kasavubu-Lumumba dispute erupted.
At this point, the ANC was threatening the northern border of Katanga
and the major military asset of the Katangan government was in danger
of being paralyzed.[34] In fact, two Katangan airplanes took to the air on
September 9, without U.N. interference.

[33] The Secretariat in New York was reproached by Katanga for its excessive
zeal in the question of the withdrawal of Belgian troops and in its attitude toward
the base at Kamina. But in contrast Katanga was overjoyed at the refusal of the
U.N. to follow the injunctions of the Lumumba government concerning elimination of European contingents of the U.N. forces in Katanga.

[34] The flight ban hit Lumumba hard and prevented him from bringing loyal
troops immediately to Leopoldville with the aid of requisitioned airplanes or with
Soviet Ilvushins.

In September, relations between Elisabethville and the U.N. were embittered because of the troubles in the north. Rajeshwar Dayal, representing Secretary-General Hammarskjöld, presented the facts in a light very unfavorable for Tshombe's forces of order, especially in regard to reprisals; while in Elisabethville, it was alleged or implied that the rebellion had gained ground under the very shadow of the U.N. presence and that massacres had taken place while U.N. troops stood passively by (except — the *ultras*, and even Tshombe, were saying — to cooperate with the Baluba or involve themselves in the pillaging).

In fact, a war of communiqués and of declarations was on, reflected in unfriendly relations, carried at times to the point of boycotting initiatives of the other side.[35] All these verbal skirmishes did not prevent a U.N.-Katanga accord on the riot-torn zones on October 17.

The most serious divergences, those which provoked the ruptures, lie elsewhere, in the conceptions of Hammarskjöld concerning the manner of "eliminating the Belgian political and military factor from Katanga."

The U.N. Secretary-General considered the unilateral aid given by Brussels to Katanga incompatible with the U.N. General Assembly resolution and requested the Belgian government "to withdraw all the military, paramilitary or civil personnel which it has placed at the disposal of the authorities in the Congo."[36] All aid must thenceforward be channeled through the United Nations. In a letter to Tshombe on October 8, Hammarskjöld felt it necessary both for the benefit of the Congo and for relations on the world scene, to "lay the groundwork for a reconciliation between Katanga and the rest of the territory of the Republic of the Congo."[37] According to Hammarskjöld, the withdrawal of the Belgians would induce the Katangan authorities — cut off from all outside aid except that furnished through the U.N. to the Republic of the Congo — to review their policy.

This demand of Hammarskjöld[38] stirred a sharp response; Elisabeth-

---

[35] Consequently, Katangan authorities refused to participate in U.N. day ceremonies.

[36] Verbal note of October 8, 1960, in *Congo 1960*, p. 784. U.N. Document, Security Council, S/4557, B, para. 1.

[37] U.N. Document, Security Council, S/4557, B, para. 5.

[38] The facts to which Hammarskjöld referred are those in the Dayal report: "In Katanga, Belgian influence is omnipresent. Virtually all key civilian and security posts are either held directly by officials of Belgian nationality or controlled by advisers to recently appointed and often inexperienced Congolese officials. Significantly, within the security forces there are, according to the latest available data,

ville and Brussels were particularly disturbed.[39] "The Belgian cadres are an essential and decisive element in the maintenance of order in Katanga," argued a Belgian representative in Elisabethville on October 11. "Their withdrawal would in 24 hours result in the collapse of the gendarmery and would be followed shortly thereafter by the collapse of the Tshombe government."

Thus, beyond the problem of the maintenance of order, the fate of the Katangan secession was at stake as was capacity to resist international pressures for reintegration into the Republic of the Congo.

This explains why Elisabethville and Brussels did everything in their power to place obstacles in the path of Hammarskjöld's request. The Belgian government, in particular, appealed for support through NATO Secretary-General Paul-Henri Spaak to the three great Western powers and to Italy (a Security Council member).

Katangan authorities were scarcely disposed to follow the path suggested by the U.N., which appeared from their vantage point like the most serious threat to Katanga's independence. The anti-U.N. reaction was reinforced in Elisabethville when the U.N. organized, at the end of October, a peace-making mission into the troubled zones — a mission entrusted to three Balubakat leaders, one of whom was Sendwe. The Katangan authorities then demanded the withdrawal of Ian Berendsen, U.N. representative in Elisabethville.

Meanwhile, in Leopoldville, relations between the College of Commissioners and the U.N. had deteriorated seriously. The international organization refused to recognize the legitimacy of the college and refused to aid it, because of the arrest of Lumumba. Dayal accused the commissioners of being, in fact, political instruments of Belgian advisers. He took the ANC severely to task for what he considered "a renewal of indiscipline." The college demanded the withdrawal of the Ghanaian and Guinean contingents of the U.N. in the Congo as well as Dayal's departure, but the U.N. did not gratify these injunctions. The college refused to receive the Conciliation Commission created on November 5, 1960, by the Consultative Committee of the U.N. Several political and military incidents with pro-Lumumbist African states had repercussions on the relations of the College of Commissioners to the U.N. in the

---

114 Belgian officers and 117 Belgians of other ranks in the gendarmery and 58 Belgian officers in the police." U.N. Document, Security Council, S/4557, A, para. 49.

[39] All the more so, since the U.N. Secretary-General's note was aimed not only at Katanga for the withdrawal of Belgians but at all of the Congo.

Congo,[40] and in particular the U.N. demanded the withdrawal of Belgian advisers in Leopoldville as well as in Katanga.[41]

In this context, the *de facto* authority in Leopoldville tried to find an ally against the new Lumumbist menace and against the U.N. At this point, Belgian advisers in Elisabethville again suggested an extra-parliamentary Round Table without Lumumba,[42] or at the very least a so-called summit meeting between Kasavubu and Tshombe, which would be prepared in late October in Brazzaville by a Kimba-Bomboko meeting. Despite Belgian pressures, the latter meeting failed on October 29.

The attempt to bypass the contradictions inherent in the double Belgian game, with the gambit of a common anti-Lumumbist and anti-U.N. front, proved in practice very difficult insofar as the contradictions were real and not erased by a simple community of antagonisms.

At this time, Katanga meant to obtain from this Round Table the recognition of a very loose type of confederation. It demanded that no government be constituted and that the Parliament not meet before a solution to the constitutional conflict were reached. In the meantime, autonomy would be recognized as a fact. These positions were defended at the time of visits to Elisabethville by Colonel Mobutu on October 16 and by Cyrille Adoula, Jacques Massa, and Albert Delvaux on November 24. In fact, the Katangan authorities felt they were in a position of political and military strength[43] with respect to the commissioners, whose zone of influence was dangerously shrunken since the Gizengist takeover in Orientale province and the rupture with Cléophas Kamitatu's provincial government in Leopoldville.

In Leopoldville, the projects for Leopoldville-Elisabethville cooperation were stalemated. Discussions in Brazzaville on the Central Bank and on economic cooperation between Leopoldville and Katanga fell through, as did the Kasavubu-Tshombe meeting in Brazzaville in November. These failures developed among the commissioners an anti-Katanga

---

[40] *Congo 1960*, pp. 899–922.

[41] Diplomatic relations were still ruptured between Leopoldville and Brussels.

[42] The Chief of State had entrusted to Marcel Lihau, Commissioner General of Justice, the responsibility for preparing a Round Table, but it did not materialize. On November 26, 1960, in Paris, Kasavubu again talked of a Round Table with Lumumba and Tshombe.

[43] Summoned by Kasavubu to Brazzaville on October 10, Tshombe adopted a dilatory attitude, then tried to organize a meeting between Kasavubu, Justin Bomboko, Joseph Mobutu, and himself in Elisabethville. At the U.N. on November 8, Evariste Kimba protested against his own inclusion in Kasavubu's U.N. delegation.

reflex which was quite clear by late November and early December. Accordingly, Leopoldville reproached Belgium severely for its support of the secession. This campaign culminated in an exchange of notes the day after the reception of Tshombe by the King in Brussels on December 6, 1960,[44] at which time the creation of a separate Katangan franc was announced to take effect at the end of the year. At this moment, the College of Commissioners planned to block all recruitment of Belgians in Leopoldville [45] if the Belgian government did not recognize the central government's monopoly in matters of technical assistance for all the provinces, including Katanga.

Despite this bitterness aroused by the Belgian position, the two Congolese groups were not at this time in a position to let their anger rise to the surface, in view of their dependence in fact on Belgian assistance and in view of the nature of their relations with the U.N.

THE CONGOLESE PARTNERS OF THE ANTI-LUMUMBA AND ANTI-U.N. AXIS

From September to December, attempts were made to achieve a rapprochement between the effective authority of the Leopoldville College of Commissioners and the Katangan authorities. In November and December, 1960, the Chief of State himself participated in the attempts, looking toward the Round Table that he wanted to organize in order to solve the problems of the structure of the state.

A first meeting between Kasavubu and Tshombe took place in Brazzaville on November 27, but, in the atmosphere of the republic presided over by his friend the Abbé Youlou,[46] Tshombe dreamed less of the former

[44] The Belgians asserted that the aid accorded Katanga "has leveled off and will not be expanded." Note for Leopoldville, December 10, 1960. In regard to the King's reception of Tshombe, some Belgian advisers let it be known in Leopoldville that aside from having no official significance, since Tshombe simply wished to offer the King a wedding present, the visit had afforded the occasion to suggest that Tshombe reach a speedy agreement with Leopoldville. This first assertion cannot be checked. It seems that reception was, for Brussels, the lesser of two evils, since a high-ranking adviser had already given Tshombe to understand that he would be invited to the King's wedding. They then sought a "compensation." The American embassy in Brussels had shown its disapproval inasmuch as the Ministry of Foreign Affairs had been alerted in advance, on December 2, about the repercussions from Tshombe's reception.

[45] Declaration of Joseph M'Beka of November 29, 1960.

[46] At this point, authorized Belgian circles believed that Tshombe had given one million Belgian francs and promised five million more to Abbé Youlou, who had in turn promised recognition of Katanga on December 15 and access "to the summit" in Paris.

Belgian Congo than of an economic and customs union of Central Africa, guaranteeing to each partner his full political independence.[47] On December 1, Katanga applied officially for admission to the Union Douanière Equatoriale, the Equatorial Customs Union. This turn of events offended leaders in Leopoldville. Brussels addressed a rather severe memorandum to Tshombe, in which the Belgian government recorded that it was disturbed by Tshombe's declarations which seemed to announce a "sudden reversal of Katangan policy" in a direction which "would, in a fashion no doubt irremediable, widen the existing rift between Katanga and the other parts of the former Belgian Congo."[48] The Belgian government declared that it could not favor a solution by force to the Leopoldville-Elisabethville problem, "even indirectly." Belgo-Katangan cooperation could not continue unless Katanga pursued in the Congo the maintenance of economic unity, financial solidarity between the regions, and a formula of political union.

Another meeting took place in Brazzaville between the leaders of the Congo, on the occasion of the Conference of Heads of French-speaking African States (Brazzaville Group), where the influence of the Abbé Youlou was great and where there was a temptation for Tshombe to be treated as a chief of state in this group of "moderate" African states. In the course of a discussion among Kasavubu, Tshombe, Ileo, and Kalonji, the old oppositions reappeared: Kasavubu and Ileo rejected the Katangan confederal formulas which no longer permitted, according to them, the existence of a real Congolese state. Ileo felt it necessary to constitute a central government before the Round Table took place.

No written accord resulted from this meeting. Tshombe, nonetheless, stated that the Round Table would take place on February 15, 1961, in Elisabethville. On January 2, 1961, Kasavubu announced the convocation of a Round Table for January 25.

A period came to a close with the meeting in Brazzaville — a period of tentative attempts at agreement, ending regularly in stalemate, despite the external pressures (especially Belgian) in favor of an understanding among anti-Lumumbist leaders in Leopoldville and Elisabethville.

Other attempts, on the whole more serious, took place during the course of the first months of 1961, and some of these ended in written agreements, each destined, however, to remain a dead letter.

---

[47] The idea of joining the French community was widely mooted in Katangan circles in late 1960 and early 1961. It was discussed in Brazzaville and constituted a means for pressure on Belgium.

[48] *Congo 1960*, pp. 973–75.

RESPECTIVE STRENGTH OF THE PARTNERS

During the latter part of 1960 and early 1961, the balance of forces leaned in favor of the dissident provincial power. This situation served to heighten Katangan demands and to paralyze negotiations.

From the point of view of legitimacy, the College of Commissioners and the Ileo government which succeeded it in February benefited from no legal recognition on the part of the great foreign powers. The U.N. held the position expressed by Dayal in his report:

ONUC [the U.N. Operation in the Congo] accordingly, while taking no position on the legality of the constitutional decree-law of 11 October 1960 creating the Council [College] of Commissioners-General, has continued to follow its policy of dealing in routine matters, with whatever authority it finds in the ministerial chairs. It has thus maintained useful contacts of an informal character on all matters of practical value in the fields of administration and technical assistance, without admitting any element of political recognition.[49]

The view of the Secretary-General was even more explicit in regard to the College of Commissioners. It was a question for him of an authority having "no basis in the constitution of the Congo."[50] This view was shared, in more extreme form, by several countries with troops in the Congo. For them, the commissioners were only usurpers.[51] It is understandable that in these circumstances the Katangan government was not induced to negotiate permanent agreements with a power whose legal basis was so disputed.

The Ileo government, installed by the constitutional decree-law of February 9, 1961, was stated to be provisional "until the date, fixed by the Chief of State, when the legislative Chambers would be in a position to convene including parliamentary deputies from each province."[52] Ileo never went before the Chambers for a vote of confidence and was assigned the same stature as the College of Commissioners by the U.N.: a *de facto* authority with which current business could be transacted, but no agreement or commitment having a legal value. The Secretary-General never addressed himself directly to Prime Minister designate Ileo nor to his ministers. He corresponded only with the Chief of State. In reports and

[49] Dayal report, U.N. Document, Security Council, S/4557, A, para. 29, November 2, 1960.

[50] Declaration of the U.N. Secretary-General, see U.N. Document, Security Council, S/PV/913, para. 41, December 7, 1960.

[51] See the telegram from Sékou Touré, U.N. Document, Security Council, S/4594, December 12, 1960.

[52] *Moniteur Congolais*, No. 5, February 9, 1961.

correspondence, he mentioned the "Ileo regime" without ever according it the name of government. The capacity of valid spokesman could not be clearly denied to the authorities in Leopoldville. In contrast, the U.N. never denied to Tshombe his title as president of the province of Katanga. The Secretary-General did not hesitate to make himself available twice to meet with Tshombe.

The reluctance of Katangan authorities to negotiate with those of Leopoldville was reinforced by the weakness and the concrete shortcomings of the center. On the military level, Colonel Mobutu's army suffered several defeats which were eloquent testimony to the limits of his authority. After the bloody defeat of his troops in Bukavu at the beginning of January, the mutiny of the Thysville military camp took place on January 13, followed by the beginnings of a mutiny at Camp Nkokolo in Leopoldville. On February 23, the offensive of the Stanleyville contingents opened at Luluabourg and officers loyal to Colonel Mobutu were routed.

In Katanga, on the contrary, the military reverses suffered in the month of January were erased by the victorious Katangan counteroffensive unleashed on February 11, 1961, against the positions held by the Lualaba government in the north. The success of the Katangan forces was rapid and total. Dayal then estimated the forces of the Katangan gendarmery at five thousand men, who were well equipped and led by non-Congolese officers and non-commissioned officers numbering, according to the U.N. representative, about four hundred.[53]

On the political level, the inferiority of the Leopoldville authorities was even clearer. After the crumbling of the College of Commissioners' power in January, 1961, the Ileo government got off to a difficult start. Not only was it provisional and incomplete — ministerial posts had been reserved for representatives of absent provinces and a vice-presidency for Katanga — but immediately after its constitution it was challenged by the PSA nationalist deputies, Félicien Kimvay and Thomas Mukwidi, and by Cléophas Bizala. The massacres of Lumumbists at Bakwanga during February discredited the group in power and shook its unity. The head of the government, Ileo, never managed to impose a political line on his ministers and abandoned the exercise of real power to persons of second rank. The authority of the government extended effectively only to Equateur and Leopoldville provinces, and even there very incompletely. In Kasai, the president of the Luluabourg government, Barthélemy

[53] Dayal report, U.N. Document, Security Council, S/4691, para. 2, February 12, 1961.

Mukenge, and especially Albert Kalonji in South Kasai had preferred to look for support from the authorities in Elisabethville, although ethnic and political affinities should have pointed them more in the direction of Leopoldville.[54] The deficiencies of the central authority inclined them to look again to a Katangan alliance.

Finally, in regard to technical assistance and political support furnished by Belgium, Katanga, although no longer wielding the near monopoly of Belgian aid which it had enjoyed during the summer of 1960, was still in an incomparably better position. Against the ten officer-advisers furnished the *Armée Nationale Congolaise*, could be counted the three hundred Belgian officers staffing the Katangan gendarmery. On the level of civilian assistance, the disproportion, without being so flagrant, was nevertheless considerable.[55] Moreover, the repugnance shown by the U.N. in dealing with the Leopoldville authorities, to whom they denied any constitutional basis, had almost totally vitiated U.N. technical assistance.

In conclusion, this brief examination of the respective strengths of the two anti-Lumumbist partners in the military, political, and technical domains illustrates the immediately advantageous position of the Katangans. This was one of the principal reasons for their refusal — apparently contrary to their long term interests — to make concessions at this point to the Leopoldville authorities. Each time they pressed their demands and stymied negotiations.

Later, after the formation of the Adoula government, as the balance of forces leaned little by little in favor of the central power, Leopoldville in turn increased its demands, driving the Katangan authorities toward concessions they refused to make until the moment of their defeat.

FACTORS OF SOLIDARITY AND UNDERSTANDING BETWEEN THE TWO PARTNERS

Since the Lumumba government had been ousted from power in September, 1960, the choices and fundamental orientation of Leopoldville and Elisabethville had been identical. Both were resolutely pro-Western. In both cases, it was the Belgian advisers, whose salaries were partly cov-

---

[54] An agreement between South Kasai and Elisabethville was signed in August, 1960. The Luluabourg government evinced its preference for Elisabethville by the December 3 accord dealing with commercial exchanges (300 million francs in each direction).

[55] In January, 1961, there were in the Congo 2,268 Belgian civil servant-technicians, and 308 subsidized lay teachers as against 1,583 in August, 1960, and more than 8,000 at independence. Out of the total of 2,576, Katanga alone had 1,168 as against 538 in the province of Leopoldville, 107 in Equateur, 116 in Orientale, 169 in Kivu, 95 in Kasai, and 75 in South Kasai.

ered by Belgium, who often inspired and coordinated the policy of the two governments. This state of affairs won both of them the distrust of the U.N., to which they responded alike by hostility and reprisals. In response to the solicitude of the Western powers and of Belgium, the two governments were unstinting in their active concern for the material interests of these powers. The capitalist system was perfectly guaranteed by both. The dangers stemmed solely from inevitable competition within the system among different capitalist groups and powers.

On the ideological level, the same anti-Communism, expanded into hostility toward the neutral powers and the countries of the Casablanca Group, characterized the established powers in Elisabethville and in Leopoldville.

Finally, over and above the identity of all their fundamental choices of action, common and immediate perils induced the leaders in Leopoldville and Elisabethville to join forces. The first and gravest of the dangers was the person of Lumumba himself, who represented the exact antithesis to the fundamental choices of the two regimes. After the death of Lumumba on January 17, 1961, Gizenga, in particular, inherited his ideology and his support, becoming in his turn a simultaneous threat for the two regimes.

After February and, more particularly, after the Security Council resolution of February 21, leaders in Leopoldville and Elisabethville began to fear that the U.N. would proceed to a disarmament of their respective military forces. This fear was unwarranted on the part of Leopoldville, since the Afro-Asian draft-resolution demanding the disarmament of Colonel Mobutu's soldiers had not passed. On the other hand, "the immediate withdrawal and evacuation from the Congo of all Belgian and other foreign military and para-military personnel and political advisers not under U.N. command, and mercenaries," as demanded by the adopted resolution threatened the Katangan gendarmery directly. The Tshombe government made no mistake about it and considered it a "declaration of war by the U.N. not only on Katanga, but also on all the former Belgian Congo."[56] Having denounced in the same remarks, "the U.N. protectorate" and "the installation of a new colonial regime," Tshombe decreed "the mobilization of all the inhabitants of Katanga."

In Leopoldville, Ileo used almost the same language and proclaimed that his government would respond "by every means at our disposal to

[56] Radio speech by Tshombe, cited in *L'Essor du Katanga* (Elisabethville), February 22, 1961.

the war which the U.N. means to declare in trying to attack our sovereignty."[57] Ileo announced likewise that he would make an appeal to the "people of the Congo to stand prepared against any eventuality and to execute the orders which we shall give to them if the situation demands."

From this point on, the authorities in Leopoldville and in Elisabethville had a concrete basis for adopting a common policy. From an identity of conception, they could pass to an identity of action against the common danger represented by the new policy of the U.N. It is probably not an exaggeration to argue that this was the principal reason for the military and political accords which were reached between Katanga and Leopoldville during February and March. By the same token, it is probable that the agreement of April 17 concluded between the U.N. and the Chief of State, removing as it did the principal basis for the accords, led to the rupture between Tshombe and the central authorities at the Coquilhatville Conference.

To these objective factors tending to bring the leaders of Leopoldville and Elisabethville together, must be added the relatively discreet efforts of Western diplomacy, and Belgian diplomacy in particular. Thus, it is on the recommendation of Belgian advisers that the Katangan government considering aiding Leopoldville financially by returning the Congolese francs collected when the Katangan currency was created.[58] During this time, other Belgian advisers tried to convince leaders in Leopoldville of the utility of adopting a very loose federal political structure and giving pledges to the Katangan government.

Factors Contributing to Opposition and Rupture

Factors arousing opposition and conflict between Katanga and Leopoldville were many, and they were rapidly revealed to be more powerful than the factors uniting them. In regard to the choice of political structures, despite the mutual concessions that the leaders on all sides were ready to make, the Katangan confederal views, based on the complete sovereignty of each member state, were still incompatible with the very loose federalism advocated by one segment of the leadership in Leopoldville. Failure to apply the Tananarive resolutions (see pp. 148–51) well illustrated this difference.

[57] Press conference of Ileo, Leopoldville, February 22, 1961; Benoît Verhaegen, *Congo 1961* (Brussels: CRISP, 1962), p. 134.

[58] This plan was not put into effect. On the other hand, the reserve of Congolese francs held by Katanga was abundantly utilized in Leopoldville during the detention of Tshombe.

The very short but eventful history of Katanga and of the independent Congo had created a rift between their respective institutions. In Leopoldville, a complete Africanization of the army and of the administration from top to bottom had occurred; while in Katanga, if certain functions in the public view were given to Africans, the great proportion of the middle and higher positions remained Belgian. This difference in structure was, for example, the basic cause behind the breakdown of General Mobutu's (see pp. 145–48) attempts to reunify the *Armée Nationale Congolaise*. The very presence of Congolese officers had a highly disturbing effect within the Katangan gendarmery, because their Katangan counterparts who did not hold the real military power demanded a thorough Africanization like that which had taken place in Leopoldville.

Another factor of discord, probably more fundamental, was the competition for the economic resources of Katanga. The sharing of these resources had become for Leopoldville the only hope for stabilizing a near desperate financial situation in the first quarter of 1961. However, the growing military and political expenses of the Katangan government during this period required the total utilization of its resources, to the point where a reduction in its portion of them would compromise the stability of the regime.

The sympathy, if not the active support, accorded almost uninterruptedly to Sendwe and his colleagues in North Katanga by the Leopoldville leadership was very badly received and construed by the Tshombe government, for whom Sendwe was the implacable foe of the Katangan regime. Consequently, the Elisabethville authorities did not hesitate to arrest Ferdinand Tumba, sent to Katanga as an official emissary by the Leopoldville Round Table Conference, for the sole reason that he was one of the Balubakat leaders. Another example of the importance of the North Katangan factor in the relations between Leopoldville and Elisabethville was provided at the Coquilhatville Conference in April, 1961, where Sendwe was admitted by unanimous vote after Tshombe announced he was returning to Katanga.

The role of advisers, of local pressure groups, and of diverse foreign influences was certainly an important factor in barring the possibility for an understanding between Leopoldville and Elisabethville. In Katanga, internally, the settlers, Belgian administrators, and mercenaries and, externally, the pressures and intervention from the Rhodesias and the Abbé Youlou acted at this time for a variety of reasons to divert the Katangan government from any real accord with Leopoldville.

In Leopoldville, the influence of certain Belgian advisers combined
with that of U.N. personnel who had retained the confidence of the Congolese leaders and that of certain embassies to favor a hard line toward
Katanga. This advice corresponded to settled conceptions or stemmed
from the conviction that the political and economic viability of the regime in Leopoldville was to be had only at this price.

ATTEMPTS AT ACCORD AND COMMON ACTION BETWEEN ELISABETHVILLE AND LEOPOLDVILLE

THE DEATH OF LUMUMBA

The transfer of Lumumba and his two companions from Thysville to
Katanga on January 17, 1961, was a concrete manifestation of the solidarity of interest between the authorities in Leopoldville and those in
Elisabethville. Several days before, on January 12, a Congolese delegation
had arrived in Elisabethville. Composed of Commandant J. Pwati, who
had the confidence of Colonel Mobutu, and of Albert Delvaux, minister
in the Lumumba government as well as in that of Ileo in September, 1960,
the delegation sought to convince the Katangan leaders to attend a Round
Table conference they were planning in Leopoldville.

On January 13, a mutiny broke out in Thysville and the rumor spread
that Lumumba had been liberated by the soldiers. Panic gripped the
leadership in Leopoldville.

On January 14, according to the account of J. Duchemin, Tshombe
asked the Leopoldville delegation, as a precondition of his participation in
a Round Table conference, that Lumumba be transferred to Katanga.[59]
Delvaux having accepted, a telegram was sent to Leopoldville that very
day. This version differs from that generally cited, according to which the
transfer of Lumumba had been decided upon by the authorities in Leopoldville in the distracted aftermath of the mutinies in Thysville and
Leopoldville. The prisoner, according to the first plan, was sent off toward
Bakwanga, where several days later seven Lumumbist leaders imprisoned
in Leopoldville were taken to be massacred. It was only at the last moment
— the airfield of Bakwanga not being secure — that Elisabethville had

[59] Account of J. Duchemin in Roger Trinquier, Duchemin and Jacques LeBailey,
Notre Guerre au Katanga (Paris: Editions de la Pensée Moderne, 1963), p. 77. It
may be recalled that Gilbert-Pierre Pongo, an official with the Leopoldville *Sûreté*,
came under strong pressure to transfer Lumumba immediately to Katanga after
his arrest on December 2, 1960, in Kasai. In September, 1960, Albert Kalonji, acting as Minister of Justice in the Ileo government had had a plan to transfer Gizenga
and Maurice Mpolo to Elisabethville.

been chosen as the destination. According to this version, the agreement of the Katangan government was given at the last minute.

Whatever the authority which took the initiative for the transfer and whatever the terms of the bargain (or of the negotiations) which ensued from this transfer, the important fact is that an agreement was reached and that concrete common action was achieved. Moreover, neither of the two parties could seriously doubt that the transfer and its aftermath, while delivering them from a common danger, might compromise them in the eyes of international public opinion and draw censure upon both. For Katanga, furthermore, this would strengthen the current in favor of the resolution on the withdrawal of mercenaries and foreign officers. The transfer of Lumumba thus marked the beginning of effective cooperation along the Leopoldville-Elisabethville axis.[60]

THE LEOPOLDVILLE ROUND TABLE (JANUARY 25 — FEBRUARY 16, 1961)

At the meeting in Brazzaville in December, 1960, Katanga demanded that the Round Table take place before a new government were constituted in Leopoldville and before the Parliament met again.[61] This was also the view of Colonel Mobutu, who wanted to see the College of Commissioners play an important role in the organization of the Round Table and in the elaboration of the constitution. In contrast, Ileo, the Prime Minister designate of the new government, and Congolese Parliament members pressed for the formation of a new government and a meeting of Parliament.[62]

As for practical arrangements, Tshombe demanded that the Round Table be held in Elisabethville on the fifteenth and that Katanga be entrusted with the material organization of the meeting. This boiled down to saying that the Katangan government would also select the participants.[63] The Katangan demands were partially satisfied. Chief of State Kasavubu agreed not to form a government before the end of the year and announced on January 2 that a Round Table would be convened on

---

[60] Questions have been raised as to the reasons which led the Leopoldville authorities to transfer Joseph Okito and Mpolo to Katanga as well. Mpolo had been named by Lumumba on September 13 as head of the *Armée Nationale Congolaise* and could set himself up as a legitimate rival to Colonel Mobutu. Okito was considered by Lumumba to be senate president replacing Ileo and could from there play a decisive role in case of vacancy in the presidency of the republic, in conformity with provisions of the *Loi Fondamentale.* For Okito, see *Congo 1960,* p. 957.

[61] See on this subject, *Congo 1960,* p. 958.

[62] *Ibid.,* pp. 958–59.

[63] *Ibid.,* p. 960.

January 25 in Leopoldville and would be presided over by Ileo.[64] The
College of Commissioners was maintained and any role for Parliament
was expressly ruled out by the Chief of State. The objective assigned by
Kasavubu to the conference was the "reform of the very structures of the
country," the solution of an "institutional crisis," rather than a "governmental crisis."[65]

These important concessions to the Katangan viewpoint were not ad-
judged sufficient, however. Evariste Kimba, Minister of Foreign Affairs
in Katanga, refused to take part in the organizational committee of the
Round Table, adding that, if the date and the place proposed by Katanga
were not maintained, Katanga would not participate in the conference.[66]

Despite the negotiations undertaken by Delvaux, Adoula, and Commandant Pwati in Elisabethville at the beginning of January, seeking a
compromise and despite Bomboko's assurance that Lumumba would not
be invited, the Katangan government hewed to its desire to see the
conference held in Elisabethville. This amounted to excluding not only
Lumumba but also the MNC/Lumumba partners, the PSA, the Cerea,
and above all the Balubakat. It seems that the hostility of Tshombe was
principally aimed at the Balubakat leaders and, in particular, at Sendwe.

Two more attempts were made to bring the Katangan leaders to the
conference. The first was to propose the candidature of Kimba for second
vice-president of the conference, for which he obtained 39 votes against
60 for Adoula. The second was to send a commission headed by V. Koumoriko, the eldest senator, to Elisabethville "to sound out Tshombe's
intentions."[67] Tshombe responded to the advances of Leopoldville by
arresting one of the members of the commission, Ferdinand Tumba
(Balubakat), and by declaring that the "preconference" in Leopoldville
was not valid.

The humiliating setback for the Koumoriko commission in Elisabethville aroused a hostile reaction at the conference toward Katanga. A
resolution passed, fixing the site of the final Round Table in Leopoldville.
However, the announcement of the death of Lumumba and his companions in Katanga provoked disarray in the ranks of the "nationalist"
delegates to the conference. It could be concluded that "the death of
Lumumba was interpreted as a victory for Tshombe, who became, from
then on, the only 'strong man' of the Congo, with whom it was necessary

[64] *Congo 1961*, pp. 3–4.
[65] *Ibid.*, p. 3.
[66] *Le Courrier d'Afrique* (Leopoldville), January 6, 1961.
[67] *Congo 1961*, p. 16.

to negotiate at any price."[68] At the end of the conference, a majority took shape, reversed the choice of site for the final Round Table, and designated Elisabethville.

This decision and the transfer of Lumumba followed by his execution clearly illustrated the predominance of Katanga on the Congolese political scene at that moment. Leopoldville, although treated harshly and with a certain disdain by the Elisabethville authorities, remained the suitor and sought out an alliance with Katanga.

MILITARY ACCORD: LEOPOLDVILLE-ELISABETHVILLE-BAKWANGA

Two events precipitated the negotiations between Leopoldville and Elisabethville: the vote of the Security Council resolution of February 21, and the arrival on February 23 of "Gizengist" soldiers in Luluabourg.[69] Several preliminary contacts had already taken place between Leopoldville, Elisabethville, and Bakwanga to effect a military accord. For Tshombe, the conclusion of such an accord, at a time when an offensive of "Gizengist" soldiers in North Katanga had just installed the government of Lualaba in Manono, was of greater importance than the Round Table Conference.

The Leopoldville view, expressed by Bomboko, provided for the creation of a single command with no political preconditions. Colonel Mobutu, who had been promoted to general of the army in this framework, would have the responsibility for the entire armed forces, of which Kasavubu would be, in accordance with the constitution, the Commander-in-Chief. This solution suited the needs of its framer, by permitting the Katangan forces to step outside the provincial borders, without justifying reprisals on the part of the U.N.

Considering that the authorities in Leopoldville were in the position of suitors, Tshombe demanded that the military accord be preceded by a *de facto* recognition of the three governments — Leopoldville, Elisabethville, and Bakwanga — on an equal footing, which amounted to recognizing independence for Katanga by Leopoldville.

On January 26, the authorities in Leopoldville under the influence of Bomboko rejected Tshombe's proposed agreement. Tshombe then turned to Kasavubu from whom he expected more understanding toward the Katanga secession. He wired him shortly after the beginning of the Round Table to insist "on the urgency of settling first the military questions,

[68] *Ibid.*, p. 18.
[69] This section is based on documents published in *Congo 1961*, pp. 21–27.

before sending a delegation to the Round Table." [70] The attempt to influence the Chief of State by the lure of Katangan participation in the Round
Table did not have the desired effect. Leopoldville sent right back a
counterproposal for an agreement between Leopoldville, Elisabethville,
and Bakwanga, aiming at "the definition of a common line of conduct
toward the regimes installed in Stanleyville and in Bukavu, the preparation and the conduct of concerted action in pacification, as well as mutual
aid in technical domains." [71] The solution of political differences was in-
tentionally put off until later.

Tshombe refused to discuss Leopoldville's counterplan. The editorial
writer of *L'Essor du Katanga*, Mikolajczak, clearly defined the Katangan
position: "To emerge from this impasse, it would suffice for [Leopoldville]
to recognize the independence of the State of Katanga and that of South
Kasai." [72]

When the resolution of February 21 became known, Katanga and
South Kasai, which felt the most threatened,[73] stirred up the Leopoldville
authorities once more.[74] The latter had, in the meantime, been profoundly
shaken by the raid of a contingent of Stanleyville soldiers at Luluabourg —
during which the superior officers in that garrison failed to offer any resistance or leadership — and they were eager to respond to Tshombe's
invitation. On February 27, a delegation led by Ileo and including Minister of the Interior Adoula and Commander Pwati arrived in Elisabethville. The next day, a protocol of a military agreement was signed by
Tshombe, Ileo, and Kalonji. Its substance was extremely meager.

The protocol stated only that the military authorities of Katanga and
of South Kasai and those under the general staff in Leopoldville would
establish permanent contacts among themselves to pool all the military
forces to fight the threat of the establishment of a Communist regime over

[70] *L'Essor du Katanga* (Elisabethville), February 1, 1961.

[71] *Congo 1961*, p. 22.

[72] *L'Essor du Katanga* (Elisabethville), February 3, 1961.

[73] As a riposte to the U.N. resolution and in particular to avoid panic among
Europeans, Katanga decreed "civilian mobilization." So that the Belgian administrators would fall under the resolution, Katanga at this moment renounced Belgian financial aid for salaries to public servants. (Letter from Jacques Masangu
to the Belgian Colonial Minister, February 22, 1961), and encouraged Europeans
to take Katangan nationality. Tshombe sent an appeal to the King in which he said:
"I know that the King will do all within his power not to let the last of his loyal
subjects be sacrificed."

[74] See telegrams from Kalonji and Tshombe of February 23 and 24 printed in
Congo 1961, p. 24.

the Congo as a whole.[75] The only clause which could have been substantive and which Leopoldville made the essential theme of its demands, namely, the reunification of the army under the command of Leopoldville, had been left out of the accord.

Nor, on the other hand, did the protocol involve any recognition — formal or *de facto* — of the independence of Katanga on the part of Leopoldville. The signers acted not as "chiefs of state," but only as simple representatives of the three regions. An official spokesman for the Katangan government was entrusted by the three signers to state the substance of the agreements. He specifically declared: "These military agreements do not mean that Leopoldville recognizes the independence of Katanga and of South Kasai, nor that Katanga and South Kasai recognize the authority of Leopoldville . . . . The formulas used in the signatures mean that the parties, in the face of a common danger, have agreed to dispense with any prior solution on questions of hierarchy." [76]

Without representing a definitive achievement of the Katangan positions, the signing of the agreement nevertheless conveyed important advantages for Tshombe; it was first of all a psychological victory, partially overshadowing the Round Table Conference in Leopoldville, since the negotiations had taken place in Katanga, on the initiative of the Elisabethville government.

In accepting negotiation on an equal footing with the authorities in Elisabethville and South Kasai, the provisional Leopoldville government in fact weakened its rights to a reunification of the Congo under its authority. By demonstrating solidarity with Katanga against the involvement of the U.N., Leopoldville rejected all cooperation with the U.N. and with it — as events of the second half of 1961 were to demonstrate — the only effective threat to the Katanga secession.

With this beginning, Leopoldville was drawn into certain types of agreements, of which the most spectacular example was that of Tananarive, from which Katanga emerged temporarily the victor. The Tananarive conference confirmed the military accord of February 28 without giving it the more concrete provisions which were to have solved the problem of reunifying the army. Resolution 4 of the conference stipulated that each one of the states would have its own gendarmery and its own police. The efforts of General Mobutu to create a single command were thus

[75] The protocol was published in *Le Monde* (Paris), March 2, 1961.
[76] These official commentaries were reproduced in *L'Essor du Katanga* (Elisabethville), March 1, 1961.

brought to nought. It was, nevertheless, only in November, 1961, under
the threat of a unilateral initiative from Stanleyville ANC troops toward
North Katanga, that he gave up on Elisabethville and unleashed in his
turn an offensive against Katanga from Kasai.

THE TANANARIVE CONFERENCE

The Tananarive Conference was set for February 28, date of the signing of the military agreement for which it was to be the political extension.[77] The only surprise registered at the beginning of the conference was
the participation of a PSA delegation led by Cléophas Kamitatu, president of the provincial government of Leopoldville. (It is true that the U.N.
representatives had not yet received the reinforcements of Indian troops
they required if they were to execute the resolution of February 21 on
the withdrawal of foreign mercenaries. But U.N. representatives hoped
that a meeting between the leaders of all the factions, including those
from Stanleyville, would be the first step toward a reopening of Parliament.
It is for this reason that they urged Gizenga and Kamitatu to go to Tananarive. Only Kamitatu responded to their urging.) The U.N. anticipated
at least a weakening of the Katangan ascendancy. This was a major error
of judgment, for Katanga was at this moment at the peak of its power
and prestige.[78]

Leopoldville, however, did not yet understand the advantage it could
draw from cooperation with the U.N. on the basis of the February 21
resolution and lacked the elementary means of exercising power. These
conditions would necessarily lead to the triumph of Katangan views.

Katangan leaders effectively had the initiative from the beginning of
the negotiations and they could impose their own conceptions in a nearly
unilateral fashion when resolutions were adopted. The treatment of Chief
of State Kasavubu is significant in this regard. Facing the reluctance of
Kasavubu to join the delegation from Leopoldville, Tshombe wired him
to come "to the last-chance Conference," threatening to draw the "consequences of his absence." [79] Kasavubu arrived late at Tananarive, accompanied by a Belgian legal adviser, Jacques Denis. Denis was expelled
within the hour by the Malagasy authorities, at Tshombe's request, yet
the Katangan president was surrounded with a whole team of Belgian and
French advisers. The compliance of the Malagasy authorities had been

[77] *Ibid.*
[78] See pp. 155–84, dealing with the military and political situation in Katanga.
[79] *Congo 1961*, p. 28.

secured, in all probability, by the French, who were trying at this point to supplant Belgian influence in Katanga, or at least to taper it off somewhat.

In his opening speech, Tshombe did not hesitate to berate members of the Leopoldville government, whose recalcitrance was in part the cause, according to him, for a new and mortal danger threatening the Congo.[80]

Tshombe assigned three objectives to the conference; the first and foremost, with an eye to the U.N. General Assembly meeting, was the denunciation of the Security Council resolution of February 21. Resolution No. 5 of the conference, on relations with the U.N., yielded Tshombe this point, reiterating forcefully the rejection of council resolutions by Congolese authorities.[81] The second goal was the adoption of a confederal political structure permitting autonomy and quasi-sovereignty of the member states. Resolution No. 3 on the relations among states supplied this objective. In effect, it provided for the creation of a confederation of sovereign states. The function of the chief of state was maintained. The Katangan delegation felt, with good reason, that the U.N. would hardly admit a number of Congolese delegations and that it was wiser to retain unity, at least on this level. However, the president of the confederation was surrounded by a Council of Member States, composed of the respective presidents. This council would "be responsible for determining the general internal and international policies of the confederation," but in order to forestall any unitary inclination, an article stipulated that the decisions would be taken unanimously. This right of absolute veto conferred on the chiefs of state would permit each to paralyze confederal institutions completely. The resolution provided that an "agency of coordination among the States — destined to replace the provisional central government — assures the execution of decisions decreed by the Council of States" in the problematic eventuality that unanimity could be reached. There is no need to demonstrate that such a political system perfectly guaranteed the *status quo* in Katanga and was equivalent to what could be called "generalized Katangism."[82]

The third Katangan objective concerned what Tshombe called "the

[80] Inaugural address, reproduced in *Congo 1961*, pp. 32–33.

[81] See on this subject the declaration made by Tshombe at Elisabethville to explain to Katangans why he had been obliged to support having a president for the confederation. — *Congo 1961*, pp. 44–45.

[82] François Perin, cited in *Congo 1961*, p. 103.

pacification of all the territory of the former Belgian Congo and the total normalization of the situation."[83] The improving military situation of the Tshombe regime permitted it to be fairly discreet in this matter. The military agreement of February 28 was confirmed, but the idea of unifying military contingents was definitely discarded: an article of Resolution No. 4, on the maintenance of order, stipulated that each one of the states would have its own gendarmery and police at its disposal.

The delegations from Leopoldville could obtain only minor changes and concessions without practical importance. The presidency of the Council of Member States was given to Kasavubu on the insistence of Ileo.[84] The resolution concerning the U.N., rejecting the Security Council resolutions of February 21, was mitigated by an affirmation of principle, according to which the confederation stood ready to "cooperate with the U.N. on condition that the prerogatives of sovereignty were respected."

Finally, Katanga won a last victory, albeit short-lived. Elisabethville was chosen as the site of the future Round Table conference, which was to approve and elaborate the measures for execution of the resolutions. Katanga hoped thus to be able to control to the very end the process of political transformation which it had initiated and, until then, directed. Katanga would be able, among other things, to select the participants and to keep out North Katangan representatives and Sendwe.

In regard to North Katanga, the Tananarive Conference had likewise turned to the advantage of Tshombe, since his rival, Sendwe — at this time on a mission in Belgium — did not participate in the conference, and Sendwe's state was not recognized among the sixteen founding members of the confederation. Leopoldville lost, as a result, one of its best ripostes to the Katanga secession.[85]

It is interesting to note that Katanga's success passed relatively unnoticed at first, even in the Congo. It was abroad that observers and the press unanimously stressed the undivided victory of Katanga. At the Bourse in Brussels, Katangan stocks rose briskly on March 13. The same day, the editorial writer of *La Libre Belgique*, Paul Struye, wrote: "Katanga separatism has now been consecrated almost officially on the legal level, or at least recognized as a reality of which it has become unreasonable not to take account. The cooperation which has been established

[83] Draft of the Tshombe resolution, *Congo 1961*, p. 35.
[84] *Congo 1961*, pp. 41–42.
[85] By telegram, Sendwe asked Kasavubu to defend "energetically the government of the Lualaba State" at Tananarive. Printed in *ibid.*, p. 42.

between Kasavubu and Tshombe is, without a doubt, a success for the second rather than for the first." The editorial writer for *Le Monde* spoke of a "great success for Tshombe and for the growing influence of Katanga in the Congo and even in Africa." In a statement made to Agence Belga, Belgian Minister of Foreign Affairs Pierre Wigny declared himself "very satisfied with the Tananarive agreements" which, he added, "correspond to a policy which we have patiently followed."

If the complete victory of the Katangan viewpoint at Tananarive is easily explained by the total disparity of forces between Leopoldville and Katanga at this point, one can nevertheless wonder how Katanga leaders could believe that an accord obtained under such conditions and tied to consequences so humiliating for the partner had the least chance of being respected. Real mutual concessions could have created lasting reciprocal ties between the two groups, which were not separated by any fundamental ideological or political differences. Perhaps we must see in the intransigence of Katanga at Tananarive the first example of behavior which would make the Elisabethville leadership during the course of the next two years refuse the often honorable exits that the U.N. and Leopoldville held open in the effort to persuade Elisabethville to abandon its fruitless course. The attitude of Katanga at Tananarive helped to push President Kasavubu and the Leopoldville leaders into the arms of the U.N., thus shattering one of the foundations of the axis upon which the conference had been based.

The Tananarive agreements, then, constituted only a moment of particularly clear crystallization of the anti-Lumumbist and anti-U.N. common front, in gestation since the *coup d'état* of September, 1960. Rapidly, they were, if not denounced, at least allowed to lapse.

THE COQUILHATVILLE CONFERENCE

Several events took place between the Tananarive Conference and Coquilhatville which radically changed the balance of power and the perspective of negotiations.[86]

In Katanga, the first contingent of Indian soldiers arrived at Kamina on April 2, marking the intention of the U.N. to apply the February 21 resolution concerning the withdrawal of foreign military personnel and the cessation of all military operations.[87] In Leopoldville, the Chief of

---

[86] A later chapter (Chapter 5) analyzes the principal changes which occurred in the general political context.

[87] On April 2, the Katangan government issued an ordinance on "the state of

State and the Minister of Foreign Affairs had signed on April 17 an agreement of principle with the U.N. by which they accepted the February 21 resolution and recognized the necessity of reorganizing the ANC with the assistance of the U.N. In Brussels, a new Lefèvre-Spaak government, Social Christian and Socialist, was to replace that of Eyskens and Wigny.

These fundamental changes in the general political context were matched with a strongly evidenced psychological turnabout. In Leopoldville, the Tananarive resolutions were completely discredited, and an aggressive hostility toward Katanga began to develop. The delegate from Katanga in Brazzaville and then President Youlou both chose this occasion to advise Tshombe to take some spectacular steps in the spirit of the Tananarive resolutions in order to win back the confidence of the Leopoldville authorities.[88]

The delegate added that the Leopoldville authorities were about to send Tshombe an appeal to halt the attacks against the Baluba, reminding him that his position as provincial president forbade him to take initiatives in external matters. It could be deduced from this that Leopoldville had already abandoned the Tananarive resolutions and even further, recognized *de facto* the province of North Katanga. Yet more disturbing to Katanga was word from the delegate in Brazzaville that the U.N. was exerting pressure on Leopoldville, with success, "to undo Katanga, which will be isolated in case of probable conflict with the U.N., which will deliberately provoke it."[89] Tshombe's source of information added, however, that Leopoldville still waited for a Katangan initiative. This impression was shared by the Belgian mission (April 11, 1961) in Leopoldville: "Tshombe must not count on Leopoldville's support to oppose U.N. designs."

It is not out of the question to think that these several days of April, 1961, were decisive in the defeat of the Katanga secession. Leopoldville recovered the two levers which would permit the central government, in Kasavubu's expression, to "corner" Tshombe, namely, the U.N. and the Baluba of North Katanga. The rest would be no more than a question of effecting concrete measures of coercion, although with many interruptions — half spontaneous, half imposed — to give the Katangan regime an opportunity to rally peacefully to Leopoldville.

---

enmity with the U.N." which forbade all inhabitants and businesses from furnishing goods and services to the U.N. forces in the Congo.

[88] Telegrams published in *Congo 1961*, p. 51.

[89] Telegram of April 14, *Congo 1961*, p. 51.

Tshombe decided to react, but he did so in the most maladroit fashion, issuing a summons coupled with threats. In a letter delivered to Kasavubu, by special mission entrusted to Justin Meli, he summoned the Chief of State:

To make known in clear and precise fashion whether the Leopoldville government cooperates frankly with Katanga, and if the answer is in the affirmative, to take immediate steps to that effect. If not, Katanga, which agreed to join the confederation uniting the various viable States of the former Belgian Congo, from a sincere desire to cooperate with its Congolese brothers, will find itself obliged to look elsewhere for alliances.[90]

All Tshombe offered in concrete terms was to discuss at the next conference the transit of Katangan goods through Matadi or Lobito. Tshombe reminded Kasavubu of the telegram which the latter had sent at the end of the Tananarive Conference to the U.N. Secretary-General, rejecting the dispatch of Indian troops to the Congo and demanding that he intervene with the U.N. to secure withdrawal of these contingents.

This letter was not suited either in substance or in form to strengthen the axis of solidarity between Leopoldville and Elisabethville at a time when an alliance with the U.N. was taking shape in Leopoldville. The threat of looking elsewhere for alliances could scarcely move the authorities in Leopoldville, who had until then gained nothing concrete from their Katangan ally. The Chief of State not only declined to submit to the injunctions of Tshombe, but also addressed a warning to him on April 14, firmly asking him to end the military operations against the Baluba in North Katanga and to normalize his relations with the U.N.[91]

On April 20, Tshombe sent one of his advisers, Belina, to Leopoldville to sound out Western diplomatic circles and to discuss the economic concessions that Katanga was ready to make. This mission was a failure.

On April 22, the Katangan delegate in Brazzaville reiterated his warnings and indicated that the Coquilhatville Conference promised to be violent, that anti-Katanga feelings were predominant, and that Albert Kalonji was ready to betray Tshombe.[92] The situation was therefore ripe for a brutal rupture. This took place at the beginning of the Coquilhatville Conference.[93]

[90] Letter from Tshombe to Kasavubu, April 14, 1961, reproduced in *Congo 1961*, pp. 51–52.

[91] Telegram from Kasavubu to Tshombe, April 14, 1961, reproduced in *Congo 1961*, pp. 56–57.

[92] Telegram reproduced in *Congo 1961*, p. 53.

[93] The Coquilhatville site was chosen by Tshombe himself, after Indian troops

The first day of the conference appeared to be a prolongation of the Tananarive Conference, with Katangan positions holding the field. The first demand of the Katangan delegation was immediately satisfied, namely, to keep in the conference hall only those delegations having participated at the Tananarive Conference, and so to preserve at the Coquilhatville Conference the character of a "summit meeting" as planned. This permitted Tshombe to exclude from the deliberations his North Katangan rival Jason Sendwe.

The opening speech by Kasavubu was followed by an extremely tough statement by Tshombe directed almost exclusively against the Chief of State. Essentially, his reproach focused on the signing by the Chief of State of the April 17 agreement with the U.N. and his acceptance of the February 21 resolution. As a condition of participating in the work of the conference, Tshombe demanded that the April 17 agreement be denounced and that participation in the conference be limited to the delegations which sat at Tananarive. After receiving no support for his motion, Tshombe declared two days later, on April 26, that he was returning to Katanga. It is at this point that ANC soldiers, among whom were several who had been ousted from Katanga by the Tshombe government in July, 1960, intervened and arrested Tshombe and his following, one of whom was Minister Evariste Kimba.

Insofar as the arrest proper is concerned, it was no doubt a question of an unforeseen accident attributable to the soldiers and not to political leaders in Leopoldville. After several days of hesitation however, the Leopoldville government endorsed the arrest and went one step further by deciding on May 9 to intern Tshombe for threatening the security of the state.[94] Bomboko declared, in response to the Abbé Youlou, that Tshombe would be "tried for the crime of high treason" and that four counts of the indictment were being brought, including the massacre of the Baluba in North Katanga and the murder of Patrice Lumumba.[95]

The vicissitudes which surrounded the internment and imprisonment of Tshombe in Leopoldville and ended in his liberation are interesting, for they permit us to assess the real allies of the Katangan president, abroad as well as among the Leopoldville leadership. They constitute the

---

had occupied Kamina, where he had initially anticipated that the summit conference preparing the general Round Table would be held.

[94] Official report on the Tshombe incident by Adoula, printed in *Congo 1961*, p. 252.

[95] *Le Monde* (Paris), May 9, 1961.

last phase of the attempts at cooperation on the Leopoldville-Elisabethville axis and are commented on in the following section.

An event whose political significance was probably greater than even the arrest of the president of the Katangan government occurred in the days which followed. Foreign advisers of Tshombe, who were arrested by the soldiers, were then expelled from the Congo by the U.N., at the request of the Chief of State. The April 17 accord was thus enforced for the first time. Among the expelled political advisers, the majority were Belgian. The pro-Katanga press in Belgium protested vehemently, but the Belgian government admitted on this occasion that the U.N. could apply the February 21 resolution to a certain extent and in certain ways, against Belgian citizens clearly linked to the Katanga secession but not working directly for the Belgian government (the so-called *occult* advisers). For the Belgians, this was the first concrete manifestation of the new policy of the Lefèvre-Spaak government.

THE MILITARY SITUATION IN KATANGA

THE NEEDS AND OBJECTIVES OF THE KATANGAN FORCES

During the second half of 1960, the Katangan government came to grips with three successive military dangers, each of a completely different nature, and each time it was forced to adapt its defenses to new adversaries.

The first danger was the mutiny of the *Force Publique* itself, which the Katangan authorities met with an appeal to the Belgian troops in Kamina. The Belgians completely occupied Katanga in the month of July and expelled all the mutineers, but they themselves were forced to evacuate their positions during August, under pressure from the U.N.

During the final ten days of August, 1960, Katanga came to grips with the second danger: invasion of Katanga by the *Armée Nationale Congolaise*. To this end, the Katangan authorities strongly seconded by Belgian military advisers,[96] hastened to organize a small Katangan gendarmery

---

[96] Former members of the *Force Publique* or from *Cométro* (the latter were regular Belgian army troops brought to the Congo in July, 1960). Pro-Katanga Belgian circles had prepared to transfer into the Katangan gendarmery the many Belgian officers already there, when the time came for regular Belgian troops to leave Katanga. Instructions from Brussels, especially from Wigny, called for the withdrawal of most of them to Rwanda, Burundi, or Belgium. These instructions were provoked by international reactions at the U.N. From Elisabethville contrary pressures were exerted in favor of sending officers from Belgium: "New officers from Belgium needed." September 13, 1961.

with some of the soldiers left over from the former *Force Publique* (200 men at most) and with volunteers chosen especially from the Lunda and Bayeke who were favorable to the government. To these must be added a Belgian officer corps. If the young Katangan gendarmery had had to face the invasion of the *Armée Nationale Congolaise* alone it probably would have been swept away. On the other hand, several groups of European volunteers led by Belgian officers still on the scene would no doubt have offered a more effective resistance.

The government in Elisabethville chose also at this point to arm the warriors of the loyal traditional chiefs and to attach political and military advisers to these troops.[97] At the beginning, in August and September, 1960, the critical need for arms was met on the one hand by former *Force Publique* depots which *Cométro*, the contingent of Belgian troops, had abandoned before its evacuation to Belgium, and on the other hand, through shipments by plane from Belgium. ANC units which had penetrated Katanga through Kongolo in early September withdrew September 18 pursuant to Kasavubu's declaration of cease-fire. But, by this time, a third threat had emerged, that of the armed insurrection of Baluba in North Katanga. By December, most of North Katanga had escaped Elisabethville's control. Against this danger, the Katangan authorities made an appeal for new military means: units composed exclusively, or in large part, of European mercenaries nicknamed the *affreux* ("the frightful ones") who were given the task of repression. The gendarmery was partly reconverted to increase its mobility (helicopters, jeeps, trucks), thanks to direct imports from Europe, imports under license into friendly territories followed by re-export to Katanga, and even supplies of matériel from local enterprises.

At the beginning of 1961, the Katangan armed forces were composed of three distinct elements: the gendarmery, which was led essentially by Belgian officers, former members of the *Force Publique* who were hired locally or recruited in Belgium for the army and the gendarmery in agreement with Belgian authorities; the warriors, who took orders from loyal traditional chiefs to whom arms and military advisers were furnished;

---

[97] "Katanga arms itself and hastily gives its warriors uniforms, arms, and a rudimentary training. Military advisers are placed with the traditional chiefs to organize an intensive grid of military support by leaning upon traditional authority." — *La Libre Belgique* (Brussels), August 1, 1960. "Approximately 400 soldiers in uniform and with rifles," composing the army of Paramount Chief Kasongo Nyembo, paraded at Kamina before three American students in 1962. — *Congo-Katanga Quest*, a report distributed by the Agence Katangaise in the United States.

and the groups of European mercenaries. In the cities must be added groups of European volunteers, composed of civilians, who came forth during the trials of strength with the U.N.

The military dangers confronting the Katangan forces in 1961 were different from those of the preceding year; the danger to the frontiers was represented, until November, 1961, solely by contingents of troops from Stanleyville. The numerical weakness of the troops sent by Stanleyville was compensated by the support that they found within North Katanga among the Baluba population — the Katangan forces no longer occupied the principal centers — and by the fact that the U.N. let them penetrate into the neutral zone established by the October 17, 1960, agreement between the U.N. in the Congo and the Katangan government.

The internal danger was twofold: the Baluba insurgents and the government of Lualaba installed at Manono, on the one hand, and the U.N. forces, from the moment they began to apply the February 21 resolution, on the other.

From the capture of Manono by the Katangan gendarmery on March 30, 1961, the significant Baluba military resistance decreased, while Katangan military strength grew in the north. In contrast, the external threat continued on the northern frontiers, and, from October on, a new threat appeared from Kasai itself. During this period, however, the principal danger came incontestably from the U.N. troops, whether it was intervention to stop a Katangan operation as was the case in Luena and Kabalo in March, or interception of contingents of Katangan forces in order to expel from them foreign officers and mercenaries. In this regard, the April 17 agreement between the U.N. and Leopoldville was even clearer than the February 21 resolution. It stated:

> The United Nations is to assist the President of the Republic so that all foreign personnel, whether civilian, military, or paramilitary and all mercenaries and political advisers who have not been recruited or recalled under the authority of the President [of the Republic], be repatriated from the Congo within the shortest possible period of time. To implement the above and to take into account recognition of the sovereign rights of the Republic and the constitutional powers which he holds, the President of the Republic will re-examine the appointments of foreign civilian, military and paramilitary personnel made under his authority and will take the necessary decisions compatible with the interests of the Republic of the Congo.[98]

[98] Agreement of April 17, 1961. U.N. Document, Security Council, S/4807, Annex I, reproduced in *Congo 1961*, p. 341.

The Katangan military apparatus was least adapted to meet a threat of this kind. In effect it would have been necessary to exclude from the gendarmery European officers and mercenaries, and this operation would have nullified its effectiveness in confronting all other dangers: mutiny, Baluba insurrection, ANC invasion.

The Katangan gendarmery was caught in a vicious circle. The external and internal dangers it was designed to combat required that it be strong and tightly knit. To be strong at this point meant necessarily to build up the European corps of officers. But the presence of foreign officers furnished the principal pretext for the U.N. to take issue with the Katangan gendarmery, heightening the danger to the whole of the Katangan system.

WEAKNESS AND INCONSISTENCY OF THE KATANGAN FORCES

In January, 1961, the Katangan gendarmery and, more generally, the very defense of the territory of Katanga still depended substantially on Belgian assistance in men and even in arms. Now, Belgian policy toward Katanga and its ability to aid Katanga were encumbered with several contradictions and destined in the long run to a total paralysis.

The first weakness in Belgian military assistance was, obviously, that it opposed the letter and spirit of the resolutions passed by the U.N. Security Council. Belgium had accepted these resolutions, agreeing moreover that no Belgian officer taking orders from Brussels would join battle with the U.N. in the Congo. Belgium could, by various artifices, delay the universal application of the resolutions, but it was unthinkable that it could long evade their execution.

Belgian troops took a month and a half to withdraw from their positions in Katanga, but they were, nonetheless, obliged to do it and at a moment when an ANC offensive on two fronts threatened the Katangan regime most dangerously. Likewise, the February 21 resolution on the withdrawal of foreign military personnel was not at first applied by Belgium. But, especially after the change of government in Brussels, the beginning of military disengagement on the part of Belgium in Katanga could be noted, particularly in the recall of certain conspicuous military advisers and by a stricter control of arms shipments from Belgian territory to Katanga.

On January 31, 1961, Brussels had warned its consul in Elisabethville that the turn of the international situation made it indispensable to rein in all military aid, at the same time promising that the regular Belgian officers and noncommissioned officers would continue to serve in Katanga.[99]

[99] "Consider official that the Belgian government wants regular officers and non-

On February 27, however, the permanent representative of Belgium was already taking a more qualified stand and declared in a verbal note addressed to the U.N. Secretary-General that steps had been taken by Belgian military authorities to recall the officers and non-commissioned officers recruited from outside the former *Force Publique*.[100] These measures involved thirty-one officers and non-commissioned officers whose staggered repatriation would be completed by March 19.

The recall of Major Weber on June 14 was another indication of Belgian disengagement in Katanga, in contrast to the forms of assistance which the situation in the second half of 1960 had called forth. Furthermore, it was evident that the international position of Belgium, her susceptibility to American influence, her political system traditionally dominated by moderates, forbade her to suppose that she could separate herself for long from the policy adopted in Washington and New York, as had France in the case of North Africa.

Belgian assistance suffered from yet another handicap, already mentioned, namely, the double game of official Belgian policy toward the Congo ever since the installation of a moderate power in Leopoldville in September, 1960. The amount of assistance furnished by Belgium to Leopoldville was not of prime importance to Katanga — there was never any real competition on this level. Katangan authorities took exception, rather, to the very principle of this support, which produced significant political repercussions within Katanga.

Since the refusal by Belgium to recognize the independence of Katanga officially, the attitude of the Belgians in Katanga had been ambiguous.[101] To the extent that they took orders from the Belgian government, they were inclined — so at least the Katangans suspected — to follow the directives from Brussels (even if, in reality, their opinions influenced Belgian policy more than the latter influenced their activities with regard to the secession). If a conflict broke out between Leopoldville and Elisabethville, nothing guaranteed the Katangans that Belgium would continue

---

commissioned officers to continue to serve." — Telex from the Minister of African Affairs, January 31, 1961.

[100] U.N. Document, Security Council, S/4752, Annex II, A. Certain officers had been detached from the regular Belgian forces in August, 1960, when the latter had evacuated their positions in Katanga. At that time, the Minister of African Affairs had asked that these officers wear the insignia of the *Force Publique*. — Telex from the Minister, September 6, 1960.

[101] Declaration of Evariste Kimba, November 24, 1960. The Katangan government cannot close its eyes to the danger of using as technicians "individuals who always consider themselves under allegiance to the Belgian government, whose game can no longer be hidden." — *Le Soir* (Brussels), November 26, 1960.

to pursue its double policy and that it would not opt for the central government. The attempts to renew diplomatic relations between the Congo and Belgium, although very hesitant, were interpreted in the sense of "casting off" Katanga and greatly disturbed Tshombe and his ministers.

To this were added the counsels of moderation and understanding with Leopoldville which irritated the Katangans and the European *ultras*, already inclined to suspect the Belgian government of unitarism. Thus, a plan of rapprochement with Leopoldville was suggested by Belgium to Tshombe and Kibwe, with a view toward a military accord, political co-operation, and financial support. To the Belgian representative who came at the beginning of February to propose this plan to him, Kibwe responded by attacking Belgium: "Belgium is responsible for the turn of events by refusing, despite promises offered repeatedly during the month of July, to recognize the Katangan state. The U.N. threat, provoked by the Belgian government so its unitary views would triumph, does not impress Katanga, which will never renounce its independence." [102]

After the constitution of a new Belgian government, the Tshombe government attributed to the Belgians and to the Socialists, in particular, the responsibility for Leopoldville's switch in tactics after the Tananarive Conference. Tshombe, likewise, suspected that Belgium supported Sendwe. During the course of an interview that he had in mid-April with an emissary of the Belgian government, Tshombe declared that he "had been warned that emissaries from the Belgian Ministry of Foreign Affairs had arrived in Leopoldville to stab him in the back."

Touching on the question of the forthcoming resumption of diplomatic relations between Belgium and the Congo, he declared that he was not opposed to it.

The emissary noted:

We understood that this was for him a source of very great dissatisfaction and that he suspected us of wanting to renew our relations with Leopoldville to the detriment of our relations with Katanga. At one point, Tshombe, raising his voice, declared he had always been a friend of Belgium and the Belgians, but that, given the attitude of Belgium toward him for some time, he could easily break off this friendship and believe what certain of his ministers said to him.

ATTEMPTS AT A SOLUTION WHICH WOULD MAINTAIN KATANGA'S MILITARY POTENTIAL

Katanga found itself in a dilemma. Its officer corps was exclusively Belgian, but U.N. pressure was mounting on Belgium to call a halt to

[102] *Congo 1961*, p. 236.

bilateral military assistance. Several expedients were tried in order to loosen Katanga's military potential from this bind: camouflage of the Belgian officer staff; hiring of non-Belgian officers — mainly French — at higher levels; negotiation with Leopoldville; and finally cooperation with the U.N., after acceptance of the February 21 resolution by the Katangan leadership that was established during the internment of Tshombe.

The only solution which could have been definitive but was not seriously considered at this point by the Katangan government was to Africanize the officer corps and to exclude foreign officers. U.N. action in Katanga, all of which after the February 21 resolution was based on the obligation to evacuate the foreign mercenaries, would have been paralyzed by a move of this nature.

The radical Africanization of the Katangan army, which the resolutions of the U.N. in fact implied, would have encountered several major difficulties, notably hostility from foreign military personnel on the spot and from *ultra* groups, as well as the distrust of European political opinion.

In addition, the type of organization adopted by Katangan forces in their struggle against the Baluba guerrillas (small autonomous units with great mobility and aerial liaison) offered little chance for successful Africanization.

The following discussion examines briefly the various strategies adopted by Katanga in order to maintain its military potential.

Camouflage of the Belgian officers began early in September, 1960, when Brussels asked that the officers of the Belgian army put at the disposal of Katanga wear the insignia of the former *Force Publique*.[103] With respect to the U.N., the official Belgian position was to make an absolute distinction between two categories of Belgian military personnel in the Congo: those taking orders from the Ministry of National Defense and those directly responsible to the Congolese authorities. On February 27, the permanent representative of Belgium at the U.N. described the two categories:

> The first category consists of a very small number of men who are still by agreement with the U.N. at the Kamina and Kitona bases. They will have left these bases before 15 March 1961.
>
> The second category may be subdivided as follows:
>
> (a) Belgian members of the former *Force Publique* placed at the disposal of the Congolese authorities under Article 250 of the *Loi Fondamentale*. The government asks that the Congolese authorities shall relieve these officers and non-commissioned officers from their task as soon as the latter can be

[103] See above, note 100.

assumed with equal effectiveness, and in agreement with those authorities, by the U.N. forces.

(b) As for the officers and non-commissioned officers, who, members of the Belgian army until the time they were made available to the Congolese authorities, had in some cases arrived after July 1, 1960, to assist the officers of the former *Force Publique* in their task of officering and training, steps are being taken by the Belgian military authorities to recall them to Belgium.

(c) Finally, a number of Belgians have been recruited — in the Congo, in Belgium or abroad — as mercenaries by various Congolese authorities. The Belgian government has no interest in these nationals of whose ventures it disapproves.[104] To the extent that some of them still have military obligations in Belgium, these will be requested to return to their country. In addition, steps are being taken — as has been publicly announced — to put an effective stop to such recruitment. These steps will be multiplied and intensified, and proceedings will be taken against the promoters of the recruitment who have contravened the laws in force.[105]

From this moment forward the tactic followed consisted in replacing if possible the Belgian officers returning under category (b) by officers of the former *Force Publique* and by mercenaries in the hope of removing the onus of the Belgian government in the eyes of the U.N. To requite the need for mercenaries, a representative of President Tshombe in Brussels was involved in a massive recruitment program,[106] for which he received the support of a private organization, Mission Marissal, named after Colonel Marissal, its director, president of the Fraternelle des Agents Parachutistes. This mission worked in close liaison with a colonel in the Belgian military *Sûreté* or security police who screened the selection of candidates, of whom 250 left for Katanga through August, 1961.

With the agreement of the Ministry of National Defense, telegrams were sent to former members of the *Force Publique* serving in the Belgian army.[107] They were informed that there were opportunities for being hired

[104] This type of declaration, even if it is not reflected in concrete action against the recruitment of mercenaries, provoked strong reactions in Katanga: "Belgium has declared that it is opposed to the recruitment of volunteers for the Katangan army which fights in the name of the West against Communism in Africa. Legal proceedings will even be undertaken against those who would take part in this recruitment. The Communists, in contrast, openly declare they mean to put their troops at the disposal of the Gizenga government, troops made up of former U.N. contingents in the Congo. There really are some people who won't open their eyes." — *L'Essor du Katanga* (Elisabethville), January 25, 1961.

[105] Oral note addressed by Walter Loridan, Belgian representative to the U.N., to Hammarskjöld. — U.N. Document, Security Council, S/4752, Annex II, A.

[106] See on this subject, *Courrier Africain du CRISP*, No. 4 (1961).

[107] *Ibid.*

in Katanga as technicians, and the letter was signed by an officer attached to the Ministry of African Affairs. The hiring of military personnel who had belonged to the *Force Publique* was enough to compensate for the withdrawal of the few officers (thirty-one) belonging to the Belgian army. Throughout the first half of 1961, the number of Belgian officers and non-commissioned officers was maintained between 230 and 250.[108] It was at this point, early in 1961, that the Belgian government sent Colonel Vandewalle, the former Administrator-General of the *Sûreté* in Leopoldville, to Elisabethville with full powers. Colonel Vandewalle would later run the consulate in Katanga.[109] It must be noted here that the threat of recourse to *ultra* elements in France placed strong pressure on Brussels, from whom Elisabethville insistently demanded pilots and platoon leaders "to lead the offensive against pockets of Baluba." Also, at this moment, the Belgian government recommended that Belgian advisers in the Congo oppose the Stevenson project in the U.N. ("to bring about conditions to stymie the American plan") which was considered tantamount to disarming the Katangan forces.

On January 23, 1961, fifty more Belgian mercenaries or soldiers arrived in Katanga by an indirect route, via Teheran, on board a Persian airlines plane, according to Agence France-Presse. On January 31, 1961, the Ministry of African Affairs reassured Belgian officers and non-commissioned officers who continued to serve, and, on February 8, it authorized Belgian pilots to utilize any Katangan airplane put at their disposal.[110]

The Belgian argument to the U.N. that military personnel having once belonged to the *Force Publique* took orders from the Congolese authorities was legally weak and not very effective. It was rejected by Commandant Weber himself who stated in an explanation addressed to *La Dernière Heure* that "the Belgian officers who served in Katanga between July 10, 1960, and September, 1961, were on special assignment. They carried out orders from the Minister of African Affairs and were all paid by the Belgian government. Like the soldiers of any country, they remained under orders of their government."[111]

[108] Major G. Weber cites the figure of 220 at the time of the Trinquier affair, that is, in February, 1961, in *La Dernière Heure* (Brussels), April 20, 1963. At the beginning of September, a U.N. report counted 187. U.N. Document, Security Council, S/4940, Annex III.

[109] At this point, Brussels was much disturbed over the tensions and carping registered at the highest levels of the Belgian military in Katanga.

[110] At the height of the so-called Fouga affair, see note 119, pp. 166–67.

[111] *La Dernière Heure* (Brussels), April 20, 1963.

Furthermore, the Belgian thesis that these were former members of the *Force Publique* was a fragile one. In effect, the *Force Publique* was at the bidding of the central authorities and thus a provincial authority could not decide on the assignment of its former officers, much less a foreign government. Moreover, the former officers of the *Force Publique* had, in the meantime, generally ceased to belong to it, having requested reintegration into the Belgian army during the summer of 1960. Besides, disguising the presence of officers in Katanga as "technical assistance" would dangerously compromise this assistance and render all other forms of aid subject to the same condemnation that the U.N. and Leopoldville would not fail to level against assistance in this military form.

As for the hiring of mercenaries, the rebuke of the Belgian government remained somewhat platonic. The Mission Marissal continued its recruitment until August, 1961, yet not a single mercenary was effectively prosecuted on the basis of Article 135 of the Penal Code forbidding enlistment for profit into a foreign army.[112]

It is likewise to be noted that the U.N. Secretary-General, while accepting in theory the artificial distinction between Belgian soldiers of the former *Force Publique* and soldiers from the Belgian army, refused to condition the withdrawal of the former upon their relief by U.N. officers and required, in fact, the immediate and unconditional withdrawal of both categories.[113]

Internationalization of the recruitment of foreign military personnel, which began at the end of 1960 was designed to break the Belgian monopoly in this respect, both to forestall a defection or a slow-down in Belgian assistance and to neutralize Belgian influence, judged by the *ultra* groups to be too moderate and too "unsure" from the point of view of the secession.

The internationalization assumed two quite distinct aspects. A first form of internationalization consisted in recruiting non-Belgian mercenaries, either to form units composed entirely of foreign soldiers or to serve as officers for small units of the Katangan gendarmery, organized for guerrilla warfare. Thus, the thirty white mercenaries apprehended at Kabalo

[112] On January 23, 1961, a spokesman for Wigny publicly condemned the recruitment for the Katangan army: "An administrative inquiry is underway and legal proceedings will be instituted in the courts." On February 8, 1961, Wigny declared: "If need be, legal action will be taken on the basis of Article 135 of the Penal Code."

[113] Oral note from the U.N. Secretary-General to the permanent representative of Belgium, March 2, 1961. — U.N. Document, Security Council, S/4752, Annex I.

on April 7, 1961, by the U.N. belonged to a unit called "the international company," composed of about two hundred officers, non-commissioned officers, and men, all foreigners, and divided into five sections.[114] These mercenaries were for the most part of South African, English, and Rhodesian origin, but Belgian officers cooperated actively in their recruitment, in their instruction, and in the direction of their military operations. The fact that these soldiers knew only English is one of the reasons that they were constituted in wholly foreign units, which permitted their instruction time to be shortened and increased their effectiveness on certain missions. Coming from communities practicing radical racial discrimination, these soldiers, if incorporated into the Katangan gendarmery, would have raised serious difficulties. The mercenaries of Belgian or French-speaking origin, however, were integrated in small units of the Katangan gendarmery.

The number in both categories of mercenaries could be estimated as no more than 500 of which about half were Belgian. On September 8, 1961, the U.N. counted 260 left, of which 175 were Belgian.[115]

This first form of internationalization in the recruitment of mercenaries, which went back to September and October, 1960,[116] with the outbreaks of guerrilla fighting in North Katanga, was not inspired at the beginning by the political concern to diminish Belgian influence. In the minds of the recruiters, the non-Belgian mercenaries did not serve as a substitute for the Belgians, but as complementary troops.

However, in late 1960 and early 1961, there developed a second form of internationalization of direct military assistance to Katanga with the goal of breaking the total dependence of Katanga on Belgium and of looking elsewhere for the necessary means and men. Often acting through Belgians directly and personally linked to Katangan leaders of the secession, Katanga began in January and February, 1961, to recruit, in Paris or in Toulouse, French mercenaries versed in the techniques of war in Indochina or in Algeria. At this point, Elisabethville considered entrusting the supreme command of the Katangan gendarmery to the French

---

[114] See the report concerning the interrogation of 30 mercenaries apprehended at Kabalo. — U.N. Document, Security Council, S/4790, April 14, 1961.

[115] U.N. Document, Security Council, S/4940, Annex III.

[116] At the beginning of November, 1960, Joseph Yav held a press conference in Paris. He had just brought 40 Katangan military trainees to Belgium and sought to recruit French, German, and British military "technicians" for the Katangan armed forces (especially, instructors, fliers, and noncommissioned combat officers. At the end of November, Yav claimed he had received numerous inquiries from volunteers in France and Germany.

Colonel Roger Trinquier, former aide to General Jacques Massu, known for his *Algérie française* positions and especially for his role in the Algiers repression. Was the initiative a scheme of the *ultras* led by Georges Thyssens and aiming to replace Tshombe with Kibwe, as the Belgians asserted? Or was it an affair on which the Katangan government was unanimous from the outset, as the colleagues of Colonel Trinquier argued? It is difficult to discern which interpretation is the more plausible.

On January 5, 1961, Colonel Trinquier received in a letter from Thyssens a proposal of the Katangan government declaring that "the State of Katanga, former province of the Belgian Congo, separated from the Congo since July 12, 1960, was recruiting outside Belgium: (1) A high-ranking French officer to take command of the Katangan army. (2) One hundred officers and non-commissioned officers, French and German, if possible." [117]

According to Colonel Trinquier, it was with the agreement of the French Minister of the Army Pierre Messmer that he left for Katanga on an exploratory mission on January 25, in the company of Thyssens. According to Colonel Trinquier, the French Minister of the Army was "particularly interested in this affair and the advantages which France and the French Community could draw from it." [118]

At the time, the observers were struck with the rapidity with which an active colonel could obtain leave for his exploratory mission and, later, his resignation or retirement. According to Colonel Trinquier, the Quai d'Orsay, on the contrary, was hostile to his trip.

From this point on, the internationalization of the direct military assistance to Katanga [119] took on a dual political aspect; internally it was de-

[117] Trinquier, et al., *Notre Guerre au Katanga,* account of Colonel Trinquier, p. 53.

[118] *Ibid.*

[119] In deliveries of military matériel and equipment, the internationalization was well under way. A particularly serious question emerged in January and February of 1961: that of the delivery to Katanga of Fouga-Magister airplanes. The arrangement had been made in September and November of 1960, between Joseph Yav, the Secretary of Defense for Katanga, and Attala, an important Lebanese business man. The contract provided for the delivery in Toulouse of nine Fouga aircraft by the French firm, Potez, within the framework of a contract concluded before Congolese independence for the Belgian Ministry of National Defense. The Quai d'Orsay is supposed to have been very disturbed on February 8, 1961, about the possible delivery of the airplanes to Katanga, and the Belgians were greatly concerned not to have to take responsibility for the matter before world opinion. Brussels published denials and was reassured by a telex from Elisabethville on February 17, 1961: "Fouga Company will take care of the assembly and in prin-

manded by the *ultra* groups, but fought by high-ranking Belgian officers and by moderate political advisers. At stake principally was the complete rupture — desired by the *ultras* — of Belgian-supported cooperation with Leopoldville, but it is probable that personal rivalries and questions of prestige likewise helped to poison relations between Belgian officers and the French.

Externally, the internationalization of military assistance via French involvement, was supported by certain French governmental authorities in the context of a general policy of support for the Katanga dissidence and in hopes of a political renaissance of the French-speaking African nations with economic cooperation.

On the other hand, the French Ministry of Foreign Affairs had reason to fear this involvement of *Algérie française* officers in Katanga, for at that time rumors began to circulate about the assassination of Lumumba and most severe measures against foreign advisers and mercenaries serving in Katanga were expected from the U.N.

On February 4, Colonel Trinquier declared himself officially charged with the reorganization of the Katangan gendarmery, and on February 9, he opened, at 29 rue Cambon in Paris, a recruitment office which was closed several days later on orders from the French Prime Minister, on the basis of Article 85 of the Penal Code forbidding recruitment on behalf of foreign armies on French territory.

The Belgian government let Tshombe know that "the conditions of the designation of Trinquier were most vigorously resented in Brussels, even in circles most sympathetic to Katanga." Locally, the Katangans looked for a way to calm Belgian reactions; Trinquier could reorganize the gendarmery but would no longer be the commander. But Belgian representatives thought it was the intention of the Katangan leaders to undertake a political operation: the creation of a "war *directoire*," having all the power, with Tshombe, Kibwe, and Munongo as ministers, Trinquier as head of the gendarmery and police, and Thyssens as political adviser.

Having heard about a plan attributed to Colonel Trinquier and his team to attempt an airborne operation against the Gizengists in Stanleyville and to carry out elsewhere mopping up operations of pockets of

---

ciple then Belgian officers will not be involved; three mechanics are already there." Three Fouga were delivered to Elisabethville on February 16, 1961. During the course of the battles between Katanga and U.N. forces in the Congo in September, 1961, the Fouga played a decisive role in the U.N. setbacks.

the Baluba rebellion, the Belgian consulate in Katanga recommended that Brussels demand from the Katangan government certain guarantees about the types of missions which would be entrusted to Belgian cadres. Thus, "all doubts would be removed on extent to which our military personnel will be authorized participate in operations against rebels and use certain matériel." [120]

These questions were all the more serious when the new American administration proposed a plan to disarm forces in the Congo. Belgium opposed it but at the risk of running into growing resistance should Colonel Trinquier and his men set foot in Elisabethville and there apply their theories on "subversive war" led, in Algeria as in Katanga, according to them, by international communism.

Until the end of February, Colonel Trinquier's prospects were uncertain. Two officers in his command — Bovagnet and Pradier — had arrived in Elisabethville and proposed to bring in the Colonel after February 21. The U.N. resolution, the conclusion of a military accord with Leopoldville and Bakwanga, and the perspectives of Tananarive all worked against the operation envisaged by Thyssens. But the Colonel came, nevertheless, to Salisbury on February 28, where the Katangan government let him know that it would not need his services.[121]

The affair amounted to a personal defeat for Colonel Trinquier, which he attributed to "the clear resolve of the Belgians not to admit any foreign officers, and particularly not the French, who could hamper their policy. The Belgians, as I have said previously, blindly hope against all good sense to maintain the unity of the Congo, solely in order to conserve the whole of their immense interests there." [122]

Despite the personal setback for Colonel Trinquier, other French officers gained a foothold in Katangan affairs, especially in the gendarmery,

[120] Telex of February 8, 1961.

[121] Tshombe feared offending the French authorities if he dismissed Colonel Trinquier and his team, after having asked for them. The Katangan president was advised to write to General Charles de Gaulle. The letter was transmitted by the honorary consul of France in Elisabethville and a response, clearly unfavorable to the designation of Trinquier as commander of the Katangan gendarmery, was received by Elisabethville.

[122] Trinquier, et al., *Notre Guerre au Katanga*, Colonel Trinquier's account, p. 101. In fact, the most authoritative Belgian position in January, 1961, was that a certain amount of French aid could be accepted in fighting units, but that any attempt at the systematic disbanding of Belgian officers to the benefit of the French in the leadership of the gendarmery would lead to a re-evaluation of the whole system of Belgian military assistance in Katanga.

where they played an important role in the operations against the U.N. in September and December.[123]

Their presence did not stop the Katangan leaders from seeking — under the influence of their Belgian advisers, with the support of Belina, a stateless person and private adviser to Tshombe — a partial solution to their military problem in an agreement with Leopoldville.

The Katangan authorities, seeking only tactical cooperation, did not get from this agreement — as we have seen — the advantages they might have gained had they accepted certain political conditions from the beginning of the negotiations. Among these conditions was the principle of a single command demanded by General Mobutu and finally incorporated into the Tshombe-Leopoldville accord of July 18, 1961. This would ultimately have spared the Katangan gendarmery the application of the February 21 resolution, agreed on by Leopoldville and the U.N. It is probable that foreign military advisers, who felt threatened by any attempt at reunification of the army, deprived the military agreement between Leopoldville and Elisabethville of all concrete political substance and also sabotaged the agreement of July 18 between General Mobutu and Tshombe.

After the internment of Tshombe and the break with Leopoldville, Katangan leaders paradoxically turned toward the U.N. to negotiate a solution to the dilemma which the Febuary 21 resolution and the April 17 agreement imposed upon their military forces. The agreement would have called for the elimination of units of mercenaries and for the gradual replacement of foreign officer personnel of the gendarmery by officers chosen by the U.N. This agreement, called the Egge plan after the Norwegian officer of the U.N. who negotiated it, is analyzed in Chapter 6.

MILITARY OPERATIONS FROM JANUARY TO APRIL 1961

During the first four months of 1961, Katanga faced two threats of a military nature. The first, in January, was an offensive of Lumumbist soldiers coming from Stanleyville; the second, in April, grew out of the attempts by the U.N. to neutralize the mercenaries and foreign officers

[123] In particular, Colonel Faulques, who was entrusted with the training of Katangan paracommandos and who was in command at Kaniama, then at Elisabethville. *Le Monde* (Paris), July 31, and August 1, 1960, wrote of him that he "had won notorious fame for his role in the interrogations which took place in the Susini villa during the battle of Algiers." (Translator's note: The Susini villa became infamous as the house in which Algerian rebels were systematically tortured during the Algerian independence struggle.)

in application of the February 21 resolution. Between the two, from February to March, a large-scale counteroffensive of Katangan forces took place in North Katanga.

On January 7 and 8, a few days after the taking of Bukavu by troops coming from Stanleyville, 600 Lumumbist soldiers crossed North Katanga and occupied Manono.[124] Meeting no resistance, they had crossed the zone controlled by the Katangan forces and that neutralized by the U.N. The same day, a government of Lualaba Province was installed in Manono under the presidency of Prosper Mwamba Ilunga. The complete and rapid success of the Lumumbist offensive in North Katanga was a gauge of how tenuous the military effectiveness of Katanga was there. The Elisabethville government concluded likewise that the agreement which had been reached with the U.N. concerning the neutralized zone had been violated and declared on January 12 that Katanga would reassume "its freedom of military action throughout the territory."[125]

In Manono, the government of Prosper Mwamba Ilunga tried during the month of January to organize the administration of the province and to prepare its defense against a Katangan counteroffensive. It could not, however, obtain the support expected from Gizenga and tried to make up for the lack of troops by organizing a band of armed youth. In fact, the arming of the Balubakat youth was a disappointment for the Lualaba government, which could never control, let alone use, this youth band. When the Katangan offensive against Manono was launched, the Lualaba government had 160 soldiers at its disposal.

On the eve of the counteroffensive, the Katangan gendarmery was estimated by the U.N. to have a force of "5,000 men, which is well equipped and strengthened by non-Congolese officers and non-commissioned officers now estimated to be some 400 strong."[126] If these figures are an accurate estimate, the European officer contingent was relatively numerous, since there was one European for every twelve Africans, whereas before independence the ratio had been one for twenty-five. This illustrates one of the paradoxical characteristics of the Katangan regime, namely, the proliferation of foreigners hired by the Katangan government concurrent with partial Africanization. It is possible, nevertheless, that

[124] According to certain observers, these soldiers, who were originally from North Katanga, hoped above all to leave Stanleyville and return to their home villages with their families.

[125] *Congo 1961*, p. 216.

[126] Dayal report, February 12, 1961, U.N. Document, Security Council, S/4691, para. 2.

the figure of 5,000 is under estimated, for four months later the Egge report gave a figure of 11,000 men led by 460 foreign officers and non-commissioned officers, including 201 Belgians. Even this proportion is high.[127]

To the gendarmery must be added the mercenaries of the "international company" of Captain Richard Browne. Although relatively small in number (between 200 and 250), these mercenaries — a majority of whom were English, South African, or Rhodesian — played an important role in the first weeks of the offensive, thanks to their training and to their superior arms.

The air force, composed of light airplanes and helicopters, played scarcely any offensive role — with the exception of the bombing of Manono on January 30.[128] However, the reconnaissance, liaison, and transport flights were extremely numerous and constituted an important element in the success of the Katangan offensive. Besides the air force, the means of transportation were plentiful: heavy and light trucks, armored jeeps, armored trains. Arms included 75 mm. antitank guns, 37 mm. cannon, mortars, heavy machine guns, and so forth.

Katangan offensive forces were put under the command of the Belgian Colonel Crèvecoeur. The Belgian Major Matthys commanded the Task Group which opened the offensive on February 11 with the capture of Mukulakulu.

The first part of the offensive, to reopen the rail line from Lubudi to to Luena and thus allow the coal production to be shipped out, ended successfully February 13. The Katangan forces pursued their offensive to the north, however, with the avowed aim of taking Manono.[129] But, on

[127] "I have at my personal disposal 15 [foreign] technicians for my 17,000 men. In Katanga, for 11,700 gendarmes and soldiers, there are more than six hundred." — General Mobutu, press conference, July 20, 1961.

[128] A high military adviser asked Tshombe on January 29 to indicate the position he chose: "(1) bombing of the stadium (of Manono) during the inaugural ceremonies of the so-called Lualaba state; (2) bombing of the government buildings in Manono (and the residence of Prosper Mwamba Ilunga) and of the military camp; (3) bombardment of the senate of Manono." Each formula, he explained, had advantages and disadvantages. The bombing of the ceremony, for example, would result in many victims among women and children, "which would probably provoke very violent repercussions in the eyes of world opinion and unforeseeable reactions in the U.N.; otherwise, it is probable that the result would be very spectacular, capable of impressing the crowds." — Unpublished letter to Tshombe, from Section G 3 of the General Staff Headquarters, *Force Terrestre*, January 29, 1961.

[129] On this point, see the statements of the Belgian Captain Protin on Febru-

February 22, the day after the vote on the resolution in the Security
Council, an agreement was reached between the Katangan government
and the U.N. representative in Elisabethville, Ian Berendsen, before the
attack on Manono could begin. The two parties agreed "not to make any
troop movement liable to lead to friction." [130]

However, the arrival of Stanleyville troops in Luluabourg on February 26 aroused a violent reaction on the part of Katangan authorities.
Tshombe declared — for the second time — that Katanga resumed "all
its freedom of action that it had voluntarily curtailed somewhat for a
week. Moreover, if the threat of the Gizenga army against the rest of
the Republic of the Congo were directed against Katanga, the forces of
the state would be obliged to occupy all positions which contribute to
their security, even if they were located outside the limits of the state." [131]

After the military agreement was concluded with Leopoldville and
Bakwanga on February 28, the offensive against Manono opened on
March 12. But the Katangan gendarmery was unable to penetrate Manono until March 30. The rather long delay contrasted sharply with the
speed of advance during the first phase of the February offensive. It does
not seem that military resistance slowed the advance of Katangan troops,
but rather the desire of Katangan authorities to avoid any combat which
could provoke a U.N. intervention and to intimidate the U.N. to the
utmost by a spectacular deployment of forces. Tshombe had declared
the day following the February 21 resolution that Katangan forces would
never attack the U.N. forces but that "the Katangan forces would defend
themselves if they were attacked." [132] Such a tactic necessitated detailed
preparation and considerable use of military matériel. This buildup occupied the entire month of March. These tactics paid off on the military level
since Manono fell without the intervention of the U.N., but proved politically disastrous for the Katangan authorities because it led to the reinforcement of the U.N. military force in Katanga, with the addition of
Indian contingents in particular.

The February 21 resolution urged "that the U.N. immediately take
all appropriate measures to prevent the occurrence of civil war in the
Congo, including arrangements for cease-fires, the halting of all military

---

ary 17. — Dayal report, February 20; U.N. Document, Security Council,
S/4691/add. 2, para. 2, February 20, 1961.

[130] *L'Essor du Katanga* (Elisabethville), February 22, 1961.

[131] *Ibid.*, February 28, 1961. Note that at this point, the Trinquier group was
alleged to have a plan of attack against Stanleyville.

[132] *L'Essor du Katanga* (Elisabethville), February 28, 1961.

operations, the prevention of clashes, and the use of force, if necessary, in the last resort." In application of the resolution, the U.N. forces in Katanga ought to have intervened. The special representative of the Secretary-General in the Congo, Mekki Abbas, who succeeded Dayal, in fact, if not in title, explained the passivity of the U.N. at this point by the weakness of its military forces in Katanga, after some contingents from the countries of the Casablanca Group had been withdrawn from the Congo.[133] The U.N. military force in North Katanga was at this point primarily constituted by the Ethiopian battalion at Kabalo, several of whose units were spread over other sectors. The disproportion between the U.N. forces and the Katangan gendarmery was obvious.

Consequently, instructions issued to the U.N. commander in North Katanga "to oppose and resist any further aggressive moves by the Katangan gendarmery" remained a dead letter.[134] Negotiations were initiated with Tshombe, who stated that "his aim was to occupy Manono by peaceful means, and that he would advance there only in accordance with the wishes of the people of Manono."[135] He, nonetheless, refused to exclude the use of military means to seize Manono. The commander of the U.N. forces in Katanga warned Tshombe on March 27 that the U.N. would oppose any use of force — a threat which was not carried out. On March 29, he warned that Katanga's advance on Manono must be halted immediately; if not, he declared, the U.N. would send reinforcements to Katanga. On March 30, Manono fell, and on April 2, the first Indian contingents arrived at Kamina.

The seizure of Manono represents one of the decisive turning points in the history of independent Katanga. On the internal level, it was the crowning achievement of Belgian military assistance to Katanga. Despite some inclination toward closer relations with France at the beginning of the year, Tshombe was the principal defender of cooperation with Belgium in Katanga. He could boast that his policy had been wise, and his prestige was considerably strengthened in relation to the *ultra* groups. The pro-French group went into an eclipse as illustrated by the renunciation of Colonel Trinquier's services. Blinded by these successes, Tshombe several days later risked going to the Coquilhatville Conference to meet publicly with Chief of State Kasavubu, in spite of explicit warnings he received from Brazzaville.

[133] Report of Mekki Abbas, April 15, 1961. — U.N. Document, Security Council, S/4791.

[134] U.N. Document, Security Council, S/4791, para. 9.

[135] U.N. Document, Security Council, S/4791, para. 10.

On the other hand, Tshombe's situation had deteriorated very seriously with respect to the U.N. After the first military reinforcement in early April, the U.N. passed to the counteroffensive. A surprise attack by Katangan forces on Kabalo on April 7, ended in U.N. capture of 30 white mercenaries at the airfield and in the destruction of a barge carrying 150 Katangan gendarmes, some of whom drowned.

These spectacular events in North Katanga constituted the first concrete application of the February 21 resolution. They were eclipsed, however, by the arrival of the U.N. troop reinforcements in South Katanga — first at Kamina, then at Elisabethville. In reply to the arrival of reinforcements, the Katangan government promulgated on April 3 an ordinance-law declaring a state of enmity and setting in motion a general boycott of the U.N.[136] In Kamina, water, electricity, motor fuel, railway, and roads were cut off by order of the Council of Ministers.

After the arrest of Tshombe at Coquilhatville, a period of calm and conciliation between the U.N. and the Katangan authorities ensued, during which the U.N. was able to reinforce its military positions in the south as well as in North Katanga without encountering resistance.

On balance, the offensive of the Katangan forces against North Katanga was all in all to the detriment of Katanga. To be sure, the Katangan forces had regained a footing throughout the north and ousted the Lualaba government, but they had been followed everywhere by U.N. troops. The U.N. had also reinforced its position considerably in the south.

EXTERNAL REPRESENTATION, RELATIONS, AND INFLUENCES

From July, 1960, the hopes of the Katangan leadership lay in rapid international recognition, at first by Belgium; then by the Western countries, friendly to or interested in the secession (especially Portugal); then by French-speaking African countries linked with France as they acceded to independence. In the hope of securing recognition — *de jure* or *de facto* — Katanga sent numerous delegations across Europe, America, and Africa.

The major disappointment came from Brussels. On July 31, 1960, the delegation led by Jean-Baptiste Kibwe was accommodated at the Chateau

[136] Ordinance-law published in *L'Essor du Katanga* (Elisabethville), April 5, 1961. The Belgian military adviser Guy Weber at this point advised Tshombe to undertake a set of measures that could paralyze the U.N. forces in the Congo (Conga plan).

de Val Duchesse [137] and was received by the King. The delegation had discussions with members of the government and the Katangan spokesman pleaded for immediate recognition of the state of Katanga by Brussels. But no country — Belgium, Western nation, African state — recognized the sovereignty of Katanga. It was not admitted to the U.N.

This lack of recognition is explained principally by the politico-judicial nature of the Katangan problem at the U.N. This does not mean that Katanga in secession — setting aside Belgian technical and political assistance — did not benefit at all from the sympathy and support of several governments,[138] or from certain relationships and informal representatives abroad.

For the most part external support and sympathy came from government officials, pressure groups or specialized lobbies, and the private economic sector. For countries like Portugal,[139] South Africa, and the Federation of Rhodesia and Nyasaland,[140] the existence of anti-Lumumbist Katanga assumed considerable value, the territory controlled by Tshombe being a barrier to African pressure directed at them. In these three territories — besides real ethnic affinities and solidarity between South Katanga, Northern Rhodesia, and the Angolan border zones — the white settlers supported the secessionist initiative. As the political observer of the Belgian government in Elisabethville noted on November 2,

[137] "Which is in a way the Belgian *Blair House*," *La Libre Belgique* (Brussels), August 1, 1960.

[138] On November 10, 1961, a letter of credit for 2.5 million dollars had been established by the Geneva bank, Imefbank, on the request of Katangan authorities payable to an American, Dr. A. P. W. The *quid pro quo* was to be recognition of Katanga by Costa Rica. The interested party had to furnish the following documents: copies of the *New York Times* or the *New York Herald Tribune* announcing the Costa Rican decision; a copy or photostat of the letter by which Costa Rica announced to Elisabethville its intention of exchanging diplomatic representatives; a declaration of the Costa Rican representative supporting the Katangan request for admission to the U.N. The authorities in Costa Rica denied having accepted the check.

[139] On June 4, 1961, the Congo had denounced the treaties signed in its name with Portugal in protest against the repressions in Angola. Portugal and Katanga had a vital interest in halting Angolan nationalist activities against the routes of communication.

[140] At any period of acute crisis, direct contacts were made by Katangan authorities with those of the federation and South Africa. Sir Roy Welensky said under no circumstances would he "impose an economic blockade on Katanga, which already suffered from the abuses of U.N. power." — Associated Press dispatch, December 26, 1961. Sir Roy always promised asylum to the Katangan leaders, in case of serious crisis.

1960: "They pride themselves [in Katanga] in the sympathy of Rhodesia and South Africa, forgetting that it derives from whites who approve a regime which appeals largely to whites." Throughout the secession, a strong community of interests existed between these countries and Katanga; it is hard to say which party found it most necessary and most useful.

For Katanga, it was a question of keeping open the routes for exporting minerals and for importing civilian and military supplies. It was a question of maintaining places of refuge for leaders in case of difficulty, of securing friendly military pressure and protected redoubts on the southern frontiers, and, as in 1961, for example, recruiting whites locally to reinforce the Katangan gendarmery.

For the countries involved, Katanga's political structure was to their liking. It also constituted an immediate physical safeguard — in particular at the frontier with Angola — as well as a hardly negligible source of profit for British capital invested in the mines and transportation systems and for commercial receipts on shipments of copper and deliveries from Europe to Katanga.

From the end of 1960, Katanga in addition benefited from the scarcely veiled support of French-speaking African nations gathered into the "Brazzaville Group," in which the Abbé Youlou's role was at that time central. This support was reflected in the "family reunion" of December, 1960, in Brazzaville, where contacts among Congolese leaders were organized under the auspices of member states,[141] and in February, 1961, when the Tananarive Conference was prepared.[142]

Later on, the Abbé Youlou reserved for himself essentially the conduct of relations with Katanga. The Katanga policy of the Abbé Youlou was based in part on long-range considerations: to avert the formation of a united Congo bordering on the balkanized former French Equatorial Africa and to constitute a confederation of anti-Communist French-speaking African states. Short term considerations also influenced the behavior of the Abbé toward Tshombe: financial aid solicited by Azume in Elisabethville from January 19, 1961, for the campaign of the Abbé during the referendum-plebiscite which he organized in Congo-Brazzaville; the promise of a Katangan contribution to financing the Kouilou

[141] Tshombe had asked on December 1, 1960, to join the Equatorial Customs Union.

[142] Appeal of the Abbé Youlou, May 4, 1961, "to the eleven Heads of French-speaking African states who endorsed the Tananarive Conference." — Agence Congolaise de Presse.

dam, deemed by the Abbé the alpha and omega for the economic development of his territory.

A "private" visit of Youlou took place on February 9, 1961, in Elisabethville with all the trappings of a visit between chiefs of state. The Abbé accepted the Order of Katanga, but no official recognition took place. The question was in fact avoided, Youlou having advised the Katangans to seek above all "the entry of Katanga into the concert of French-speaking African nations."

On the Western side, direct or indirect support for Katanga was expressed at the U.N. in the positions taken by the British and French, though always within a certain limit, viz., the exercise of the veto against proposed resolutions, accepted by the United States, although conflicting with the claims of Katanga. After the rupture between Kasavubu and Lumumba, the French adopted at NATO a position favorable to a Kasavubu-Tshombe understanding, but with the accent on support for the Chief of State. The British position was no different, except that London was more directly involved locally and was led to compromise its position because of South African, and, more especially, Rhodesian activities. The British set their hopes on non-violent solutions which would maintain the Tshombist order in Elisabethville and protect Northern Rhodesia from political upheavals which could not help but spread from Katanga should the secession be violently dissolved. The United States, for its part, chose — after several weeks in 1960 — to support the moderates in Leopoldville as well as the position of the U.N. Secretary-General and not to cut itself off from the African and Asian states hostile to Tshombe. That implied, in Washington, a reintegration of Katanga into the republic but without leaving a void the Gizengists could fill.[143] With the new Kennedy administration, the element of "pressure" in favor of reintegration was strengthened at the expense of the circumspection and discreet support previously accorded the Katangan authorities. This tendency — from the Stevenson plan in February, 1961, to the Truman mission in December, 1962 — became gradually more pronounced.

In the majority of the Western countries, groups or organized lobbies tried to influence government policy in favor of Katanga, often benefiting

[143] That is why, for example, the Department of State in January, 1961, exerted pressure so that the U.N. in the Congo would not facilitate Stanleyville's task in North Katanga. Its position as principal financial provider for the U.N. forces in the Congo gave increased weight to the U.S. position.

from the support of private financial or commercial groups linked to the secession or threatened in case of its collapse.

In Belgium, important segments of the press and spokesmen for the Social Christian party and the Parti de la Liberté et du Progrès (PLP) provided widespread support.[144] In addition, Katanga was bolstered during the early months of the secession by groups of former settlers or organizations oriented toward defense of settler interests. Of this type was the Comité d'Action et de Défense des Belges d'Afrique (Cadba), constituted on July 8, 1960, at the height of the Congolese crisis; it campaigned initially for Belgian military intervention. Another was the Rassemblement pour la Défense des Belges au Congo, which was created at the same time by former leaders of the Association des Fonctionnaires et Agents de la Colonie (Afac); it organized public demonstrations in Brussels during July, 1960. These two organizations — anti-U.N., anti-Lumumbist, violently hostile to Belgian ministers responsible for African policy — acted as pressure groups and demanded the recognition of Katanga. Their influence remained limited. The first group turned into an activist political movement of the European nationalist type, close to the theses of the OAS, the Mouvement d'Actio Civique (Mac), and later, Jeune Europe. The second transformed itself into an obscure group, the Rassemblement pour la Défense de l'Oeuvre Belge au Congo.[145]

Little political groups of the right also professed their faith in Katanga: the Parti National Belge, of a type inspired by Charles Maurras,[146] counting among its adherents former *Force Publique* commander General Janssens; as well as tiny independent parties — Parti Indépendent, Parti Social Indépendent, Rassemblement National, Centre Indépendent — but the real channel for pro-Katanga activities ran through the traditional parties, Social Christian and Liberal (PLP).

A group was organized in early 1961 to "promote, encourage, and sustain by all the means at its disposal . . . the ties of friendship with Katanga." Amitiés Katangaises was constituted as a non-profit organiza-

---

[144] Together, these two parties constituted the parliamentary majority on which the Eyskens government, in power from 1960 to the beginning of 1961, was constructed.

[145] On these movements and tendencies of the extreme right, see *Courrier Hebdomadaire du CRISP*, Nos. 140, 141, and 142.

[146] Translator's note: Refers to Charles Maurras, writer and leader of the Action française, a French fascist movement which gained a following after the Dreyfus case. It was a major element of ultra-nationalist opposition to the Third Republic, and during World War II was a mainstay of the Vichy government. Maurras was condemned in 1945 as a collaborator.

tion on February 10, 1961. Its president was Paul Laloy, a young, little-known student, but its important members included a representative of a Belgo-Katangan company as treasurer, and Edouard A. Mendiaux, a former colonial magistrate who was violently anti-Communist.

The activities of Amitiés Katangaises focused principally on propaganda in favor of the Tshombe regime (meetings, publications, protests, anti-U.N. demonstrations). The association tried, nevertheless, to collect under its banner and to aid those repatriated from Katanga, as well as to unite the most active elements of pro-Katanga opinion. Thus, among the orators and editors for Amitiés Katangaises figure Belina, Tshombe's adviser who was expelled by the U.N. at the time of the Round Table in Coquilhatville in 1961; Albert Pirard, Radio-Katanga reporter, expelled at the same time as Belina; Jo Gérard, reporter for *Europe-Magazine* and contributor to *La Libre Belgique*; Joseph Pholien, former Belgian Prime Minister; A. Decoster, editor in Brussels of *L'Echo du Katanga* weekly digest; Roger Jaspar, alias "Jean sans Peur" of Radio-Katanga.

Blamed in newspaper reports for the pro-OAS activity in Belgium, Amitiés Katangaise denied all contact with the *ultras* in France or elsewhere.[147] It is certain that the official leaders of Amitiés Katangaises are not in fact the ones who recruited the *affreux*, furnished arms to Tshombe, or trained officers and parachutists for Katanga. Neither Elisabethville nor Brussels would leave these tasks to the nonprofit organization of Laloy and Mendiaux.

According to the society's journal, it had 1,500 members. *Liberté*, their publication, set forth the following positions:

"Katanga remains the principal bastion of the West in the center of Africa." (No. 1)

"Katanga is to the heart of Africa what Berlin is to East Germany, namely, the bastion of the West." (No. 4)

"The goal of Adoula is to put the resources of Central Africa at the disposal of the Communist bloc." (No. 3)

"Hitler-Nehru-U Thant." (No. 5)

It also spoke for a federation of the Congo, the departure of the U.N. from the Congo, technical assistance on a provincial basis (J. Pholien in No. 6), and for a competition between African states aided by the West and those aided by the East (No. 5).

Objectively speaking, it must be conceded that the Amitiés Katan-

[147] *Liberté*, No. 2 (February, 1962).

gaises was the fruit of a pro-Katanga current of opinion rather than the creator and manipulator of this current. In Belgium, lobbying for Katanga operated on another level, by groups with a different capacity for exerting pressure. At the time of the trial of strength in Katanga, numerous and important voices expressed themselves against the U.N. in the Congo: that of the Senate president Paul Struye and those of the most respectable patriotic and colonial organizations in the country.

Belgium was not the only country to know pro-Katanga lobbies. In France, there existed in 1961 an Association France-Katanga presided over by Jean Baylot, an ex-prefect of police and right-wing spokesman, whose activities consisted of protests to Maurice Couve de Murville against U.N. action in the Congo, several banquets and meetings with the participation of Katangan representatives, and the dispatch of a delegation to Katanga. In activities favoring Katanga in France, it is not always easy to dissociate the political from the commercial motives. Thus, in the action undertaken to break the monopoly of Sabena by the creation of a line run by Union Aéro-maritime de Transports (UAT) between Brazzaville and Elisabethville, the eagerness of the Abbé Youlou to ensure regular air service between the two cities is apparent,[148] as well as that of the Katangan authorities to be linked to Brazzaville and to South Africa for certain purposes. However, expansion of the war between the airline companies, and in Katanga the UAT was not the only one to be involved, may also be discerned. Very revealing in regard to this mercantile-political amalgam is an unpublished report of a visit to France from Friday, March 24, to Thursday, April 6, 1961, by a Katangan delegation under the leadership of Minister of Economic Affairs Salomon Tshizand. Besides the portion of the report which constituted a "digest" of the good eating, good lodging, and good living in France from Paris to the Côte d'Azur, the report notes the pro-Katanga declarations made by all the organizations and companies visited (including UAT, Compagnie française de l'Afrique Occidentale, Centre National du Patronat française). But on each visit there was demonstrable eagerness to sell in Katanga, to be assured of an outlet down there for French goods and services, and none seemed disturbed that the Belgian monopoly might suffer by their counsels.

---

[148] "We knew that President Fulbert Youlou himself insisted that links be established between Katanga and Brazzaville." — Speech by Bonaventure Makonga in Elisabethville at the inauguration of the UAT line.

In the United States,[149] the Katangan lobby had at its disposal a powerful organization: "The American Committee for Aid to Katanga Freedom Fighters." Founded in November, 1961, it defined its objectives for the first time on December 14, 1961. On this date, a full-page advertisement — $6,000 at normal rates — appeared in the *New York Times* and in seventeen other important newspapers in the United States. Under the headline, "Katanga is the Hungary of 1961," the advertisement called on United States citizens to write to President John F. Kennedy and Adlai Stevenson, demanding the withdrawal of American financial aid to the U.N. mission in Katanga. According to Max Yergan, its president, this appeal had brought gifts of money from more than 3000 commercial and industrial companies. Persons such as former President Herbert Hoover, former Vice-President Richard Nixon, Senators Barry Goldwater, Thomas J. Dodd, Thruston B. Morton, and Everett M. Dirksen publicly took a position in favor of the committee's objectives. The committee demanded a congressional investigation of the makers of American policy in Central Africa, requested President Kennedy not to subscribe to the U.N. loan, and asked Congress to oppose it if the President did subscribe. Thereafter, the committee set up important channels for propaganda against the activities of the U.N. in Katanga.

To these activities were added those of conservative or isolationist organizations: the Young Americans for Freedom,[150] an organization of young anti-Communists; the Committee for One Million, which had taken upon itself the task of collecting one million signatures against the admission of mainland China to the U.N.; the John Birch Society founded by Robert Welch. Regional committees were established: the American Friends of Katanga in Indiana and the New England Committee for the Aid to Katanga Freedom Fighters. On March 7, 1962, the committee organized a meeting in Madison Square Garden in New York. Senator Goldwater attended it and $80,000 for the pro-Katanga struggle was collected. The committee benefited from the support of Max Yergan and George Schuyler, journalist and editor-in-chief of the *Pittsburgh Courier* and spokesman for a section of Negro Americans.

Apart from these efforts to form public opinion, support for Katanga

[149] See Jean Ziegler, "Le Katanga-Lobby aux Etats Unis," *Courrier Africain du CRISP* (March 21, 1963). We borrow our information here from this study.

[150] In 1961, at least, for after May, 1962, the Young Americans for Freedom no longer participated in demonstrations favoring Tshombe. — Ziegler, in *Courrier Africain du CRISP* (March 21, 1963).

was demonstrated in Washington by a limited number of senators and representatives, won to the secessionist cause. Among these, Senator Thomas J. Dodd, Democrat from Connecticut, who was a prosecutor at Nuremberg, must be mentioned first. For him, Tshombe was the anti-Communist rampart in Africa. In the House of Representatives, one voice espoused the same views, that of Donald C. Bruce of Indiana.

The Katanga lobby did not succeed in changing the line of the Kennedy administration toward the Congo and toward Katanga,[151] but its influence was felt to the extent that by articulating the theme of defense of the free world in Africa it did create some resistance to U.N. activities in the Congo. The White House had to take this into account, particularly when Tshombe and his Assembly backed out of agreements concluded, according to them, under American pressure.

Other countries experienced concerted pro-Katanga activities: for instance, Sweden invited to a *Katangakommit* in September, 1962, Rector Frenkiel, of the State University of Elisabethville. Frenkiel spoke in Scandinavian university circles and distributed widely an article written by Belgian doctors in Katanga against the U.N. in the Congo after the trial of strength in 1961. Struye contributed the introduction to this article. In Great Britain, right-wing conservative circles, whose capacity to influence opinion is particularly strong in the press, supported Tshombe's policy and by the same token reinforced pressures that were being applied by British economic circles linked to the Copperbelt and to Katanga in the hope of averting a collapse of the Tshombe regime and its replacement by the forces from Stanleyville or even from Leopoldville.

FOREIGN REPRESENTATIVES

While Katanga was not officially recognized, it nevertheless had permanent informal representatives in certain capitals, and in particular, in Brussels, Paris, and New York.

In Brussels, a Katangan delegation to the Common Market (Delperkat) headed by Jacques Masangu, a Balubakat senator who rallied to Tshombe, was inaugurated in the presence of representatives of the Belgian Ministers of Foreign Affairs and of African Affairs. This delegation occupied quarters on rue Marie de Bourgogne, in Brussels, in a building belonging to a Congolese parastatal organization, and was closely involved in recruitment for Katanga. Its principal adviser was a former Belgian provincial commissioner in Katanga. When the Belgian government demanded the

---

[151] The Department of State refused a visa to Tshombe early in 1962.

removal of this delegation after the re-establishment of normal diplomatic relations between Leopoldville and Brussels, the delegation was in fact replaced by a Cultural and Economic Office (Ocekat) headed by "Minister [Odilon] Mwenda of Ocekat in Brussels." [152]

In Paris, Dominique Diur established Katangan representation, without any mandate from Elisabethville.[153] This representation played an important role at the time of Katanga's attempts to internationalize assistance and recruitment of European civilian and military personnel.[154] His political adviser was Delègue, a French jurist, formerly a chief of mission in Southeast Asia who had been asked at the end of 1960 to advise Tshombe, replacing Bartelous. At that time, Delègue had contacted UMHK and the Belgian authorities in Brussels, with the agreement of the Quai d'Orsay. Diur's military adviser was an officer serving with Trinquier.

In New York, Michel Struelens, Katanga's representative[155] bearing the title "Chief of the Katanga Information Services" (Katinfor), had been since October, 1960, a member of Professor Clémens' entourage. Struelens was on the rolls of the Belgian technical assistance mission until the end of July, 1961. According to *Newsweek*, he had spent $140,000, on "operating expenses" in the lobbies of the Capitol, but Struelens asserted that his budget did not exceed $100,000 and that his actual expenses in 1960 were $40,000. Struelens was received at the Department of State on July 29, 1961, in company with President Tshombe's brother. On October 4, 1961, the American authorities notified him of the cancellation of his visa but he was not expelled, having taken advantage of a subpoena issued October 6 by the Internal Security Subcommittee of the Senate.

In fact, no expulsion took place, and on February 28, 1963, Tshombe was able to thank Struelens for the "remarkable work" accomplished in the United States. Struelens published his final issue of *Katanga Calling* on March 29, 1963, under the headline, "The time has come to say *au revoir.*"

[152] *L'Essor du Katanga* (Elisabethville), June 19, 1962.

[153] Kibwe asked the Katangan Council of Ministers if anyone knew where this initiative came from. Kimba and the rest of the council did not know. Minutes, Council of Ministers, Katanga, January 3, 1961.

[154] Diur had been received by French Premier Michel Debré in late March, 1961.

[155] "Struelens . . . head of the official office of Katanga in the United States with quarters in New York, in the KLM Building, Apartment 718, 48th Street and Fifth Avenue . . . is empowered to receive applications from candidate-immigrants to Katanga from the United States." *L'Essor du Katanga* (Elisabethville), April 14, 1961.

For an unrecognized "state" like Katanga, relations on a less official, less public basis than those at Brussels, Paris, and New York assumed a considerable importance. Through his Service de la Centralisation et de la Coordination du Renseignment (Sccr), Tshombe established a permanent liaison in Brazzaville, in Usumbura, and in Brussels (at Delperkat), and listening posts in Luanda and Salisbury. Contacts existed with the counterpart intelligence services in Brussels, Paris, Munich, and Brazzaville as well as in Angola, South Africa, and Rhodesia.

Locally, in Katanga, attempts to establish secret services were not lacking, but, by definition, they escaped observation. Nevertheless, what can be noted is a very particular interest on the part of the French SDELE (formerly the *deuxième bureau*) in Katanga.[156] In *Congo 1961*,[157] Benoît Verhaegen cited a French overture, relatively official, to the Katangan authorities. Bistos, an official entrusted with a mission by French Prime Minister Michel Debré, was in Katanga in April, 1961, where he declared that France would support recognition of Katanga by members of the Brazzaville group while France herself would open a consulate-general in Elisabethville: "From consulate to embassy is but a step, which will be soon taken," concluded Bistos. It seems actually that Bistos had played a role in this affair. He said that he was "attached to the cabinet of the president of the Council of Ministers for coordination between departments on the problems of the former Belgian Congo." He received visitors in the offices of the former Ministry of Overseas France and he was in Katanga with Diur. His relations with Debré and certain French services involved in Africa seemed intimate. It is probable that France was not alone in acting via such agencies; in Elisabethville, it was generally believed that Mr. D——— was the American CIA agent, and his positions concerning the Tshombe regime were said to differ from those of Consul Cannup.

[156] Translator's note: The *deuxième bureau* was the French intelligence agency.
[157] *Congo 1961*, p. 305.

CHAPTER 5 · *Before the Trial of*
Strength in Katanga

FROM TSHOMBE'S ARREST TO HIS LIBERATION

A T the end of April, 1961, relations between Leopoldville and Elisabethville were hardly promising for Katanga. President Tshombe and
his Foreign Minister, Evariste Kimba, were imprisoned by the central authorities; the expulsion of political advisers [1] began in a rather spectacular
fashion in Coquilhatville; while in Kabalo on April 7, the first thirty
mercenaries were captured by U.N. troops. The occupation of Katanga by
U.N. troops was methodically pursued and U.N. forces inflicted their
first important defeats on the Katangan gendarmery, notably at Kabalo.
On their side, Leopoldville authorities unanimously asserted their cooperation with the U.N. by virtue of the April 17 accord and Justin Bomboko even concluded: "The accord with the U.N. implies the automatic
disarmament of Katangan troops. . . . Congolese and international authorities are agreed on studying means of cooperation between the ANC
and the U.N. forces in the execution of certain missions." [2] This clearly
set the stage for the trials of strength which took place in the second half
of 1961.

On every point, Katanga's position was unlike that which Commandant
Guy Weber had described to Tshombe several weeks earlier. The Belgian
adviser then wrote:

The position of Katanga has perhaps never been so strong as it is today.
You are considered as the ideological leader of the former Belgian Congo

[1] The Belgian press favorable to the secession maintained at this time that some
of those expelled, such as L. Hason, were simply private individuals. Hason, in fact
a Turkish merchant and spokesman for the Zionist association in Elisabethville,
had accompanied Evariste Kimba to New York in 1960 and figured in the files of
the *Sûreté* as a Conakat adviser before June 30, 1960.

[2] Justin Bomboko, declaration at the Coquilhatville conference, cited in *Le Courrier d'Afrique* (Leopoldville), May 4, 1961.

185

thanks to your Tananarive initiative. You have proved to the world that you are capable of restoring order in your own house AGAINST the wishes of the U.N. [Bukama and Manono operation]. The military instrument which you possess is the ONLY capable one in the former Belgian Congo. You possess your own currency. You must retain the INITIATIVE.

In seeking to maintain the initiative on the political and military front, Tshombe and his regime rapidly found themselves in an extremely precarious situation, but by the end of June, the balance was redressed somewhat in their favor.

In Katanga, a triumvirate composed of Godefroid Munongo, Jean-Baptiste Kibwe, and Joseph Kiwele exercised power in the absence of the head of government and succeeded, internally, in avoiding a breakdown of institutions that the majority of observers had anticipated and, externally, in establishing a *modus vivendi* with the U.N.[3]

In Leopoldville, dissensions within the government and between the government and the army combined with wholesale political inertia to slow any continuation of the first successes over Katanga achieved in Coquilhatville. More and more, it appeared that Tshombe's adversaries in Leopoldville lacked the conviction and support to press their advantage to the full. Moreover, Tshombe was not without support among the people of Leopoldville, in particular among the Bakongo, and even among members of the government. In the final analysis, the presence of the common danger constituted by the Gizenga regime in Stanleyville stimulated the Leopoldville leaders to moderation in regard to their former ally.

In Brazzaville, the Abbé Youlou and his French advisers did not make any bones about the direct support which they accorded to the prisoners in Leopoldville.[4] They also provided facilities to Katangan emissaries, who, with the aid of a group of Belgian mercenaries, tried to operate out of Brazzaville.

The first plan to liberate Tshombe was to organize a commando raid to divert the boat which would transfer Tshombe from Coquilhatville to Leopoldville, and perhaps afterwards to try a coup "à la Skorzeny" in Leopoldville itself.[5] The latter involved halfway serious schemes, at the very least short on caution, but demonstrating the support on which the prisoners could count. In analyzing the problem, the effect of attempts

[3] All the acts of the triumvirate had to be initialed by the Assembly president, Charles Mutaka.

[4] Note that at the end of March, 1961, Tshombe had promised to participate in the financing of the Kouilou dam in Congo-Brazzaville.

[5] On this subject, see *Congo 1961*, p. 268.

at corruption with Congolese bank notes must not be overlooked. These bank notes had been withdrawn from circulation in Katanga and spent freely by the Katangan emissaries in Leopoldville.[6]

And finally, those active in the U.N. were far from unanimous in their opposition to the Katangan regime. Western pressures in favor of "friendly" negotiations with Katanga's leaders did not slacken. They were based on the idea that only cooperation with the Conakat in meetings of Parliament in Leopoldville could neutralize the influence of the Gizengists. This meant making the imprisoned Tshombe mediator in the situation, because the formation of a "moderate" parliamentary government depended in the final analysis on him.

In Leopoldville at the beginning of June, leaders were divided over the fate to be reserved for the Katangan prisoners. Ileo seemed won to the idea of freeing Tshombe, and several ministers were favorable to immediate release without conditions — Albert Delvaux, former Resident Minister in Belgium; Jacques Massa, Minister of Economic Affairs; and Jean Bolikango, Vice-Premier, who intervened personally with the Chief of State. But, General Mobutu posed several conditions, among which were the reunification of the army, the export of copper through Matadi, and the return to Leopoldville of Congolese bank notes exchanged in Katanga. The U.N., which was in the process of negotiating the participation of Stanleyville in the meeting of Parliament, was not opposed to the liberation of Tshombe, but insisted that he remain in Leopoldville and that an accord be concluded with him as well on the subject of reopening Parliament. The American embassy, reluctant at first, gave the green light to releasing him when a real or imaginary threat of a *coup d'état* by *ultras* was raised in Elisabethville.[7]

In Milan, Mario-Philippe Cardoso and Julien Kasongo, envoys of the Ileo government, made contact with a Katangan delegation led by Jacques Masangu. According to the latter, the discussions ended on June 8, with an agreement in principle on the liberation of Tshombe, to whom a ministerial portfolio in Leopoldville would even be offered. "All will depend, however, on the financial aid which we can bring to the government in Leopoldville," added Masangu.

[6] Translator's note: After its declaration of independence, Katanga called in all the Congolese currency in circulation in Katanga and exchanged it for Katangan bank notes. The Congolese currency collected was then spent elsewhere in the Congo to buy support for the Katangan regime.

[7] On the subject of the preliminaries to the freeing of Tshombe, see *Congo 1961*, pp. 273–77.

From abroad, numerous interventions were made in favor of the prisoners: two interventions by the Abbé Youlou with Kasavubu, with Hammarskjöld, and with the heads of French-speaking African states; an official intervention of the British government with the U.N. in New York trying at least to ensure humane treatment to Tshombe and his companions, and on this point London had the support of the West.

Tshombe was freed on June 22. He was able to leave Leopoldville on June 24, after having signed — with the approval of his Minister of Interior Godefroid Munongo, who had come to Brazzaville — an eleven point agreement with the central government.[8] If the Tananarive resolutions reflected the Katangan point of view almost entirely, the June 24 accord expressed, with a few concessions, the position of Leopoldville. Unification in customs, fiscal, monetary, diplomatic, and educational matters was guaranteed. The opening of Parliament and the formation of a parliamentary government which would act until the adoption of the new constitution, after three months, were announced by the agreement. Katanga undertook to cooperate in the execution of the April 17 accord on the recruitment of foreign technicians and to free all political prisoners.[9]

Simultaneous with the political negotiations, a military agreement was concluded between General Mobutu and Tshombe, which was to take effect immediately. The substance of this accord was revealed in part at the press conference held by Tshombe in Leopoldville before his departure for Elisabethville. Under the terms of this accord, the reorganization and staffing of the Katangan gendarmery would be accomplished under the authority of General Mobutu; the execution of this plan would begin by the dispatch to Katanga of 102 Congolese officers newly trained in Belgium and placed under the orders of Colonel Eugene Ndjoku. Colonel Ndjoku and nine officers of the ANC accompanied Tshombe, then, on his return to Elisabethville.

On his arrival in Katanga, Tshombe explained the significance of the

[8] The agreement is published in *Congo 1961*, pp. 277–79.

[9] "A large number of Baluba and of members of other tribes loyal to Patrice Lumumba have already been imprisoned." — *La Libre Belgique* (Brussels), May 2, 1961. In mid-June, a hunt for those Africans living without residence permits had again taken place in Elisabethville. The Katangan Council of Ministers had refused on December 27, 1960, to liberate political prisoners except by decision on individual cases reached in council. On Tshombe's return to Elisabethville, according to Katangan sources, 706 political prisoners were amnestied and "a second group of 250 were about to be freed." Note that a ministerial *Arrêté* dated May 4, 1962, and signed by Godefroid Munongo, declared, "All political detainees still interned at this time . . . are liberated as of May 12, 1962." — *Moniteur Katangais*, No. 6, June 15, 1962.

agreements reached; that is, he deprived them almost completely of any practical meaning.[10] Concerning the military accord, he stated that "Colonel Ndjoku and the nine officers who arrived at the same time as he did, will remain in the Katangan army if they are capable. Colonel Ndjoku will take command if he demonstrates his capacity and if he is loyal." Furthermore, Tshombe would not confirm Katangan participation in the parliamentary session: "Before defining the future political line for Katanga, I want to meet with my government." It could not have been more clearly implied that the June 24 agreements would remain a dead letter, in both their military and their economic and political provisions.

The Leopoldville authorities made virtually no further allusion to the agreements when it appeared that Katanga would not respect them. The hypothesis cannot be discarded entirely that the signing of the political accord, for the execution of which no guarantee was provided, had been only a "gimmick" to make the liberation of Tshombe acceptable in the eyes of Congolese public opinion. No one in Leopoldville — except perhaps General Mobutu in regard to the military accord — could have supposed that the Katangan authorities would feel bound by the agreements. It would always be possible and plausible to invoke the fact that they had been accepted under moral and physical duress. The detention of Tshombe had become of less interest for Leopoldville from the moment the Katangan institutions had demonstrated that they could maintain themselves in the absence of the head of government and when it was clear the leaders remaining in power were in no wise inclined to give up the independence of Katanga to obtain his liberation. Finally, the prospect of an imminent meeting of Parliament motivated some Leopoldville leaders to seek support among the Conakat members of Parliament to neutralize the "Gizengists."

PRELIMINARY NEGOTIATIONS FOR THE MEETING OF PARLIAMENT (JUNE AND JULY 1961)

The June 24 agreement concluded between the Leopoldville authorities and Tshombe provided for the opening of Parliament, at which the central government, with the assistance of the U.N., would guarantee the security of the Parliament members. The prospect of forming a parliamentary government had made Tshombe an arbiter of sorts between the groups of Leopoldville and Stanleyville.

[10] Tshombe press conference on June 26, 1961, reported by Agence France-Presse and reproduced in *Congo 1961*, pp. 280–81.

Tshombe, realizing the role he could play in Leopoldville, was probably sincere when, at Leopoldville, immediately after his liberation, he declared in a press conference that the Katangan members would participate in the meetings of Parliament, provided that he would be allowed the time needed to form his delegation.[11] On his return to Elisabethville, Tshombe formulated a more evasive response. For he found that some of his ministers (Munongo and Kibwe), some members of Parliament, certain *ultra* pressure groups and their allies abroad were much more reluctant to cooperate with Leopoldville.

On June 19, in fact, twenty members of Parliament from Katanga had sent the Chief of State an open letter setting conditions for their participation in the meeting of Parliament. They demanded that the "meeting of the *confederal* Parliament be held in Kamina" under the protection of U.N. contingents recruited from countries of the French community, Nigeria, Liberia, and Cameroun.[12]

As the likelihood of participation by members of Parliament from Stanleyville became more certain, distrust grew among the Katangans. They feared that a Leopoldville-Stanleyville understanding would be reached at their expense. To the schemes for meetings of Parliament, the Katangan leaders opposed the idea of a "summit conference" in line with the Tananarive Conference resolutions. To this summit meeting would be invited Gizenga, Tshombe, Albert Kalonji, and Kasavubu, but not Ileo.

Tshombe's position toward the June 24 agreement continued to be somewhat erratic. In a press conference held on June 29, he declared: "These agreements were not signed under duress and I am not a man to sign agreements in thin air."[13] The same day, during the course of an interview with the special correspondent of *La Libre Belgique*, Tshombe and Munongo declared: "The agreements signed under duress in Leopoldville will not be honored."[14]

The provincial Assembly in Katanga dissipated any uncertainty by contesting the validity of the agreement:

[11] Tshombe press conference in Leopoldville on June 22, 1961, in *Congo 1961*, p. 280.

[12] Declaration of 20 Parliament members from Katanga, Elisabethville, June 19, 1961. — *Congo 1961*, p. 283.

[13] Agence Belga dispatch published in *La Libre Belgique* (Brussels), June 30, 1961.

[14] *La Libre Belgique* (Brussels), June 30, 1961.

The members of the National Assembly [of Katanga] have studied the protocol and have determined that President Kasavubu, sole legal authority in the former Belgian Congo, had not signed this document. They have furthermore determined that at the moment when President Tshombe and Minister Kimba signed the accord, the Chief of State [of Katanga] was not in a position to exercise power in reality and that his Minister of Foreign Affairs was not in full possession of his functions either.

Having made these determinations, the Assembly members reject *in toto* and unanimously the protocol signed in Leopoldville.[15]

The U.N. intervened at this point to uphold the Katangan proposal for a summit conference preceding the meeting of Parliament. The U.N. saw in the summit meeting the only means to avoid a violent coalition against Katanga; it continued to hope, despite past disappointments, that the latter would be peacefully reintegrated into the Congo. At this juncture, the U.N. policy coincided perfectly with that of the moderates in Leopoldville, the Western powers, the Belgians, and even with the point of view of the "reasonable" Katangans. The special correspondent of *La Libre Belgique* summed up the situation correctly in these terms:

Katanga, in any case its moderate elements, is not hostile to such an attempt at conciliation. But the government has not yet given a positive response. Its abstention dangerously strengthens Gizenga. It is only too clear that in the next few days, major political decisions will be taken which could permanently crystalize the division of the Congo into two violently hostile blocs and could soon lead to grave incidents. If Katanga really wishes to do so, it could still save the situation without sacrificing its essential positions.[16]

After numerous tergiversations over the site of the conference and after Katanga had given its approval to the choice of any site, it did not even take place.[17] At this point, it seems that the U.N. abandoned support for the scheme because of Gizenga's reluctance. For the Katangans, this was the pretext not to go to Lovanium, where the Parliament met.[18]

The absence of Katangan representatives in the Parliament at Lovanium deeply disturbed the West. It was pointed out to the Katangan leaders and their advisers that the absence of Parliament members from Katanga would lead to Gizenga's triumph and, consequently, to Katanga's loss, whereas an accord between Leopoldville and Elisabethville might provoke

---

[15] *L'Essor du Katanga* (Elisabethville), July 5, 1961.

[16] *La Libre Belgique* (Brussels), June 30, 1961.

[17] See the declarations of Tshombe and Munongo of July 17 and 19, in *Congo 1961*, pp. 285–86.

[18] Secrétariat Général de l'Assemblée, Katangaise, Communiqué, July 25, 1961, quoted in *L'Essor du Katanga* (Elisabethville), July 27, 1961.

Gizenga's refusal to come to Lovanium, which would in turn put him in the position of secessionist to be condemned before world opinion.

The principal efforts were undertaken by the American embassy. Early in July, a letter was sent to Elisabethville noting that the Americans, because of international tension, needed support from the Afro-Asians and that they would prefer eventually to sacrifice the interests of Katanga rather than lose standing in the Stanleyville camp, recognized by thirteen countries, mainly Afro-Asian.

The same note underlined the identity of views of the U.N. and the United States on the Katanga problem and pointed up the fact that if American influences had worked *in extremis* in favor of Tshombe's release, it was because the United States feared Katanga would sacrifice its president and shut itself off in total resistance. From Washington and New York, the Katangan mission, whose adviser was Michel Struelens, shared the same point of view and counseled moderation.[19]

These different pressures brought Tshombe to Brazzaville on July 29. The Chief of State and General Mobutu, disturbed over the formation of a "nationalist" Parliamentary bloc at Lovanium, tried to contact Tshombe in order to negotiate the participation of the Conakat.

At this point, the intervention of the Abbé Youlou and the Katanga *ultras* was conclusive in foiling attempts at contact. Tshombe returned to Elisabethville on August 1, in an atmosphere of general pessimism. A decisive new course had been set, without Katanga. Already, it was clear it would be oriented against Katanga.

This final episode in relations on the Leopoldville-Elisabethville axis illustrates the fundamental solidarity which existed between the Katangan positions, those of the moderates in Leopoldville, those of the West, and even those of U.N. leaders, who did not hesitate to be compromised in the scheme for the "summit conference" just as they had already been com-

---

[19] According to Senator Thomas J. Dodd on August 3, 1962, Struelens, accompanied by Pweto, Henri Ndala Kambola, and Thomas Tshombe (the President's brother), had been received at the State Department on July 28, 1961, by Sheldon B. Vance, Director of the Office of Central African Affairs. Vance proposed to the visitors the drafting of a text which could lead to Katangan participation in the Lovanium conclave (this text appeared in *Congo 1961*, p. 289). Struelens, Dodd's account continued, had been invited by a U.S. adviser to return to the Congo to suggest to Tshombe that he send Conakat Parliament members to Leopoldville immediately. In Brazzaville, the Katangan representative to New York held discussions with U.S. Ambassador Blanche and R. Eisenberg, Deputy Director of the Office of Central African Affairs in the State Department. In Elisabethville, Struelens and Eisenberg finally convinced Tshombe; it was August 3, and the Adoula government had been constituted the day before.

promised at Tananarive. All these powers were in league up to the last minute to bear with the Katangan authorities and to urge them to accept spontaneously cooperation with Leopoldville.

On the other hand, this period demonstrates that certain contradictions had developed within Katangan institutions to the point where the actions of the head of government were paralyzed. It is probable that Tshombe glimpsed, during his detention, that it was in the interest of Katanga to be represented in Leopoldville in the central institutions. He had been able to take stock of their weaknesses and to assess their fundamental similarity of orientation with those of Katanga. This choice, which he shared with certain of his Belgian advisers, met with the complete assent of the U.N. and Western powers, particularly the Americans, the British, and the Belgians. That explains the patient and incessant efforts that these powers undertook to meet the Katangan demands, short of a rupture with Stanleyville.

Nevertheless, in Katanga, this new move of the head of government was fought by *ultra* groups, whose power had been further strengthened during his detention.

CHANGES IN OUTSIDE PRESSURES AFFECTING THE KATANGA SECESSION

On May 2, the government of Katanga, represented by the triumvirate which assumed power in the interim during Tshombe's internment, addressed an open letter to the U.N. Secretary-General announcing to him that it was "ready to hold discussions immediately on the means for applying the Security Council resolutions of February 21, 1961." [20] Minister of the Interior Munongo, who supposedly represented the *ultra* clique in the government, himself took the initiative in measures of appeasement and of conciliation in regard to the U.N. [21] Thus Katanga's relations with the U.N. entered upon a period of apparent respite. During this time, however, profound transformations took place in external political determinants which, until then, had permitted or favored the Katanga secession.

THE NEW AMERICAN POLICY IN THE CONGO

On the day of his transfer from Leopoldville to Katanga, January 17, 1961, Lumumba was assassinated. In fact, since August, 1960, the Prime

[20] Open letter reproduced in *Congo 1961*, pp. 270–71.

[21] Thus, in May, the lifting of the boycott on Kamina, instituted at the beginning of April (Conga plan) to protest the sending of Indian troops to the U.N. in the Congo.

Minister of the Congo had been condemned politically. The United States, in June and July, 1960, had demonstrated its readiness to summon, then to maintain, a nationalist in power even at the expense of the Belgians. After early August, 1960, however, it did not wish to risk maintaining in Leopoldville a power such as that of Lumumba, who was criticized for psycho-political instability and for his orientation and whose acts they feared as much for their effect on the U.N. as on East-West relations. Since then, United States policy regarding the Congo had been inhibited to the great advantage of the Katanga secession. Mobutu's *coup d'état* in September, 1960, by installing in Leopoldville a power even weaker than that of Ileo and compromised in world opinion to boot, postponed for six months the real American options in the Congo. It was understood that the Washington "line" consisted in recognition of Kasavubu and *de facto* support for the moves and forces judged capable of neutralizing or at least containing Lumumbism or Gizengism. During this respite, Katangan disaffection organized.

At the beginning of 1961, three events occurred which were to permit a complete recasting of American policy in the direction of unity for the Congo:

1. With the disappearance of Lumumba, what Americans called the risk of seeing installed in the Congo a neutralist regime leaning by preference toward the Communist powers was decidedly reduced. With the aid of the U.N., the installation of a moderate power — necessarily favorable to the West, from which it received the means for its administration — became possible. A meeting of Parliament could from that point on be envisaged without too much fear.

2. In Leopoldville, the most visible traces of the military *coup d'état* were erased by the establishment in February of the Ileo government (second model), which the Western powers had unanimously recommended. In the eyes of the United States, it was not yet the ideal regime, since it did not command any high regard among the most active neutralist Afro-Asian countries. But there was already a means for getting negotiations underway, firstly toward an agreement between the Chief of State and the U.N., and secondly toward a meeting of Parliament with the approval of the Chief of State and the vigilant cooperation of the United States.

3. In Washington, finally, a new Democratic President and administration took over from the Republicans.

All the conditions were present to strike out on a new Congolese policy

— the "American plan" for the Congo.[22] The essentials of the plan consisted in the neutralization of all military forces on Congolese territory — including, to be sure, those of Katanga — and the formation of an enlarged government formed under the direction of the Chief of State. For the execution of the plan, the U.N. in the Congo would have to be considerably strengthened both financially and militarily. The plan failed in its initial form, partly because of the hostility of the Soviet Union and the extremely violent reactions caused by Lumumba's death in Afro-Asian countries and partly because of very marked resistance from the principal European NATO allies of the United States.

The general conception of the plan continued, however, to inspire American policy, which aimed to install in Leopoldville a moderate legitimate power, to which would rally, willingly or otherwise, the Katangan dissidents. In the minds of the Americans the dominant pressures on Tshombe were to come from the UMHK ceasing to pay him his taxes, duties, and mining royalties and from the U.N. in the Congo being in a position to oust foreign officers from the Katangan gendarmery.

The American or Stevenson plan aroused the mistrust and hostility of the Belgian government, which at this point still lent its preference entirely to the Katangan government and took comfort from the Tananarive agreements.[23]

The African Brazzaville states also opposed the American plan. President Philibert Tsiranana of the Malagasy Republic took the initiative by warning all member states that the American projects for neutralization of the Congolese army were contrary to the Brazzaville conference resolutions of December, 1960.

SECURITY COUNCIL RESOLUTION OF FEBRUARY 21, 1961

Before the announcement of Lumumba's death, the position of the U.N. Secretary-General was still close to the principles of non-interference in the internal affairs of the Congo and renunciation of the use of force to execute its mandate, the scope of which, however, he envisaged possibly broadening.[24] When the death of the Congolese Prime Minister became

[22] On the subject of the "American plan" see *Courrier Africain du CRISP*, No. 7 (1961) and *Congo 1961*, p. 320.

[23] A telex from D'Aspremont Lynden had made clear his hostility to the plan. Belgian efforts in this direction were made at the NATO Council meeting on February 10, 1961.

[24] Declaration of the Secretary-General at the February 1 session of the Security Council, U.N. Document, Security Council, S/PV/928, para. 70, reproduced in *Congo 1961*, p. 321.

known, the atmosphere of the Security Council changed. Without following the lead of the Soviet Union in its attack against the Secretary-General
— a move which might, they felt, permanently paralyze the U.N. — the
Afro-Asian countries demanded, on the contrary, that the mandate be
strengthened.

Nkrumah addressed a plan to the Secretary-General in which he argued:
"The interpretation of the Security Council mandate, namely, non-
interference in the internal affairs of the Congo, is no longer tenable. . . .
If certain factions will not cooperate, force must be used." [25]

Without incorporating all the Nkrumah proposals, the resolution finally
adopted by the Security Council on February 21, 1961, picked up, with
certain refinements, the two strands of Nkrumah's argument. Resistance
to them was almost nil at this point, following the assassination of Lumumba. Recourse to force was authorized by the council, with the condition as stated: ". . . if necessary, in the last resort." [26] Interference in
internal affairs was also sanctioned since the resolution requested "that
Congolese armed units and personnel should be reorganized . . . and
arrangements be made . . . to the elimination of any possibility of interference by such units and personnel in the political life of the Congo."

The resolution contained a direct threat to Katanga, for it asked at
Point 2 that measures be taken for "the immediate withdrawal and evacuation . . . of all Belgian and other foreign military and paramilitary
personnel and political advisers not under U.N. Command, and mercenaries."

In fact, the resolution was strong enough to authorize the Secretary-
General to strike at the roots of the Katanga secession; no one could
deny that, even in the short run, secession could not survive the removal
of foreign military personnel. The U.N. force in the Congo had sufficient
military means at its disposal; both the international diplomatic context
and the Secretary-General's personal interpretation of the local and
world situation encouraged it to utilize the freedom of movement the
Security Council had accorded.

Negotiations with certain Afro-Asian countries were undertaken by
the U.N. Secretariat immediately after the resolution to strengthen the
military potential of the U.N. in the Congo considerably and to compensate for the withdrawal of troops by the countries of the Casablanca group.

[25] "Nkrumah plan," U.N. Document, Security Council, S/4725, February 18, 1961.
[26] Security Council Resolution of February 21, 1961, U.N. Document, Security
Council, S/4741; see also Appendix II, pp. 330–32.

India agreed to put forth the largest effort. Its troops arrived in Katanga at the beginning of April.

But before the vise which began to tighten around the Katanga secession could close completely, the tacit accord, if not support, of two forces had to be obtained: the Leopoldville authorities and the Belgian government.

NEW BELGIAN POLICY

In Brussels, a Lefèvre-Spaak coalition (Social Christian-Socialist) succeeded the Eyskens-Wigny government (Social Christian-Liberal) at the end of April, 1961. The new government intended to disengage itself gradually from the policy of the preceding government and asserted a preference in principle for Leopoldville. Orders to this effect were given to Longerstay, the official Belgian *chargé d'affaires* in Leopoldville, who tried to improve relations locally between the Belgians and the U.N. and to make the U.N. admit, in implementing the February 21 resolution, the distinction between Belgian civilian and military technicians recruited by the central government and those working for the Katangans. An agreement on this basis could be obtained fairly easily from Sture Linner, chief of U.N. civilian operations in the Congo, and from Robert Gardiner, delegate of the Secretary-General in Leopoldville, "to facilitate a complete and rapid application of the February 21 resolution . . . and to lay out the direction and the details of plans for reorganizing the Congolese army." [27]

This agreement was, however, never made official. It did not conform to the letter of the Security Council resolution and to the interpretation that the Secretary-General made for Kasavubu.[28] But it did have, in the eyes of the U.N. representatives in the Congo, two important advantages. In the first place, it forced Belgium to the wall and made her stop playing both sides of the fence by furnishing civilian and military technical assistance simultaneously to Elisabethville and to Leopoldville. In the second place, this agreement, by reassuring both the Belgian technicians working for Leopoldville and the Congolese leaders to whom they reported, removed one of the principal obstacles to a rapprochement between the U.N. and Leopoldville. The Belgian technicians involved understood it was in their interest to cooperate with the U.N., and they tried to bring Leopoldville leaders around to this point of view.

[27] *Congo 1961*, p. 333.
[28] Letter from the Secretary-General to Kasavubu, February 27, 1961, U.N. Document, Security Council, S/4752, Annex IV, and in *Congo 1961*, pp. 331–33.

In Brussels, the special envoy of the Secretary-General, Ambassador Taieb Sahbani, tried, but with less success, to clarify the policy of assistance. What had been easy in Leopoldville was rendered difficult in Brussels by the presence of a vigilant Katanga lobby, by the activities of the pro-Katanga press, and by the lukewarm attitude of the high administration and of Belgian political circles in regard to a sudden shift in policy for which they could not clearly see the necessity nor the interest.

In Katanga itself, during this period from April to July, 1961, relations between the Katangan government and the Belgian government were bad. The Katangans accused Spaak, or at least his political friends (meaning in particular, Arthur Doucy, Director of the Institut de Sociologie of the Université Libre de Bruxelles), of having plotted with Justin Bomboko the arrest of President Tshombe and of his advisers in Coquilhatville.[29]

Several events occurred in this atmosphere of mistrust toward Belgium. The first Katangan lists of Belgians to be "repatriated" were drawn up. A member of the *cabinet* of Belgian Minister Henri Fayat was arrested by Munongo's police in Elisabethville on July 7. He had been sent to inaugurate the exposition in Elisabethville and perhaps also — this is what Conor Cruise O'Brien, in any case, asserts — to present to the U.N. the first list of advisers whose expulsion the Belgian government would accept, eleven names in all. The Katangan gendarmery sacked the Belgian consulate in Elisabethville at the same time and for the same reasons. The interim Katanga triumvirate (serving during Tshombe's internment) sent a letter demanding the departure of Crener, the Belgian consul general and his assistant.[30]

However, the only notable event to mark down as a Belgian government initiative was the recall to Belgium of Commandant Weber on June 14, 1961. He had been linked to Tshombe since the very first day of the secession and appeared in the eyes of world opinion as the symbol of a Belgian political adviser in Katanga.

As for the more delicate problem of civilian advisers in Katanga, the absence of official Belgian protest on the occasion of the expulsion or departure of Belgian advisers Clémens[31] and Thyssens[32] in July, 1961,

---

[29] There is no evidence to support this accusation. It was, moreover, abandoned fairly rapidly, even by those favoring it in Katanga.

[30] The measure was withdrawn by Tshombe, who also presented his apologies for the sacking of the consulate.

[31] "Requested" to leave Katanga by the U.N. on the basis of the February 21 resolution, Professor Clémens obtained an extension by invoking the need to give examinations to students at the University of Elisabethville. His departure was, in fact, only temporary. After a sojourn in Belgium during which he recommended

must be mentioned. The Belgians nonetheless underlined the need to draw up in short order an exhaustive list of advisers to expel, in order, it was said in Brussels, to pay off the reckoning and to reassure the Europeans of Katanga who might, in case of an incomplete list, continue to fear a broadening of the criteria for expulsion, acted upon by the U.N.

U.N.-LEOPOLDVILLE AGREEMENT

While the U.N. reinforcements were arriving in Katanga, relations between the U.N. and the central government progressively improved in Leopoldville.

A first overture from Kasavubu was made on March 6, before the Tananarive Conference. In a letter to the Secretary-General, the Chief of State of the Congo proposed five steps for reorganization of the army.[33] Kasavubu's plan which clearly departed from his earlier declarations and met most of the requirements of the February 21 resolution, produced no reaction from the U.N.

After Dayal's departure, all the credit of mediation fell to Gardiner, who effected on April 17, after three weeks of negotiations, an agreement on principle with Kasavubu.[34] This agreement nullified the interpretation that the Secretary-General had made of the February 21 resolution in his letter of February 27 to Kasavubu. The new agreement specified that "all deleterious" foreign influences would be eliminated; Point 3 stated that "the U.N. is to assist the President of the Republic so that all foreign personnel, whether civilian, military or paramilitary, and all mercenaries, and political advisers who have not been recruited or recalled under the authority of the President, be repatriated from the Congo within the shortest possible period of time."

This agreement was of capital importance in every regard:

1. For Leopoldville, it nullified the dangerous consequences of the Security Council Resolution;
2. It diverted the U.N.'s political and military efforts to Katanga alone;
3. It made of the Chief of State, or Leopoldville, not only the arbiter of

---

breaking diplomatic relations with countries associated with the U.N. operation in the Congo, he again made contact, in Rhodesia and in Katanga itself, with Tshombe in the field. The press noted his active presence in Kolwezi in January, 1963.

[32] Thyssens figured, according to O'Brien, on the Spaak list of advisers who could be expelled by the U.N. in July, 1961. He was expelled on July 5, 1961.

[33] This letter is reproduced in *Congo 1961*, p. 335.

[34] U.N. Document, Security Council, S/4807, Annex I, and *Congo 1961*, pp. 340–41.

the operation, but the initiator, since the U.N. accorded him their full assistance in realizing the objectives of the resolutions.

In fact, Kasavubu received, without having formally called for it, what had always been refused to Lumumba in 1960: military and political assistance to put an end to the Katanga secession.

Tshombe knew what he was about when, several days later at Coquilhatville, he summoned Kasavubu to retract and to break the agreement. No such break occurred. What is more, the agreement went into effect immediately through the arrest and expulsion, by the U.N., of several foreign political advisers of the Katangan president.

The accord was confirmed and later applied by the Adoula government in August, 1961. Upon it hinged, essentially, a policy designed to reduce the secession of Katanga by force. If it was not used until August 28, 1961, this is to be explained by delaying maneuvers, both in Leopoldville and at the U.N., in hopes of a peaceful reintegration of Katanga.

The respite for Katanga that the Western powers, the U.N., and Leopoldville leaders accepted or even helped to prolong, until the end of August, 1961, was not, in the final analysis, used to advantage by Elisabethville, except to strengthen her combat capabilities which were to be put to the test in August-September and December, 1961.

INTERNAL PROBLEMS OF KATANGA

INTERNAL STRUCTURE OF THE GOVERNMENT

Composed of ministers elected in June, 1960, by the provincial Assembly of Katanga, then enlarged by appointed ministers and secretaries of state,[35] the government presided over by Tshombe (according to Agence Belga, on December 4, 1960), was on the verge of a major change in structure in early December, 1960. The President would have concentrated in his person the Ministries of Economic Affairs, Foreign Affairs, and Justice, each of which would, in fact, have had at its head a European — two Belgians and one Swiss, chosen by Brussels.

In fact, rumors of governmental reform were the expression of uneasiness in Elisabethville, where Western observers thought they perceived

---

[35] Several ministers died: at the end of May, 1961, in Brazzaville, Salomon Tshizand, Minister of Economic Affairs; on November 14, 1961, Joseph Kiwele, Minister of National Education; on November 19, 1961, Lucas Samalenge, Secretary of State for Information, whom the authorities alleged had been a victim of a hunting accident near Jadotville, but whose "presumed assassin" was arrested when he was about to pass into Rhodesia.

serious tensions between "moderates" and *ultras*, the former represented by Tshombe, the latter by Jean-Baptiste Kibwe. Belgium had hoped that the Belgian members of the ministerial staffs or *cabinets* would maintain, by and large, at least a double loyalty, but it had to be recognized that the influence of private advisers — Belgians indeed, but recruited locally because of their pro-Katanga position — remained generally predominant. The ministers tended, as a result, to align with the so-called hard or *ultra* secessionist views. Thus, in November, 1960, a political observer with the Belgian consulate noted: "President Tshombe directs matters less and less and, despite his desire for moderation, he too frequently lets himself be led by the Kibwe wing." The idea of reorganizing the government was in fact the idea of "moderate" advisers. It was not implemented and conflict between "moderates" and "hard-liners" intensified during the Trinquier affair.

There were certainly tensions, but they were often the expression of conflicting temperaments. The "moderate" President was also a man quite open to influence, very naturally inclined, after a first outburst of violence or anger to find formulas for "settling" matters and capable of spectacular shifts in outlook. The "hard-liners" — Munongo and Jean-Baptiste Kibwe — were undoubtedly of more violent temper, more intransigent, seeking to impose their views on adversaries by bringing pressures to bear by threats or face-to-face confrontations rather than by compromise. This interpretation of internal tensions remains open to doubt, for on the Katangan ministers in question, we have only the rare accounts of Belgian representatives, inclined to class men by their attitude toward advice given them or by the leanings attributed to their influential advisers. To illuminate Munongo's character, however, one may recall his role in Lumumba's death.

For all matters of importance and at crucial moments, decisions were taken by an inner committee of ministers, a kind of war cabinet where the dominant personalities were Tshombe, Kibwe, Munongo, Evariste Kimba, and, to a lesser extent, Joseph Yav. Some Europeans sat in on these meetings, especially Clémens, but also in early 1961, Belina, Vandewalle, and Major Weber.

On April 17, 1961, Munongo demonstrated to President Tshombe his displeasure with the certain types of interference, involving the office of the president in other departments:

Whatever the motives invoked to act otherwise, desire for personal power, coordination, or unification of government regulations, I am convinced that the dissensions now coming to light between the presidency and the various ministries must cease as early as possible. . . . It is high time for you to take hold of yourself. . . . No one appreciates better than I the present danger of a partisan policy based on personal imperatives and ambitions.[36]

This tension was manifest, then, on the eve of Tshombe's arrest in Coquilhatville, and of the constitution, by ordinance-law of May 11, 1961, of a governmental triumvirate composed of Kibwe, Munongo, and Joseph Kiwele.

Many observers in early May, 1961, expected a seizure of power by Munongo, who would then have exercised the combined functions of President, Minister of Foreign Affairs, and Minister of the Interior. After May 11, the same observers thought they could detect signs of rupture within the triumvirate, and in Leopoldville it was imagined that the Katangan triumvirate would collapse in the absence of Tshombe or be carried to all manner of extremes.

Nothing happened. The triumvirate, on the contrary, adopted a moderate position, appealing for calm, proclaiming its loyalty to Tshombe, negotiating with the U.N. in the Congo on the withdrawal of advisers and mercenaries, lifting the anti-U.N. boycott at Kamina, and maintaining its solidarity under all circumstances.

The moderation of the triumvirate toward the U.N. had distinctly anti-Belgian[37] overtones, deriving from a notion of the role of the Belgians at Coquilhatville and the advice of the Abbé Youlou who emphasized to Ministers Albert Nyembo, Munongo, and Salomon Tshizand the urgency of replacing the Belgians who were the targets of the February, 1961, resolution of the U.N. by Frenchmen.

RELATIONS BETWEEN THE GOVERNMENT AND THE ASSEMBLY

This subject has scarcely been touched upon during the period of the secession. It is, however, revealing of tendencies and currents of opinion that prevailed in non-governmental Katangan political circles.

On the whole, the Assembly always voted by a majority of those present for what Tshombe wanted: independence, adoption of the constitution, support at Tananarive, anti-U.N. motions, rejection of the accords of June, 1961, between Tshombe and the Ileo government, and so forth. Nevertheless, the Assembly displayed — on points not jeopardizing the status of Katanga — a very critical attitude toward the government, in

---

[36] By letter, reference 1057/CAB.

[37] Again drawing upon the triumvirate in Katanga, the Belgians concerned launched an accusation of an *ultra* policy.

particular through its president Charles Mutaka and through a Conakat spokesman, André Kapwasa.

The opposition crystallized around several points: non-representation of Haut-Katanga in the Tshombe government,[38] the demand for the creation of a Prime Minister responsible to the Assembly, and grievances over Kibwe's budgetary policy.

In regard to the Prime Minister: The constitution prepared by Clémens made of the President a chief of state who was not responsible to Parliament but who was given broad political power; the Assembly demanded the creation of a Prime Minister who would have to report to it. From September 6, 1960, Mutaka, second highest ranking official in Katanga, declared he was against the creation of the post of Vice-President of State which was to go to Kibwe, and on November 8, 1960, he took the position — along with his counterpart on the Grand Council of Chiefs — in favor of the post of Prime Minister, threatening to censure the government if it still refused to bow to the Assembly on this question. Mutaka said he was threatened with prison at this time by the government.[39]

On April 5, 1961, the Assembly called again for creating the position of prime minister. The position must be "created during the course of this session," demanded Mutaka, while Kapwasa argued, in behalf of his colleagues, that it "must be someone who is responsible to the Assembly and serves at its pleasure." The proposal passed by 34 to 6 with 2 abstentions. The Council of Ministers devoted a special session to this question on April 7. Kimba declared that it was "dangerous for a country to have one individual holding all the power," and he was supported by several ministers who opted in principle for the creation of the position, but not at that particular juncture. What emerged was the feeling that "the idea of the creation of this position was a trap; it was wished for solely to overthrow the government afterwards."[40]

The Assembly did not abandon its claim, but it could not carry the day.

The Kibwe affair: The Assembly complained many times of having no precise information on finances from Kibwe. On this basis, it adopted three motions of censure against Kibwe — by twenty-nine votes to six on

[38] The government promised to name later a representative of Haut-Katanga, probably Jean-Chrysostome Mwewa. — Minutes, Council of Ministers, Katanga, April 7, 1961.

[39] Abstract of the Proceedings, Katangan Assembly, November 8, 1960.

[40] Minutes, Council of Ministers, Katanga, April 7, 1961.

April 14, 1961, and by unanimous vote of those present on May 29 and July 29, 1961. "The position of Minister of Finance is vacant," the motion proclaimed, but Kibwe remained a minister nonetheless and even a member of the ministerial triumvirate which replaced Tshombe after Coquilhatville.

Tension between the government and the Assembly president reached its peak in November, 1961. Mutaka was accused of playing the U.N.-Leopoldville game. With Lasimone,[41] a French officer of the Katangan gendarmery participating, a closed session of the Assembly took place.[42] Mutaka, accused of mismanagement, of exceeding the budget, indeed, even of "embezzlement" of funds, was released from all responsibility for management on behalf of the Assembly and was ordered by his peers to reimburse the total amount of the deficit before the end of the legislative session.

It is interesting to note that the Assembly — not confronted with the problems of running the state as the government was — heartily echoed criticisms of Tshombe for using too many European experts and advisers. "The entire wealth of Katanga is to their exclusive profit. . . . [The government] permits the Whites to perpetuate a policy of domination here," Prosper Muyumba declared on April 7, 1961. "It is the Belgian mercenaries who guide our country," Thomas Kabwita Tshombe said on the same day. "We must clean all the Belgians out of the government," Kapwasa argued on September 5, 1961. In the face of the offensive launched by the Assembly members, the Council of Ministers was obliged to pronounce: "In view of the critical period through which Katanga is now passing, the employment of Belgians in the administration is necessary."[43]

[41] Captain Lasimone was first in the service of Albert Kalonji in South Kasai. Kalonji fired him in May, 1961, accusing him of having committed excesses in the tribal wars (letter of May 31, 1961, from Kalonji to Ileo). Lasimone then passed into the service of Katanga, where he played a front-line role in the September, 1961, fighting against the U.N. He was expelled by the Katangans in November, 1961, and went from there to Leopoldville, where the press revealed that he was working for General Mobutu. (In fact, he made a report of some usefulness to the ANC.)

[42] This session is summarized in Abstract of the Proceedings, Katangan Assembly, November 9, 1961.

[43] Minutes, Council of Ministers, Katanga, April 7, 1961. Criticism from the Katangan side also bore upon the survival of customs from the colonial period in the relations between the races. In education, for instance, the Katangans always resented the fact that the International Institute (an interracial secondary school) accepted from Elisabethville, Jadotville, and Kolwezi only 373 Africans for the 2,778 Europeans enrolled.

Throughout 1960–61 and 1962, the Assembly was handicapped by the constitutional quorum. Because of the absence of the Cartel members [44] and parliamentary absenteeism, numerous sessions could not take place. The Assembly would have liked to change this situation, but in vain. The government even decided, on April 7, 1961, to see to it that the Grand Council of Chiefs no longer sat with the Assembly. But the "contagion" was already at work. Despite the governmental acts in favor of traditional authority,[45] Mwenda Munongo, spokesman for the chiefs, declared on April 7, 1961, in the Assembly: "Nothing has changed in the situation of the traditional chiefs." They demanded direct compensation from the moment when the CSK was taken over, salary increases, and the right to re-establish a head tax in order to support local treasuries.

KATANGAN FINANCES

Describing in the CEPSI *Bulletin*, the problems of Katanga's industry, Grosjean and Clémens noted a dual strain on the Katangan budget during the secession: the transformation of a provincial administration into a state administration and the existence of "non-productive expenses imposed upon it by the demands of the external political situation."[46]

The extent of the strain in these two cases is scarcely comparable and there were other pressures exerted on the budget. But it is true that budgetary considerations loomed large for Katanga and that the response given by Elisabethville to Leopoldville during talks on eventual reintegration, including its financial aspects, was affected by them.

The key argument of partisans of Katangan independence, before June 30, 1960, lay in a comparison between the contribution of the province to the Congo budget and the total amount remitted to it by the consent of the central colonial authorities. With receipts of about four billion Belgian francs, Katanga in secession should logically have had very large surpluses. On the Belgian governmental side, more or less discreet appeals were made in this direction to Tshombe, for, if all the revenues were

[44] Charles Mutaka even sent a letter to the director of the central prison in Elisabethville about the incarcerated members of the Assembly from the Cartel. Mutaka asked for a solution "to permit the Assembly to vote the budgets with the required majority." Abstract of the Proceedings, Katangan Assembly, June 2, 1961.

[45] On April 6, 1961, Tshombe had, for example, decided that at the administrative level of the *chefferie*, the traditional chief with his council of notables would be the sole authority, to the exclusion of universal suffrage or other forms inspired by the European electoral system. Authority, at this level, would be exercised "within the framework of custom" on condition of respect for public order.

[46] *Bulletin du CEPSI*, No. 57 (June 6, 1962).

spent or even obligated, it would be difficult to cooperate financially with other provinces, if a Congolese confederation were to be restructured upon Elisabethville. But these appeals were scarcely heeded.

TABLE 5
The Katangan Budget*
(in millions of francs)

	Operating budget		Capital budget	
	Estimates	Expenditures	Authorizations	Expenditures
1961 Expenditures	4,173.4	4,355.5	1,137.8	1,129
1962 Expenditures	3,999.6	4,803.6	223.2	160.3

*See Appendix II, pp. 342–45.

The deficit in the operating budget is due principally to costs of the gendarmery.[47]

In revenues, estimates which had anticipated 4,006 million Belgian francs were scaled down to 3,763 million Belgian francs in 1962.[48] On December 31, 1962, the accumulated deficit in the Katangan treasury was three billion Belgian francs.[49]

Even in foreign exchange, the Katangan situation was vulnerable: revenues of 13.47 billion in 1961, but expenditures of 13.51 billion Belgian francs (7 billion spent by mining companies; 3.9 billion on imports; 2.35 billion on European technicians, travel costs, and so forth).

Thus, in respect to both budget and balance of payments, Katanga had rapidly consumed the anticipated surplus. That explains Kapwasa's statement in the Katangan Assembly on April 14, 1961: "The wealth of Katanga which once was enough for the entire Congo now no longer even covers the needs of Katanga." This situation singularly reduced the flexibility of Katanga's leaders in negotiations with Leopoldville. It was practically impossible for them to make an important gesture without upsetting their own situation and without affecting the whole political structure of Katanga.

[47] 660 million Belgian francs in 1961; 961.7 million Belgian francs in 1962.

[48] Contribution of the UMHK: 2,617 million Belgian francs in 1960; 2,096 million in 1961; and 1,485 million in 1962 (declaration by Henry Fortemps of the UMHK, July 24, 1963).

[49] Despite the fact that the Katangan law of August 8, 1960, that created the National Bank of Katanga limited advances of the Treasury to one billion francs. — Article 6, II, para. 2.

All this was due, in good part, to rising military expenses, which in the 1962 operating budget represented 32 percent of estimated expenditures and 47 percent of those spent, while the budget of the Ministries of Labor and Economic Affairs [50] represented, respectively, only 41.6 million or 1.04 percent and 20.8 million Belgian francs or .52 percent. [51] Nonetheless it is difficult to believe that military expenses alone can explain the flight of foreign exchange and evaporation of revenue. Immediately after the central authorities took over the National Bank of Katanga, a vast European network was discovered which permitted the establishment of substantial "dummy accounts" opened by various banking correspondents. At that time, more precise information was received about the close relationship existing between Tshombe and the French financier Vicomte Olivier de Ferron, vice-president of Imefbank (Banque d'Investissements Mobiliers et de Financement), 6 rue de Petitot, in Geneva, as well as data on the nature of the Swiss corporation, Change BNKSA, located at the same address with a jurist, J. Hoeschstatter, acting in principle as director.

Whatever the case, despite flourishing exports, the budgetary situation and the Katangan treasury were the constant preoccupation of Katanga's financial experts and various measures aimed at improving the situation were taken or envisaged. For example, the exporter was obliged to turn over an advance in foreign exchange to the National Bank of Katanga (BNK) on all exports at the moment when the products crossed the border; an ordinance-law on November 6, 1962, created a "special contribution to independence" of 5 percent "on all funds or securities deposited with any authorized banking agency" (Article 3) and on all property of corporations and individuals. [52]

In this context, the UMHK's direct contribution to the Katangan state was vital to Elisabethville not only because of its size but also because of its "demonstration value" for all the other Belgian companies. That explains why, after November, 1961, when the Katangans thought they

[50] Budget reduced in a state which leaves to the private sector the real direction of social and economic policy.

[51] Police, 7.53 percent; Agriculture, 2.15 percent; Public Health, 5.59 percent; Foreign Affairs and Foreign Trade, .69 percent; Parliament, 1.85 percent; primary, secondary, and technical education, 15.8 percent; Munongo's *Sûreté*, .69 percent.

[52] This ordinance-law was repealed November 11 since "the manner in which it was intended by those who prepared it, and the manner in which it was adopted during a troubled period, might cause a loss of confidence." — Ordinance-law No. 50-296, November 11, 1962.

could detect a desire on the part of the UMHK management in Brussels to renew relations with Leopoldville, Tshombe, his ministers, and his advisers let the UMHK understand that they would not tolerate negotiations by the company alone with the U.N. or with the Congolese Monetary Council. Pressures, accompanied by direct threats concerning the installations, were maintained and increased after U Thant took over the U.N. Secretariat. The new U.N. Secretary-General saw the UMHK payments to Katanga as the necessary condition for the state of secession and intended to deprive Tshombe of the customs receipts and foreign exchange brought to Katanga by copper, cobalt, and other metals exported by the UMHK.

THE GOVERNMENT AND BALUBAKAT OPPOSITION

While the Katangan Assembly seemed at every turn to be seeking contact with its Balubakat members and recommended their participation in the government,[53] no inclination in this direction was evinced by the government. "The Katangan government cannot reconcile itself with a Communist, . . . a traitor," like Sendwe and, moreover, "the majority of the Baluba have rallied" to the authorities in Elisabethville, "only force will prove that we are masters in Katanga."[54] We have already seen how force was exercised in North Katanga during the course of the gendarmery offensive against Kabalo, Manono, and the Baluba centers.

Simultaneously, so-called rallying campaigns were undertaken: "Some of you followed Mwamba Ilunga believing that he was a Muluba. Well . . . we know now . . . [that he is a] Kanioka from the province of Kasai," claimed a tract of January 24, 1961. "The fact that this tract falls into your hands from the heavens proves that we have the strength and the means to break your senseless revolt . . . enough bloodshed . . . this is our final and fraternal appeal before the irreparable." This tract, dated January 31, 1961, was signed by Tshombe, "your Katangan brother."

In this context, any attempt at conciliation was out of place. Two attempts were, however, made by the Cartel at the beginning of 1961.

[53] On July 15, 1961, for example, it was proposed in the Assembly to give 6 portfolios to the Cartel as against 14 to the Conakat; while on July 4, 1961, Mutaka was elated at the amnesty accorded several Balubakat members of the Assembly imprisoned in Elisabethville and at their presence in the Assembly (Hubert Ngoye and Ismael Banza).

[54] Communiqué, Secrétariat d'Etat de l'Information, Service de Presse, Katanga, published in *L'Essor du Katanga* (Elisabethville), January 30, 1961.

The first occurred following a meeting of chiefs and the Balubakat leaders held in Manono, in the presence of Sendwe and U.N. representatives. An appeal was launched on February 8, 1961, for a meeting of the Conakat and the Balubakat which would be held at Kamina base ("by preference") under the auspices of the U.N. The appeal was signed by Sendwe, Mwamba Ilunga, André Shabani, and some twenty other Balubakat leaders.

The second attempt was made in Brussels in late February and early March, 1961, by a substantial delegation from the province of Lualaba, headed by Sendwe and Isaac Kalonji, which asked the Belgian government to encourage a meeting with the representatives of Tshombe "to conclude an armistice and to re-establish normal life throughout Katanga."[55] According to the Lualaba spokesmen, it was a matter for outright Belgian meditation.

These proposals had no echo, except to set off in Elisabethville some uncomplimentary commentary on the proposed mediators. At this point, the bulletin of the *Sûreté* in Katanga attributed to the Balubakat advisers the blackest designs against the Tshombe regime.[56] It even insinuated that it could have been under their influence that in Paris an ordinance was promulgated broadening the conditions under which French nationals who served in a foreign army could lose their nationality.[57] During this period, Elisabethville's sole concern was to keep Sendwe from the Tananarive discussions and accords. No change in attitude occurred after Tshombe's arrest.

[55] See *Congo 1961*, pp. 311–15, two notes from the delegation of the provincial government of Lualaba sent to the Belgian Minister of African Affairs.

[56] No. 112, Appendix 3 (February 10, 1961).

[57] *Journal Officiel*, February 4, 1961. This measure was related to the Trinquier affair.

CHAPTER 6 · *The Trials of Strength in the Second Half of 1961*

HAVING waited too long to authorize Parliament members from the Conakat to participate at the Lovanium conclave, Tshombe found himself on the evening of August 2, 1961, without Conakat representation in the Adoula government of broad national union, which appeared without any doubt whatsoever as the legitimate government. It profited — at least for a time — from the unanimous support of Parliament and from United Nations recognition. In his program, Adoula expressed himself clearly against the secession: "Neither Tshombe, nor certain of his ministers, nor the Union Minière, nor the Belgians who are behind the Katanga secession will stop the Congolese people from recovering their heritage." [1] Simultaneously, the reunification of the *Armée Nationale Congolaise* was to begin. From the moment that reunification took place between Leopoldville and Stanleyville without the Conakat, it was only to be expected that the new government would take a fairly "hard line" against the secession.

U.N. forces in the Congo had been greatly strengthened in Katanga, especially by Indian contingents, but they had no air force at their disposal, if fighting came. Politically, the U.N. was in a position to apply its February resolution, after the agreement concluded with Kasavubu and with the prospect of the new, legitimate Congolese government.

For Katanga, the only paths open, then, were: on the one hand, negotiation with the U.N. and, if possible, with Leopoldville on the military and political level; or on the other, a confrontation which could only be violent and which would place in the balance the very foundations of Katangan authority.

[1] Abstract of the Proceedings, Chamber of Representatives, Congo Republic, August 2, 1961.

THE THEMES OF NEGOTIATIONS IN JULY AND AUGUST 1961

The U.N. resolution of February 21, 1961, provided in paragraph A.2,[2] for measures "for the immediate withdrawal and evacuation from the Congo of all Belgian and other foreign military and paramilitary personnel and political advisers" not under U.N. command "and mercenaries." The only collective "evacuations" which took place were in North Katanga for the mercenaries and in Coquilhatville in April for the advisers of the Tshombe government.

Katanga could have evaded the execution of the resolution relative to military personnel by voiding it of any substance, either by accepting replacement of foreign military officers and mercenaries with soldiers designated by the U.N. or by providing for the reintegration, at least formal, of its gendarmery into a reunified ANC under the command, nominal at least, of General Mobutu. For the advisers, the way to make sure that the resolution would not wreak too much havoc was to accept withdrawal of some advisers who were too obvious or too notorious and to have Leopoldville cover the others within the framework of Katangan participation in the central government.

All these formulas were tried or planned by the Katangans, in June, July, and August, 1961, particularly after the announcement of cooperation with the U.N. made at the beginning of June by the triumvirate which replaced Tshombe. But the attempts or declarations of intentions were not fruitful, either because they had rapidly appeared, in the eyes of Elisabethville authorities and their *ultra* advisers, to be leading too far along the path of dependence on the U.N. and on Leopoldville or because concurrent actions, such as taking on non-Belgian technicians and mercenaries, negated them.

THE QUESTION OF ADVISERS

This question was in reality highly complex. The U.N. resolution was aimed at a category of Europeans employed in political functions by the state of Katanga, whether they operated within the framework of Belgian technical assistance or had been taken on as individuals by the Katangans. The resolution did not, however, aim at European "technicians" in the public or private sectors of Katanga.

But how was one to distinguish objectively between a political adviser and a technician when the latter's task was vital to the secession and to

[2] From whence came the appellation *Adeuxiens* given to those expelled by the U.N.

Tshombe's policy? How was one to monitor the private adviser operating independently elsewhere without any relationship to the state? And where did political "advice" begin?

Furthermore, in the event of withdrawal or evacuation of political advisers, how was the U.N. to avoid letting others — sometimes more dangerous and more inclined to take a "hard line" — succeed them? How were those expelled to be prevented from returning to Katanga after several days, with other identity papers and other tasks, or from continuing to give advice from Rhodesia, or from Europe, by telephone, by letter, or by courier?

These problems were not simple and were discussed at length at U.N.-Belgian meetings in Brussels in June, 1961, during the visit of Sahbani.

In any case, it rapidly became clear that Belgian civilians would be expelled or sent back from Katanga, some because they really were political advisers or considered as such by the U.N., a greater number under the pressure of a quite tangible anti-Belgian feeling in Katanga, arising especially after April, 1961.[3]

At the time of Tshombe's arrest, an important Belgian observer advised Brussels to take steps, in accord with the Katangan government, "to recall as soon as possible about 400 to 500 Belgian technicians if Belgium did not wish to see all traces of the Belgian presence in Katanga disappear," for, according to him, "as a whole, leading circles in Katanga are impatient to escape the tutelage or control of Belgian technicians."[4] In mid-May, a Katangan list bearing the names of a hundred Belgians to be repatriated had been drawn up. This provoked such disquiet that it had to be denied on May 29, but on June 15 the suspension of forty-four Belgian technicians for budgetary reasons was announced. Munongo hoped to be rid of all the Belgians as soon as he could replace them with others, noted O'Brien after his first meeting in June with the Katangan leaders.[5]

[3] See above, pp. 102–5, for the reaction of the Katangans elected to the Assembly. See also the story by Pierre Davister in *Pourquoi Pas?* and by J. K. in *La Libre Belgique* on "the Europeanization of the cadres" in Katanga, reprinted in *Congo 1960*, pp. 795–97.

[4] At this point, the cost of Belgian technicians in Katanga was, for that portion charged to the Belgian budget, 15 million Belgian francs per month. The number of civilian technicians — 750 not counting teachers — was at least equal to that of Belgian officials in the province before June 30, 1960, and they were more concentrated in urban centers and in southern Katanga.

[5] Conor Cruise O'Brien, *To Katanga and Back, a U.N. Case History* (London: Hutchinson, 1962), p. 105. In this regard, the Katangans said they wanted to recruit French: " 'France,' said Mr. Kiwele, 'was the Eldest Daughter of the Church.' "

The Belgian view on the withdrawal of advisers was outlined and debated in the Spaak-Hammarskjöld discussions in Geneva on July 12, 1961. Its essentials were not to rock the boat in Katanga permanently and not to maintain uncertainty among the ten thousand Elisabethville Europeans who feared "an open season on whites." The list of "advisers" was to be determined by the U.N. in the Congo after consultation with the Katangan authorities; it was to be definitive and exhaustive; no evacuation of Belgians was to be ordered without prior consultation with Brussels through U.N. channels.

At this point, the U.N. in the Congo decided on the removal of some advisers, in particular, René Clémens,[6] who obtained a delay on the request of the rector of the university[7] and of Georges Thyssens, who provoked a lively incident with the U.N. in the Congo. According to O'Brien, Muller, who was a special envoy of Fayat, Deputy Minister of the Belgian Ministry of Foreign Affairs, presented Consul Crener with a list of eleven names of Belgians whom the Belgian government agreed the U.N. could expel.[8] Besides authentic advisers, noted the U.N. representative in Katanga, there were several individuals of second rank, teaching at the University of Elisabethville, known as Catholics of the right, and linked ideologically to Clémens, but whom the U.N. refused to categorize as political advisers.[9]

Munongo's riposte to the list was to arrest, then to order the immediate expulsion of, Muller. His police sacked the Belgian consulate, and the ministerial triumvirate, remaining in power despite the return of Tshombe,[10] demanded in writing the departure of the Belgian consul and his deputy. Tshombe had to intervene to settle the difference, so that the Elisabethville Fair, which was just opening its doors, would not be boycotted by the consul. Anti-Belgian feeling ran so high that a news-

[6] Clémens was at Tshombe's side in Kolwezi during January, 1963.

[7] After the secession, on September 14, 1960, Ordinance 800-162, issued by Tshombe, dealt with the creation of a state university in Elisabethville. It would be established with the aid of the Belgian Technical Mission, and it was given the plant and facilities of the former official university created by decree in 1955. Rector Frankiel and Professor Clémens played an essential role in this university and in Tshombe's Katanga.

[8] O'Brien, *To Katanga and Back*, pp. 131–32.

[9] "People like M. de Vos and M. Michel would undoubtedly give bad advice if they were asked, but no one would dream of asking them." *Ibid.*, p. 131.

[10] He and Kimba found that they were granted an additional leave of one month on their return. Tshombe ended his after two weeks.

paper, such as *L'Essor du Katanga*, judged it wise to publish details under the headline: "Let us distinguish between Belgians and Belgians."

From these incidents came a mixed U.N.-Katanga commission, headed by Albert Nyembo, Minister of the Civil Service; this commission was to try to draw up a list of *Adeuxiens* to expel. According to O'Brien, Nyembo's list was the longest[11] and the Katangan minister particularly insisted, in secret and repeatedly, to the U.N. in the Congo that his own *chef de cabinet* Brodur must figure on the list to be evacuated.

From these dealings, the U.N. selected eleven names on August 4. Practically all were *chefs de cabinet* to Katangan ministers. Four were to leave by priority: Tignée, Onckelinx, Ugeux, and Huyghe, respectively, *chefs* or *attachés de cabinet* to the Ministries of Interior, Foreign Trade, Information, and Defense. The others were allowed a delay, namely, Bartelous, Bastin, Brodur, and Frenney, *chefs de cabinet* to the president and to the Ministries of Finance, Civil Service, and Public Health, respectively, as well as Van Roey, director of the National Bank of Katanga,[12] and Jaspar of *La Radio*. This was to be, according to the U.N., an "exhaustive list of all who are political advisers employed in the Katangan administration."[13] Belgian civilians were also expelled, most often on the accusation of being private or *occult* advisers. Thus, on August 26, Decoster, editor of the daily *L'Echo du Katanga*, which had announced the death of Lumumba under the headline "The people have rendered justice," was expelled.

The U.N. operation dealing with advisers did not stop Tshombe from again using regularly the services of Belgian advisers, recruited locally among the independents, even in the private sector, or those living outside Katanga, mainly in Rhodesia, Belgium, or Switzerland.

THE QUESTION OF MERCENARIES AND FOREIGN MILITARY PERSONNEL

Early in June, there arrived in Katanga a Swedish officer, Colonel Bjørn Egge, who was responsible for preparing implementation of the February 21, 1961, resolution concerning foreign military personnel and mercenaries in the Katanga gendarmery. This matter was undertaken by Munongo and decided by him on June 8 with General Sean MacKeown, against the advice of the majority of Katangan ministers who agreed to

[11] "All Belgians are political advisers," Nyembo had declared to O'Brien (*To Katanga and Back*, p. 182).

[12] He was still on the job January 14, 1963.

[13] *L'Essor du Katanga* (Elisabethville), August 4, 1961.

it only the following day, after they were guaranteed that the general staff of the gendarmery would take part in studying the means of implementation.

The basic idea was progressively to replace the military personnel referred to in the resolution by officers and staff — probably mostly Tunisian — named to these positions by the U.N.

Colonel Egge discussed the problem with the head of the Katangan gendarmery, Major Crèvecoeur,[14] and a plan was drawn up at the end of June.[15] Out of 11,000 men in the Katangan gendarmery, 512 were affected by the U.N. resolution. Of the latter, 52 were not part of the officers corps and 460 occupied positions as officers and non-commissioned officers (144 Katangans at this point occupied such posts). Among the 460 foreign officers and non-commissioned officers, 201 were Belgians of so-called *Minaf* status, that is, they took orders from the Belgian Ministry of Foreign Affairs and were assigned by the ministry to Katanga; the others were mercenaries of various nationalities.

The Egge plan of June, 1961, provided for the withdrawal of the 460 officers and non-commissioned officers, according to a program which would allow them to be replaced by U.N. personnel who spoke French or — for those called into direct contact with the ranks — Swahili and Lingala. In retrospect, this plan appears favorable to the Katangans, since, contrary to the U.N. resolution, it did not provide for immediate application but gradual replacement, with a delay ranging from eight to ninety days, depending on the position to be filled. But at that point, those interested in the fate of Katanga did not pause to consider the possible merits of the plan; they merely seized on it as an occasion to denounce the lack of realism of the U.N. in the Congo and to deplore the harmful economic and social repercussions which a withdrawal of European officers and non-commissioned officers from the Katangan gendarmery would entail.

Why did Katanga and Belgium not exhibit support for this plan? On the Belgian side the press argued that the plan had become known in Brussels only in August, but that seems improbable since the problem of applying the U.N. resolutions was discussed in Geneva by Spaak and Hammarskjöld.

[14] He had left Katanga at the end of July, 1961. O'Brien, *To Katanga and Back*, p. 184.

[15] Published in an appendix to Pierre Davister and Phillip Toussaint, *Croisettes et Casques Bleus* (Brussels: Ed. Actuelles, 1962), pp. 230–34.

On the Katangan side, there is practically no mention of it. It seems that they did not seek to apply the Egge plan: (1) because it provided not only for the progressive withdrawal of foreign military personnel but also for the dissolution of mobile Katangan units in the north and the dispatch of the effective core of the gendarmery, the paracommandos, toward a central point in the Congo, where they would form a corps within the ANC; in short, because it deprived the Katangan government of a relatively effective military tool; (2) because the Katangan authorities thought in July, 1961, that it would be possible to halt the U.N. action based upon the February resolution by arranging with Leopoldville for a formal reintegration of the gendarmery into a unified Congolese army. This matter was far advanced; with a mandate from President Kasavubu, General Mobutu went off to Elisabethville on July 12, and there concluded on July 18 an agreement with Tshombe.[16] Under its terms, General Mobutu was to be designated as the future supreme commander of the unified army; Katanga immediately acknowledged his authority and implemented the accord by setting up a command in Elisabethville and giving it to Colonel Ndjoku. Katanga agreed to contribute to the financing of the unified army; the Katangan air force was to be the core of the future Congolese air force, and, in the meantime, a liaison aircraft was put at the immediate disposal of the General.

"As of the present, there is no longer a rebel army," declared General Mobutu on July 20, and the gendarmes operating in the north "have become soldiers in the unified national army and are all therefore at the service of the people." Thus, he asserted once more that he alone had the authority to decide the fate of the European officers. These views perfectly suited the Elisabethville authorities. But, General Mobutu also announced a rapid Africanization and the concentration of all the European military personnel in Leopoldville. On July 26, invoking the apprehensions of Katanga over the agreement, he suspended it, saying, nevertheless, that it was "a good agreement, above all for Katanga." He then recalled his officers to Leopoldville. Despite an affirmation by Munongo on July 27 that "General Mobutu remains commander-in-chief of the unified army," the accord remained "suspended." Katanga had meanwhile sulkily refused to attend Parliament in Lovanium despite Western and U.N. pressures. On July 20, Munongo, in response to an incident with the U.N. in the Congo and to tensions between himself and the Belgian

[16] Text and outcome of the Tshombe-Mobutu agreements in *Congo 1961*, pp. 241–43.

government, had threatened — but unconvincingly — to deal directly with the countries of the East [17] and with Gizenga.

The failure of Katanga to participate in Parliament rendered the agreement untenable, while a temporary Leopoldville-Stanleyville union was being effected at Lovanium. One incident aggravated General Mobutu's new frame of mind toward Katanga. Determined to play a mediator's role between Tshombe and Leopoldville and especially to get the Conakat members of Parliament to participate in the conclave, the General went to Brazzaville, where the Katangan president was visiting at the pressing invitation of the Abbé Youlou. The General was practically ejected when he disembarked in Brazzaville, and he was deeply humiliated by the experience.

By the time Tshombe asked to meet Adoula on August 4, and had decided to authorize the Conakat members of Parliament to sit in Leopoldville on August 6, the military accord had ceased to exist. No basis remained on which to escape the implementation of measures for the withdrawal of foreign military personnel.

For the U.N. in the Congo as well, the application of the Egge plan posed difficult problems: how — without in fact directly supporting the secession — was the U.N. to provide officers for the gendarmery to replace European officers and mercenaries and how could Leopoldville and its government of national union accept such a move by the U.N.?

While negotiating on Lovanium and the future unified army, and for withdrawal of advisers, of Belgian officers on *Minaf* status and mercenaries, the Katangans made numerous foreign contacts to sound out the possibilities for aid and support. In this way, they hoped to resist pressures too overtly exerted in favor of a radical change in the Katangan policy toward Leopoldville and towards the convocation of Parliament. Thus, at the end of June, secret discussions took place in Elisabethville with the secretary of the Rhodesian Minister of Foreign Affairs. In July, the Katangan president's brother headed a mission which was received with Michel Struelens at the U.S. Department of State; the outcome was described in Chapter 5. Evariste Kimba went to France, Italy, and Germany. Jean-Baptiste Kibwe and Gabriel Kitenge went to South Africa and Rhodesia. Daniel Tshombe (another brother of the president) visited Luanda, and the president himself went to Brazzaville to see the

[17] The Ministry of Information of Katanga confirmed on July 28 that Tshombe had previously agreed with Munongo on these threats.

Abbé Youlou, after having made many contacts locally, with the Western consuls and some of their visitors.

In the absence of either a political and military settlement with Leopoldville or an agreement with the U.N. in the Congo on the Egge plan, it became inevitable at the end of August, 1961, that something would be done by the U.N. forces in Katanga to implement the February resolution. On August 24, an ordinance issued by Kasavubu declared undesirable all non-Congolese officers and mercenaries serving in the Katangan forces and ordered their expulsion from the Congo.

OPERATIONS OF AUGUST 28 AND SEPTEMBER 1961

The goal of the U.N. operation of August 28 in Katanga was to force the departure of those whom President Kasavubu called "the undesirables" in his ordinance of August 24, 1961, and whom the February 21 resolution destined in principle for "immediate evacuation." [18]

On the Katangan side, Kimba and Munongo reacted to the threat of expulsion of white military cadres by asserting on August 25 and 26 that the U.N. wanted to disarm the Katangan gendarmery and open the way to the ANC. The U.N. merely denied this charge and implemented on August 28 a plan for occupation of strategic points in Katanga. In the north, this was rapidly reflected in the arrest and transfer to Kamina of numerous white officers. In Elisabethville at daybreak, the vital centers were controlled by the U.N. forces: the radio was temporarily controlled by O'Brien's assistant, Michel Tombelaine, and the residence of Munongo was surrounded. Tshombe, confronted with the *fait accompli*, "bowed to the U.N. decisions," appealed for calm, claimed the right of Katanga to self-determination, thanked the foreigners who had served in the gendarmery, and announced total Africanization, at all echelons, of his armed forces.

The U.N. in the Congo was highly pleased with the peaceful character of its "Operation Rumpunch" which had had no casualties; the foreign officers had been asked by Tshombe, on the one hand, and by their

---

[18] In this work, dealing in particular with the secession of Katanga as a political phenomenon, it seemed proper not to treat as such the military operations: neither those of North Katanga, nor those which set the Katangan gendarmery in opposition to the U.N. in September and December, 1961. We give to those subjects the minimum information necessary for comprehension of their repercussions on the destiny of the secession. For an account of the operations, see *Congo 1961*, pp. 511–51, or works such as those cited previously of O'Brien, or of Davister and Toussaint.

own governments on the other, not to offer resistance, and the expulsions produced satisfaction among Africans in the Katangan gendarmery.

Under these conditions, the Western consuls, presided over by Crener, Consul General of Belgium, asked O'Brien to stop the arrests. The arrests could be dispensed with since the consular corps could, in the person of Crener, take charge of the repatriation of the foreign officers and mercenaries in the Katangan gendarmery. It would be better to avoid any risk of an incident, and the U.N. accepted Crener's suggestion, suspending arrests on August 28 at 3 P.M.

According to O'Brien and the U.N. report,[19] the consul's undertaking concerned *all* mercenaries and foreign military officers, but on August 29, Crener told O'Brien that on instructions from Brussels he could take responsibility only for the repatriation of Belgians, and, among them, Crener was to distinguish between those on *Minaf* status whom he could "order" to return to Belgium and the others, simple mercenaries whom he could only "advise" to leave. The U.N. gave those concerned twenty-four hours to present themselves to the U.N. for repatriation, after which time the U.N. would recommend arrest before expulsion. This decision provoked loud protests in Belgium, including the governmental level where the "internment" of *Minaf* officers was opposed. The U.N. in the Congo authorized seventy Belgian officers to remain in the consulate building until transportation was ready for them. Some left on August 31, saluted by the consul ("you have struggled for a just cause, with an ideal of peace") and by Joseph Yav, Katangan Secretary of Defense. In Brussels, the first to arrive were met without ceremony by an army car, driven by a corporal.[20]

The balance sheet of the operation is spectacular:

On September 8, 338 mercenaries and foreign officers out of a total of 443 were repatriated or awaited repatriation. For the career Belgians (*Minaf*), only 10 out of a total of 177 failed to respond to the U.N. appeal.

However, apart from Belgians on *Minaf* status, 95 mercenaries had not been expelled: 11 of 21 French officers on the list failed to appear, as did 54 out of 175 Belgian mercenaries and 30 of the 60 mercenaries of other nationalities. The hard core remained and, moreover, the U.N. had only the power to "evacuate" the military *Adeuxiens* not to stop

---

[19] U.N. Document, Security Council, S/4940, September 14, 1961.

[20] The next day, following protests from *La Libre Belgique* against the absence of an official welcome, four *attachés de cabinet* were at the airport to await the remaining repatriated Belgian officers.

them from re-entering clandestinely and from reinfiltrating the gendarmery. And, now that the initial moment of surprise was past and
the consuls had obtained a delay, what was to prevent the mercenaries
from abandoning Katangan uniforms for civilian clothes and, provided
with all the required official papers, blending into the mass of European
technicians legitimately working in Katanga?

After the August 28 operation, differences setting O'Brien and Tombelaine against Munongo dominated relations between the U.N. and the
Katangan authorities in Elisabethville. Munongo was accused on August 31 by the U.N. in the Congo of having intended to foment attacks
against U.N. personnel, and O'Brien asked for his suspension or dismissal as Minister of the Interior. The accusation was based on the testimony of a Belgian mercenary, one Crémer, whose assertions were denied
and whose moral integrity was questioned by the Katangans.[21]

Whatever the basis of the accusation, on September 1 it resulted in
a breakdown of relations on the spot between the U.N. representative
and the Katangan authorities. At the same time, following the arrest of
R. Bintu,[22] a Muluba from Kasai and resident minister of the Mining
State in Elisabethville, and the operations led against the Baluba suspected of cooperation with the U.N. in the Congo, hundreds, then
thousands, of Baluba asked the U.N. troops for asylum — 10,000 by
September 4, 25,000 by September 8. Thus was born the human inferno
of the "Baluba camp," which was rapidly to pack together tens of thousands of refugees.[23] Meanwhile, anti-U.N. demonstrations took place on
September 6 and 7 in Elisabethville; the Katangan Assembly proclaimed
once more its support for Katangan independence on September 6, and
Tshombe declared on September 9 that an invasion of Katanga was imminent, with the ANC benefiting from U.N. aid. Tombelaine was the object of an attempted abduction on September 9, while the U.N. reinforced
its garrison by dispatching a battalion of Gurkhas to Elisabethville.

While the U.N. tried again on September 11 to encourage a meeting

[21] Later transferred to Leopoldville, Crémer was killed trying to escape.
[22] Accused of maintaining suspicious relations with other provinces and accused
by Munongo of embezzlement.
[23] The Katangan authorities accused the U.N. in the Congo of having deliberately provoked panic among the Baluba to use them, at an opportune moment,
against the Tshombe regime. The U.N. in the Congo, to the contrary, accused Munongo's *Sûreté* of provocative operations against the Baluba. A report on this problem, written by a U.N. official working on social questions in Elisabethville, with a
Katangan commentary, appeared in an interesting brochure: *Le Camp des Baluba*
(Brussels: Charles Dessart, 1962).

between Tshombe and Adoula, then direct contact between Tshombe and the Secretary-General on September 13, in Leopoldville, the Katangan gendarmery encircled an Irish U.N. company in Jadotville, and O'Brien ordered the expulsion of Europeans in Munongo's *Sûreté*.

On September 13, a direct confrontation took place in Elisabethville between the Katangan forces and those of the U.N. in the Congo. From an operational point of view, the U.N. tried to repeat its August 28 operation and to make itself master of the strategic points. The surprise effect this time was nil and fighting was bloody, especially at the post office and Radio Katanga. Kibwe agreed to cooperate with the U.N. but his appeals had practically no effect, Tshombe, Munongo, and Kimba having escaped the U.N. dragnet.[24] The military aspect of the operation was unfavorable to the U.N. In Elisabethville, little Katangan groups — officered by Europeans, mostly French, and assisted by white civilians — grappled with the U.N. forces. A Fouga ("the Lone Ranger") wrought havoc upon the U.N. forces and met no resistance; while in Jadotville, the Irish remained surrounded, and at Kamina, the Katangans turned to the attack.

Politically, the operation was disastrous for the U.N. in the Congo and bad for Leopoldville as well.

Brussels,[25] London, and all the countries which sought to avoid the overthrow of Tshombe demanded a cease-fire. They condemned the U.N. military action and by their actions in Katanga did not hide where their sympathies lay. The Rhodesians massed troops on the border of Katanga. British pressure was to be exerted on Hammarskjöld in Leopoldville by Lord Landsdowne. The Abbé Youlou refused Hammarskjöld's plane permission to land at Brazzaville. U.S. Senator Thomas J. Dodd in Elisabethville supported Tshombe. Paris accused the U.N. of undertaking an action against the U.N. Charter. The Extraordinary Commissioner for Katanga, Egide Bocheley-Davidson (MNC/Lumumba) was blocked at the airport and could not go into town where martial law had been decreed.

On September 16, the military position of the U.N. in the Congo had deteriorated in both Jadotville and Elisabethville, and the U.N. Secretary-

---

[24] According to O'Brien, Tshombe was at the home of the British consul, then went to Rhodesia, with the assistance of the consul.

[25] The U.N. in the Congo accused snipers of firing on the U.N. troops from the Belgian consular building. Brussels vehemently denied this. Belgian doctors working in Elisabethville denounced "the U.N. atrocities" and the Red Cross was aroused over them.

General proposed to meet Tshombe at Ndola to negotiate a cease-fire. During the night of September 17, the plane carrying Hammarskjöld and his deputies crashed in Rhodesia. The negotiations on the cease-fire began again on September 19 in Ndola between Tshombe and Mahmoud Khiari. The 158 encircled Irish troops of the U.N. forces surrendered to the Katangans and the Indian reinforcements sent to relieve them turned back. The U.N. forces' casualties numbered twelve dead and sixty wounded.

On September 20, Khiari and Tshombe came to an agreement on a cease-fire which provided for an exchange of prisoners. Adoula protested the accord.

It seems that on the U.N. side, the operation had been undertaken under very equivocal conditions. O'Brien thought he was beginning an operation "to liquidate" the secession, including, among other things, the execution of warrants issued on September 9 by the Leopoldville court for the arrest of Tshombe, Munongo, Kimba, Kibwe, and Charles Mutaka.[26] The U.N. representative declared that he had received instructions establishing this line of action from the Tunisian Khiari; while in Leopoldville, Hammarskjöld confirmed to the British representative that the operation underway was a simple repeat performance of that of August 28, to expel the last *Adeuxiens*; he had already sought contact with Tshombe to put an end to the fighting.

From the military point of view, the U.N. had underestimated the capacity for resistance of the gendarmery. A number of foreign military personnel had been able to hold onto their posts until September 13 or to return after a round trip to Europe, thus organizing the resistance of the Katangan gendarmery.

BETWEEN TWO ROUNDS

In the sequel to the September operation in Katanga, the participants reacted perforce in different fashions.

With the agreement of the Secretary-General, ad interim, who met with the Consultative Committee on this point, the U.N. Secretariat accepted the agreement of September 20 on the cease-fire and its corollary of October 13, with the prime object of obtaining the release of U.N. forces taken prisoner by the Katangans in Jadotville. A change of U.N. personnel took place in Elisabethville, in a direction which was to give the Katangan authorities the feeling of chalking up an additional point.

[26] A copy of the warrant for arrest appears in O'Brien, *To Katanga and Back*, p. 248.

Meanwhile, the countries having contingents in the Congo and the Secretariat were determined not to be caught again in a position of military weakness. Aircraft were requested from several countries (including India, Norway, and Sweden) to avoid being once more at the mercy of the Fouga or Fougas of the Katangan air force.

Moreover, the pressure in favor of a change in the mandate grew in October and November, 1961. From the U.N. point of view, the weakness of paragraph A.2 of the February 21, 1961, resolution and of Kasavubu's ordinance of August 24, 1961, was that they in fact permitted those expelled to return without too much difficulty. The Adoula government on the one hand, the members of the Consultative Committee on the other, felt that the only effective means would be not to expel the mercenaries, but to transfer them to Leopoldville, where they would be turned over to the Congolese authorities and imprisoned. Kasavubu issued an ordinance to this effect on November 13, 1961, and Minister Christophe Gbenye asked the U.N. to take it into account.[27] On November 24, the Security Council adopted a resolution which provided that the future *Adeuxiens* would either be expelled or apprehended and placed in detention while awaiting legal proceedings. The same resolution explicitly authorized the Secretary-General to employ "a requisite measure of force . . . if necessary" against the *Adeuxiens*.[28]

The Central Government: Adoula and his ministers bitterly criticized the cease-fire agreement accepted by the U.N. in the Congo. Leopoldville announced through the government and through the Chief of State on October 19, 1961, that it would use "its own means" to reduce the secession. Concretely, that meant a military attempt against Katanga. Two battalions from Thysville and Leopoldville were sent to Kasai on September 21 and at the end of October, battle took place within the Katangan frontiers, but without profound repercussions. Also, the ANC from Stanleyville penetrated Katanga and on November 14 reached Albertville, which had been abandoned several days earlier by Tshombe's gendarmery and had passed into Balubakat hands.[29]

In fact, the double offensive was marred by serious defects: mutiny at Luputa and violence against Europeans in Luluabourg (November 1 to 3); mutiny in Albertville and massacre of 13 Italian aviators at Kindu.

[27] *Congo 1961*, pp. 473–74.
[28] See text of the resolution of November 24, 1961, in Appendix II, pp. 332–33.
[29] Prosper Mwamba Ilunga was there before the arrival of the ANC.

These events weakened the political position of Adoula. On its part, the U.N. concluded from this that everything should be done to avert armed conflict between the ANC and the Katangan gendarmery. The United States concluded from the offensive that Gizenga must not be left with a monopoly over action against the secession and that the U.N. in the Congo should meet a substantial part of Adoula's demands concerning Katanga. At the end of November, Adoula announced, moreover, that Jason Sendwe would be the Extraordinary Commissioner General to Katanga.

The Katanga authorities: The cease-fire concluded with the U.N. in the Congo was interpreted as a victory by the Katangans and their advisers.[30] Exaltation was great in the gendarmery where the glory of the new Commander-in-Chief was celebrated: "Muké the victorious."[31] In the political sphere, the Katangan leaders had the feeling "of the elements of strength in their position," and the offer to reopen negotiations made to Adoula on October 17 set forth Katangan proposals on customs and economic union, monetary and military union, and on the resumption of exports via the "national routes" and on aid in Congolese francs to Leopoldville.

These offers could perhaps have seduced the Leopoldville authorities in December, 1960, or in March, 1961. But, they had no chance of being taken into consideration by the Adoula government, nor by the Congolese Parliament. Leopoldville declared that it was simply impossible, morally, legally, and politically, for it to deal with Katanga on bases other than the provisional *Loi Fondamentale* of May, 1960, that is, with Katanga as a Congolese province.

On the Belgian side: With the Spaak-Lefèvre government, official opinion could be summed up as follows: on the one hand, the Katanga se-

---

[30] Tshombe's adviser, a native of Liège, wrote to him on October 17: "Our group is very happy with the arrangements in the definitive agreement on the cease-fire. . . . And we hope that all will be settled within the shortest possible time to permit its application. Besides control of Luano and of the telecommunications installations, it appears to us of capital importance, in the accord, that the control of entry to the Elisabethville airport is well in the hands of the Katangan authorities, to guarantee freedom of external movement both for technicians in the private sector and for technicians of your choice in the public sector." — From an unpublished letter.

[31] Minutes, Council of Ministers, Katanga, January 3, 1961. Tshombe's answer to Kimba, who was astonished to see Yav wear the uniform of a colonel: "We were going to name the Adjutant Muké, but he does not have an imposing figure. That is how we came to make Minister Yav a symbol."

cession had failed in the sense that no recognition abroad had been forthcoming to consecrate it and international pressures were being exerted against it, especially from the Eastern bloc, from numerous Afro-Asian countries, and from the United States. The existence of the Adoula government rendered more and more improbable a diplomatic success for Tshombe. The new outlook for Belgo-Congolese relations promoted a desire at the Belgian governmental level for a certain degree of disengagement from Katanga.[32] On the other hand, the order established by Tshombe in Katanga was supported rather widely in Belgium and very strongly in Katanga by those who identified it with Belgian interests, while the balance of forces remained temporarily favorable to an understanding which would not necessarily entail a fundamental revision of the situation that obtained in Katanga.[33]

The Belgian government's view, favoring reconciliation based upon a certain balance of forces, rejected any military solution in Katanga, since a settlement through use of arms might provoke reactions of panic or bring casualties among the Europeans of Katanga with all that implied as a reinforcement for anti-U.N. and pro-Katanga groups in Belgian opinion.

As for reconciliation between Leopoldville and Elisabethville, Brussels was rapidly persuaded that it could not result from direct Belgian mediation[34] and probably not from a spontaneous initiative of the parties involved. Spaak felt, in addition, "that by charging the U.N. to play an important role in trying to reconcile the Katangan government and the central government, a grave error had been committed."[35]

Under these conditions, the Spaak view was that it would be necessary "to encourage conciliation."

Having failed in his request — formulated without any illusions of success, it seems — to introduce an appeal to reconciliation in the Security Council resolution of November, 1961, Spaak then took an ini-

[32] Spaak kept his distance vis-à-vis the secession, especially in his speeches to the Security Council on November 17, 1961. Several days earlier, the Belgian government had met Congolese criticism by withdrawing the passports of Belgian mercenaries still in Katanga: "I think, of course, that this was not very effective, but I can do nothing else," he declared in respect of this to the Belgian Chamber of Deputies on December 19, 1961.

[33] It is not without interest to note that at the end of November, 1961, changes occurred in the highest echelons of the Société Générale de Belgique that certainly did not strengthen the "secessionist" inclinations of the company.

[34] Declaration by Spaak to his party, October 14, 1961.

[35] Abstract of the Proceedings, Belgian Chamber of Deputies, December 12, 1961

tiative, in concert with Lord Alexander Douglas-Home in London, on November 30.[36]

The idea was to define a possible basis for reconciliation (reintegration of Katanga into a Congolese state of an accentuated federal type) and to entrust to a mediator, who could have been Leopold Senghor, the task of proposing it to Leopoldville and Elisabethville. A basis could easily have been elaborated by Brussels and London, whose points of view converged, but it had no chance of being carried out unless it won American backing at the U.N. and above all support in Africa, where logically the mediator would be recruited.

At this juncture, the United States was reluctant, fearing "to give too much importance to Tshombe in the resolution of the problem."

KATANGAN MILITARY FORCES

To the extent that there existed after the September confrontation a chance of a renewed struggle between the U.N. and the Katangan gendarmery and insofar as the ANC was trying to operate against Katanga on two fronts, from Kasai and from Kivu, the questions posed in October–November, 1961, were the following: exactly what did Tshombe's military force represent, and on what foundations did it rest after the expulsion of many of its foreign military officers?

Personnel: The gendarmery, 11,000 strong at the minimum, were grouped in five sectors (Elisabethville, Jadotville, Kamina, Kongolo, Kolwezi) with headquarters in Elisabethville, under the command of General Muké. In Jadotville had been set up an operational general staff of Europeans (Lasimone and de Claem, in October, 1961), while Colonel René Faulques headed a special force. The Europeans at this point included the *Adeuxiens* against whom the U.N. had not been able to move in August and September or who had returned after expulsion. There were those who had been newly recruited[37] and brought in by

---

[36] The text of the Spaak plan appeared in the *Courrier Hebdomadaire du CRISP*, No. 184, and the *Courrier Africain du CRISP* (renamed *Travaux Africains*), No. 17. On November 29, Sir Roy Welensky let it be known that Tshombe was favorable to such mediation.

[37] At the beginning of 1962, Ropagnol, a former French parachutist lieutenant, released from active duty after the barricades episode in Algiers, then recruited in Katanga in 1961, was arrested for recruiting mercenaries in Toulouse for Katanga. A Belgian who provided "financial" liaison with Geneva was likewise arrested. Further, two more centers for recruitment were revealed in 1962: one in Johannesburg and one in Bulawayo in Southern Rhodesia.

Union Aéro-maritime de Transports (UAT) or by Sabena; the "volunteers" recruited locally to whom the Katangan authorities furnished an "order of mobilization," as well as occasional soldiers called up during the course of action. A European who had to escape the U.N. search could, with the agreement of Tshombe and of the *Sûreté*, have a borrowed identity, a permanent resident's card ("registration") and a permit to carry arms. In certain cases, mercenaries were camouflaged by attaching them to the Ministry of Public Works.

In addition, Lunda and Bayeke warriors as well as Baluba loyal to paramount Chief Kasongo Nyembo had been armed with Fal, Mausers, and sub-machine guns of Belgian origin in readiness for guerrilla activities.

Equipment: Military equipment for the gendarmery was generally brought in by air[38] or water, especially around Lobito or Pointe Noire, by commercial agents who could obtain licenses in countries friendly to Katanga (Congo-Brazzaville, South Africa, Spain, Portugal) whereas civilian equipment was treated as any other kind of supplies for Katanga. The gendarmery was given small arms (rifles and carbines) and field weapons (Bazookas, cannons, and sub-machine guns). Transport was abundant, of French, German, and British make. Radio communication was maintained by Japanese-made equipment and that furnished by local industry. Airplanes — Pipers, Harvards, Klemms, and Dorniers — were furnished, even after August, 1961, through South Africa, Angola, and the Rhodesias, originating in Central Europe. However, deliveries of the Fougas were blocked.

In Katanga, enterprises worked on defense projects: one company made Mammouth tanks and produced bombs for planes;[39] another furnished explosives and lent its demolition experts and equipment for laying mines or destroying bridges; another furnished vehicle armor, while "on requisition" — real or fictitious — another provided new landing strips for airplanes. By requisition, the authorities secured the services of civilian

[38] The Katangan affair drew attention to relations with certain airlines. Thus, on June 11, 1961, discussions took place in Luxembourg between Katangan delegates and the "Seven Seas Airlines" which ran flights from Luxembourg to Brazzaville to Elisabethville. An airplane belonging to this company was seized in Leopoldville. Earlier, in April, 1961, there was a report of an airplane transporting arms to Africa — the plane belonged to a private company in West Germany. — U.N. Document, Security Council, S/4789, April 14, 1961.

[39] The UMHK denied on December 8, 1961, that it had produced bombs and tanks.

airplanes of Air Katanga (Sabena-Sobelair) for the dispatch of reinforcements, as in July, 1961, or for tasks for which the planes had obviously not been designed.[40] This applies very broadly with regard to means of transport, nominally the property of private firms, large or small.

OPERATIONS OF DECEMBER 1961 AND THE KITONA AGREEMENTS

The ANC march into the region of Albertville had once more touched off a wave of anti-U.N. feeling in Elisabethville in November. Munongo had accused the U.N. troops of being nothing but mercenaries in the service of the central government. But this wave assumed tidal proportions after the vote on the November 24 resolution authorizing the use of force to arrest or to expel foreign military personnel and advisers in Katanga.

Tshombe, on November 25, berated the U.N. before a Katangan crowd at the Elisabethville stadium: "Tomorrow or the day after," he declared, "there will be a test of strength. . . . As each successive path becomes impracticable, no U.N. mercenary can feel secure, wherever he is." At the same time, a certain "Colonel Alain, Commander of the Movement for Independence and Resistance" — publicly disavowed by Tshombe — distributed provocative proclamations against the U.N. threatening reprisals such as "collective poisoning of the U.N. colony," launching appeals to General Charles de Gaulle in the "Free French" style, and asserting that any armed U.N. patrol in Elisabethville would be attacked by his commandos.

In this atmosphere, incidents erupted: arrests of U.N. officials by the Katangan gendarmery on November 28; skirmishes at the airport on December 2; gunshots fired from a Katangan roadblock at a U.N. car on December 3. The U.N. troops demanded in vain complete freedom of movement and the dismantlement of the roadblocks, and, on December 5, invoking legitimate self-defense, the U.N. undertook to force the issue.

At this point, Tshombe was absent. On December 2, he had gone to Brazzaville without revealing whether he sought contact with Adoula or an exchange of views with the Abbé Youlou, and, on December 3, he was in Paris.

[40] Katangan Ordinance 221/156 of September 26, 1960, already provided for payment of personnel flying Sabena planes on military missions at the request of gendarmery headquarters. Reparations were also provided for planes damaged in the course of these missions. — Ordinance 081/237 of December 13, 1960.

In Katanga, the military situation was not at all comparable to that of September. The U.N. this time had jets at its disposal and used them. The Katangan gendarmery was not so well led and less effective.

The Katangan leaders threatened a "scorched earth" policy (Kimba, on December 6) and to provoke the killing of all the U.N. troops in Elisabethville (Munongo on December 6). In Paris, Tshombe was tough with the UMHK: "I know that the Union Minière has abandoned me and now deals with the central government. This company will pay dearly for its treason. We are all set to blow up every Union Minière installation in Elisabethville, Kolwezi, and Jadotville."[41] He rejected in any case the idea of any negotiation at this juncture and accepted the military challenge of the U.N. in the Congo.

The situation was far from being brilliant for Tshombe in Elisabethville. Two thousand gendarmes out of three thousand in Elisabethville refused to fight.[42] Two burgomasters in Albert and Katuba communes adopted a position for which they were suspended by the Katangan government.[43] The fighting turned to the advantage of the U.N. Sir Roy Welensky, supported by London, firmly requested Tshombe to return immediately to Katanga.

At this point, a lively campaign was launched in the press against the military acts and methods of the U.N., which struck at civilian buildings, factories, and residential areas, and caused civilian casualties. Doctors, professors, Belgian groups of all kinds protested in Elisabethville against "the savagery" of the U.N. operation[44] and these denunciations provided fuel for indignant protests against the U.N. operation in the Congo in all the Western capitals.

Spaak protested in the U.N. with the approval of the whole Belgian Parliament. He could not "discover the political line, nor find the legal basis" for the war operation launched by the U.N. But above all, he recommended a cease-fire and a renewal of plans for conciliation. On this point, London, Paris, The Hague, Athens, Ankara, and Lisbon supported him at the NATO Council meeting in Paris on December 12, and in

[41] Remarks of Tshombe in Paris, reported by E. Rouleau in *Le Monde* (Paris), December 8, 1961.

[42] Mutaka in Abstract of the Proceedings, Katangan Assembly, January 19, 1962.

[43] *Arrêté Ministériel,* 3022/17 and 3022/18 of January 31, 1962. The two burgomasters were suspended on a charge of abandoning their posts on December 2 and of having tried at this point to overthrow the Katangan government by subversive propaganda.

[44] The term comes from the rector of the University of Elisabethville.

Africa several heads of French-speaking states made pronouncements
to the same effect, including the Abbé Youlou and Presidents Tsiranana
and Senghor. Tshombe on his part continued to appeal for all-out war
(on December 13), but he would agree — under certain conditions — to
see Adoula in a "neutral" city, in a country within the Union of African
and Malagasy states,[45] which indicates either that he was not yet aware
of the real situation or that he believed he could count on some effective
support.

Lord Home and Spaak exerted pressure in two ways. Through U Thant
they tried to get the U.N. to propose or decide upon a cease-fire.[46] Then,
they brought pressure to bear on Tshombe to discuss with Adoula in
Leopoldville the basis for a federal state, in the presence, if possible, of
a "Mr. Good Offices." Neither Thant, nor President Kennedy would
accept the idea of a cease-fire before the U.N. had realized its objectives,
although one could not tell whether they meant simply restored freedom
of movement for U.N. troops, or a complete application of the U.N. resolutions on mercenaries[47] and on the reintegration of Katanga.

The pressures on Tshombe eventually worked as a result of military
developments: the Katangan president wired President Kennedy on December 15, 1961, that he was ready to meet Adoula provided that the
United States could give him a guarantee of safety and that the fighting
would stop in Elisabethville. President Kennedy made Ambassador Edmund Gullion in Leopoldville his personal representative in this matter.

Ambassador Gullion met first with the central authorities, before joining Tshombe at Ndola, where the latter had arrived with the three consuls
from the Western countries on the Security Council. The U.N. in the
Congo did not accept the cease-fire, but agreed to suspend operations
and not to act except in case of Katangan attack.

[45] Telex to Senator Norbert Hougardy, December 15, 1961.

[46] "The cease-fire was a good way to escape defeat for Katanga and conquest
by the U.N., for our soldiers were at the end of their tether." — Mutaka in Abstract
of the Proceedings, Katangan Assembly, January 19, 1962.

[47] During the events of December, *La Libre Belgique* (Brussels) wrote on December 15, 1961: "The Europeans take up arms against the U.N. troops and are
fighting in ever increasing numbers at the side of the Katangans. Who could say
they are wrong? They are no longer mercenaries, but people outraged by the
crimes of the U.N. who line up beside the victims of one of the greatest injustices
in history." Nyembo, Minister of the Civil Service, recognized the presence of
foreign soldiers in the fighting, but he described them on December 6, 1961, as "a
little group of idealists come from different countries who, in the face of so many
horrors, massacres, rapes, and pillages of churches, offered to aid Katanga."

The site for the meeting was the base at Kitona, close to the mouth of the Congo. On December 20, the delegations met, and in the evening, Ralph Bunche for the U.N. and Ambassador Gullion for the United States were invited to take part in the discussions. On December 21, about 2:30 A.M., Tshombe issued an eight-point declaration; it reflected the balance of forces which had been momentarily established by the November 24 resolution and by the U.N. operation of December 5:

1. Accepted the application of the *Loi Fondamentale* of May 19, 1960.
2. Recognized the indivisible unity of the Republic of the Congo.
3. Recognized President Kasavubu as Chief of State.
4. Recognized the authority of the central government throughout the republic.
5. Accepted the participation of representatives from the province of Katanga on the governmental commission, on January 3, 1961, in Leopoldville, to study and examine the draft of the constitution.
6. Promised to take all steps necessary to permit deputies and senators from Katanga to carry out their national mandate in Parliament after a certain date which was to be determined later.
7. Agreed that the Katangan gendarmery be placed under the authority of the President of the republic.
8. Promised to respect the resolutions of the General Assembly and the Security Council and to facilitate their execution.

Tshombe wrote the same day to Bunche. The Kitona declaration would have to be approved by "the competent Katangan authorities" on his return to Elisabethville, for, because of his precipitous departure, these authorities had not been able to give him a mandate to speak in their name. Those who had gone through the business of the Leopoldville accords of June, 1961, after the liberation of Tshombe, were not sanguine about the chances for application of the eight points.

In Elisabethville on December 22, the Council of Ministers declared itself incompetent and sent the question to the Assembly. The president's office published a communiqué regreting the intervention of Ambassador Gullion in the Kitona discussions and insisting on the fact that the eight point declaration, presented by Ambassador Gullion, had not been signed by Tshombe, who did not under the circumstances have a mandate to bind Katanga.

Adoula accused "Tshombe and his henchmen . . . of once more betraying" their given word. In London, the Foreign Office promised its aid to implement the Kitona accords. The U.N. considered the declaration as a Katangan commitment without any reservations. Ambassador Gullion felt that Tshombe would be completely discredited if he did not implement the December 21 accord.

Meanwhile, in Elisabethville, the fighting ceased and the situation improved for the Katangan government. Two points of the declaration could be implemented right away: the dispatch of the Conakat members of Parliament to Leopoldville and of experts in constitutional law. For the rest, Katanga did not consider itself bound so long as the Assembly had not pronounced itself. One serious event for Tshombe was to determine its position: on December 31, 1961, the ANC attacked in the north and the gendarmery had to evacuate Kongolo.

CHAPTER 7 · *From Kitona to Leopoldville:*
The Adoula-Tshombe Talks (December 21, 1961
to June 26, 1962)

O N December 21, 1961, Tshombe had transmitted to the assistant
Secretary-General of the U.N. the eight-point declaration adopted
at Kitona, whereby he recognized the unity of the Republic of the Congo
as well as the authority of the central government throughout the territory, and he agreed to take steps to reintegrate the province of Katanga
into the republic.

In fact, the adherence of Tshombe to the eight points of Kitona was
barely formalized: from December 21, he let it be understood that he
did not have the power to make a valid commitment on behalf of the
Elisabethville authorities and Katangan ministers — especially Kimba —
questioned the conditions under which the accords were reached, namely
American pressure exerted at Kitona on Tshombe in favor of the central
government.

At the beginning of 1962, the eight points of Kitona had not been
officially denounced, but the Katangan government had not endorsed
them. It was content to pass them on to the Katangan Assembly for judgment. The Assembly — as it was composed on June 30, 1960 — was convened at Kamina by Kasavubu (Ordinance 104) to allow participation of
Assembly members from the Balubakat, while the first Conakat members
of Parliament and Katangan experts arrived in Leopoldville to take part
in the commission for reform of the constitution. Meanwhile, the ANC
made progress in the northern part of the province, and the Katangan
gendarmery there had to evacuate Kongolo.

THE KITONA ACCORDS AT THE KATANGAN ASSEMBLY

Whether the Balubakat members would be present when the Katangan
Assembly decided on the Kitona accords was a particularly important
question for the parties involved. The site of the meeting was itself deci-

sive in regard to participation. Kasavubu had chosen Kamina. Tshombe
held out for Elisabethville, invoking in a letter of January 1, 1962, to
the Chief of State, the illegality of Ordinance 104.[1]

The Katangan Assembly was therefore convened in Elisabethville. On
January 3, the Assembly had to adjourn after ten minutes. Nineteen deputies out of sixty-nine were in session and Tshombe himself was absent
from Elisabethville. On January 8, the Assembly approved an appeal
made through the U.N., to a specialist in international law, and encouraged the Foreign Affairs and General Policy committees in the task of
examining the Kitona accords. On February 15, the Assembly adopted
by a vote of thirty-five out of forty-two present a resolution in which
it accepted the eight points of Kitona "as a possible basis for discussion"
and mandated the Katangan government to seek a solution with the
central government "in the spirit of the proposed declaration." The Assembly also formulated certain demands (that the ANC not be sent and
that the province of North Katanga not be recognized; right of initiative
of the gendarmery in North Katanga; cancellation of the nomination of
the high commissioner for Katanga; amnesty for all Katangan officials)
and reserved for itself the right to accept or reject final agreements concluded with the central authorities.[2]

This position of the Assembly was interpreted by Adoula on February 26 in a broadcast speech: "Inspired by the speech of the President,
the provincial Assembly ratifies the declaration signed by Tshombe at
Kitona, but hedges it about with reservations which in effect nullify it
and render it without substance. It is a clever trick, consistent with the
policy followed up to now by President Tshombe."

During the course of the debate on February 15, Tshombe had arisen
to inveigh against the activities of the ANC in North Katanga, to denounce
"the methods of the Americans who have financed and continue to finance
the war and disorders in Katanga" and the Department of State in Washington "under the thumb of voracious financiers," who are sworn to
eliminate the competition of Katangan copper. The Katangan president
clearly demurred from the Kitona accords, falsified, according to him, by
the foreign intervention.

The day after the February 15 resolution, Tshombe brought together
in Jadotville the traditional chiefs who supported his government, led

[1] *Second livre blanc du gouvernement central sur la sécession katangaise*
(Leopoldville: Central Government, 1962), pp. 84–87.

[2] Text of the resolution, in *Congo 1962* (Brussels: CRISP, 1963), pp. 334–36.

by the Mwata Yamvo and Chiefs Kasongo Nyembo and Mwenda Munongo. Here again there was opposition to the penetration of the ANC, to
the activities of Jason Sendwe, the Commissioner of State, and to the
freedom of movement of the U.N. in the direction of Jadotville.

It was with the support of this dual "mandate" from the Assembly
and the chiefs that Tshombe proposed in a letter to Adoula that they
meet at the base in Kamina "to reach a solution in the spirit of the Kitona
declaration." Despite the disappointment caused by Tshombe's speech
of February 15 and by the reservations contained in the Katangan Assembly resolution, Adoula invited Tshombe to Leopoldville for discussions which were to begin February 21.

The reciprocal invitation involved an important legal and political
question: for Adoula, it was an invitation addressed to a provincial president within the framework of regular contacts between central and provincial authorities, while, in Elisabethville, contact on the level of "heads
of government" was sought.

RELATIONS BETWEEN ELISABETHVILLE AND THE U.N. AND THE MERCENARY QUESTION

After the Kitona discussions, the U.N. in the Congo lent its support
to any step which could provide for application of the accords.

Thus, the U.N. in the Congo guaranteed the persons of all members
of Parliament from Katanga who would agree to sit in the capital, during
their stay, and guaranteed their freedom to return to Elisabethville. This
applied also to the Katangan officials who took part in the Leopoldville
discussions on the revision of the constitutional structure of the Congo.

Thus, the U.N. received a request from Tshombe to provide the elected
Katangan Assembly members all necessary assistance to participate in
the Assembly session which was to decide on the Kitona accords. The
U.N. acted in addition as an agency of communication between Kasavubu
and Tshombe on the question of a site for the meeting of the Katangan
Assembly.

Thus, the U.N. in the Congo furnished to Elisabethville, following
their request on January 5, the services of a legal expert: Constantin
Stavropoulos, adviser to the U.N. Secretary-General. The central government had approved legal assistance provided that the U.N. jurist
claimed no right to judge the acts of Leopoldville.[3]

[3] On March 28, Kimba invoked the U.N. legal assistance to justify the regularity
and legality of the motion of the Katangan Assembly of February 15, 1962. —
L'Essor du Katanga (Elisabethville), March 29, 1962.

Simultaneously, the relations locally between the U.N. and Katangan authorities improved on several scores. This change in atmosphere was demonstrated in particular by the exchange of prisoners on January 15 (15 members of the U.N. forces as against 33 of the Katangan gendarmery and police); by the return toward Elisabethville of 120 members of the Katangan gendarmery who had asked protection of the U.N. near Albertville; by the organization of mixed patrols in the most troubled sections of Elisabethville and by the joint expulsion of Baluba or Tshokwe who illegally occupied homes in the residential sections of the city [4] and whose presence aroused uneasiness among the Europeans.

The Katangan press and the authorities there gave credit for the change in U.N.-Katanga relations to Georges Dumontet, the new U.N. representative in Elisabethville.

Nevertheless, on two important points, the situation remained confused and the disagreement between the U.N. in the Congo and the Katangan government complete:

1. U.N. forces did not enjoy freedom of movement and the only cities or centers in which it had contingents posted were Albertville, Manono, Kamina base, and Elisabethville.

2. In regard to foreign mercenaries in Tshombe's hire, no real progress had been accomplished and the application of the Security Council resolutions of February 21 and November 24, 1961, continued to run into the same obstacles.

During the course of the fighting in Elisabethville in December, 1961, six foreign mercenaries were killed, some others arrested, but the majority escaped the U.N. forces and fell back toward Kipushi, on the Rhodesian border.

In addition, according to the U.N. in the Congo, recruitment of mercenaries for Katanga and arms deliveries had not stopped: thirty-five mercenaries recruited in the south of France were transferred through Brazzaville on January 8, 1962, by air, to Ndola in Northern Rhodesia, while Portugal, in behalf of Angola, and Rhodesia refused to receive U.N. observers who could have maintained surveillance of several airports and communication routes used by traffic to Katanga.

[4] On January 12, the operation ended in the evacuation of 1300 "squatters" from the Lubumbashi quarter. — U.N. Document, Security Council, S/5053/Add. 1, para. 35. Early in January, the Katangan press had accused U.N. contingents — especially the Ethiopians — of taking part in pillage. — *L'Essor du Katanga* (Elisabethville), January 3, 1962.

According to the U.N.,[5] on January 20, 1962: "No positive measures have as yet been taken by the Katangan provincial authorities to facilitate the implementation of the relevant clauses in the Security Council resolutions" concerning mercenaries.

On the basis of this situation, Valerian Zorin, permanent representative of the Soviet Union to the U.N., demanded an immediate meeting of the Security Council to examine what he considered "sabotage" of the U.N. resolutions and of Adoula's efforts to restore territorial integration. The Soviet demand provoked on January 28 an expression of public regret by Adoula who, at this point, hoped for rapid progress in the implementation of the Kitona accords and feared, in addition, some maneuver involving Gizenga.

On January 24, a discussion took place in Elisabethville between Tshombe, Evariste Kimba, and Godefroid Munongo on the one hand, and three high U.N. officials on the other. On this occasion, Tshombe affirmed his intent to resolve "once and for all" the question of mercenaries; moreover, according to him, it was all settled since no foreign officer served any longer in the Katangan gendarmery which, under the exclusive command of General Muké, would no longer accept the presence of these foreign mercenaries or officers. Tshombe furnished a seven-page list of officers and mercenaries with indications of the separation payments which had been given to them. In regard to the "hard core" of mercenaries grouped together around several French officers, the Katangan president declared that they had been "discharged" and that Colonel Faulques had been led to the frontier under military escort, during the preceding week.

The U.N. was not convinced by these arguments and affirmations of good faith. Sture Linner demanded application of the Security Council resolutions "not only in Elisabethville, but also at Kolwezi, Jadotville, Kipushi, and in all other such centers which, he had reason to believe, might be used by the mercenaries if they chose to launch military operations again."[6] Once more, Tshombe promised to resolve the problem immediately and completely.

The next day, Tshombe confirmed in writing that all "the former foreign officers of our *gendarmerie* left Katangese territory for good on August 28, 1961."[7] This statement was in direct contradiction to one

---

[5] U.N. Document, Security Council, S/5053/Add. 1, para. 32.
[6] U.N. Document, Security Council, S/5053/Add. 3, A, para. 4.
[7] U.N. Document, Security Council, S/5053/Add. 3, Annex I.

made January 24 on the subject by Colonel Faulques, Labourdonnaie, and their cohorts. Tshombe proposed at the same time to create a mixed U.N.-Katanga commission to uncover the mercenaries who were still hidden in Katanga; the elimination of "mercenaries who are still in Katanga" was to be carried out by Elisabethville authorities the following month.[8]

Through these contradictions, a Katangan position emerged: we want to expel the mercenaries; some have already left (willingly or by force); others are still hiding in Katanga; it will be the task of the mixed commission to see that the measures for disbanding and expelling them are implemented.

Tshombe sought at this point to gain time, for the ANC was operating in North Katanga,[9] and the reconsideration of the Kitona accords again posed the whole question of ways and means in relations with Leopoldville.

The U.N. in the Congo refused the one-month delay proposed by Tshombe. Two mixed commissions were set up early in February. The press noted the expulsion of nine Belgian and French mercenaries on February 9. Tshombe declared once more that these were the last.

At the same time, a question arose linked to that of the mercenaries and that of control over mining installations and resumption of the UMHK activities at Lubumbashi. The U.N. was of the opinion that it was impossible to settle the problem of the mercenaries without control of the UMHK factories and offices, considered as the base for secessionist activity, while the Katangan government and the company argued that the presence of the U.N. in the mining cities would precipitate the departure of Europeans and block all industrial activity. This affair turned entirely on the resumption of work in Lubumbashi-Elisabethville. The factory, which employed fifteen hundred workers, had closed its doors on December 4, 1961, during the course of fighting, and it was occupied by Ethiopians in the U.N. forces.

The UMHK had hoped to resume work on January 15, but despite discussion with the U.N. in Leopoldville and Elisabethville, Linner maintained his viewpoint: "The Ethiopian troops which now occupy the Union Minière installations would not be withdrawn, in order to keep the installations from again assuming the important role which they played

---

[8] *Ibid.*

[9] The massacre of missionaries by ANC soldiers in Kongolo, on January 1, 1962, aroused Western opinion at this juncture.

during the December events. This surveillance need not, in any case, halt normal activity in the installations." [10]

On February 6, in the course of a press conference, Jean Gonze, the UMHK director general, accused the U.N. of obstruction, but, on February 9, Tshombe announced the reopening of the factories "under the control of U.N. civilian officials," seeming to indicate that the U.N. had renounced military control at Lubumbashi and no longer predicated resumption of work on the prior guarantee of free circulation for the U.N. in Kipushi, Kolwezi, and Jadotville. Now, the U.N. considered this problem of prime importance and at this point — on February 8, 9, and 10 — a rumor circulated through Elisabethville that the U.N. was preparing an attack against the mining cities.

It seems that the Katangan government had done everything to keep the U.N. in the Congo from occupying the mining centers. At the meeting of traditional chiefs from February 16 to 18, the final motion, inspired by Tshombe, constituted a radical stance against the U.N. presence: "We do not wish a U.N. presence, be it symbolic or not, in the aforementioned localities, seats of our principal industries." Finally, on February 17, 1962, a U.N. spokesman announced activities in Lubumbashi were to resume February 19. Control of the factory would be assumed by a civilian commission of the U.N. This announcement was not matched by any decision on the part of Katanga to guarantee free circulation to the U.N. in the Congo.

At another time, the lack of a solution acceptable to the U.N. in the Congo on the problems of free movement and expelling mercenaries would perhaps have led to a new outbreak, inasmuch as the Katangan gendarmery was resuming its operations in the Kongolo region and sending armed patrols through the streets of Elisabethville. It seems that the U.N., in spite of several tough declarations, wished to avoid new tensions, at the moment when decisive discussions between Adoula and Tshombe were anticipated in Leopoldville.

This does not mean that there were no incidents between the U.N. in the Congo and the Katangan authorities. To the contrary, in February, March, and April, 1962, there were numerous protests on the part of both the Katangans and the U.N. Some examples may be cited: Elisabethville accused the U.N. of having machine-gunned a shed of the Katangan gendarmery at Kapona on February 28, 1962; contradictory

[10] Reported in *La Libre Belgique* (Brussels), January 27, 1962.

versions circulated in regard to the arrest of an Indian U.N. soldier on
March 13, 1962; incidents and exchanges of gunfire took place between
an Indian patrol and the Katangan gendarmery on April 12, 1962; Munongo protested against the theft of Katangan flags; vehicles were halted
and incidents occurred at Katangan and U.N. road blocks.

During this period, the nervousness of Katangan authorities and their
supporters was exacerbated to the point where any incident, even minimal, was amplified and generally interpreted as the signal for a new
extensive operation against the Katangan regime. The example of incidents in Kamina early in March, 1962, is revealing in this respect:

1. On March 5, President Tshombe revealed that an attack had been
   launched by surprise against the Katangan garrison in the city of
   Kamina by twelve hundred U.N. troops from the base at Kamina.
   There were dead and wounded on both sides and the Katangan garrison resisted the attacks.
2. The same day, "from private sources in Brussels," Belgian newspapers
   of March 6 reported that the Katangan garrison had passed to the
   counterattack, but that the U.N. in the Congo had also attacked at
   Lubudi, halfway between Kamina and Jadotville.
3. On March 6, despite denials by the U.N., *La Libre Belgique* vehemently accused the "ambassadors of peace" of having broken the
   truce, pushed by a "murderous madness" and guilty of "having again
   gone beyond the pale."
4. On March 8, the same Belgian newspaper — citing Katangan sources,
   the Associated Press, and Agence France-Presse — noted without
   commentary that the Kamina affair had in fact been a simple skirmish
   in which nine U.N. troops had participated (and not twelve hundred),
   with no casualties.

PREPARATIONS FOR THE LEOPOLDVILLE DISCUSSIONS

Adoula on February 16, proposed a meeting with Tshombe to examine the means of implementing the Kitona accords: "Let it be Leopoldville,
February 21." On February 20, Adoula repeated his invitation. The same
day, Tshombe declared in Elisabethville that he was ready for sincere
cooperation, but that two facts obstructed Katanga's good intentions:
the lack of effective authority over a great part of the territory which the
central government nominally controlled and the total failure to adapt
the provisional *Loi Fondamentale*, to which Leopoldville continued to
make reference.

Several days later, the delegation of the Katangan government in Leopoldville — Henri Ndala Kambola and Gabriel Kitenge — published a declaration outlining the reasons for which "the presence of President Tshombe in Leopoldville is not for the moment indicated": unfavorable reactions of the Katangan population; maintenance of the state of exception decreed by Leopoldville against Katanga; installation of an "illegal" government in Albertville; and so forth.

Tshombe continued to maintain that he would go to Leopoldville, but made ever more precise demands regarding personal security. He asked and successively obtained from the U.N. full guarantees of security for himself and his delegation during the stay in Leopoldville (February 20, 1962); full guarantees for the stay and the round trip (February 21); full guarantees for the stay, the trip, and complete freedom of choice in timing his return to Elisabethville, even in case of opposition from the central government (February 23); a promise that the U.N. would, if necessary, oppose the execution of the warrant for his arrest issued in Leopoldville on September 8, 1961 (March 3). Thus reassured, Tshombe agreed to visit Leopoldville on March 15.

The Katangan delegation included Tshombe, Jean-Baptiste Kibwe, Gabriel Kitenge, Kishiba, Henri Ndala Kambola, and Justin Meli. The central government was represented by ministers Cyrille Adoula, Jason Sendwe, Jean Bolikango, Christophe Gbenye, Justin Bomboko, Cléophas Kamitatu, and Joseph Ileo.

The discussions began on March 18. They took place over two intervals, from March 18 to April 16, when they were interrupted, and from May 25 to June 26.

POSITIONS AT THE OUTSET

Before even touching on the legal views presented by the two parties during the discussions in Leopoldville, the political positions ought to be situated precisely.

For Adoula, "Katanga is a province which withdrew from the national community at a certain stage and which must now return to it. There has never been and there never will be a Katangese State,"[11] and any eventual agreement on state structures and on the division of resources must be immediately sanctioned by measures which visually manifest the end of the secession — measures such as the abrogation of the Katangan

[11] Press Conference, March 29, 1962, quoted in U.N. Document, Security Council, S/5053/Add. 10, Annex II, para. 15.

constitution, an ANC presence in certain Katangan centers or the establishment of Leopoldville's administrative services in Katanga.

Does this mean that Adoula adopted toward Katanga Lumumba's attitude of August, 1960? The essential differences are that the Adoula government sought an agreement by way of discussion, that Adoula agreed
to a certain extent on the priority of an institutional or constitutional solution to the Congolese crisis, that he accepted the prospect of Katangan
"reintegration" with its Conakat leadership (whereas the first central
government intended to arrest and try the "traitors"), and that he accepted the principle of a provisional *modus vivendi* on appropriation of
receipts and foreign exchange.

For Tshombe, Katanga constituted a "state" prepared "to renounce
absolute sovereignty" and content with "internal sovereignty."[12] But
Tshombe intended essentially to keep the type of political order which he
had erected since July 11, not allowing the central power to act directly
in Katanga without his personal mediation. He wished also to secure
himself financially, beforehand, against an eventual inflationary "epi-
demic" spreading from Leopoldville.

In addition, Adoula was persuaded that Tshombe did not really seek
conciliation, that his first objective was to gain time to strengthen his
military machine with the support of "double-dealing" countries (on April
24, 1962), and that time worked in favor of the secession.[13] Under these
conditions, the central government felt it was authorized to use pressure
to effect reintegration, to gather with "the heads of sister countries in
Africa and Asia and of other friendly countries . . . [the means] to
terminate the secession" and to prepare the Congolese people "for the
trial of strength to which madmen and rebels in the pay of foreign business
interests wish to subject us."[14]

From their perspective the secessionist leaders thought or claimed that
the central authorities only awaited a propitious occasion to intern
Tshombe and his ministers. They saw Sendwe (Balubakat), Kamitatu
(PSA), and Bomboko, as irreconcilable adversaries of Tshombiste Katanga, at the very core of the Leopoldville delegation. They questioned

[12] Letter from Tshombe to Adoula, April 6, 1962, cited in U.N. Document, Security Council, S/5053/Add. 10, Annex VIII.

[13] "The balance of forces, which at that time [the beginning of the secession] was
in favor of the Central Government, is now completely reversed to Tshombe's
benefit," Adoula speech of April 24, 1962, cited in U.N. Document, Security
Council, S/5053/Add. 10, Annex XIII, para. 21.

[14] *Ibid.*, para. 26.

Adoula's capacity as a valid spokesman, [15] and their automatic reaction was to reject a priori anything that might suggest, to the peoples of Katanga and to the Europeans in its service, the disruption of their established positions in the administrative, political, and military domains.

These positions — fundamentally at odds — were clearly expressed from the first discussions onward and were reflected in the first proposals offered for discussion. If agreements were reached, they were often the fruit of U.N. mediation or of "advice" given to the two parties by interested Western countries. Furthermore, it must be noted that many agreements on precise points were not reached — exactly as had been the case at the Belgo-Congolese Round Table in January and February, 1960 — except by a formula leaving to each a broad area for interpretation. Besides, these compromises were not enough to open up the discussions, which ended on June 26, at 5:30 A.M. in a declaration of bankruptcy with the parties refusing even to sign a joint communiqué. [16]

THE SUBSTANCE OF THE NEGOTIATIONS

The discussion in Leopoldville dealt both with the future Congolese constitution which was intended to solve the institutional crisis which had begun in June, 1960, and with the transitional period between the eventual accord and final adoption of the constitution.

To understand the evolution of negotiations on substantive issues, one must examine the abundant documentation published on this subject by the U.N. [17] and by the central government which, in its *Second livre blanc sur la sécession katangaise*, published extracts from its own minutes of the sessions.

THE CONSTITUTIONAL REFORM

a. *The first Adoula project* did not use the term "federalism" to define the anticipated regime, but, like the resolutions drafted at the 1960 Round Table and the provisional *Loi Fondamentale* of May, 1960, it effected a fairly precise distribution of powers between the central and provincial

[15] Tshombe declaration, May 17, 1962, cited in U.N. Document, Security Council, S/5053/Add. 10, Annex XXX, para. 6.

[16] For details on the practical unfolding of the discussions, see *Congo 1962*, pp. 349–52; report of Gardiner to the U.N. Secretariat, June 27, 1962, in U.N. Document, S/5053/Add. 10. Note the interruption between April 17 and May 25 during which the U.N. maintained some liaison contacts between Leopoldville and Elisabethville.

[17] U.N. Document, Security Council, S/5053/Add. 10, with annexes June 27 and 28, 1962.

authorities. The list of powers conferred on the central government was practically identical with that of the provisional *Loi Fondamentale*, and they were listed in the same order; the only addition concerned "the fiscal system," which was not cited in the law of May 19, 1960. In regard to the provinces, the enumeration was less precise than in the provisional *Loi Fondamentale*, but this can be explained insofar as the Adoula plan, unlike the *Loi Fondamentale*, expressly reserved to the provinces "the residual power," namely, "all the powers not expressly attributed to the center." A Court of Constitutionality was provided to ensure that the division of powers would be respected. A formula was likewise recommended that conferred upon a representative of the central authority the exercise of its powers in the province. Subsequent changes in the distribution of powers could not enter into effect until approved by *all* the provincial assemblies.

b. *Concessions by the Central Government*: On April 30, the U.N. chief in the Congo submitted to the Katangans a modified version of the first Adoula plan. For the first time, it was a question of a federal constitution for the Congo (Art. 2). Compared to the version of April 16, 1962, the April 30 plan contained several innovations:

1. The central government agreed to stand or fall according to the vote on the projected federal constitution.
2. The list of powers reserved to the central authorities was reduced, both by simplification and by transfer of certain powers to the provinces (in matters relating to nonuniversity education).
3. Parliamentary immunity was recognized for members of the provincial governments on the same basis as that enjoyed by members of the central government.
4. The powers of the ANC to intervene in a province were restricted to very limited cases: request by provincial authorities; refusal to execute a decision of the Court of Constitutionality; incapacity of the provincial authorities to secure public order, to be sanctioned after an injunction remains without effect and after a declaration of a state of emergency by the Council of Ministers.
5. The procedure by which the central authority could take steps to make a province implement a law or ordinance was precisely determined: a finding of non-compliance; a prior declaration of a state of emergency.
6. The central government was allowed, at the request or with the consent of the province, "to delegate" administrative functions to officials of

the provincial government who would act in such cases under the authority of the representative of Leopoldville in the province concerned.

7. The right of provinces "to use" foreign technicians whom they require was recognized, but within the framework of national regulations or international accords concluded by the central government.

8. The provincial frontiers of June 30, 1960, were confirmed, unless the provincial Assembly gave its assent to a change by a majority of two thirds of its members.

c. *Katanga objections*: At the outset, Katangan delegates submitted no proposals but formulated objections, and demanded guarantees.

After the first Adoula plan, they demanded:

1. Maintenance of the territorial integrity of Katanga and abandonment of all Leopoldville support for Lualaba province;

2. Maintenance of all forces of order under the sole authority of the provincial government;

3. Exercise of all administrative services (including those in the competence of the central authority) by agents of the provincial government;

4. U.N. guarantees, in regard to the essential clauses of the accord, to intervene between Elisabethville and Leopoldville.

After the transmission of the amended Adoula plan, the Katangan delegates:

1. Challenged the right of Leopoldville to have a special representative in the province and "to apply its own decisions directly against the wishes of the provincial authorities";[18]

2. Objected to the principle of "two administrations," that is, to the existence of two types of administrative officials (federal and provincial) within the same territory;

3. Rejected as "absolutely laughable" the provincial powers defined by Adoula;

4. Opposed radically any right of intervention by the ANC;

5. Feared that the central government would oppose "a certain type of technical aid," for which the Katangan government felt the need;

6. Interpreted the addition of the term "federal constitution" as a purely formal addition, "presumably to please President Tshombe or perhaps to deceive him about the central government's real intentions."[19]

[18] *Ibid.*, Annex XVIII.
[19] *Ibid.*, Annex XIX.

The Katangan note of May 2, 1962, concluded in these terms: "Adoula's new draft does not differ from the old one in any way."

d. *Katanga proposals*: On the insistence of the U.N., in the Congo, the Katangan representatives formulated counterproposals on May 3, 1962, then presented two plans on May 5 and 6, which may be schematized as follows: [20]

Federal Organization: A president, an Assembly (equal number of members from each state in the federation), a federal executive (each state would be equally represented here). The new constitution would be voted by the Chambers in joint session, sitting publicly (not in closed session), then submitted to referendum (it would have to be "approved by each of the states"). After the referendum, general elections would be organized.

Distribution of powers: The differences in relation to the Adoula plans are patent:
1. Each state (province) would reserve the right to maintain economic representation abroad.
2. The president of each state would by law control the contingent of the army stationed on his territory and, furthermore, would have disposal of his own forces for the maintenance of order.
3. Each state could have its internal *Sûreté* to be "coordinated into the security services of the federation."
4. The electoral regime for the provinces would be established by each state involved.
5. Radio broadcasting would be under provincial jurisdiction.
6. The jurisdiction of Leopoldville in social services would be limited simply to "coordination."
7. A fairly broad range of "concurrent" powers would exist, but, contrary to the system instituted by the *Loi Fondamentale*, the central view would not prevail in case of conflict — "the federal authority shall enact no legislation on these matters save with the consent of the state concerned." (Among these concurrent powers were: higher education, information, basic legislation on energy and mines, means of communications vital to the national interest, judiciary organization.)
8. The president of each state would ex officio be the representative

[20] *Ibid.*, Annex XXIV.

of the federal authority within each state and officials of the federal services would come under his authority.

Analysis of these views indicates that the Katangan version tended to constitute a federation quite close to confederation, with a weak central power, dependent on member states, and aimed, on essentials, "to consolidate the internal regime instituted in Katanga," in July, 1960, while admitting limited cooperation where prior agreement had been obtained.[21] Yet, on the strictly institutional level, the central government held out for the formulas of May, 1960, while continuing to offer guarantees to the provinces, especially in regard to the use of force and intervention of the ANC and in renouncing punishment for the secession and for acts on its behalf.

The Transitional Period

While the constitutional proposals of Leopoldville and Elisabethville diverged profoundly, the differences were even deeper in regard to the so-called transitional period, before the new constitution was laid down.

For Adoula:

Plan I: While awaiting the new constitution, the *Loi Fondamentale* remained in effect throughout; the Katangan constitution of August 5, 1960, was withdrawn; Leopoldville would assume control of the Katangan gendarmery which would be integrated into the ANC command; and the U.N. in the Congo and the ANC would control Kolwezi, Jadotville, Kipushi, Baudouinville, and Sakania; the Katangan *Sûreté* would be under Leopoldville's control; the Katangan franc was to be withdrawn from circulation; the customs and treasury officials would report exclusively to Leopoldville; radio service would be a central function; the Katangan Assembly would sit in its form as of June, 1960, and the Katangan government would be obliged to dismiss the ministers who were "named" and not elected by the Assembly.[22]

Plan II: The same arrangements were provided, except in regard to military problems (the ANC was no longer to control urban centers, and, in addition, the Katangan gendarmery "divested of all foreign elements and, as now organized" would be "transferred to the control of the central

---

[21] "The mission of a central government . . . is to orchestrate fair and active cooperation between the governments of the diverse political units which constitute the Republic." These words of Tshombe on April 8, 1962, faithfully reflected the conception of power that was held in Elisabethville.

[22] U.N. Document, Security Council, S/5053/Add. 10, Annex IX.

power," but without mention of integration into the ANC). Otherwise, for the *Sûreté*, the taxes and customs services, the formula was less harsh.[23]

For Tshombe: [24]

1. There must be a guarantee that Lualaba province will not be created or supported during the transitional period, and the authority of the Elisabethville government must be recognized throughout Katanga;
2. The gendarmery must remain an entity directly under the provincial government, just as the ANC reports directly to the central government;
3. Katanga will freely recruit "technicians necessary for the smooth functioning of administrative services" and will communicate to Leopoldville the names of these technicians;
4. The Katangan passport will be as equally valid as that of the Congo republic during the whole transitional period;
5. "The [administrative] structures of the Katangan state shall be maintained in their existing form together with the personnel currently serving";
6. Traffic, including air traffic, will be free throughout Katanga;
7. Katanga will participate in political life in Leopoldville, but will lay claim to ministerial portfolios in the central government, "including some of major importance . . . the portfolios of Foreign Affairs, Finance, and Defense." [25]

To these demands must be added those concerning customs and foreign exchange.

BUDGETARY AND MONETARY PROBLEMS

Views for the Transitional Period

For Adoula: Withdrawal of the Katangan franc and its replacement by Congolese currency; return to the Monetary Council of the Congo the Congolese currency withdrawn from circulation by the Tshombe-Kibwe government; search for a provisional arrangement on the distribution of

---

[23] *Ibid.*, Annex XVI.

[24] *Ibid.*, Annexes XXIV and XXV.

[25] This requirement, formulated in the plan of May 5, 1962, no longer figured in that of May 6, 1962.

financial jurisdiction between the central and provincial authorities.[26] In the meantime, the taxes and duties were to be collected exclusively by agents of the center.

For Tshombe: The export duties continued to be collected by Katanga, but a percentage of the customs, of the royalties and rentals for agricultural, forest, and mining concessions would be remitted to the central government; the Katangan currency and the policy on foreign exchange would continue to be under the sole jurisdiction of the province until such time as a coordinated economic policy would permit the unification of the currency without harm to the economy of the federation and the member states.[27] Katanga undertook to transport "a major proportion of its products and the bulk of its imports" coming from the Atlantic by the "national route," whereas the Congo would export and import, via Katanga, products to and from South Africa, the Rhodesias, and the Indian Ocean.

The terrain was not much explored by the two parties. It is necessary to distinguish the problem of finding resources for the financing of budgets from that of raising foreign exchange (the question of exchange rates and allocation). Likewise, the physical problem of levying duties and taxes must not be confused with the problems of allocation. In this field, the U.N. was particularly involved, as well as other specialized agencies (for example, the Monetary Council).

Views on the Permanent Settlement

In this area, the documents of the central government and Katanga concerned only the broad principles.

For Adoula: Currency and foreign exchange policy were in the domain of the central government. Leopoldville alone could collect royalties and payments on leases or concessions, with the revenue to be divided according to a pre-established percentage (30 percent for the province, out of the receipts from development of mineral deposits and from concessions). Only the central power fixed and collected the customs duties, and con-

---

[26] In the revised plan, Adoula undertook "to convene within a month, a Conference of the Presidents of the Provincial Governments with a view to determining an equitable division of public revenues between the State and the Provinces." — U.N. Document, Security Council, S/5053/Add. 10, Annex XVI.

[27] "It would serve no purpose to drown the Katangan franc, which is still worth something, in the present devaluation of the Congolese franc." — Tshombe declaration, June 12, 1962, U.N. Document, Security Council, S/5053/Add. 10, Annex XXXVII.

currently with the provinces it had the right to levy and to collect personal income taxes and taxes on certain activities. Special laws (to be voted at the same time as the constitution) would be elaborated to delimit the respective financial domains of the state and of the provinces.[28]

For Tshombe: He "had said that he feared that, if the central government was granted the right to collect taxes in Katanga, the money would be wasted, squandered, and lost to both parties."[29] Katanga wanted all national legislation on customs and monetary matters to be submitted to prior consultation with the provinces and not to be implemented until after the approval of the Assembly of each member state. In addition, the federal budget would be supplied by a percentage of the state receipts, with an equal contribution from all the member states; the states would themselves fix and levy taxes, mining royalties, and customs. The federal government would have to obtain the agreement of each province to contract loans. Subsequently, the Katangans insisted that a substantial share of foreign exchange generated by exports be reserved to them, in order to meet the economic needs of the province.

THE U.N. ROLE IN THE ATTEMPT AT RECONCILIATION

After Kitona, and even more after the qualified acceptance in principle of the eight points of Kitona by the Katangan Assembly, the U.N. in the Congo worked openly in 1962 in favor of a final agreement between Katanga and the central government of the Congo. Twice it gave to Tshombe all the guarantees that he desired for his personal safety during the discussions in Leopoldville.[30] The U.N. in the Congo offered its good offices to the two parties in striking formulas and by "whatever means may be deemed necessary and appropriate";[31] its representatives — who did not sit in on the first phase of the discussions, but did on the second — took the initiative in seeking compromise wordings or in memoranda to bring the points of view together.

[28] In this regard, there existed plans of U.N. experts. — U.N. Document, Security Council, S/5053/Add. 10, Annex XXXIII, June 28, 1962.

[29] Katanga-U.N. meeting in Elisabethville, May 2, 1962. U.N. Document, Security Council, S/5053/Add. 10, Annex XXI, para. 17.

[30] On April 18, an incident permitted the effectiveness of this protection to be judged: Tshombe was able to leave Ndjili, thanks to the personal intervention of Gardiner.

[31] Letter from Gardiner to Tshombe, April 12, 1962. — U.N. Document, Security Council, S/5053/Add. 10, Annex VII.

Robert Gardiner revised, in accord with Adoula, the first central government proposals. He introduced the principles of possibly delegating to provincial officials administrative functions normally under the central administration and limiting ANC powers of intervention in Katanga and in provincial affairs. It was his idea to guarantee the maintenance of the Katangan gendarmery as then organized, so long as it took orders from the central government and did not violate U.N. resolutions.[32] Gardiner also made repeated efforts to show the Katangans that certain demands would lead to a denial of central authority, and it was he who entrusted to the experts the job of preparing the proposals on budgetary resources and foreign exchange. Listed below are several proposals or important modifications which seem, according to the documents, to have been the work of the U.N. drafter, where he either took the initiative to facilitate compromise or acted in response to an external demand (generally Katangan, Western, or private):

1. Purge of the Katangan gendarmery of all "foreign elements" but maintenance of its present organization.
2. Abandonment of the ANC presence in the urban and mining centers of Katanga, mentioned by Adoula on April 16, 1962.
3. Creation of the province of Lualaba impossible during the course of the transitional period, or later, without the agreement of two thirds of the members of the Katangan Assembly.
4. Conditions placed on the exercise of strict legal rights of the central authorities, in regard to application of national laws in the provinces.
5. Possibility of delegating to provincial officials tasks normally assigned to federal agents, but refusal in principle of a general obligatory delegation.[33]
6. Refusal to limit the scope of central legislation, in social matters, to mere coordination.
7. Refusal to consider the radio as a provincial or concurrent area.
8. Introduction of the principle that "each member state of the federa-

[32] "It is a concession obtained at the cost of much effort," Gardiner noted in this regard May 2, 1962.

[33] "The Katangese could insist that their Minister of Finances — Mr. Kibwe in the present instance — would act as the agent of the Central Government [for the collection of money], which would mean that the revenue from the taxes would in fact remain in the hands of the Katangese," declared Gardiner, in a discussion with Tshombe, Kibwe, Munongo, Kitenge, and Muhona, on May 2, 1962, in Elisabethville. — U.N. Document, Security Council, S/5053/Add. 10, Annex XXI, para. 18.

tion would be furnished with foreign exchange to meet its economic
needs, in proportion to its contribution to the economy of the nation."

9. Control, with U.N. assistance, of the troops and arms of the provincial
police — during the transitional period, the military potential of Katanga would not be increased and imports of arms, munitions, and
military equipment would be prohibited.

10. Political amnesty throughout Katanga.

11. Allocation of the import duties to the central government and a
fifty-fifty division of the export duties between Leopoldville and the
provinces of origin of the products.

12. Assessment, collection, and allocation by the central government of
corporation taxes by share and by province for other enterprises.

13. "Revenues from the Congolese portfolio must go, in totality, to the
central government; that would include the stocks held by the Comité
Spécial du Katanga as well as revenues deriving from parastatals and
mixed enterprises."

Despite these attempts at conciliation, the discussions failed and on
June 26, the delegations recorded this failure: Leopoldville — aware that
it held the major trump cards in the last resort against the secession —
was not disposed to accept the Katangan proposals, which had scarcely
been influenced at all by the profound change in the balance of political
and military forces since December, 1961.

Another parallel approach to settling the Katangan problem failed as
well: the plan to organize a meeting of *all* the members of Parliament from
Katanga. A delegation from Leopoldville, composed of Thomas Banza
and Atter Ngoy-Luongwe, had discussions in Elisabethville with Charles
Mutaka, President of the Katangan Assembly, who declared in the April
26 session, "The reconciliation between the Balubakat and the Conakat is
well underway and on the point of yielding concrete results." Cléophas
Kamitatu, Minister of the Interior in the central government, proposed on
April 12 to convene the Katangan Assembly "within the framework of
a conclave identical to that in which the Parliament met at Lovanium," to
examine "the practical means to end the secession." Mutaka opposed the
formula, which he judged "vexatious" and illegal, arguing in addition that
Katanga had a valid negotiator throughout the whole affair in Tshombe.
Matters rested at this point.

CHAPTER 8 · *The Thant Plan for*
National Reconciliation

THE GENESIS OF THE PLAN

THE financial burden for the U.N. in the Congo was heavy for the
countries which supported it, and the deficit in the Congolese budget
was taking on highly disturbing proportions. The American government
in 1962 expressed the desire to see the Belgians make a greater financial
effort in the Congo. Declining the request, Paul-Henri Spaak maintained
that the Belgian budgetary situation did not permit it. In the corridors of
the Atlantic Council in Athens in June, 1962, a common agency for
financial assistance to the Congo was agreed upon: the United States,
Great Britain, and Belgium would be the principal supporters, with the
possibility of contributions from other countries, Western, and, if possible,
Asian. This agency could approve loans to the Congo to re-establish the
balance of payments, the sums to be contingent on the application of
certain measures for budgetary and administrative reform in Leopoldville.

Such a fund could function well only if the central government were not
continually in a weak position, both in regard to its internal opposition and
to other African states, and only if this government were in a position to
implement the necessary reforms without running the risk of scuttling
themselves in the process.

In the minds of its promoters, the fund would be more effective if the
canker of secession were reabsorbed; for the Belgians and British, this
reabsorption would be worthwhile only if it were done by peaceful means,
without a brutal political upset in Elisabethville and without the destruction or paralysis of mining enterprises and transportation.

In May and June, despite differing judgments on the situation, the
United States on the one hand, Great Britain and Belgium on the other,
put their hopes on the success of the Adoula-Tshombe discussions, or at
least agreed to await their outcome.

After June 26, when the Leopoldville meetings broke down, the three most committed Western states jointly sought a practical formula, permitting them to exert pressures for peaceful reintegration of Katanga. Their effort would not, however, call into question certain situations of fact and thus render reunification intolerable for Elisabethville and its European supporters. The divergences among the Western powers concerned eventual resort to economic pressures and sanctions; for the Americans, it was essential to obtain an agreement from the Union Minière to cease paying its taxes and mining royalties to the Tshombe government, so that the secession would be deprived of its sources of income. The British and the Belgians leaned toward political pressure without threats of economic sanctions toward Katanga.

The Western discussions in New York and Washington, during late June, and July, and early August, 1962, took place in close liaison with the Secretary-General of the U.N., who, on July 31, declared that he was thinking of exerting "economic pressure upon the Katangan authorities of a kind that will bring home to them the realities of their situation and the fact that Katanga is not a sovereign State. . . . This could justifiably go to the extent of barring all trade and financial relations. . . ." He later commented, "In pursuance of this, a formal request would be made by me to all the Member Governments to apply such a ban especially to Katangan copper and cobalt."[1]

Thant had met Spaak and Stevenson on June 20 and 25, then had gone to Europe in July. He had likewise convened the Consultative Committee on the Congo (twice, June 29 and July 31), and launched a number of appeals to get the application of pressure on Katanga underway. In regard to the Union Minière which, according to him, "was implicated in the political activities aimed at dislocation" of the Congo, the Secretary-General asked Spaak in a letter, August 2, 1962, to do everything he could to persuade the company not to turn over its mining royalties and taxes to the Katangan government. The U.N., declared Thant, would offer effective guarantees to the UMHK both for the safety of its installations and for its legal status, provided that it put its returns into a special account, temporarily blocked and out of Tshombe's hands.

On its side, Leopoldville had officially announced at the end of July its intention to prepare a federal constitution for the Congo. In return, the central authorities had obtained from the U.N. the closing of Katangan airports. In addition, the vote on the law establishing a North Katanga

[1] U.N. Document, Security Council, S/5053/Add. 11, Annex II, B, para. 90.

province, especially its immediate promulgation, on July 11, 1962, by the Chief of State, had seriously heightened antagonisms between Leopoldville and Elisabethville.[2]

At the Western diplomatic level, Washington was the scene of intense diplomatic activity to set in motion a "plan of persuasion" to be applied in the Congo. At the beginning of August, the whole press reverberated with this "plan," originated by Americans, and with the British and Belgian opposition to clauses which provided for sanctions on Katanga. Opposition revolved around the plans for economic and military sanctions. The Western discussions were formally justified by a letter from Thant to the member governments on July 31 and by the necessity to respond to it. In fact, the Western initiatives were to furnish the very substance for the Thant Plan.

Publicly, a solution was thus found: the so-called Thant Plan made no allusion to sanctions, but the letter accompanying Gardiner to Elisabethville set a certain time period for Katanga's acceptance.[3] Another document had meanwhile been elaborated — a "Course of Action" which fixed a procedure binding the Western countries and was issued by Thant himself on November 26, 1962.

THE PLAN FOR NATIONAL RECONCILIATION

The so-called Thant Plan dates from August 10. It constitutes a practical program attempting to ensure the peaceful reintegration of Katanga. The program can be summarized as follows in its essential points:

1. Drafting and parliamentary approval of a Congolese federal constitution was prescribed, with consultation of the "states" and of political groups in the Congo.
2. Powers of the center were briefly enumerated but were substantial, while residual power was reserved to the provinces.
3. A law was provided dividing the revenues, which would take into account the economic and financial means and needs of the individual

---

[2] *Moniteur Congolais*, No. 19 (August 6, 1962). — Text in *Congo 1962*, pp. 216–17.

[3] Note that many newspapers published on August 22, 1962, what they called "the unabridged text" of the Thant Plan. In reality, it was a commentary given by Thant in his last report of activities. The Thant Plan dates from August 10, 1962, and it is this text, stripped of any details on sanctions, that was presented to Adoula and to the Katangan government. — U.N. Document, Security Council, S/5053/Add. 13, Annex I.

states and which should "so far as possible secure to the individual states the maximum of the revenues originating in their regions."

4. For utilization of foreign exchange, needs relative to the activities of industries producing revenues and foreign exchange would be taken into consideration (for the transitional period, the revenues deriving from foreign trade and mining royalties would be shared equally between the central authorities and Katanga, while Katanga would dispose of at least 50 percent of the foreign exchange resulting from Katangan production.

5. The International Monetary Fund would work out a "phased plan for currency unification."

6. After a maximum of ninety days, integration and unification of military forces and gendarmery troops would be effected.

7. External representation (foreign affairs, diplomacy, and consular corps) would be the exclusive domain of the central government, and the other types of representation (economic or commercial, for example) would be subjected to the agreement of the central government.

8. General amnesty would be voted.

9. The central government would include the Conakat representatives.

We should mention that Elisabethville raised questions on the text. The French (official) text differed from the English, which is today accepted as the working document. Thus in the French text, representation, apart from the diplomatic or consular, is subject *à l'accord des autorités centrales*, while in the English text it is permitted "with the concurrence of the national government." In the financial section, the French text omits all reference to the fairly detailed report of the financial commission of June, 1962, while the English text mentions it.

This plan was considered by Thant as a final attempt at conciliation:

Should progress toward that solution not come quickly, I am inclined to believe that the U.N., both because of a virtually inevitable deterioration in the Congo and its own financial limitations, may soon be confronted with the necessity of deciding whether to withdraw its military force from the Congo or to go to the other extreme of specifically authorizing ONUC [the U.N. Operation in the Congo] to seek, by all necessary measures, to end Katangese efforts at secession.[4]

The Thant Plan was "not a basis for negotiation," but constituted a "non-negotiable whole" to be accepted or rejected in its entirety. The role

[4] U.N. Document, Security Council, S/5053/Add. 11, Annex II, A, August 20, 1962.

of the mixed commissions provided for in the Plan was not to bring about negotiation starting from it, but simply to elaborate the practical details of its military and financial arrangements.

To bring about the implementation of the Plan, the Secretary-General of the United Nations had in his program a "Course of Action," in four phases:

Phase 1

a. Presentation of the Plan to Adoula and if he accepts it, presentation to the Katangan authorities by Gardiner;

b. A ten-day period for Elisabethville's acceptance, with the promise — if it is accepted — of a U.N. guarantee for an equitable application;

c. Intervention in favor of the Plan in Elisabethville on the part of interested governments;

d. Belgo-Congolese negotiations attempting to obtain Belgian cooperation in collecting in Belgium duties on products exported from Belgium to Katanga; contact between Leopoldville and the Union Minière;

e. Furnishing of a modest amount of American military equipment for the ANC, and U.N. aid for carrying out an urgent modernization program for the ANC;

f. Strengthened provisions against arms smuggling and mercenaries in Katanga.

Phase 2

a. In case Katanga did not accept within the allotted ten days, the interested governments would notify Elisabethville of their intention to boycott Katangan copper and cobalt, if Leopoldville requested it, and would accept provisions for more severe measures in case the boycott did not work.

Phase 3

a. Request by Leopoldville to the governments involved to cease purchases of copper and cobalt in Katanga;

b. Favorable response to this request by the governments.

Phase 4

a. If the first three phases did not end in the reintegration of Katanga, the U.N. and the governments would concert further action.

On August 20, the Plan was presented to Adoula by Gardiner; then, with the agreement of the Congolese Prime Minister, on August 24, a copy was sent to Evariste Kimba, Jean-Baptiste Kibwe, and Godefroid Munongo, representing Tshombe who was absent.

On August 23, Adoula made known his answer: "We appreciate this gesture of good will but" reserve "freedom of action in case, though its substance may be acceptable, its execution raises difficulties." [5]

On September 2, Tshombe let it be known that he welcomed "enthusiastically the decision to endow the Congo with a federal constitution" and that he "wholeheartedly" supported "the Plan as a whole, which sets out the general principles governing the solutions which will have to be formulated. . . . The proposals of the Plan lay the foundations of a Congo that can survive." Tshombe solicited the powers which supported or approved the Plan "to guarantee in form and in fact its faithful execution." [6]

On September 5, Thant interpreted the responses of Adoula and Tshombe as an acceptance of the Plan by the two parties, adding, however, that "the acceptances are a necessary and important step forward, but they are no more than that. Their true significance will be revealed only as the specific provisions of the plan are put into effect." [7]

APPLICATION OF THE PLAN: PHASES 1 AND 2

On September 10, Thant sent a letter to the Leopoldville and Elisabethville authorities, detailing the program for execution of the Plan. It provided for:

1. Completion before the end of September, 1962, of the proposed federal constitution and its subsequent presentation to Parliament.
2. Preparation of a financial law on the distribution of revenues and foreign exchange, to be written into the constitution and to be submitted to Parliament.
3. An oath of allegiance to the president of the republic, to be taken immediately by the commanders of all the Katangan military units.
4. The proclamation of an amnesty by the central authorities.
5. The suppression of the "Ministry of Foreign Affairs" in the Tshombe government and of Katangan missions abroad.

[5] *Ibid.*, Add. 13, Annex III.
[6] *Ibid.*, Annex IV.
[7] *Ibid.*, Annex V.

6. The renewal by Adoula of the offer of participation made to Conakat in a reconstituted central government.

According to Gardiner's reports this is the way the question of execution of the Thant Plan evolved during September and October, 1962:

ELABORATION OF A FEDERAL CONSTITUTION

A draft of the federal constitution, different in many respects from the draft of the *ad hoc* Congolese commission, was presented by a group of experts furnished by the United Nations.[8] This is the text which was to have been discussed and adopted by the Congolese Chambers of Parliament meeting together and sitting as a Constituent Assembly. A government bill would have eliminated the procedure of ratification of the constitution by the provincial assemblies;[9] Adoula therefore sent to the provincial governments and assemblies, as well as to political groups a note inviting them to make known their views on constitutional matters. On August 24, this note was sent to Elisabethville. Katanga replied on September 24 with several "first preliminary remarks" carrying strong reservations. The draft of the constitution was submitted to Adoula on September 27, and, according to Gardiner, it was transmitted by him to the officers of the two Chambers of Parliament on October 13, 1962. This plan was submitted to the conference of provincial presidents in Leopold-ville between October 16 and 23, but the Katangan authorities, although invited, did not attend this meeting.[10] The constitutional plan made of the Congo a "sovereign federal State" with substantial powers at the center, residual powers granted to the provinces, and a broad zone of matters of concurrent jurisdiction. "The draft is more centralized than the former *Loi Fondamentale*," a Katangan communiqué was to assert on November 12, 1962.[11]

WORK OF THE MIXED COMMISSIONS

Led respectively by Joseph Ngalula, Congolese Minister of National Education, and Joseph Yav, the delegations of the central government and of Katanga began work on September 22 in Elisabethville. From the

---

[8] *Congo 1962*, pp. 307–24.   [9] *Congo 1962*, pp. 305–7.

[10] The President of the Assembly in Elisabethville, Charles Mutaka-wa-Dilomba, refused to go to Leopoldville, the invitation having been addressed to him as "President of the South Katanga Assembly," a province whose legal existence as such he rejected. — *L'Essor du Katanga* (Elisabethville), October 17, 1960.

[11] U.N. Document, Security Council, S/5053/Add. 13, Annex XIX-a.

outset, the views diverged. For Ngalula, it was simply a question of applying the Thant Plan; for Yav, the Thant Plan had to be considered as a
"basis for discussion." These divergences weighed heavily on the evolution of the discussions, to such an extent that on October 3, Ngalula, in a
letter to Yav, said it was his "painful impression that the meetings are
degenerating into idle talk." [12]

In the commission on foreign exchange, no accord was concluded on
the precise percentage of foreign exchange to allocate to Leopoldville and
to Elisabethville; however, it was agreed that the Monetary Council could
fix, with a delegate from the Bank of Katanga (André Van Roey), the
details for making the exchange control procedures uniform. It was agreed
in principle that the foreign exchange receipts from Katanga could be
turned over to the central government, in accordance with methods to be
defined by the agreement between the Monetary Council and the Bank
of Katanga. It was understood that the needs of Katanga would be given
priority when the available foreign exchange came to be allocated.

In the commission on revenues, agreement was reached on the principle
of centralization of control over customs receipts and on rapid resumption of transportation via the Katanga-Matadi "national route," to
the full extent technically feasible. The Katangan delegation agreed to
turn over to the central government its share of the customs duties. Yet,
during the transitional period, Katanga wished to limit the central government's share in the duties, taxes, and mining royalties to 25–30 percent
of the net revenues, while the Thant Plan fixed it at 50 percent.

In the military commission, the agreement concluded on October 16,
in Elisabethville and published by the local press on October 17 — a
cease-fire halting troop movements and arms deliveries in North Katanga
— was rejected in Leopoldville by the Adoula government. Adoula felt
that such an accord, which did not apply to South Katanga, would in
reality have constituted recognition of Tshombe's authority over North
Katanga, whereas the law of July 11, 1962, had created a new province
of North Katanga. In addition, Adoula objected to "the scandalous interference" of certain "consular missions" in Elisabethville.

Thus, at the end of October, the application of the Plan was hardly
begun.

At this point, Thant, noting "the lack of any substantial progress in
the actual implementation of the Plan" and the ensuing risk that the

[12] *Ibid.*, Annex XIII.

August proposals might lapse, tried to relaunch them by addressing to the two parties on November 1 and 2 a document entitled, "An Assessment of the Requirements of the Plan."[13] Gardiner's covering letter explained, "The main burden of action falls upon the Katangese authorities, although the importance of the actions which the Central Government is obliged to take must not be minimized."

What the Thant document considered incumbent upon each party concerned is as follows:

For Katanga

1. Agreement to share equally between Leopoldville and Elisabethville, the taxes and duties on exports and imports, and all royalties from mining concessions.[14]
2. Deposit of all foreign exchange resulting from Katangan exports with the Monetary Council of the Republic, with the understanding that the council would refund at least 50 percent of it to Katanga to cover its needs.
3. Oath of allegiance from the Katangan military commanders, without any precondition.
4. Completion of the plan for rapid integration and unification of all military, paramilitary, and gendarmery units.
5. Elimination of the Ministry of Foreign Affairs and of foreign representatives for Katanga.
6. Freedom of movement for the U.N. in the Congo and application of measures aimed at the mercenaries.

For the Central Government

1. Decree of immediate amnesty and, if need be, a bill in Parliament.
2. Renewal by Adoula of the offer of participation by the Conakat in the central government.

The relaunching of the plan came to nothing.

On November 10, Adoula reiterated the "complete agreement" of his government, but drew attention "to the risks which failure to respect the

---

[13] *Ibid.*, Annex XVII.

[14] And not to divide the net revenues with 70 to 75 percent for Katanga and 25 to 30 percent for the central government, as accepted by the Katangan delegation. It is clear also that the Katangan proposal made at the end of June, then again on October 11 and on November 12, to offer 100 million francs to the central government did not correspond to the Plan, even as an intermediate solution.

time sequence of [the] Plan might entail."[15] The Prime Minister confirmed the offer for governmental participation by the Conakat in a letter
to Tshombe on November 13, 1962, letting it be understood that this
offer would be applicable when South Katanga had renounced its state
of secession. On November 26, the Chief of State proclaimed "that a
general and complete amnesty will be granted to all those who return to our
country, . . . whatever political offenses they may have committed."[16]

On November 28, in the Chamber, Adoula confirmed this promise of
amnesty, but, on November 30, Tshombe objected to the fact that it had
not been given legal form by Parliament.

On November 12, Tshombe responded to Gardiner, pleading not guilty:
"I was astonished and even pained [by this document]. . . . Our willingness to carry out the Plan of National Reconciliation has been shown
in innumerable ways since September 3. We are still willing to put this
Plan into effect despite the difficulties placed in our way. We shall not
deviate from this. Katanga has no separatist attitude."[17] Tshombe felt
that it was Adoula who thwarted the work of the mixed commissions
and who sabotaged the Plan. In an attachment to this letter, Tshombe
analyzed what, according to him, had been done by Katanga to further
the Plan[18] and the shortcomings of Leopoldville in this respect, but he
took upon himself none of the obligations defined for Katanga by "An
Assessment of the Requirements of the Plan."

In addition, the same day, a Katangan communiqué openly accused
the U.N. of preparing military action against Katanga.[19]

"If the object of your reply is to prove Katanga's desire to put the
U Thant Plan into effect, I am very much afraid that your reply will mis-
lead and disappoint not only the Secretary-General but all those who have
up to now counted upon you to play a constructive part in the solution of
the Congo's problems," Gardiner responded to Tshombe on November 16,
1962.[20] The chief of U.N. operations in the Congo concluded:

The only way to convince the Secretary-General and the world at large
that Katanga has decided to give up its secession is to fulfill the following
conditions:

[15] U.N. Document, Security Council, S/5053/Add. 13, Annex XVIII.
[16] *Ibid.*, Annex I.
[17] *Ibid.*, Annex XIX.
[18] In particular, the reopening of rail traffic over the Lubilash bridge in order to
resume transportation over the "national route."
[19] U.N. Document, Security Council, S/5053/Add. 13, Annex XIX-a.
[20] *Ibid.*, Annex XX.

1. To send the senior officers to Leopoldville without delay to take the oath of allegiance there, it being understood that the U.N. is prepared, if necessary, to provide the transportation of these officers to Leopoldville.

2. The announcement of immediate measures for the application of the provisions of the Plan dealing with revenues, finances, and foreign exchange.

3. Authorization for customs and immigration officers of the central government to discharge their functions to Katanga as in the rest of the Congo.

4. Granting of absolute freedom of movement to all U.N. personnel in Katanga, including Jadotville, Kipushi, and Kolwezi.

5. Cooperation with the U.N. to eliminate all mercenaries from the gendarmery.

In fact, from this moment forward, no solution by conciliation seemed practicable for Leopoldville, Elisabethville, and the U.N. in the Congo. The question was whether the situation was going to pass into the subsequent phases of the "Course of Action" or to all forms of effective pressure on Katanga. The Western powers again stepped into the picture, consulted and acted together in November. U.S. Undersecretary of State George McGhee tried to unclog the apparatus and to relaunch the Plan in a conciliatory form, obtaining from Tshombe "not a fulfillment of the Thant Plan, but certain gestures" such as the deposit of two million dollars in Leopoldville, the reopening of the Lubilash bridge, and the resumption of Elisabethville–Leopoldville telecommunications.[21] But at the end of the month, the affair was the object of discussions between Spaak, Thant, and Gardiner on November 26; Spaak and Kennedy on November 27; and Spaak, Thant and Stevenson on November 28. The idea of a final conciliatory attempt (a meeting in New York with the participation of Adoula, then of Tshombe) was submitted to Leopoldville on December 4, but was rejected by the Congolese Prime Minister.

The threat of economic sanctions against South Katanga, coinciding with the seizure of Kongolo by the ANC on December 4, increased political tension in Elisabethville, while the destruction of the bridge over the Lualaba at Kongolo by the South Katangan gendarmery, hardened the positions adopted by Leopoldville. The U.N. strengthened its military forces; while affirming that it would take no initiative in any military offensive, the U.N. meant to ensure for itself total freedom of movement in Katanga by dismantling the roadblocks. Meanwhile, the pro-Katanga "lobbies" were particularly active in Brussels and London.

In late November and early December, two public warnings were addressed to Katanga. The first came from President Kasavubu who, recall-

---

[21] Declaration of Spaak to the Belgian Senate on December 4, 1962.

ing his position of non-violence in principle and his preference for a peaceful settlement, nonetheless put Elisabethville on guard against "the continued harmful influence of colonialism" which prevailed in Katanga and to which the Congo intended to put an end.[22]

The second warning emanated from Spaak: November 15 had been fixed as the date for settlement of the Katangan affair by the Thant Plan and on December 4 the Plan was still stymied. Under these conditions, if there were no solution by December 21, Thant would have to return to the Consultative Committee and to the Security Council, and there "one would have to expect tough resolutions . . . against Katanga."[23]

KATANGAN PROBLEMS DURING THE SECOND HALF OF 1962

THE PROBLEM OF THE REFUGEE CAMP IN ELISABETHVILLE

At the end of December, 1961, the U.N. refugee camp in Elisabethville included tens of thousands of men, women, and children, especially of Baluba origin. "Between 50,000 and 100,000," noted the U.N. with significant vagueness.[24] The interpretation of the phenomenon diverges sharply, depending on whether U.N. or Katangan sources are consulted. According to the U.N., the refugees had come spontaneously since August–September, 1961, to solicit protection from the U.N. against persecution by the Katangan authorities and the police, and, "having established that the danger they feared was real, ONUC gave them the protection they requested."[25] For the Katangan authorities, this camp was the sinister fruit of a U.N. political operation (especially of O'Brien and Tombelaine), which had sought to provoke a violent reaction in world opinion against Minister Munongo, accused of being the perpetrator of the Baluba persecutions.

In any case, this camp was a running sore, a center of misery, of banditry, and of violent opposition to the established authorities. Appeals by the U.N. and Katanga to persuade the refugees to return to their homes in the Elisabethville communes were to no avail. The great majority of the refugees demanded repatriation to their birthplaces.

The repatriation of 71,266 refugees to South Kasai, North Kasai, Kabinda, and northern Katanga took place from May 8 to July 30. On the

[22] U.N. Document, Security Council, S/5053/Add. 13/Add. 1.

[23] Minutes, Belgian Senate, December 4, 1962.

[24] U.N. Document, Security Council, S/5053/Add. 11, I, E, para. 45, August 20, 1962.

[25] U.N. Document, Security Council, S/4940, para. 7, and *ibid.*, para. 44.

morning of August 1, 1962, the population of the camp had been reduced to 1,500 refugees. The U.N. turned over the camp to the Elisabethville authorities in an official ceremony on the morning of August 1, 1962, after Elisabethville had guaranteed the safety of the refugees and their progressive reintegration into the communes.

RELATIONS WITH THE U.N.

After the Leopoldville discussions, difficulties with the U.N. resumed on the occasion of the July 11 celebration, the anniversary of the secession, with the participation of two thousand soldiers and eight hundred Katangan policemen in Elisabethville.

The prospect of completion of the Thant Plan, with persisting rumors, then overt declarations, concerning eventual economic pressures or sanctions against Katanga, provoked a violent anti-U.N. and anti-American reaction in Elisabethville. The first violent incident that can be linked with the conjuncture of the Thant Plan was the demonstration, on July 17, of several thousand Katangan women at the U.N. control post on Avenue Tombeur in Elisabethville. Twenty-one members of the U.N. force were wounded; a Katangan woman was said to have been killed and six others injured. Tshombe then, reportedly, declared "that the United Nations was in a state of war with Katanga . . . [and that] the U.N. forces would be subject to harassment tactics."[26] U.N. members were arrested; vehicles were confiscated by the gendarmery. Stores refused to sell to U.N. personnel, who could not leave their homes after sunset, and so forth. The press dispatches according to which Thant characterized Tshombe and his colleagues as a "band of clowns" were often cited in Elisabethville in the polemic with the U.N. There were numerous incidents between U.N. patrols and the Katangan gendarmery: for example, on September 12, when the Katangans accused the U.N., and in particular the Indian contingent, of provocative attacks against the gendarmery positions; on September 24, when a U.N. patrol fell victim to land mines; on September 20 when a U.N. Dakota was shot down at Kamunzu on a reconnaissance mission, without anyone's knowing whether it had been hit by the ANC or by the Katangan gendarmery; on September 22 and on October 5 and 24, kidnapping of a total of four Tunisian soldiers, explained by Tshombe as desertion; then on December 4, the arrest of two civilian officials of the U.N. in the Congo. This type of incident would be multiplied in December until the final trial of force.

[26] U.N. Document, Security Council, S/5053/Add. 11, I, C, para. 39.

THE MERCENARIES

Despite the most solemn declarations of the Elisabethville authorities, mercenaries continued to serve in the Katangan armed forces and, in the face of the ANC threat in North Katanga, especially since the beginning of August, troops and equipment were reinforced by the Katangans. The number of mercenaries present the first half of 1961 was again equaled and even surpassed. The Katangan air force had been strengthened in 1962 with at least five Pipers, three German Klemms (furnished, according to Gardiner, by the Belgian Colonel Cassart), seven Harvards for instruction and combat, and probably with Mustangs and Harvards from South Africa and with four Vampires piloted by Australians.[27]

To these precise charges of the U.N., Tshombe merely replied: "The affair of the mercenaries is like the tales about sea serpents or the Abominable Snowman. It is being used against Katanga once again, just as it is whenever . . . the truth and justice of our cause and the moderation of our position gain new public understanding. . . . [The] mercenaries are the pretext put forward before each new resort to force."[28]

RELATIONS WITH LEOPOLDVILLE

On his return from Leopoldville, at the end of June, Tshombe was careful to give the impression that these discussions had not been unfruitful, in the fear that the "hard-liners" in Leopoldville and in the U.N. might too hastily conclude that failure there had tolled the knell for attempts at conciliation and that the only way left open was a trial by force of arms.

This was reflected on June 28, 1962, by a gesture of the Katangan government (a promise to deposit 100 million francs in Leopoldville to combat unemployment in the capital) and by declarations: "I feel that the work done in Leopoldville was extremely constructive."

Almost at the same moment, however, Tshombe adopted an attitude which could not fail to offend the Leopoldville leadership. The gift of 100 million francs ("transmitted" declared the Katangan president) was given through U.N. channels to avoid having it squandered by "the Leopoldville politicians [who] have already profited from Katangan money to clamber into power."[29]

The creation of a province of North Katanga at the beginning of July

[27] Gardiner report, in *ibid.*, Add. 12, C, para. 30 and 51.
[28] U.N. Document, Security Council, S/5053/Add. 12, Annex VI.
[29] *L'Essor du Katanga* (Elisabethville), July 2, 1962.

and the discussions over the plans ascribed to the Americans and to Thant served to harden Tshombe's position. He broadened the scope of the July 11 festivities (on the anniversary of the secession). He accused Adoula of not being a "valid spokesman," his government of "being only a fiction . . . sailing under an illegal flag."[30]

At this point, Tshombe appropriated the arguments of the anti-Adoula opposition in Leopoldville, which rallied the MNC/Lumumba, the PSA, the Balubakat elements, the MNC/Kalonji, the Parti de l'Unité Nationale (Puna), and the Conakat. This opposition cartel denied any legal basis to the government reconstituted by Adoula, which on July 16 had received 66 votes against 44, with 6 abstentions, in the lower Chamber. The opposition maintained that the minimum required for a new government was sixty-nine votes, or half of all the members of the lower Chamber. Adoula held that half of those present was enough for a vote of confidence in a continuing government, even if it was reconstituted.

The attitude of the Conakat in Leopoldville, where it supported the opposition (even in the Gizenga episode), helped to poison relations between the central authorities and Elisabethville, especially in June and July, 1962, at a moment when the Adoula government was weakened by the momentary passage of the Abako into the opposition. In spite of concrete proposals made to the Conakat on June 19 and 22, the Conakat did not participate in the reconstituted government. This is understandable, after the breakdown of the Leopoldville discussions. Rather curiously, therefore, in July, 1962, Tshombe seemed to be casting his lot on the collapse of the Adoula government and on the creation of another government in Leopoldville including the MNC, the PSA, the Puna, and the Conakat. He arrived at a similar calculation in December, 1962, when the opposition cartel sought to avoid letting the Adoula government be strengthened by the prestige which would redound to it from ending the Katanga secession. Jean Bolikango (Puna) was to declare to Adoula on November 28, 1962, in the lower Chamber: "Without you, Katanga would come back with no problem and without loss of human life or dispersion of the national inheritance." Up to the very end, Elisabethville believed its salvation could come from an anti-Adoula climate in Leopoldville and overlooked naught in stimulating it.

In late July, 1962, the Elisabethville position was influenced by several additional facts:

[30] *L'Echo de la Bourse* (Brussels), July 25, 1962.

1. The closing of Katangan airports, on the request of Leopoldville, and the prohibition of direct "radio" contacts outside Katanga.
2. The obligation imposed by the central authorities on foreign enterprises to choose between Elisabethville and the Congo:

Mining companies, commercial firms, plantations and other enterprises will no longer be authorized to continue, on the one hand, to support subversion and secession in South Katanga, and, on the other, to draw economic advantages from their activities in other regions of the Congo. The central government has decided to create a special commission to study and propose legislative measures and other steps which are necessary to implement effective action against the enterprises which fit into the category described above.

3. ANC offensive in North Katanga, especially after August 20.

This fundamental opposition did not stop discussions from taking place on the Thant Plan nor prevent steps from being taken such as the re-establishment of Elisabethville-Leopoldville telecommunications in mid-October or, at the same time, the resumption of rail traffic over the Lubilash bridge, which in turn reopened the "national route" for the export of Congolese copper. These initiatives reflect the fact that Katangan authorities could not ignore the attitudes of the world at large. A certain amount of "good will" had to be displayed to the U.N. in the Congo to provide the friends of Katanga with some arguments for proving Katanga's good faith in seeking reintegration and understanding with Leopoldville.

THE SITUATION IN NORTH KATANGA

The military situation in North Katanga had developed unfavorably for the Katangan gendarmery in early 1962.

On December 31, 1961, in fact, Kongolo was controlled by the ANC, and it was later learned, on January 19, that nineteen missionaries had been massacred on January 1 in this region.

On February 17, Tshombe's gendarmery had reoccupied Kongolo,[31] while the ANC, receiving reinforcements from Luluabourg, based its operations on Kabalo and Albertville, where General Victor Lundula declared he was "determined to pursue the military operation until the Katanga secession was liquidated." Albertville served as the political capital of North Katanga and was, moreover, regularly visited by politi-

---

[31] Yav claimed, on February 26, 1962, that the gendarmery found on their arrival "880 bodies of civilians killed by ANC soldiers." This assertion was never again repeated by Elisabethville.

cal leaders from Leopoldville: Adoula, Cléophas Kamitatu (at the beginning of March), Jérôme Anany, Joseph Ngalula, and others.

During the Adoula-Tshombe talks, a military lull prevailed in North Katanga, but, early in July, resumption of military activity in the Kongolo region was announced, which each party accused the other of instigating.

After Leopoldville had rejected the cease-fire agreement concluded on October 16 in Elisabethville by the mixed military commission of Ngalula and Yav, the situation in the north developed favorably for the ANC. The ANC reoccupied Kongolo on December 4; but, before retreating, the Katangan gendarmery blew up the bridge over the Lualaba, stirring protests both from Leopoldville and the U.N.

Politically, North Katanga was the object of a struggle between Leopoldville and Elisabethville as tense as that on the military level. During the first six months, Jason Sendwe, Vice-Prime Minister and Extraordinary Commissioner General for Katanga, tried to organize a local administration with Balubakat leaders who had remained in the province and to secure the resumption of regional economic activity, especially in Manono, through talks in Brussels with directors of the companies concerned (Géomines, Cimental, Plantkaf, Filtisaf, Messageries Automobiles du Sankuru, Bunge, and Compagnie des Chemins de Fer du Congo Supérieur aux Grand Lacs Africains). Circulation of the Katangan franc was barred in North Katanga, in regions controlled by the ANC or by the Lualaba government; while in regions still under their control (Kabongo, Kamina, Kongolo, Luena), the Elisabethville authorities imposed their currency and granted special credits to launch social and commercial activities anew (100 million Katangan francs on April 13). In fact, in the economic and social domains, the situation in North Katanga was difficult, often even disastrous, except for the great mining enterprises in Manono.

During the last half of 1962, the legal and political situation of North Katanga was fundamentally changed by the creation of the province. It was granted an assembly and a government. Sendwe had even made an appeal for a government of provincial union to Evariste Kimba, "Minister of Foreign Affairs" in Elisabethville, who was guaranteed his personal safety and a "position." The appeal met with no response. Simultaneously, Elisabethville encouraged more than ever the pro-Tshombe "Baluba rallying movement" whose manifestos and proclamations appeared with increasing frequency in the Katangan press; their practical import continued to be very little.

APPLICATION OF THE THANT PLAN: PHASES 3 AND FOLLOWING

The attempts of Gardiner, Thant, and McGhee, as well as those decided upon in Washington at the time of the Spaak-Kennedy talks, virtually failed in that the Thant Plan was not implemented after the long process of conciliation. Consequently, the central Congolese government and the U.N. Secretary-General felt it necessary to pass into the subsequent phases of the "Course of Action." This decision led to a series of initiatives of which the first took place on December 10 and 11: Thant's official warning to Elisabethville that the final phases of the Course of Action were to be implemented because of the lack of any serious step on the part of Katanga towards implementing the plan;[32] a letter from Adoula to seventeen governments asking them temporarily not to authorize the importation of Katangan copper and cobalt;[33] a letter from Thant to Spaak asking him to "exert all possible influence on the Union Minière to cause it to desist forthwith from paying revenues to Katanga province."[34]

The days from December 10 to 20 were, therefore, decisive. The Adoula government, supported by Thant, unleashed Phases 3 and 4 of the Course of Action, with threats of an embargo on copper and cobalt. Governments could render this embargo ineffective, but some of the most important — the United States, Belgium, and the United Kingdom — were so linked to the drafting of the Course of Action that they could not very well disavow it, even supposing they wished to do so. Brussels and London, acting in concerted fashion, in Europe, locally in Africa, and even at NATO (Council of December 14), continued to plead for negotiation or at least conciliation. Still they knew that the concession South Katanga had to make was to accept the solution proposed by Thant on the division of revenues and foreign exchange. The United States sent the Truman mission to the Congo, both to furnish necessary equipment to the U.N. in the Congo with the assumption that a trial of strength was imminent and to impress Tshombe and his entourage by a manifestation of the support that the Americans were prepared to furnish immediately to the U.N. in the Congo.

At this point, Tshombe and his followers were isolated.[35] The hope of linking secessionist Katanga to the Pan-African Freedom Movement of

[32] U.N. Document, Security Council, S/5053/Add. 14, Annex XII.
[33] *Ibid.*, Annex XVII.
[34] *Ibid.*, Annex XIII.
[35] "Tshombe can no longer be considered as a statesman, but as a very powerful rebel." — Paul-Henri Spaak at the Université Libre de Bruxelles, December 11, 1962.

Eastern, Central, and Southern Africa (PAFMECSA) grouping collapsed, although it had never really had any substance elsewhere than in the minds of European advisers in Elisabethville and the policy makers in London or Brussels. Rhodesian aid, discussed by Sir Roy Welensky and Jean-Baptiste Kibwe on December 13 in Salisbury, lost its importance in the medium and long run when London accepted the principle of the break-up of the Federation. The UMHK was conscious that the secession was weakening, even if its directors hardly dared act openly in accordance with the belief. Gaullist sympathy was at this point strictly platonic. In Leopoldville, the opposition on which Tshombe seemed to count for allies could not anticipate taking over in the short run.[36]

On December 13, it appeared as if Tshombe had recognized his situation. Belgian authorities in Brussels sent Rector Marcel Dubuisson on a special mission to Tshombe seeking to keep the door to conciliation still ajar. Tshombe said he was ready to authorize the UMHK to deposit its foreign exchange with the Monetary Council, provided that the Katangan provincial government could count on 250 million francs each month. Tshombe advised Thant of this decision on December 13, and, on December 15, the Belgian government advised the UMHK to argue on the basis of the Tshombe letter to the U.N. and to take the initiative and, without beating about the bush, to send representatives to Leopoldville to deal directly with the problem. The UMHK management hesitated and consulted with Elisabethville, but on December 18, Tshombe cut the knot: "It seems futile for the Union Minière alone to deal with the implementation of our proposal"; the Katangan government would itself designate negotiators with Leopoldville.

From then on, no solution could be reached by conciliation. Tshombe declared at Kolwezi on December 19 that he would resort to a "scorched earth" policy rather than accept reintegration by force. Anti-American demonstrations erupted in Elisabethville. The U.S. military mission arrived in the Congo on December 21. Thus, after several days, economic-financial pressures and threats were bypassed by events, and the end of the secession was to be found after a trial by military strength.

[36] In Elisabethville, at the beginning of December, government circles and the press made much of the activities of Jean Bolikango and of certain members of the opposition to whom "Katanga assured all its support." — *L'Essor du Katanga* (Elisabethville), December 10, 1962. Simultaneously, a pro-Tshombe Belgian newspaper such as *La Libre Belgique* the same day hopefully posed the question, "Bolikango's Hour?".

CHAPTER 9 · *The Final Trial of Force*

THE state of tension prevailing in Katanga after December 15 was almost bound to give rise to incidents which could degenerate into a trial of strength between the U.N. in the Congo and the Katangan gendarmery. Elisabethville was at this point in a volatile state. The Americans directly supported the U.N. on the political level and in military matters; the Belgian government still spoke of the necessity for "conciliation," but meant by this term, pure and simple acceptance by South Katanga of the clauses of the Thant Plan concerning money and finances. The ANC chalked up serious victories in the north.

On December 24, incidents broke out which were to ignite the powder. Accounts differ greatly, with the U.N. in the Congo and the Katangan authorities each offering its own version. The U.N. in the Congo accused the gendarmery of firing on a reconnaissance helicopter, shooting it down (one Indian officer dead), and of having then, on December 25 and 27, opened fire sporadically against U.N. positions. According to the Katangans, the first shot came from the Ethiopians of the U.N. forces and the occupants of the helicopter had fired on the Katangan gendarmery before the latter answered.

On December 28, the U.N. in the Congo tried to get Tshombe to give orders to the gendarmery for the immediate dismantlement of all road blocks in Elisabethville and in the surrounding countryside, in order "to ensure freedom of movement for the U.N. forces."[1] The Katangan president said he agreed "in principle," but refused to sign the prepared document; he said he would have to consult his government.[2] The U.N. then decided to dismantle the Katangan roadblocks itself.

[1] U.N. Document, Security Council, S/5053/Add. 14, Annex XXVII.

[2] According to the British consul, Tshombe had given the order for a cease-fire at 6. A.M., but this order had not been observed. Tshombe declared that this agreement would "have handed the country over without resistance to the troops, which without any right are seeking to impose by force the political solution of foreign imperialism." — U.N. Document, Security Council, S/5053/Add. 14, Annex XXVIII.

Tshombe then made an inflammatory declaration, calling on the people to struggle against the U.N. forces by all means, "ambushes, poison, spears and poisoned arrows," and threatening to destroy the economic potential of Katanga if the U.N. pursued its action.[3]

On December 28, at 4:15 P.M., the U.N. forces began to clean out the road blocks in Elisabethville. The Katangan gendarmery put up no resistance, or almost none: generally, they dispersed into the brush, sometimes taking with them the local population. Without difficulty, the U.N. forces occupied the post office, the presidential palace, the railroad station, the Radio-Katanga studios, and the gendarmery headquarters. On December 29, the Ethiopian and Irish forces advanced on Kipushi, while six Swedish fighters attacked the Kolwezi-Kengere airfield (one Harvard shot down, another burned; one Dove and one Harvard destroyed on the ground along with a Vampire and a Piper Comanche, according to the U.N. report). At Ngule airport, a Katangan Dragon Rapide was destroyed. In Kasapa commune, the Gurkhas met a certain amount of resistance. In Albert commune, there were civilian casualties from automatic arms and mortars.

In an appeal over the radio, the U.N. in the Congo declared: "The cause for which Tshombe has armed you is that of foreign interests, who maintain the secession to draw a profit from your natural wealth." The U.N. in the Congo invited the gendarmery to lay down their arms in order to "safeguard the honor of the Republic."[4]

Tshombe left his home and, according to Radio-Katanga Libre, he directed operations not far from Elisabethville. South Katangan refugees crossed the Rhodesian frontier. London invited Thant to secure an immediate cease-fire and to permit the resumption of discussions to implement the plan for reconciliation. This would be done, as Tshombe proposed on December 28, by sending to Leopoldville a delegation charged with discussing the equitable distribution of revenues.[5] "What is happening has nothing to do with the Thant Plan," declared Spaak. He added, "It is not beyond the realm of possibility that the U.N. is taking advantage of circumstances to try to find a solution to the Katangan problem by a method of which I never approved."

On December 30, Kipushi — hub on the route toward Rhodesia and

[3] *Ibid.*

[4] *Le Monde* (Paris), January 1, 1963.

[5] On December 28, Tshombe accused the U.N. of not having transmitted to Adoula his offer of December 13 concerning the division of foreign exchange.

Jadotville and a mining center on which Jadotville depended — was occupied by the U.N. in the Congo without a fight. The Swedes and the Ghanaians of the U.N., operating from Kamina base, occupied the city of Kamina. The Elisabethville zone, that is, the city and the zone within a radius of 20 kilometers, was entirely under the control of the U.N., whose air force had destroyed two more Harvards on the ground.

That afternoon, Tshombe was in Salisbury, where he met with Sir Roy Welensky and held a press conference. He announced his return to Katanga. He said he was ready again to practice a "scorched earth" policy. According to a Foreign Office spokesman, Tshombe was informed by Great Britain that the U.N. would guarantee his personal safety if he returned to Katanga.[6] Numerous reactions hostile to the proposal for a cease-fire made by the Macmillan government were heard: an official protest from Adoula; rejection of the idea by Gardiner, who declared that the U.N. would not commit the error this time of permitting Tshombe's gendarmery to regroup; opposition from British Labor leader Harold Wilson; telegrams from leaders of the PAFMECSA meeting in Leopoldville, and others. Spaak declared on his part that he was in favor of a cessation of military operations and the resumption of discussions to apply the Thant Plan.

On December 31, the U.N. forces pushed forward over the route to Jadotville where gendarmery and mercenaries were entrenched. Nowhere did the population organize resistance against the U.N. in the forms Tshombe hoped for. Mixed patrols of U.N. forces and Katangan police were organized in Elisabethville to ensure order. U.N. officials took over the Bank of Katanga, and in Leopoldville a United Nations spokesman declared that the Katangan gendarmery would be considered as a hostile force, so long as its officers would not take the oath of allegiance to the central authorities.

It was at this point that Thant announced that "the ONUC operation, which had begun on the afternoon of December 28 to remove all of the road blocks of the Katangese gendarmery in the Elisabethville area, has been completed" and that he would allow a period of two weeks in which to implement his Plan, "before other measures might have to be weighed."[7] This unexpected declaration by Thant — supported by Washington — seemed to indicate two things:

[6] "Unless he instigates acts of hostility against the United Nations Operation and its personnel," declared Thant, January 2, 1963. — U.N. Document, Security Council, S/5053/Add. 14, Annex XXXII.

[7] *Ibid.*, Annex XXXI.

1. Military operations were ended; the position of the U.N. force, according to Thant, was that it would not let itself be attacked in the future, "without responding quickly and sharply."
2. For two more weeks, the relaunching of the Thant Plan would be tried on a properly political basis, and, for Katanga, the legitimate spokesman for the discussions would be Tshombe.[8]

It is certainly in this fashion that the text was interpreted by the governments of Belgium and Great Britain: in Brussels, "one can only rejoice over the halting of these operations"; and supported the measures recommended by Thant to the Katangan authorities and to Adoula; in London, it was recalled that a "procedure of this nature to avoid new fighting has always been recommended by Her Majesty's Government." Through their consuls, the two Western powers encouraged Tshombe to return to Elisabethville at this point to take advantage of the new two-week delay, while Leopoldville complained that Tshombe was only being furnished a new chance to "drag up dilatory measures for renewed consideration." Events were to unfold in a very different manner in fact than that hinted at by the Thant declaration of December 31.

On January 1, 1963, the U.N. resumed its march toward Jadotville, despite the blown-up bridges and mine fields, and, at mid-day on January 3, the U.N. forces entered the city.[9] For forty-eight hours, on January 8 and 9, it was thought that, in view of Tshombe's return to Elisabethville from Kolwezi[10] and his peace-making role in the occupation of Sakania by the U.N., it would be possible to avoid a direct operation against Kolwezi, where the Katangan ministers had repaired along with the last knot of mercenaries and available gendarmery units under General Muké.[11]

[8] Thant amended this on January 2, 1963, by explaining that, in his opinion, new official discussions with Tshombe were useless at this stage; the problems to be settled were technical and concerned the application of the plan.

[9] U.N. headquarters in New York was caught by surprise with this operation. Subsequently "the stress and strain of action," created by this military operation, revealed "serious deficiencies in communications and coordination between the United Nations Headquarters in New York, Leopoldville Headquarters of the ONUC [U.N. in the Congo], and the military detachments in action in the field." — Gardiner report, U.N. Document, Security Council, S/5053/Add. 14, para. 74, January 11, 1963.

[10] Tshombe returned to Elisabethville, coming by the Kipushi road in the car of the Belgian consul, Vandewalle. His safety during the stay was guaranteed by the Belgian and British consuls. For an account of his return, see *L'Essor du Katanga* (Elisabethville), January 9, 1963.

[11] Relations between General Muké and the mercenaries had become very bad.

The risk of an operation against Kolwezi lay especially in the fact that the vital economic installations, in particular the Delcommune and Le Marinel dams and the Lufira power generators, had been mined by a South African munitions specialist and were thus threatened with destruction.

Despite Belgian and British suggestions, Tshombe again refused to let the U.N. into Kolwezi peacefully and still threatened to practice a scorched earth policy. Surreptitiously, he left Elisabethville on January 12, when he no longer felt it safe to remain in his residence, under the U.N. control, and returned to Kolwezi, where he found his old adviser, René Clémens, and his principal ministers. He was joined there by Houart, the Belgian consul in Salisbury.

On January 14, 1963, at 9 A.M., the Katangan ministers addressed to Spaak a declaration in which they said they were "ready to proclaim to the world that the Katanga secession is ended . . . and ready to allow the United Nations troops freedom of movement throughout Katanga . . . ready also to return to Elisabethville to arrange for the complete implementation of the Thant Plan." [12] On January 15, the UMHK signed in Leopoldville an agreement on foreign exchange, [13] while the last mercenaries, disengaging from Kolwezi *in extremis* by the Dilolo train, took refuge in Angola. On January 21, the United Nations troops entered Kolwezi. On January 23, Joseph Ileo, Resident Minister of the Central Government, arrived in Elisabethville. [14]

The white population feared excesses on the part of the Katangan gendarmery and saw in the mercenaries a bulwark against eventual excesses. On this subject, see the report of Pierre Davister in *Pourquoi Pas?* of January 18 and 25, 1963. He asserts that at Kolwezi, the mercenaries had proposed to "protect" the Delcommune dam in exchange for 200 million francs from the UMHK.

[12] U.N. Document, Security Council, S/5053/Add. 15, Annex V.

[13] The agreement provided that the UMHK would turn over all its gross receipts in foreign exchange to the Monetary Council, which would then hand back to the UMHK the foreign exchange corresponding to its needs, with a maximum of 425 millon Congolese francs per month and 38 percent of the total receipts per year. The UMHK furnished the council with accounts permitting a check of the receipts and expenditures of foreign exchange.

[14] For an account of the operations, see U.N. Documents, Security Council S/5053/Add. 14 and 15, and S/5240.

Concluding Observations

THROUGH the unravelling of events and the analysis of facts, it is possible — at the conclusion of this work — to formulate several interpretations of the Katanga secession and of the behavior of its actors, in response to the leading questions which are inevitably asked and which have been the source for abundant polemics.

First question: Is the Conakat simply a creation of the European settler community, nothing more than the instrument for the secessionist tendencies latent or overt in this sector?

Inclinations toward autonomy in Katanga do not date from the birth of the Conakat and the race to independence in the Congo. The new fact, which emerged in 1958–59, is that these leanings ceased to be a monopoly of the Europeans living in Katanga and began to occupy first place in the program of the Conakat and of the local ethnic associations led by Tshombe, Godefroid Munongo, Jean-Baptiste Kibwe, and their colleagues.

At this point, the only chance politically for the autonomist secessionist view was to have it spread and defended by Africans, with broad support in local European society. After the fact, if we use the test "Who profited from the secession?" we are sometimes tempted to explain totally the Conakat phenomenon by the strongly felt need of the Europeans to have at their disposal a transmission belt into African circles.

The reality is more complex. It is correct that, in conscious fashion, the leaders of the settler community, after 1955, adopted the strategy of organizing a black *bourgeoisie* which, socially and politically, would play the protector's role for the entire middle class in Katanga.

But elsewhere another phenomenon was developing. Ethnic groups in Katanga — the very same who proclaimed themselves "authentic Katangans" — had the more or less spontaneous feeling that industrialization and urbanization were benefiting them less than "stranger" Africans, especially Kasai immigrants. This feeling was strengthened after the elections of December, 1957 in which these "strangers" won burgomaster posts in Elisabethville and Jadotville.

The spokesmen for the groups in the urban centers then took the initiative, or let themselves be persuaded, to set up a united front of Katangan ethnic groups in opposition to those from Kasai. Pressures in this direction grew at the end of 1958. The announcement of the imminent arrival of the parliamentary Working Group from Belgium to prepare a report on the political evolution of the Congo and, in this context, the desire of future leaders of the Conakat to appear as spokesmen for a representative organization were important catalysts; so also was the desire among important segments of the administration, not suspect of complacency toward settler views, not to leave the monopoly of inter-tribal organization to the Kasaians in Fédéka. One can also discern a desire or a willingness among Europeans to see "moderate" views defended by Africans, as a counterpoise to the "extremists" in Leopoldville.

Objectively, it must be recognized that the groups constituting the Conakat were not, therefore, without African roots; so that, until mid-1959, the Baluba were even included. Nonetheless, from the outset, the Conakat was destined to turn to more or less virulent forms of xenophobia directed against "strangers" coming from other provinces of the Congo, rather than toward their Lunda "racial brothers" from Rhodesia. By the same token, the Conakat was bound to welcome favorably the confederal views of the settlers in the Ucol and the Union Katangaise as the only formula permitting the Conakat to stake their claim for keeping all powers and all leading offices for authentic Katangans alone, at the expense of the Kasaians.

By no means were the links between Conakat and the settlers in 1959 simply ideological. The community of interests was reflected in technical and financial assistance from European *ultras* to the Conakat, especially in 1959 and early in 1960, a period during which the Conakat counted the Union Katangaise among its member associations and received the essential portion of its financial support through this channel. After the Round Table, when new sources of financing and assistance came to the fore, both in Katanga and in Belgium, and even in Western circles desirous of reinforcing or of securing their future position, the Conakat sought at times to back off from its settler advisers, taking stock of the harm done by past identification with European interests, both in Balubakat Cartel circles and in the eyes of nationalist opinion in the Congo and elsewhere in Africa.

The loosening of ties between the Conakat and its *occult* settler advisers was never complete; some of the principal ones were to be found in the entourage of ministers in Tshombe's government from July, 1960, until the end of the secession. Besides, the nearer the time for the elections of May, 1960, and independence came, the more European support for the Conakat was diversified and intensified; European society in Katanga was very broadly attracted by the Tshombe party, both because he proclaimed his attachment to Belgium and to her King and because it appeared to them as "the party of calm people," respectful of authority and tradition, pitted against the Kasai "agitators" or against the Abako and the MNC "revolutionaries."

Locally, the European support, both administrative and private, played a major role in the elections. It appears that the UMHK — until then its Brussels management had acted cautiously — began to favor the Conakat, especially when strikes broke out in Katanga during April and May, 1960. Despite the appeals of Jason Sendwe to resume work and the condemnation of wildcat strikes by the Balubakat, Europeans accused the Kasaians and the Katangan Baluba of being the ringleaders. Locally, the decisive argument of the UMHK management would have been that it was necessary to compensate for, neutralize, or reduce Baluba and Kasai social agitation by a Conakat-dominated governmental authority, in that this party also appeared as the irreconcilable adversary of Lumumbist-type nationalists and as the local political force apparently the most attentive to the arguments of the industrial world. The UMHK behavior may come as a surprise to those who know the numerical importance of Kasaians among the personnel of the mining enterprises. The surprise may diminish when it is recalled that at the end of May, 1960, the Conakat made an alliance with the MNC/Kalonji, whose main roots lay in the diamond-bearing zone of Kasai. One could hardly maintain, however, that this alliance was an explanation rather than a result of the UMHK position. It was in any case decisive in the political contexts of June and July, 1960.

Second question: Were there really attempts at secession in Katanga in the months which preceded independence?

From the end of 1959 until June, 1960, secession was at the same time a means of pressure on the Belgian authorities, a temptation for the *ultras* in the white settler community and in the Conakat, and a political program in these same circles. Secession schemes were rendered vain by the balance of strength at the time, which was clearly in favor of the "united Congo" view (unitary or moderately federal), then defended by Belgian political circles in Brussels, by the parliamentary majority as well as the opposition. This view was also advocated by Congolese nationalists and by Belgian quarters traditionally influential in Congolese matters, especially the Catholic Church and the large companies.

As a means for pressure, secession for a long time proved to be a dangerous weapon for those who wielded it; at the Round Table in January, 1960, it isolated the Conakat from the Congolese federalists grouped in cartel by the Abako, by tarnishing the Conakat's confederal views with strong shades of separatism and with conservative European influences.

Analysis of the facts and accounts reveals that in December, 1959, in March and April, 1960, the idea of the Conakat leadership and of their advisers was essentially to prepare for the possibility of proclaiming an independent Katanga. This proclamation was to take place before the establishment of central institutions and immediately after the installation of provincial institutions; the latter were to have powers as extensive as possible (hence the Conakat position at the Round Table and at the political commission) and to be as strong as possible (hence the presence of leading personalities of the Conakat in the provincial elections). The idea was that it would thus be possible to hedge against future eventualities. Katanga would have cooperated to a certain extent with Leopoldville to prepare a confederal constitution but, in case of serious disagreement, the local provincial institutions could act as organs of an independent state. That explains fundamentally why the Conakat tried hard in June, 1960, to set up provincial institutions immediately and why its adversaries, on the contrary, did everything to adjust the calendar in favor of the central institutions.

On the official Belgian side, the seriousness of the secessionist threat in Katanga was always underestimated, and an erroneous or complacent interpretation was given for the threats of the Conakat in June, 1960. The anger against the Cartel does not explain the Scheerlinck affair, in which all the most influential leaders and occult advisers to the Conakat were involved. It was a question then of proclaiming independence at the provincial level, not before the establishment of the Lumumba government, since that was impossible, but before that government could come into full possession of its powers.

"The impatience of Conakat leaders to proclaim independence for Katanga during the final days of Belgian sovereignty stemmed from the fear of not being able to do it, once the Congo became independent," wrote Minister Ganshof van der Meersch.[1] Our analysis confirms this conclusion from experience. The failure of attempts to do so can be explained: the promoters seriously underestimated the importance of the stake committed at the central Congolese level by the great Belgian forces — economic, political, and religious — and many backers of the secession did not understand that in this context, there existed no chance for a secession of Katanga.

Third question: Does evidence exist of a desire on the part of the colonial authority to recoup Katanga for itself after June 30, 1960, thanks to the secession?

Personally, in discarding what would be simple presumption of intention or explanation a posteriori, we have found no decisive proof in this direction, and what evidence others have been able to marshall does not generally bear up under scrutiny. Thus it could be argued that the scheme for division of the CSK portfolio and the convention concluded by the Belgian authorities on the eve of independence with the Compagnie du Katanga clearly showed the secessionist intention of the Belgians. This argument is in contradiction with the origins and the sequence of events in this affair. If the accepted formula were that desired by the secessionists, it would be necessary to conclude that the Balubakat and its advisers, who signed an agreement on this point with the other Katangan delegations, were accomplices in this maneuver.

In fact, we have shown that the formula adopted for the CSK, was — quite simply and in keeping with the reasoning of the Belgian government of the time — the one that assured the largest possible share in the UMHK to the private sector, which, in the general shareholder's assembly, was left in a clear majority and independent of any African authority, even Katangan.

Is this to say that the secession was not hypothetically considered, among other methods, as an eventual means of defending the private sector, so strongly implanted in Katanga and Rhodesia?

This was certainly an issue among interested industrial leaders and came through in March, 1960, in the declarations of Sir Roy Welensky. In June, 1960, the local business leaders would have had at least a per-

[1] Ganshof van der Meersch, *Fin de la Souveraineté belge au Congo*, p. 92.

missive attitude toward secession. But it was understood on June 30, 1960, that secession was entirely contingent upon the collapse of the central power and of the means of repression at its disposal, and no one seriously believed that this collapse was imminent.

Meanwhile, a government dominated by the Conakat was set up in Katanga, and it would be in a position — to use Tshombe's phrase — to profit from a favorable opportunity to proclaim independence.

Fourth question: What were the most important sources of external support for the Tshombe regime?

The decisive aid, ensuring the very existence of the regime in July, 1960, was that which the Belgian soldiers gave to Katanga on the eve of, and just after, the proclamation of independence. Without it, the Katangan state would not have been able to exist. With it, Katanga was provided with an assurance of order which permitted the resumption of economic activity; by it, the resources of the secessionist state were temporarily guaranteed.

After the rupture in relations between the Congo and Belgium, Belgian aid was still of primary importance, at least until the beginning of 1961. This included the technical assistance mission of D'Aspremont Lynden, whose legal position constituted at the very least a bold and dubious innovation; the direct provision of arms and defense matériel, especially in late August and early September, 1960; a daily supply of political and military information; diplomatic support for a position of forbearance toward the status quo (a position defended in the U.N., NATO, and through bilateral contacts with Western allies); the acceptance of Katangan representatives and missions, working in liaison with semiprivate Belgian missions for the recruitment of military personnel and mercenaries.

On the diplomatic level proper, Belgium held positions which often had the support of France and Great Britain, both because of the ties traditionally existing between these capitals and Brussels and because of positions taken by those countries in Africa with which Paris and London had special relations (Congo-Brazzaville and Rhodesia). To the extent that Katanga constituted a shield against pressure from anticolonialist countries, Portugal and South Africa facilitated the solution of certain Katangan problems (transport, supplies, recruitment), often by normal commercial routes, sometimes by tolerating clandestine traffic.

During the first two months of the secession, a number of Western countries adopted toward Katanga an attitude of benevolent neutrality, corresponding to the distrust that these same countries felt toward Lumumba. This was true for the United States, which, after the month of August, treated the Tshombe regime with caution, while waiting for the central authority to be exercised by "moderates." For the United States, it was not so much a matter of giving support to the secession, but of accepting the consequences of a diplomatic position which sought not to play the Lumumbist game.

From the end of 1960 to the beginning of 1961, aid to Katanga had a tendency to be internationalized. First of all, this came on the pressing request of the Katangans themselves, who were indignant or disturbed to see in Belgian hands positions vital for the secession, when these Belgians were liable to be brusquely withdrawn at any given moment, under pressure from the U.N. or following a change of governmental policy in Brussels. Then there was the advice of the Abbé Youlou and of his French entourage, who pointed out — in a fashion which was not always disinterested — the fragility of Belgian support to Tshombe in the context of a resumption of relations with Leopoldville. Internationalization was supported locally by the European *ultras*, who felt an ideological solidarity with Algiers, as well as by those whose solidarity extended southwards into the Rhodesias, Angola, and South Africa. The relative internationalization which developed was also encouraged by pressure from the Security Council resolutions and the apparent intentions of the Secretariat, prodding Belgium to renounce its monopoly of personnel and to exercise prudence in certain forms of assistance.

Fifth question: Did the UMHK make the secession or did Tshombe save the UMHK?

In July, 1960, Katanga could not secede without the support of the UMHK which had to provide its essential resources, directly or indirectly. But the UMHK could not maintain its activities at this point, unless a certain degree of order were re-established locally, both by the Belgian army and by the Katangan government. The Union Minière and Tshombe were inseparable and lived in direct symbiosis for several months. It is this symbiosis and convergence of interests that created throughout nearly all of sub-Saharan Africa the image of Katanga as a mere creature of the UMHK, sacred ground for neocolonialism, in the dual sense that Europeans remained in a dominant position and had managed also to skim off the cream of the spectacular wealth of the former Belgian colony.

In Katanga, this symbiosis was prolonged well beyond the time when the management in Brussels had hoped to bring about a certain disengagement to take account of developing events: the failure to recognize Katanga, the reinstallation in Leopoldville of an indisputably legitimate central government of national union, and the appearance of new governments in Washington and Brussels.

For a very long time, the management in Katanga maintained pressure on the top executives in Brussels and the latter generally obtained purely formal concessions on the part of its influential managers in Katanga. Even on questions of internal Katangan policy, the symbiosis continued locally without shocking anyone in Katanga (anti-U.N. action, support for the forces of order, etc.), but all was done with respect for certain formalities, by means of requisition, mobilization, or even by resort to taxation or to regulation of foreign exchange.

After the trials of strength of September and December, 1961, which gave rise to grave mutual accusations between the UMHK and the U.N., the UMHK management found itself in a very delicate position. The United States and the U.N. demanded from the company a serious gesture (the payment of taxes to the central government) — a gesture which, according to the UMHK, could not fail to lead to retaliation by the secessionist authorities, which could be costly to mining installations for a long time.

In 1962 — and here is a very important element in the negotiations on the so-called Thant Plan — the question at issue was whether a solution should be forced by demanding that the UMHK cease to pay its taxes, duties, and mining royalties to Tshombe, or whether, on the contrary, a new situation could be created by political means in order to make it possible for the company, without serious risk, to make payments directly to the central authorities.

If Belgian diplomacy, with British support, did obtain a substantial concession in July, 1962, it was that the United States and the U.N. cease to require in the Thant Plan that the first gesture be made by the UMHK. At this point, the UMHK was no longer master of the situation. Until January, 1963, the company was buffeted by contradictory forces, including those exerted from Elisabethville on the one hand, and those from Brussels, Washington, and New York on the other. Finally, at the decisive moment in mid-December, the UMHK was incapable of acting promptly, consulted Tshombe, and almost had to pay with a "scorched earth" policy for its position in 1960, 1961, and 1962. The UMHK found itself the chief scapegoat at the end of the secession, confronting unanimous rancor and hostility. But its legal status was unchanged. Its resources in foreign exchange were guaranteed to a sufficient extent by an agreement with the Congolese Monetary Council; its installations were practically intact and its personnel on the job.

Sixth question: Was Katanga a country of order and good government, the perfect antithesis of Congo-Leopoldville?

The essential difference between Katanga and the other provinces of the Congo in July and August, 1960, lay in the maintenance of a strong core of European personnel in Elisabethville and in the protection of relatively normal economic activity by the Belgian army. European personnel in Katanga were found above all in the ministerial *cabinets,* the administration, and the security forces; objectively, Europeans constituted at that moment the very backbone of independent Katanga. This situation explains why the Katangan and Belgian authorities reacted in common toward the U.N. projects for withdrawal of Belgian assistance in October, 1960.

Where European influence was exercised to a lesser degree, the situations in Katanga proved to be about the same as those in Leopoldville. This is particularly apparent in the Katangan Assembly where the concerns, the forms of expression, and the ambitions bear a singular resemblance to those of other Congolese assemblies.

The documents used in this work bring out certain information and revelations: the number of European deaths in Katanga, following the mutinies, was the highest in the Congo; the number of political prisoners there remained regularly at several thousand; the Baluba or Kasai urban population, especially in Elisabethville after July, 1961, sought to escape at any price from the control of Munongo's police; the repression in North Katanga took on forms of extreme cruelty comparable to that of "rebel" actions such as Katangan propaganda described; in addition, corruption was not a monopoly of Leopoldville.

"Katanga has become a paradise for adventurers and pack rats of all kinds who make fortunes by selling no matter what to the State . . . and by sharing the benefits with certain leaders," wrote the special correspondent of *La Libre Belgique* on July 8, 1961. This judgment may seem severe. Figures made public here on the subject of the treasury and of the Katangan budget confirm, in any case, singular shortcomings in management, even if one wishes to make allowances for the squandering of public monies, without any real control or discretion, to build a gendarmery by all accounts more ruinous than effective, as the occasion proved in December, 1961, and in December, 1962.

Seventh question: What future did the promoters and the supporters of the secession envisage for Katanga?

After the break in diplomatic relations between Leopoldville and Brussels, the prevailing Belgian government view leaned toward support (rather than "recognition") of the Katangan state. Following the rupture between Kasavubu and Lumumba, the Belgian government pushed for reconstruction of the Congo along confederal lines, with the support of Katanga, if possible starting from Katanga as a base (the so-called Rothschild view — "Katangalization").

Concretely, this view sought to maintain and to institutionalize the strong position of Tshombe in Katanga, while achieving, if possible, the legitimacy of an endorsement from Kasavubu. This objective presupposed an understanding between the moderates in Leopoldville and the authorities in Elisabethville, to which the Kalonjists in Bakwanga would be a party. The cement for this alliance was, until August, 1961, anti-Lumumbism and all it represented, the common hostility toward the U.N. based especially on the fact that the world body wanted to eliminate Belgian personnel from the Congo, and opposition to the Eastern bloc and Afro-Asian countries such as the United Arab Republic, Guinea, Ghana, and India.

The Belgian government had in mind, then, a Congolese confederation of which the member states would be essentially in the hands of Congolese, friends and "moderates," and the borders — insofar as possible — those of the former colony or even of the former Belgian sphere in Central Africa.

But, there prevailed elsewhere a tendency (called "Clémens") to try every means for making Katanga a real state, with internal and external sovereignty. For this faction, negotiations with Leopoldville were to be circumscribed entirely within a context in which the weak partner would be led to a settlement (Tananarive). They were to secure for Katanga a reinforcement in prestige, real autonomy, and defense capacity. Other attempts were to be made simultaneously to obtain recognition by any state (Costa Rica? Congo-Brazzaville?). An independent Katanga could then join a confederation or an economic grouping not limited to the territory of the former Belgian Congo. Katangan leaders dreamed of, and were often encouraged by Brazzaville or Paris to imagine, a French-speaking confederation in sub-Saharan Africa in which Tshombe and the Abbé Youlou would play the leading African roles, or even — as Mario Spandre, Tshombe's adviser, suggested to him — the future birth of a frankly bilingual state including Katanga and Northern Rhodesia.

In fact, Katanga never achieved the status of a state, despite generous financing of the expenses of sovereignty. Its territory was disputed by the ANC again and again, as well as by "the rebellion" of the Baluba which created permanent pockets of insecurity or even independent territories within a territory.

Its external relations were never those of a recognized state, even with Brazzaville, and were based on ambiguities, semi-clandestinity, or on *de facto* situations allowed by political complaisance. Even if the expression is harsh, Spaak was right in declaring that Tshombe was not a chief of state but a powerful rebel at the head of what the royal message of July 21, 1960, called "entire ethnic groups" — the only ones who, even at the moment of strongest anti-U.N. passions in Elisabethville, ever exhibited the "Katangan faith."

Tshombe and his regime committed the error of not understanding quickly enough that the fall of Lumumba would lead eventually to the disappearance of the psycho-political basis for their action. They were confronted with a common Leopoldville-U.N. front and the understandings which made this possible. Their only chance was for them rapidly to accept substantial concessions within the framework of a Congolese federal state.

This was the path that Spaak advised Katanga to take after July, 1961, in place of seeking — as Tshombe's Belgian advisers recommended in April, 1961 — to profit from the temporary military weakness of the U.N. in the Congo and the political weakness of Leopoldville.

If Spaak's policy contained a new element, it is less the acceptance in principle of the progressive withdrawal of certain Belgian advisers or soldiers on *Minaf* status, than the search for a negotiated solution between Leopoldville and Elisabethville, on the basis of a peaceful reintegration of Katanga into the republic. This reintegration was to secure for the center a reasonable portion of the fiscal receipts and of strong foreign exchange and to guarantee to Tshombe the maintenance of his government and the adoption of a federal structure for the Congo. According to Spaak, mediation via Jaja Wachuku or Leopold Senghor could assist in the solution, and he sought British support for this idea. The trials by force between the U.N. and Katanga constituted serious handicaps for Spaak. But in 1962, when the Thant Plan was elaborated, Spaak again launched the idea of a practical formula for an understanding between Leopoldville and Elisabethville: sharing of receipts; more or less formal integration of Katanga; maintenance of the "Tshombist order"; plan for a federal constitution; amnesty for the leaders of the secession; formula for nonpenalization of the UMHK; Senghor mediation.

For Spaak, it was a question then of helping to reconstitute a federal Congo within the borders of June, 1960, and of fostering an attempt to get back on an even keel with "moderate" authorities. The Thant Plan was based on these assumptions, something Tshombe's advisers never seemed to understand.

Eighth question: Has not the importance of Katanga in the Congolese crisis been overestimated, both from the point of view of relations with Belgium and with the U.N.?

As we have already pointed out in the conclusions of *Congo 1960,* after the proclamation of Katanga's independence on July 11, political developments throughout the Congo and the behavior of the principal protagonists — Belgium, Congolese governments and authorities, the United Nations, the United States, Great Britain, and African countries concerned — were determined by the fact of the secession.

It is the secession and the support which Belgian military personnel gave to it rather than the military intervention as such which provoked the rupture between the Congo and Belgium. This is brought out in the telegrams from Kasavubu and Lumumba in July, 1960, and in the details which we have recalled ensuing from the refusal of landing rights in Elisabethville by Munongo on July 12 to the Congolese Chief of State and Prime Minister.

The essential political objective of the center then became the reabsorption of the Katangan dissidence which threatened to extend to other provinces and inclined Leopoldville toward allies that could help — the United Nations first of all, then, in the face of the initial failure of the U.N. to intervene in Katanga, the Soviet Union, and friendly African countries. Although the appeal to bilateral aid from all quarters did not succeed, the U.N. nonetheless had to change its position. Before May, 1961, and especially after the elimination of Lumumba, its primary objective in the Congo was to obtain a political success, especially in the Katangan affair, and this led inevitably to a relative overshadowing of problems of technical assistance. The reorganization of the ANC was impracticable in this context; the appeal for Belgian technicians was ambiguous and a priori political; the U.N. financial effort in the Congo was marked by a priority on military expenditures in keeping up with Katanga.

The Katangan problem not only jammed the workings of the United Nations and compromised the efforts of Belgium in the Congo, but it likewise consummated the fall of the Lumumba government, because of the priority that this government had to accord external problems to the detriment of administrative and economic reorganization, and because of the international support that it had to seek, and the opposition which lined up against it as a result of its rupture with Belgium.

However, the "moderate" powers later installed in Leopoldville likewise ran afoul of the Katangan dissidence. Unable to impose itself on Katanga either by force or by negotiation, the central government in Leopoldville — until August, 1961 — revealed its weakness and its dependence on the West. Neither Afro-Asian opinion nor Congolese nationalist opinion was fooled.

In Belgo-Congolese relations during these years, the lowest points, the moments of sharpest tension correspond nearly always to Belgian acts favoring Katanga, even when these acts were relatively minor in themselves.

These observations do not mean that the whole Congolese problem lay in the secession and its mercenaries, as has too often been written. The crisis had other profound causes as well, but the secession definitely aggravated it, especially in 1960. It is equally true that reintegration, because of the real situation of the Congo and of Katanga, could not constitute by itself an immediate solution to the financial, economic, and political problems of the republic.

The questions which I have answered here probably cover the main problems of the secession and the Katangan regime from 1960 to the end of 1962. Other queries remain on more particular points; the text itself has shed a certain degree of light on them. It must be noted, however, that all these events will shortly merit reconsideration and further analysis, taking into account additional factors which are coming to light in all the countries of Central Africa, and especially in Rhodesia and Angola.

APPENDIXES·INDEX

APPENDIX I · *Documents for Part I*

I. CONAKAT OR THE CONFEDERATION DES
ASSOCIATIONS TRIBALES DU KATANGA

FOUNDED
October 1958, in Elisabethville
July 11, 1959, creation of the Rassemblement Katangais,
political party of the Conakat.

LEADERS

Godefroid Munongo: Born November 20, 1925, in Bunkeya (Katanga); descendent of Msiri. Ethnic group: Bayeke. Classics in the Catholic mission at Kapiri. Entered the grand seminary in Baudouinville in 1947, remaining two years. Diploma from the School of Administrative Sciences in Kisantu. Joined the municipal administration in 1954. Successively named court clerk, police judge for the tribunal responsible for identity cards, department chief in the Pensions Service, and finally territorial agent in 1958.

One of the Conakat founders, he was the first president in October, 1958, but when Belgian authorities pointed out the incompatibility between his civil service position and his Conakat post, he stepped down in favor of Tshombe. Named administrator for the Inga Public Corporation, he participated in the workings of the council in Brussels in November, 1959. Member of the *Collège Exécutif* for the governor of Katanga during the first half of 1960. Elected provincial deputy in Elisabethville territory. Minister of Interior in the government of the "State of Katanga."

Moise Kapenda Tshombe: Born November 10, 1919, in Musamba. Ethnic group: Lunda. Primary school at the Methodist mission in Sandoa. Teacher's diploma after four years' study in the school for teaching assistants of the Methodist mission in Kamene lez-Kinda. Holder of a diploma in accounting. Belonging to a family of merchants and plantation owners, Tshombe was himself a trader before entering a political career. In June, 1960, his police record listed four convictions.[1]

[1] In regard to one commercial failure of Tshombe, *L'Essor du Congo* (Elisabeth-

He was regional chairman of the Association des Classes Moyennes Africaines (Acmaf) in 1958, and was president of Groupement des Associations Mutuelles de l'Empire Lunda (Gassomel). President-general of the Conakat in the second half of 1959, he headed the Conakat delegation to the political Round Table conference and to the economic Round Table. Visited the United States in May, 1960, on the invitation of the American government. Elected provincial deputy from Elisabethville territory. After the secession, became President of the "State of Katanga."

Jean-Baptiste Kibwe: Born March 3, 1924, in Kilwa (Katanga). Ethnic group: Batabwa. Completed primary school, four years of high school, three years of law and four years of sociology and political science in evening classes at the Institut St. Boniface in Elisabethville. In 1947, employed by the CSK. In 1948, worked in the Banque du Congo Belge. From 1949 to 1956, in the territorial administration. In 1954, served as assistant judge (*juge assesseur*) in the court of Elisabethville territory, then presiding judge in the evening courts in Elisabethville. In 1956, left the administration and was named representative on the "traditional" courts. Member of the Conakat delegation to the political Round Table. Member of the Political Commission attached to the Minister for the Congo, where he represented Katanga. Elected provincial deputy on the Conakat list in Elisabethville. Vice-President of the Conakat since July, 1960. Vice-president and Minister of Finance in the government of the "State of Katanga."

Bonaventure Makonga: Muluba from Katanga; editor in chief of *Etoile Nyota* in 1957; losing candidate for the presidency of the Balubakat and excluded from this group on April 23, 1958; founding member, then executive committee member for the Conakat. Clerk in the Information Services in 1958, founding member of the Union Culturelle Katangaise. Elected as "nontraditional" senator to national Parliament for the province of Katanga. Named Secretary of State for Foreign Trade in the government of the "State of Katanga."

Evariste Kimba: Born July 26, 1926, in the territory of Bukama. Muluba from Katanga. Primary and intermediate schooling and five years

---

ville), stated on February 3, 1954: "These natives thought themselves as capable as their white brothers of going into the wholesale merchandise business." Tshombe retorted in the same newspaper on February 23 by detailing the services rendered by his company during the war.

of evening courses in sociology, law, and political economy at the Institut St. Boniface in Elisabethville. Reporter since 1954, then editor on *L'Essor du Congo*. Supporter of the Catholic trade unions, then secretary late 1955 of the Association des Parents et Amis de l'Enseignment Catholique. In 1958, Kimba was accused of "treason" by the Baluba of Kasai because he was connected with a newspaper which opened its columns to the Union Katangaise. Traveled to Belgium in 1958 and to Germany in 1959. Conakat candidate for Katuba commune. Deputy *chef de cabinet* to Minister Ganshof van der Meersch. "Nontraditional" senator then provincial minister in June, 1960. Minister of Foreign Affairs in the "State of Katanga."

Henri Ndala Kambola: Former Apic [Association du Personnel Indigène de la Colonie] leader; member of the Conakat central committee before June 30, 1960; author of a declaration in favor of nationalizing the UMHK in October, 1960. Member of the Board of Directors of CEPSI in 1962.

Among the Conakat leaders who were prominent after 1960, the next two must be cited:

Charles Mutaka-wa-Dilomba: Born September 9, 1932, in Mutaka, Lubudi territory. Primary school in Mokabe, secondary schooling in Kapiri and three years of philosophy in the Baudouinville grand seminary. Clerk third class in 1953; dismissed after his apprenticeship. Clerk in Kikula-Jadotville in 1958; dismissed by its burgomaster. Chairman of the Conakat section in Jadotville in 1959. Alternate at the political Round Table. Elected in May, 1960, on an individual pro-Conakat slate in Kambove territory. Spent the month of May, 1960, studying Belgian Parliament. President of Katangan Assembly.

Joseph Yav: Born on August 15, 1929, in Musumba-Kapanga. Ethnic group: Lunda. After a year of philosophy at the grand seminary, worked in administration. Communal secretary of Albert Commune in Elisabethville in 1957. With Tshombe, led the Conakat delegation to the economic Round Table. Spent short training period at Union Minière headquarters then at the Ministry of Social Welfare in Brussels. Minister of Economic Affairs in the Lumumba government, he resigned on July 16, 1960. In September was named Secretary of State for National Defense in the government of the "State of Katanga."

PROGRAM

— For autonomy of Katanga and union with Belgium.

— For the monopoly of public functions by "authentic Katangans."

— For measures favorable to the authority of traditional rulers.

1. That Katanga opts for an autonomous and federated state where the reins of political command must be in the hands of authentic Katangans and of all men of good will who demonstrate and have demonstrated by their acts that they will cooperate sincerely for the progress and rapid emancipation of Katanga, under conditions which will be determined by the future government of the autonomous Katangan state; that the condition *sine qua non* for the constitution of a federal Congo consists in equitable representation proportional to the economic importance of each autonomous state;

That for the moment, while awaiting new legal dispositions, in Katanga, only the Conakat, whose basic support and legitimacy are undeniable (namely, in its traditional chiefs, its history, its populations living and dead, its land, in short, its whole patrimony), and no one and no group else, can pretend to represent and speak for Katanga.

(L'Essor du Congo, May 26, 1959, "Conakat position.")

2. Since the creation of the Conakat section in Kolwezi, on June 14, 1959, rumors against this association have been spread throughout the African quarters by certain non-Katangan Congolese. They allege that the Conakat was created to evacuate or chase out all people from other provinces.

This is not the case and is an illusion pure and simple on the part of these non-Katangans. Here are our goals:
  a. Union of all the original residents of the province of Katanga, black and white, without racial discrimination, who by their behavior have shown that they have been integrated into the province;
  b. Protection of the legitimate rights of the original residents of this province;
  c. Reciprocal benefits in the moral, material, physical, and intellectual evolution of the province and of its inhabitants;
  d. To struggle henceforth against seizure of any power in this province by a non-Katangan;
  e. To cooperate actively with Belgium toward the goal of accession to independence, but with order and calm and above all without precipitate haste.   *(Phare du Katanga*, July 3, 1959.)

3. Federal System, unifying the great Congolese provinces and Belgium within the framework of a Belgo-Congolese community, each constituent party exercising internal autonomy;

Increase in the productivity of rural regions by the adoption of a well-prepared plan of action to modernize tools now at the farmer's disposal;

Development of trunk roads to permit remote regions to participate more fully in the economy;

Development of education of all types in the interior, especially agricultural and secondary education;

General application of the formula: Equal work, equal pay;

Frank and sincere cooperation between African and European to develop together the true potential of this country, for the greatest benefits to both peoples;

Respect for the vested rights of traditional authorities.

(Document of Conakat Central Committee, July 13, 1959.)

4. The Confederation of natives of the Province of Katanga, in its entirety, eager to take charge of the destinies of the province in peace and calm, having learned through last year's elections that in certain urban centers Katangans were not held in great respect whereas they should have enjoyed the highest degree of esteem, have hereby brought to your attention that the Conakat does not intend to see persons who are neither Katangan natives, nor civilizers in Katanga, participate in elections.

The administration of Katanga ought to be in the hands of Katangans and of our civilizers and not in those of people who come from other provinces. Our idea is along the same line as that set forth in the law of October 18, 1908, on the government of the Belgian Congo when it stipulated in Article 21: "No one can be named as Governor-General if he is not a Belgian by birth or by full naturalization . . . ." (Conakat Memorandum, October, 1959.)

5. In our opinion — and here we feel that the moment has come when we cannot mince words — the Congolese state must necessarily assume the form of a federal state which will reconcile the unity of all Congolese with a maximum number of powers reserved to the member or federated states.

Based on the formula set out above in regard to structure, we are naturally led to consider what should be the institutions of states which comprise the Congolese whole.

And in order to respect the wide, constitutionally guaranteed autonomy, which the provincial states must enjoy, these institutions would, of necessity, include the following organs:

  a. An assembly of provincial Councilors, providing especially for equitable participation by traditional authorities. The method of designation of these Councilors need not be uniform for all the provinces. It is up to the provinces themselves to exercise this choice.
  b. An executive power, including Secretaries of State having the rank of Ministers, and headed by an elected President.
  c. A representative of the King, called the Royal Commissioner, without direct administrative powers, except possibly during a transitional period as short as possible, if authorized by the competent provincial Assembly . . . .

. . . .

As regards the division of powers between the federal state and the federated states, the following principles, which derive from the very nature of federalism, must be respected:

— The federal constitution will be based upon the principle according to which internal sovereignty belongs to the federated states, the federal state having no other powers than those which are expressly defined and delimited by the Constitution.

— Within the limits of its authority the federal state will enact laws which shall be binding on all member states and on their citizens.

— The federated states will be empowered to complement the federal law by their own legislation.

— Conflicts between the federal law and law of the federated states will be regulated on the basis of the constitution, by a federal Supreme Court whose composition will be determined by the federal constitution.

The Institutions of the Federal Congolese State:

These institutions will include a bicameral federal Parliament, a federal Executive responsible to Parliament and a federal Court.

The federal Parliament will include a Chamber of Representatives and a Senate.

The Chamber of Representatives will ensure representation from the Congolese Nation, according to a method of election based on provincial parity determined by the Constitution.

The Senate will represent the different federated states on an equal footing. Each state sovereignty determines the method of designation for its Senators.

The two Chambers of Parliament will share the same powers and all federal laws must receive an absolute majority of the votes of each Chamber.

The federal Executive (Government) will be named, during a transitional period, by a Royal High Commissioner, and eventually by the Congolese Chief of State.

The composition of the federal Government must assure equal representation to each of the six federated states . . . .

In order not to compromise the very existence of the edifice which is created, it would appear necessary to provide that the full assumption of certain particular powers — Foreign Affairs, National Defense, etc. . . . — should follow an appropriate timetable which takes into account the capabilities of the new State. This should be done during the period preceding the adoption of the final constitution for the Congo.

Seat of the Central Institutions:

The central institutions must be established in what is called a neutral federal territory situated outside any provincial capital. It would seem easy to find such a place near Kamina which enjoys a healthy climate, excellent food supplies, and a complete communication network.

Belgium-Congo Association:

The Congo has every interest in remaining associated with Belgium. The person of His Majesty the King of the Belgians can very happily form the symbol of association between the two countries.

The protocol of co-operation could usefully provide for the possibility that each federated state would conclude regional accords directly with Belgium. (Conakat proposals on January 30, 1960, at the political Round Table.)

ADVISERS AND EUROPEAN SUPPORT BEFORE INDEPENDENCE

The best known advisers of the Conakat before independence were those who had been active in Ucol and in the Union Katangaise,[2] especially:

Achille Gavage: Born in Complain-au-Point, Belgium, on March 21, 1906; settled in the Congo since 1929, former civil servant in the Agricultural Service who became a merchant, selling agricultural machinery; founding member of the Union Professionnelle Agricole du Katanga (Upak) and of Ucol; active member of the Walloon cultural circle "Amons nos autes"; elected Elisabethville communal councilor in December, 1957; founder of the Union Katangaise in 1958 and president until its dissolution at the end of March, 1960.

Joseph Onckelinx: Born in Landen, Belgium, on April 16, 1909; businessman in the Congo; was member of the Conseil de Province of Katanga and of the Conseil du Gouvernement-Général; an active member of the "Vlaamse Vriendenkring"; Ucol vice-president and adviser to the Katanga Acmaf; attended meetings of the central committee of the Conakat; advised the Conakat in Brussels on the sidelines of the political Round Table; chosen as *chef de cabinet* to the Minister of Foreign Trade in the "State of Katanga"; expelled by the U.N. in the Congo in August, 1961.

Georges Thyssens: Born in Liège, Belgium, on April 21, 1900; retired civil servant formerly with the public prosecutor's office of Elisabethville; secretary of Ucol-Katanga and adviser of *La Voix du Katanga*, edited by Rodolphe Yava (Conakat) with the assistance of Ucol. Carried out special missions in the context of the secession (especially, the Trinquier affair). Expelled by the U.N. operation in the Congo in 1961.

Jean Humblé: Born in Antwerp on October 25, 1906; lawyer at the Elisabethville bar; was president of Ucol until his resignation in June, 1960; official adviser of the Conakat during the political Round Table;

---

[2] In the list of names of people, we have scrupulously followed the rules of discretion, citing only the names which were or are in the public domain; the Katangan question has not yet settled down to the point where it can be treated as an object for pure study and investigation.

on April 19, 1960, published a declaration in *L'Essor du Congo*, asserting that he had had no further political involvements since the end of the Round Table.

Rémy Calonne: Born in Hasselt, Belgium, on January 4, 1906, doctor-dentist; president of the *Ligue des Familles Nombreuses* and member of the *Comité* [executive] of Ucol in 1960; vice-president of the Union Katangaise until its dissolution in March, 1960.

Besides these people whose functions as advisers were quasi official, there were, if only because the Union Katangaise was admitted as a member association of the Conakat, other individuals who influenced African leaders with their advice: notably, M. S., lawyer, member of the Union Culturelle Katangaise and of Ucol; A. B., lawyer, expatriate, Ucol, expelled by the U.N. in the Congo in April, 1961; L. H., Turkish merchant, Zionist Association and Ucol, expelled by the U.N. in the Congo in April, 1961; J. P., former lawyer sought for embezzlement.

In Brussels besides the individuals establishing contacts on behalf of important Belgian companies and assuring financial assistance to the Conakat, there is one more adviser who came very near to playing an important role at the end of June, 1960:

François Scheerlinck: Born in Voorde, Belgium, on March 27, 1901; former *Sûreté* agent for the eastern Congo (during the war); personnel chief of Messageries Automobiles du Sankury, then a settler; Conakat adviser in Brussels during the Belgo-Congolese economic conference in May, 1960; called to Elisabethville and charged with the mission of "Ambassador" for the "State of Katanga" by Tshombe and Munongo at the time of the secession attempt (late June, 1960).

Seats Won by Conakat in 1960 Elections

Lower Chamber: 8 elected out of 16 for Katanga and out of 137 for the whole of the Congo.

Senate: 7 seats out of 14 for Katanga and out of 84 for the whole of the Congo.

Provincial Assembly: 25 seats out of 60
    9 in Haut-Katanga
    3 in Haut-Lomami
    6 in Lualaba
    3 in Tanganika

1 in Jadotville

3 in Elisabethville

II. THE CARTEL KATANGAIS: BALUBAKAT, FEDEKA, ATCAR

FOUNDED

End of 1959 — beginning of 1960, by a Cartel of Balubakat (created in 1957), of Fédéka (end of 1958), and of Atcar

Balubakat = Association des Baluba du Katanga.

Fédéka = Fédération des Associations des Ressortissants de la Province du Kasai au Katanga.

Atcar = Association Sociale et Culturelle des Tshokwe du Congo, de l'Angola et de la Rhodésie.

In November, 1959, the Balubakat had, on the political level, a special title: Parti Progressiste Katangaise (PPK), foreshadowing the Cartel.

LEADERS

Jason Sendwe: Born in 1917 in Kabongo. A Muluba from Katanga. Ten years of study with the Methodists, five years of nursing courses in Stanleyville and at the State School for Male Nurses in Elisabethville. A certified nurse, he finished his studies at the Ecole des Assistants Médicaux Indigènes in Leopoldville. Member of the Protestant Council of the Congo. Founding member and treasurer of the Amitiés Belgo-Congolaises in Elisabethville. President of the Balubakat and of the Balubakat-Atcar-Fédéka Cartel at the political Round Table. Delegate from the Cartel to the economic Round Table. In May, 1960, made a study trip to the United States at the invitation of the American government. National deputy elected on the Cartel slate, with 20,283 preferential votes in the Elisabethville district. Proposed for the post of Commissioner of the central government for the province of Katanga, at the end of June, 1960. Extraordinary Commissioner to Katanga in 1961. Vice-president of Adoula's Council of Ministers (censured December 28, 1962).

Rémy Mwamba: Born in 1921 in Vulnea; four years of intermediate school in St. Boniface, two years of advanced secondary education. Chief clerk of the court in Elisabethville, member of the Kenia Communal Council. Co-founder and vice-president of the Balubakat, President of PPK, member of the Balubakat Cartel delegation to the political Round Table. Member of the *Collège Exécutif Général* in Leopoldville. Elected "non-traditional" senator from the province of Katanga. Minister of Justice in the Lumumba government and in the first Adoula government (until July 11, 1962).

Prosper Mwamba-Ilunga: Provincial deputy of the Balubakat Cartel from Elisabethville territory. President of the Cercle d'Etude Balubakat. Spokesman for the Cartel in the provincial Assembly in June and July, 1960. Forbidden to remain in Katanga by the secessionist authorities. Sought refuge in Stanleyville. President of the government of Lualaba Province (October 20, 1960), then of the North Katanga Province (July, 1962).

Isaac Kalonji: Born September 9, 1914, in Lusambo; a Muluba. Clerk in the Banque Belge d'Afrique. Provincial president of Acmaf (1958). Leader of Fédéka. Represented the Balubakat-Fédéka-Atcar Cartel at the economic Round Table. Traveled from December, 1956, to March, 1957, in the United States. Elected "nontraditional" senator from the province of Katanga. Proposed by Lumumba as Commissioner of the central government in Kasai. Went to Brussels in February, 1961, as provincial government delegate from Lualaba-Katanga (Manono). President of the Senate.

Ambroise Muhunga: Born in 1920. Ethnic group: Tshokwe. National deputy. Atcar president. On October 20, 1960, in the proclamation of Lualaba Province, was designated State Administrator of Companies. Secretary of State for Mines in the first Adoula government.

Among the other leaders of the Cartel, are the following: Joseph Kahamba, secretary-general of the Balubakat; Albert Kalikoni, treasurer; Pierre Umba, assistant secretary-general.

PROGRAM

Congolese unity (against separatism) with decentralization of powers.

Goals of Balubakat (as defined in 1958 by Jason Sendwe)

1. Promote Baluba unity.
2. Harmonize to the maximum the relations between the Belgian administration and traditional authorities.

The entire association, through its president, insists particularly on the apolitical nature of the work which it proposes to accomplish.

The broad lines of its activities:

1. To attain its first goal, Baluba unity, the association desires at the very outset to attack the cultural problem. This work can be summed up under

several headings, not necessarily listed in the order of importance, the study
of which overlaps, and must often be concurrent:

a. The systematic study of all the ancestral customs of the various Baluba
groups;

b. A profound analysis of all these customs will permit a judicious choice
of those which it will be useful to preserve for posterity . . . ;

c. Promote education in the "good customs" . . . ;

d. Introduce in the Ecole sociale in Elisabethville as a first effort a course
in Kiluba . . . ;

e. Kiluba-French dictionary and a Kiluba grammar.

2. To attain the second goal, harmony of relations with the Belgian administration:

a. Begin tireless activity to interest the administration in the work of the
board of directors of the association to obtain an urgent examination
on all questions touching the great Baluba community.

b. Obtain a commitment from the administration that it will no longer
decide by itself the choice of chiefs in the *chefferies* and *circonscriptions
indigènes* against the wishes of the population and contrary to the traditional methods of designating chiefs.

(There was a recent case in the Kinda *chefferie* where the administrator selected a chief who was recognized neither by the notables nor
by the population.)

In these cases, the Belgian administration must have perfect confidence
in the association and must request its opinion on one or several candidates.

c. Obtain the aid of experienced researchers knowing Kiluba to look into
the history and development of each of the Baluba *chefferies*, where the
complexity of the various regimes in effect results almost daily in actions
by the administration which, although undertaken in good faith, are apt
to be misinterpreted by the population.

(Unpublished text of Jason Sendwe.)

Positions of Atcar

The Association Sociale et Culturelle des Tshokwe du Congo, Angola et
Rhodésie (Atcar) supported candidates in the elections who agreed to defend
the following points heading their program:

1. Favor all action to bring about independence or autonomy for the
Congo in the shortest time possible.

2. Defend the principle of a Unitary Congo with equality of rights for all
its inhabitants — a guarantee of a certain degree of decentralization, all provinces receiving equal budgetary support.

3. The *circonscriptions* (cities, territories, communes, traditional areas),
with representatives elected by universal suffrage and eventually supplemented
by delegates of traditional authorities, must have full rights to contract and
to guarantee loans for the *circonscription* and mortgages on property it owns
or taxes.

4. *Circonscriptions* would recognize the right of permanent residence (citizenship) for "strangers" established on their territories.

"Established" means exercising his principal activity and having the majority of his investments there. This rule would be valid pending the creation of the Congolese nation.

These same elected authorities would guarantee the security of persons and property in the territories which elect them.

The Central Committee of Atcar,

<table>
<tr><td>Secretary-General,</td><td>President,</td></tr>
<tr><td>Jean Mushidi.</td><td>Herman Ambroise Muhunga.</td></tr>
</table>

(Appeared in *L'Essor du Congo*, September 16, 1959.)

Memorandum of PPK Sent to the Minister of the Congo (Elisabethville, December 1, 1959)

Dear Sir,

In the name of the Parti Progressiste Katangais and of its parent, the Balubakat, we are happy to be able to welcome you to this our Katanga soil from the bottom of our hearts.

We express the same sentiments in regard to the members of your Cabinet who accompany you.

The ministerial declarations of October 16 and 31, 1959, following that of January 13, have won our support and we were founded to affirm as of the present that Belgium — by means of its representatives — has proved its clear, wholesome determination to lead the Congo toward total emancipation; in doing this, Belgium has a perfect right to our lasting friendship.

We therefore desire peace in Katanga, this country so very dear to us. In this domain, we are persuaded that the local Administration is conscious of its burdensome task to see to it that we can get through this alarming epoch in peace. We would wish, however, that the responsible authorities redouble their vigilance to maintain peace and that the trouble makers such as "rumor-mongers" be immediately silenced.

After these simple words, we ask you to find attached herewith the program that our movement would desire to execute if one day it is called to power.

Elisabethville, December 1, 1959.

For the PPK,

President,
Rémy Mwamba

President-general,
Jason Sendwe

Political program of PPK: (Balubakat)

·   ·   ·   ·   ·   ·   ·   ·   ·   ·   ·   ·   ·

By way of introduction to the following chapter, PPK has elaborated this program taking into account a transition period which the Congo must necessarily pass through before entering upon total independence.

C. Political problems
1. Form of government: united Congo with broad decentralization of provincial powers.
2. Levels:
   — Native *circonscription* (traditional chief)
   — Territorial Council
   — Chief of administrative zone (district)
   — Provincial representative Assembly deciding on questions of local interest.
   — Head of provincial government: Governor assisted by a permanent deputation.
3. Central government
   a. Parliament:
      i. — Chamber of Deputies: 120 members by universal suffrage
         — Mandate: 5 years
         — Legislation and sanction
         — President: to be elected by the Chamber itself
         — Eligibility: minimum age 25 years (four years of post-primary study)
      ii. — Senate: 80 members — minimum age 35 years (educational requirements same as for Chamber)
   b. Executive power:
      — Premier designate of government proposed by the president of the Senate and named by the King.
      — Council of Ministers presided over by the Prime Minister assisted by the Royal High Commissioner.
   c. Portfolios and allocation of responsibilities:
      i. Ministry of General Administration
      ii. Ministry of Public Health
      iii. Ministry of Justice and Religion
         Five year term
      iv. Ministry of National Commerce and Industry
      v. Ministry of Public Works
         To be provided: Legislation and sanctions
      vi. Ministry of Political and Social Relations
      vii. Ministry of Agriculture
      viii. Ministry of Lands, Waters and Forests
      ix. Ministry of Education
      x. Ministry of the Interior
      xi. Ministry of National Defense
      xii. Ministry of National Economy
         Higher education: Belgium
         External Defense: Belgium
         Currency: Belgium
         International Trade: Belgium
D. Elaboration of the Congolese Constitution: by special commission.

E. Relations with Belgium — for the transition period:
   Community (modeled on French policy).
   Duration: undetermined.
F. Total independence:
— Employment of technicians.
— Commercial exchanges (by treaties).

Address to the King against Separatism (December 24, 1959).

Sire,

The unexpected arrival of your Majesty constitutes for us an immense hope.

Thus, in the name of all the members and supporters of the Balubakat and of the Parti Progressiste Katangais as well as on our own behalf, we are honored to welcome Your Majesty in our province of Katanga.

The arrival of Your Majesty constitutes for us proof of the unshaken attachment of the Royal Family to the great tasks undertaken by Your Illustrious Forbear, His Majesty King Leopold II.

The great foresight of Your Majesty enabled You to make the gesture for which we dared no longer hope: to come to take note of the real situation existing in our country.

Will Your Majesty permit the work of destruction now in progress, that seeks to dismantle the immense country created at the price of so much effort by your predecessors?

Do You not think, Sire, that they would rise from their graves to defend the unity of the Congo, acquired at the price of so many sacrifices, if the Congo continues to be threatened?

Powerful financial interests wish to dismember our beautiful country and do not hesitate, in reaching their ends, to pit our ethnic groups one against another.

Sire,

Hear its plea, the Congo does not want to be mutilated. . . .

.   .   .   .

It would be a crime to permit the achievement and spread of such a policy in the Congo, for it is a manifest sign of ingratitude in the mind of the promoters toward Him (Leopold II) who organized this immense Country which is the Congo.

We regret the fate of our Congolese brothers who encourage such a policy, for they — involuntarily perhaps — are damaging their own future.

Our policy, based on the hope of future cooperation between the Congo and Belgium, does not, however, admit the separatist ideas which have been wrongly inculcated in the minds of certain Congolese, under a "federalist" form.

We are not, however, against a federal system when this is conceived in its true meaning, when it does not hide the separatist idea. The Congo must be considered as a whole.

We know that the majority of Whites have come to the Congo with a humanitarian goal. Very few have come to pursue the grand scheme of the

Great King Leopold II. These will be good citizens in an Independent Congo if they will withdraw from Congolese politics.

With the support of Your Majesty, we know that Independence will not be a vain word and that with the interests of Belgium and the Congo both safe-guarded, we shall be able to march together towards a better future, happy and prosperous.

This is the wish of all Congolese.

The Balubakat expresses the desire to see its representatives invited to Belgium to defend its program in the Parliamentary setting.

We are convinced that Your Majesty will see nothing improper in this plan, given the fact that this important political party in Katanga owes to itself the task of carrying its stone to the building of a great, unified Congo of tomorrow.

Long live the King,
Long live Belgium,
Long live the Independent and Unified Congo.

Secretary-General	President-general
J. Kahamba	J. Sendwe

ADVISERS AND EUROPEAN SUPPORT BEFORE INDEPENDENCE

Among the first advisers of Balubakat in 1957: Mme. L. Brabon; A. Maurice, secretary of the University of Elisabethville; A. Lambert, a liberal, editor-in-chief of *L'Echo du Katanga*; Father Floribert, who became Mgr. Cornélis. Later, advisers to the Balubakat or the Cartel included: Mme. Perin-Hockers, research assistant at the Institut de Sociologie Solvay; G. Ryckaert, from Tournai, secretary of the Cartel in 1960. It is to be remembered that A. Decoster, publisher of *L'Echo du Katanga*, was solicited as an adviser by Fédéka: he declared on June 7, 1960, that he had never been "political adviser to the Cartel."

At the time of the Round Table, the Cartel appealed to Arthur Doucy, born at Marchienne-au-Pont on October 16, 1917, professor at the Université Libre de Bruxelles and director of the Institut de Sociologie of the ULB, founded by E. Solvay; member of the Académie des Sciences Coloniales; author in 1957 of an important study "Sociologie Coloniale et Réformes de Structures au Congo"; a socialist.

SEATS WON BY BALUBAKAT CARTEL, 1960 ELECTIONS

Lower Chamber: 7 seats out of 16 for Katanga and out of a total of 137 for the Congo.

Senate: 5 seats out of 14 for Katanga and out of a total of 84.

Provincial Assembly: 23, of which:

4 from Elisabethville-Jadotville
7 from the district of Tanganika (1 in cartel with
    MNC/Lumumba)
3 from Lualaba
9 from Haut-Lomami

III. UCOL-KATANGA

FOUNDING AND STRUCTURE

Founded in May, 1944, to promote the development of European colonization. (923 members in January, 1959, out of a total of 3,065 settlers in Katanga). Founding member of Fédacol which federated the provincial organizations of settlers in the Congo and Rwanda, Burundi since 1960.

LEADERS

Jean Humblé, Georges Thyssens, Joseph Onckelinx, Achille Gavage: (see pp. 299–300) the documentation relevant to Conakat, "Advisers and European Support Before Independence."

POLITICAL PROGRAM

1. "Our policy," by the Central Committee of Ucol:

Decentralization:

Colonies have revolted against direction by the metropolitan power, when the latter did not concern itself with regional differences nor take into account the legitimate aspirations of the colonial peoples.

Belgians revolted in the last century, because an administration which was too centralized disregarded their aspirations, their desires, their needs.

In the Congo, the centralization of power hinders the administration from considering regional requirements. A measure judged worthy in Brussels, based on party considerations or on the report of *missi dominici* passing through the Congo with meteoric speed, may prove disastrous in its application. Another measure judged excellent in Leopoldville, is revealed to be catastrophic in its effects on Katanga, whose economy is clearly different from that of the other provinces. A political conception in Leopoldville, based on a certain ethnic unity, will be inapplicable in Katanga where the population is an amalgam of races and tribes from the most diverse origins, with the most disparate social structures.

Decentralization is therefore indispensable. It runs the risk of remaining only a wish, an affirmation of principle, and of not being realized, if practical measures are not taken such as the granting of a certain degree of autonomy to the provinces or the re-establishment of Vice-Governors-General.

Local authorities must be given enlarged powers.

This decentralization will permit the inhabitants to be more readily consulted.

Higher levels, either in Belgium or in the Congo, must limit their intervention to the establishment of general policy and to the coordination and the harmonization of the rights and duties of each region. . . .

Geography:

Ucol cannot refrain from drawing attention to the geographical position of Katanga, a country in large part arid and unpeopled at the arrival of the first Europeans, a country whose economy was created by Europeans, a country in which only the Europeans could, and only they for some time to come, develop and whose natural riches only Europeans could bring forth and put at the disposal of humanity.

Katanga is wedged between stabilized colonies, and has a high rate of immigration, which exerts an ideological and social influence upon it.

Autonomist tendencies have appeared and discontent with the excessive centralization of the *Gouvernement-Général* has increased.

A policy which ignores the vested interests of the settlers, the most numerous and established in the Congo, would be dangerous and could have regrettable repercussions.

Immigration:

We demand a policy of extensive immigration. Far from infringing the interests of the natives, it would accelerate economic development of the country and in this fashion assure to the natives, on a parallel route, full and better employment opportunities and a more harmonious, more rapid and more complete social evolution.

(From *Eurafrica,* organ of
Fédacol, No. 1, September, 1957.)

2. Motion of the General Council of Fédacol (Bukavu, January 13 and 14, 1960).

With a view to avoiding the breakup of the Congo, Fédacol wishes to see the provinces of the Congo given a status of autonomy within a federation placed under the aegis of the Crown. This federation would conclude with Belgium an economic and political union which would assure to the Congo its place in the Common Market.

(*L'Echo du Katanga,* January 18, 1960).

IV. UNION KATANGAISE

FOUNDING AND ORGANIZATION

Political arm of Ucol-Katanga; created in May, 1958, by Gavage; principal sections in Elisabethville, Jadotville, and Kolwezi; 500 to 600 members officially; dissolved in May, 1960, after a period of membership in the Conakat, dating from June, 1959.

LEADERS

President: Achille Gavage, merchant

Members of the Committee: Benjamin Amato, industrialist
Joseph Onckelinx, business man
Stanislas Herman, lawyer
John Elleboudt, doctor

Treasurer: Hector Vander Biken, retired colonial administrator

For Gavage and Onckelinx, see (pp. 299–300) the documentation relative to Conakat, "Advisers and European Support before Independence."

POSITIONS AND PROGRAM

1. In the face of the awakening of a Katangan national conscience, and the cruel doubt which hovers over the political future of the country, before this crisis of confidence which is compounded by economic recession, before the urgent necessity to combine all efforts to realize the Eurafrican community in the Congo, before the imperative need for the great Congolese regions to choose the path best responding to their own aspirations, Katangans belonging to diverse social milieux have decided to form the party of the Union Katangaise.

. . . the new group will admit, as effective members, all Belgian and foreign Europeans settled permanently in the country, whether self-employed or on a payroll, and all those who have decided to choose the Congo as their new homeland. It will admit as well on a footing of perfect equality, all Africans from Katanga and all those from other provinces having definitely become one with the Katangan people.

Political and Administrative Organization — Elective System

Division of the Congo into large territories enjoying internal autonomy with a Council and a permanent executive committee under the authority of the Royal Commissioner, Representative of the Crown; elimination of the *Gouvernement-Général* in Leopoldville, replaced by a Royal High Commissioner, with no direct administrative power. Federation of large territories with Belgium as equal partners. Central agency of the Federation in Brussels.

Extension of the communal organization to the European centers of some importance and to the *circonscriptions indigènes*, with the election of communal councilors. In the native jurisdictions the traditional chief would automatically become burgomaster.

Meeting of burgomasters and other delegates in a Territorial Council, presided over by the representative of the Administration, the territorial officer. Designation of European and African members to the district council, in equal numbers, headed by the current District Commissioner.

Finally, a Higher Council of the Grand Territory, bringing together equal numbers of European and African members of the district and city councils.

For all these councils, full authority to decide all questions within their competence.

Immigration — Nationality — Military Obligations

Encouragement to immigration, not massive, but enough to furnish the country with necessary technicians and to favor the entry of new capital. Priority to Belgian candidates but call extended to people from Western nations.

Creation of a Belgian nationality with Congolese status, rendered accessible without long and costly formalities to all those, Belgians or others, settled in the country and desirous of enjoying to the fullest their political rights.

Extension of obligatory military service to subjects of Belgian nationality with Congolese status and to Congolese of European status.

Reinforcement of the contingent of Belgian volunteers for service in the Congo and assignment of garrison troops in all the large centers in Katanga, with a view to permitting these young elements to judge, in full knowledge of the facts, if they are fit to respond to the appeal of this new country.

Economic Policy — Investments

Industrialization and diversification of the economy is imperative. To this end, creation in each large territory of an Official Economic Commission, offering wide access to private interests.

Exemptions from taxes for new activities and for reinvested profits. Supplementary taxes on expatriated profits.

Obligation for all public agencies (savings banks, pension funds and family allowances, colonial disability funds, etc.) to reinvest the capital in the regions from which they have come. Obligation for the same agencies to establish regional headquarters.

Setting up a system of preferential transport duties and tariffs, in order to afford maximum protection to local agriculture and industry.

Creation of a Steel Industry in Katanga

Decentralization of the powers of the *Société de Crédit au Colonat et à l'Industrie* and extension of the grant of credits to rural native communities to accelerate mechanization and to increase productivity.

Increased reliance upon private enterprise for all public works, with the administration restricting itself to regulation.

Agricultural Policy

More aid to benefit native rural communities with a view to increasing their resources, ameliorating their health and their food, perfecting their equipment and their work methods, and maintaining soil fertility. Study of possible means for promoting acquisition of small private property.

Integration of Europeans within native milieux to ensure the success of the plans for mechanization and for processing of products. Extension of use of draught animals in native lands and of the introduction of small scale single cash-crops.

Opening of available land and encouragement of middle-sized European mixed farms.

Protection of local production, native as well as European.

(Extracts of the program, published by *L'Essor du Congo*, May 28, 1958.)

2. Gavage statement

. . . we must agree in all honesty that the country is at a turning point in its history.

Two routes are open to us: on the one hand, the *status quo* of our political organization, with eventual accession to independence of a unified Congolese State having Leopoldville as capital and as the seat of central government. This would be indisputably the end of the expansion of European settlement with all the disastrous consequences which will flow from it for the further promotion of interests of the inhabitants of this country. On the other hand, we have an indistinct vision of a Congo divided into regions of settlement and into regions of exploitation, with, as a corollary, the creation of great territories enjoying total internal autonomy, but joined in a federation remaining tightly bound to Belgium. The central agency of this federation would be situated either in the Congo or in Belgium, but in any case, would no longer administer the extensive functions of the present *Gouvernement-Général* in Leopoldville. In each large territory, a grand council could be established following a formula yet to be determined, which would choose the executive committee which would supervise all that dealt with the internal life of the territory. These grand councils would be constituted by equal numbers of Europeans and Africans in a fashion to realize that equitable collaboration which, alone, can lead the country toward its true destiny to achieve that Eurafrican community we all desire. . . .

That Leopoldville fears a different disposition of the returns from "the good Katanga cow," we can well understand. But let us be free to say that the mining wealth of Katanga will not last indefinitely and that we have, we the inhabitants of Katanga, the sacred tasks of benefiting from the period of profitable mining exploitation to create in the field of agriculture and industry activities which will permit Katanga to pursue its development when the plentiful mining receipts diminish. But let Leopoldville reassure itself; in the meantime, we shall never act as miserly relatives and we shall always be ready to render assistance in the federal framework to the territories which are less favored than we are. The Bas-Congo will have the Inga, but the rest of us must also be assured our economic and social future.

Judicious utilization of our resources would permit us to attain this goal in good time.

The author of the article which appeared in *Présence Congolaise* describes as simplistic our arguments speaking of the climatic and ethnographic characteristics of Katanga as the basis for the creation of autonomous territories. This is proof of his lack of talent for analysis.

Who would deny today that, although European settlement is possible in the east and south of the colony, it is by no means so in the vast regions of the Central Basin and the Bas-Congo? Who would deny that the territories of the industrial Haut-Katanga were only sparsely populated when the Whites arrived in this country? Who would dream of denying the rights of citizenship to all the Europeans who are the very foundation of the improvement of our regions? Who would think today that it is still possible to apply to such immense territories as the Congo a single political status, when the differences among the regions which compose it are no longer even debated?

It is, nevertheless, precisely this that people in the Bas-Congo would ignore, in the secret hope of seeing their region continue to drain to the maximum the economic profits of the Congo. When one is sitting at the cheese-board, one does not willingly leave one's place.

(Article by A. Gavage, *L'Essor du Congo*, April 2, 1958.)

3. Manifesto-Memorandum of Union Katangaise (early December, 1959).

The Minister was skeptical as to the viability of a truly Katangan state. We were unable to agree with him in this matter.

The Minister wishes to see emerge from the discussions next January, the principal reforms in structure that will shape the Congo's future. We have expressed doubts as to the real value of conclusions which would be arrived at by such a small number of people (the Minister foresaw 12 or 15).

That, then is where the situation stands and less than one month remains to collect the opinions of all those among you who would like to help us in the choice of a clear and firm attitude.

The opinion to which we have made allusion above derives from the fact that in Katanga everyone gathers the impression that the Belgian government has considered no propositions other than those which have come to it from the Bas-Congo; that under such conditions, there is only one possible solution for Katanga: to act on its own initiative.

And the idea is gaining ground that the choice must take place in calm and legality, following a perfectly democratic formula, which would consist in empowering the elected provincial delegates to call a Constituent Assembly for Katanga, with the mission of studying and adopting the future Katangan constitution and of establishing the first government of the State of Katanga, which could then deal with the other Congolese states and with Belgium to spell out terms of association which would no longer compromise the freedom of action of any of the participants.

The gravity of the hour escapes no one. But we do not wish to push the implementation of such a program until we can know with virtual certainty that the mass of Katangans are with us.

We ask you therefore to return to our Post Office Box 81 in Elisabethville immediately the answer to our appeal, which you can easily fill in on the last page of this letter. We ask especially the cooperation of those still called "strangers" but who in a new state would have access without difficulty to the new nationality.

We guarantee to all those who answer, the greatest discretion. After tabulation, all the answers will be destroyed and an official report on the validity of the proceedings will be drafted by a commission drawn from our midst.

KATANGANS, LISTEN TO OUR FINAL APPEAL AND RETURN YOUR ANSWER BY DECEMBER 31 AT THE VERY LATEST!

For your information, here is the whole text of the memorandum submitted to Minister de Schrijver.

OUR VIEWS ON THE SUBJECT OF THE NEW INSTITUTIONS.

Preamble:

The goal of the new institutions must be threefold:

1. To accord to the great Congolese regions a maximum of internal autonomy, permitting them to administer themselves.
2. To assure political and economic unity of the new Congolese State, with respect for regional aspirations;
3. To preserve between the Congo and Belgium ties of association, in the framework of a community.

Regional nationalism, often of tribal origin, exists. It would be useless to ignore it and more so to combat it. The Congo can never form a great, politically stable country as long as the new regime does not take account of this fact. To wish to establish overly powerful central institutions would be tantamount to opening the door to dictatorial power from some quarters or to encourage secession.

A federal structure alone can adequately contain and channel the great thrusts of a regional nationalism which already exist in the Bas-Congo and in the Haut-Katanga and which will not be slow to develop in the other great Congolese regions. The present provinces can serve as bases for the new organization. . . .

V. POSITIONS OF THE BELGIAN AUTHORITIES ON THE STRUCTURE OF THE CONGO

Far from imposing on these people wholly European solutions, we intend to favor original adaptations, answering to the character and to the traditions which these people hold dear. In this regard, a broad decentralization, in conjunction with an extension of the electoral system and the abandonment of all discrimination between European and African, will permit the burgeoning development of the different regions to be hastened along their diverse paths according to their geographic, cultural, and racial particularities as well as to their different levels of economic development.

(Royal Message, January 13, 1959.)

The extensiveness of the territory and the development of its organization require an effort at deconcentration and decentralization, which will bring the administrators closer to the administered and the elected, to the electors.

(Government Declaration, January 13, 1959.)

Political decentralization would contradict the unitary heritage of the Congo. . . . The arguments in favor of this decentralization pale before the consideration that it could, under certain circumstances, promote secession and, under others, compromise the political, economic, and social progress which Belgium means to pursue for the benefit of the whole territory. . . .

> (Report of the *Groupe de Travail pour l'Etude du problème politique au Congo*, Belgian Parliamentary Documents, *Chambre des Représentants*, No. 108, January 20, 1959, pp. 58–59.)

No region of the Congo, no matter what it be, could hope to become a prosperous country in isolation from the rest of the country. . . . Moreover, a step in this direction [separatism] would risk entailing others, and, instead of forming a rich and powerful Congo, we would end up with a mosaic of little states. . . . To commit an offense now against the unity of the Congo would be to err in our essential duty to its 13 million inhabitants and, if we should act thus, *the descendants of those who, in certain regions, perhaps, dream of it*[3] would be later the first to reproach us for it.

> (H. Van Hemelrijck over Radio Congo Belge, March 12, 1959.)

It is therefore vain to cast doubt on the unity of the Congo and to place before public opinion programs which consecrate its division; the balkanization of the Congo would deprive it forever of the possibility of occupying a preponderant place in Central Africa.

> (Minister of the Congo, June 24, 1959.)

Katanga, under the impetus of its European population,[4] has always been marked by a lively particularism. The province is very rich and sparsely populated so that it fears that a unitary structure would bring it more sacrifices than advantages: it does not wish to remain forever, as it has felt itself for some time to be, the provider for the poor regions of the Congo. The most forward spirits periodically play with the idea of separatism, but by and large a federal structure would be considered as a sufficient guarantee.

> (Report on federalism by Alain Stenmans, secretary of the government in Leopoldville, August 24, 1959.)

It would then seem necessary to concede a federal structure, but to insist on the unity of the country. The only formula "with any chance of success" is one which gives "full powers to the provinces, with the exception of delimited and enumerated matters to be delegated to the central power."

> (Harold d'Aspremont Lynden, deputy *chef de cabinet* of the Prime Minister, August 30, 1959.)

Belgium . . . hopes that the Congo recommends institutions adapted to local customs and preferences and corresponding to the needs of the country. . . .

> (Royal Message, December 17, 1959.)

[3] Author's italics.
[4] Author's italics.

VI. COMITÉ SPÉCIAL DU KATANGA (CSK)

The Comité Spécial du Katanga (CSK) was created on June 19, 1900, by convention between the Congo Free State and the chartered company, the Compagnie du Katanga, for the management of the undivided assets of the two associates.

The Compagnie du Katanga was founded in April, 1891, at a time when the claims of Leopold II's Free State over the Congolese southwest were disputed and the state was incapable of organizing the necessary expeditions by itself. In exchange for the responsibilities assumed (to annex, occupy, organize, administer and to create the economic infrastructure), the Compagnie received a third of the unoccupied lands of the territory thus occupied, the other two thirds remaining the domain of the state. The 15 million hectares of the Compagnie did not constitute a single region but were divided into several thousand checkerboard sections of 12,500 hectares, symmetrically dispersed among similar (but twice as numerous) squares, belonging to the state. This checkerboard pattern had been tried by the state to avoid an overly concentrated improvement of the land.

In addition to the lands ceded, the Compagnie benefited from a concession of 99 years over the exploitation of the subsoil of "its own" territory and from an option for 20 years over the eventual concessions from the subsoil of the state.

This checkerboard system soon proved impractical and, finally, CSK was created for the management of all the land. The CSK took over the obligations accepted by the Compagnie, but in 1910, the costly responsibilities in the realm of administration and politics were withdrawn from it without reducing the interests of the CSK.

CONVENTION CREATING CSK

Article 1

A special *Comité* is created to guarantee and direct the exploitation of all the lands belonging to the domain of the State and of the Compagnie du Katanga bounded by a line extending from the eastern frontier at 5° South due West to 24° 10′ East, then proceeding southwesterly to the point 6° South and 23° 54′ East, then due South to the southern frontier of the State.

The *Comité* will have full powers of administration, of management and of alienation [of land], without limitation or reservation. It will issue decrees by a majority of its members.

Article 2

The *Comité* will be composed of six members: four of these members, including the President, with tie-breaking vote, will be named by the State of the Congo and two by the Compagnie du Katanga.

. . . .

Article 5

All interests and profits accumulated through exploitation covered in Article 1 and all the costs, or losses . . . will be divided by the *Comité*, with ⅔ for the State of the Congo and ⅓ for the Compagnie du Katanga.

RELATIONS WITH TANGANYIKA CONCESSIONS, LTD.

Shortly after its constitution, the *Comité* entrusted a British businessman, Robert Williams — who was soon to become one of the leading figures in

TABLE 6

Percentage of Shares Held by CSK in Other Companies

Companies	On June 1, 1960 (before decree of dissolution)	On July 1, 1960 (after withdrawal of ⅓ reverting to Compagnie du Katanga)
Union Minière du Haut-Katanga	35.73%	23.82%
Géomines*	48.30	32.20
Charbonnages de la Luena	28.23	18.82
Compagnie Foncière du Katanga	14.00	9.34
Tanganyika Concessions Ltd.	0.15	0.1
Sogefor (hydroelectricity)	10.11	6.74
Sogelec (electricity)	11.05	7.37
Sermikat (mining research)	36.00	24.00
Grelco (large stock-raising)	11.70	7.80
Pastorale du Lomami (Albertville cement)	19.50	13.00
Cimental	15.45	10.30
Cobelcat (Colonization Society)	55.95	37.30
Métalkat	12.19	8.13
Auximokat (apartments)	15.00	10.00
Van Gysel Marungu (stock-raising)	19.95	13.30
Mutuelle Immobilière du Katanga	15.00	10.00
Sclkibara (stock-raising)	15.00	10.00
Pierkat (building materials)	14.28	9.52
Saruc	4.95	3.30
Sarma. Kindelunga (stock-raising plantations)	19.95	13.30
Ciments Métall. Jadotville (CMJ)	10.11	6.74
Minsudkat (mining)†	39.80	25.20
Charbons de la Lukuga‡	64.50	43.00

*Géomines: The CSK held voting rights in it equal to one third the outstanding shares, or 350,000 in addition to the 105,066 shares held in the CSK portfolio.

†Minsudkat: Through its "B" shares, the CSK controlled a third of the votes.

‡Lukuga: In voting certificates, CSK controlled a third of the votes that could be cast in addition to its votes through share holdings.

the famous Tanganyika Concessions, Ltd. — with prospecting for minerals throughout southeast Katanga. . . . The convention between the *Comité* and Williams — the latter negotiating on behalf of Tanganyika Concessions — stipulated that each one of the two participants in the contract would provide half the necessary capital for the development of the mineral deposits to be discovered and would name half the administrators in the companies to be created, while 60 percent of the profits would go to the *Comité* and 40 percent to the Williams group, i.e., Tanganyika Concessions. From this association, the Union Minière du Haut Katanga (UMHK) was born in 1906. . . . Shortly after the conclusion of the convention by which CSK entrusted Robert Williams with the prospecting, a new accord was negotiated between the same partners, on the subject of railroads to be built in Katanga. . . . It was agreed in 1901, for the railroads as for the mines, that the Williams group, namely Tanganyika Concessions, would participate in 40 percent of the creation of a railroad company, the Compagnie du Chemin de Fer du Katanga, founded the following year.

(J. Van Bilsen, "La grande féodalité du Katanga,"
Revue Nouvelle, October 10, 1950, pp. 314–21.)

Joint Declaration of the Katanga Delegations Relative to the Comité Spécial du Katanga

THE DELEGATIONS OF KATANGA express their desire to promote to the maximum, as of next June 30, economic activities of all sorts throughout the whole territory of the Congo and especially of Katanga.

In regard to land and property rights

The delegations feel that the land rights which have not been allocated or are revocable must be returned to the province. They mean by non-allocated rights those not conceded as of now, and by revocable rights, those bearing upon concessions not actively exploited as well as those contractually liable to cancellation. This problem must be resolved immediately. As of the present, all allocations of land must cease and preparatory measures taken with a view to possible cancellations.

Concerning the CSK portfolio

They want, assuming there is provision made for a general audit, a reasonable redistribution of this portfolio, that is, attributing a third to the Compagnie du Katanga, a third to the Congolese State, and a third to the province of Katanga.

Concerning the situation of the monopolies

They demand the immediate re-examination of certain monopolies by a commission which will include a fair representation from Katanga and from the interested parties.

Concerning the subsidiary services

They demand that the CSK subsidiary services [5] be attached to the province; each of the three to whom the portfolio was divided paying his part of the costs of these services.

Concerning the statutes of the CSK

They declare that it is up to the province of Katanga to readapt the statutes of the CSK to the new situation. The CSK will administer the lands of the province. It will retain all personnel without distinction with all their rights.

Concerning the private sector

They recognize solemnly the rights vested in the private sector, namely in the Compagnie du Katanga. They hold it inadmissible that any negotiations, touching the rights of the private sector, be conducted by the Belgian State with the Compagnie du Katanga.

Léon Ilunga	Chief Kasongo Nyembo	Joseph Yav
Balubakat Cartel	Katanga Chief	Conakat
Raphaël Senga	Jean-Baptiste Kibwe	Joseph Kalala
Union Congolaise	Member of Political	Acmaf Katanga
Katanga	Commission, repre-	
	sentative of Katanga	

RESOLUTION NO. 10 OF THE BELGO-CONGOLESE ECONOMIC CONFERENCE (MAY, 1960)

Subject: Concessionary Companies

The Conference:

maintains that the *Loi Fondamentale*, relating to the structures of the State of the Congo will not abrogate the powers delegated to CNKi, CFL, and CSK;

strongly hopes, nevertheless, that the Congo will exercise from the first day of its independence all its concessionary powers and the rights of management in the public domain;

considers that there is cause, therefore, to review immediately the conventions concluded with the aforementioned agencies and approved by decrees, and to proceed with this revision under conditions which, while fully respecting the rights of the Congo, do not prejudice either the legitimate interests of the private groups associated with the concessionary companies, or good relations between Belgium and the Congo;

declares that this result can be attained if, before June 30, simultaneously and by common accord between the Belgian and Congolese governments:

[5] Translator's note: The CSK operated a certain number of subsidiary services for research and prospecting as well as some social welfare activities, such as dispensaries.

1. one or several decrees proposed by the competent minister withdraw the concessionary powers from the aforementioned companies, revise their status while guaranteeing the permanence of the existing services, and divide, in accordance with resolution 9, paragraph b, of the political Round Table, the disposable assets and stock in securities, especially in the case of the CSK, respecting the rights both of the Congolese authorities, central and provincial, and the private interests.
2. an equitable ruling be made with the interested groups on the subject of compensation, to the extent it is necessary, taking account of vested interests and of expenses for improvement, but excluding any compensation for property which was not improved and for rights which were not exercised or not conceded;

asks the competent minister to take the steps in his power and use his influence to realize the objectives aforementioned if this equitable ruling is established;

takes note of the joint declaration of the delegations of Katanga as well as noting the reservations expressed on this subject by the other delegations;

decides to entrust to an Economic Commission, which will work in conjunction with the political Commission, the task of preparing the necessary conventions on this subject in the framework outlined by the general treaty of friendship, assistance, and cooperation.

VII. SOCIÉTÉ GÉNÉRALE DE BELGIQUE IN CENTRAL AFRICA

The Société Générale de Belgique is beyond doubt the most important financial group in the Congo. It is generally admitted that it controls, directly or indirectly, 70 percent of the Congolese economy (subsistence production not included). It must be added that its influence is practically absolute in certain mining industries (copper, cobalt, diamonds, uranium) and in transportation by water and rail. Its mining activities are especially concentrated in Katanga and Kasai.

The Société Générale also has interests in two companies which carry on their activities in territories bordering on the Congo, but are linked financially to the Congolese companies: Tanganyika Concessions, Ltd., and the Compagnie des Diamants de l'Angola.

The Société Générale carried on its activities in the Congo either by direct stockholding in the most important industrial companies: the Union Minière du Haut-Katanga, Forminière, Minière du Bécéka, Chemin de Fer du Bas-Congo au Katanga, or by the intermediary of two specialized holding companies: the Compagnie du Congo pour le Commerce et l'Industrie (CCCI), which holds stock in fifty-odd Congolese companies and twenty Belgian and foreign companies, and the Compagnie du Ka-

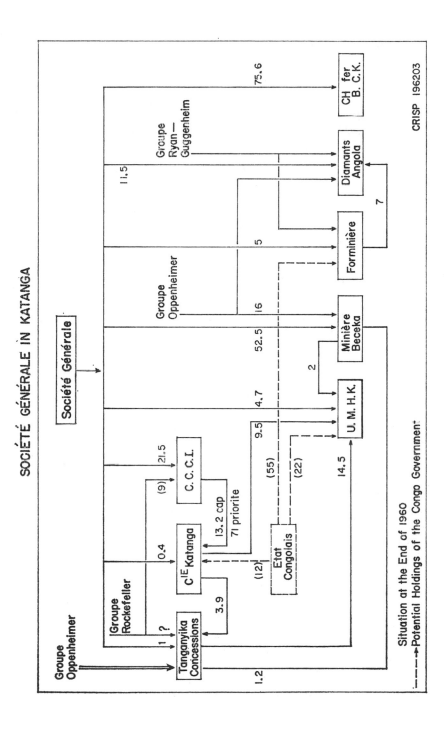

SOCIÉTÉ GÉNÉRALE IN KATANGA

Situation at the End of 1960
------ Potential Holdings of the Congo Government

CRISP 196203

tanga, having interests direct and indirect in Union Minière du Haut-Katanga. (See diagram, p. 321).

The relations between the diverse companies are complex and one must refer to the diagram in order to understand them. The percentages indicated give the proportion of capital of one company controlled by another company following the direction of the arrows. It can be seen that the pyramided ownerships are numerous (for example, the Société Générale to the CCCI, to the Compagnie du Katanga to the UMHK, or the Société Générale to the Minière du Bécéka to Tanganyika Concessions, Ltd., to the UMHK).

Union Minière du Haut-Katanga (UMHK)

The Union Minière is the world's leading producer of cobalt and the world's third largest producer of copper after two American companies, Kennecott and Anaconda. The production of the UMHK surpassed its own records in 1960. Production of uranium was practically halted after saturation of the market and the exhaustion of the richest deposits.

TABLE 7
UMHK Production

	1960	1959
Copper	300,704 metric tons	280,403 metric tons
Cobalt	8,240 metric tons	8,431 metric tons
Zinc	192,000 metric tons	118,000 metric tons
Germanium	26,100 kilograms	13,643 kilograms
Silver	124,100 kilograms	148,307 kilograms
Uranium oxide	1,079 metric tons	2,110 metric tons
Cadmium	214 metric tons	99 metric tons

The Union Minière du Haut-Katanga is the most important employer in all of Katanga: it had on its payroll as of December 31, 1960, 1,755 management personnel (of whom 86 were Africans) and 20,876 manual laborers.

The UMHK is capitalized at 8 billion francs. Assets total nearly 20 billion; the value of the capital stock amounts to 1,875 billion francs (as of December 31, 1960).

Although closely connected to the Société Générale, the UMHK seems to enjoy, in fact, a certain autonomy. This probably derives from the diversity of its stockholders. In the extraordinary general assembly of the

Union Minière du Haut-Katanga, held on May 25, 1960, the principal stockholders present may be seen in Table 8.

TABLE 8
Principal Stockholders in the UMHK

Companies	Shares	1/10 shares	Registered bonds	Number of votes
CSK	315,675	—	99,093	248,400
Tanganyika Conc.	179,760	—	61,384	134,016
Société Générale	57,685	—	39,523	31,584
Compagnie du Katanga	18,400	1,000	—	—
Congométaux	4,000	—	—	—
Electrorail	3,370	—	—	—
Congovielmont	3,000	—	—	—
Minière du Bécéka	598	19,020	—	—
Miscellaneous	1,394	2,592	—	—
Total	583,882	22,612	200,000	414,000

The capital of the UMHK is represented by 1,242,000 shares. Registered bonds total 20 million francs (two hundred thousand 100-franc bonds).

The Union Minière holds interest in seventeen Congolese companies, ten companies in Belgium, and five foreign companies. The majority of the stocks of these companies is found elsewhere in the portfolios of other companies belonging to the group of "la Générale."

The most important block of Belgian shares held is the 47.7 percent holding in the capital of the Société Métallurgique Hoboken.

Among the companies in which the Union Minière owns important interests, yet in which other companies in the Société Générale complex are also shareholders, the following can be cited:

— La Compagnie Foncière du Katanga (Cofoka);

— Société Générale des Forces Hydro-Electriques du Katanga (Sogefor), which exploits the power station at the Francqui dam and manages three other power complexes belonging to the UMHK (two billion kw.-h. in 1960);

— The Société Générale Africaine d'Electricité (Sogelec): industrial production and public distribution of electricity in Jadotville, Kipushi, Kolwezi, Elisabethville, and its affiliates — Comelco and Entrelco — electrification projects;

— Société Métallurgique du Katanga (Metalkat): production in Kolwezi of zinc, cadmium, electrolytic germanium, and sulfuric acid;

— Société Générale Industrielle et Chimique du Katanga (Sogechim) in Jadotville (sulfuric acid, sodium chlorate, water purification) and its commercial affiliate (Congochim);

— Charbonnages de la Luena: 247,000 tons of coal in 1959;

— Société de Recherche Minière du Sud-Katanga (Sud-kat), production of manganese. Minsudkat (mining of copper deposits) ceased its activities in 1960;

— Société Africaine d'Explosifs (Afridex) and its affiliate (Afrimeches) with the Poudreries Réunies, Poudrerie Royale de Wetteren, Olin Mathieson (United States), Dynamit Nobel A.G. (Germany), Nobel Bozel (France), and others;

— Minoteries [flour mills] du Katanga in Jadotville, Elisabethville, and Kolwezi;

— Société d'Elevage [stock breeding] de la Luilu (Elvalulilu);

— Société de Colonisation belge au Katanga (Cobelkat).

The Union Minière holds shares in Ciments Métallurgiques de Jadotville, Société de Recherches et d'Exploitations des Bauxites du Congo (Bauxicongo), Compagnie des Chemins de Fer Katanga-Dilolo-Léopoldville (KDL), and others.

The Union Minière is one of the principal shareholders in Rhodesian coal mines: Wankie Colliery Company, Ltd., in Bulawayo.

TABLE 9
Quotations of UMHK Shares on the Brussels Stock Market

Period	High	Low	Period	High	Low
(whole share)			($\frac{1}{10}$ share)		
1937	4,820	3,000	1956	7,320	5,530
			1957	6,300	3,525
($\frac{1}{10}$ share)			1958	4,260	3,080
1949	15,425	12,175	1959	3,675	2,430
1950	19,750	14,200	1960	2,730	1,492
1951	28,800	18,300	1961	1,994	1,044
1952	28,700	22,225	1962	1,572	1,074
1953	27,950	23,050	Nov. 1, 1963	1,528	998
1954	49,235	26,450			
1955	7,970	4,480			

TANGANYIKA CONCESSIONS, LTD.

This holding company has its headquarters in Salisbury, Rhodesia. It is capitalized at £9,507,448. Very large financial groups are interested in it, notably, Tanganyika Holdings, Ltd., in London, Lazard Frères, in Paris, and Société Générale (directly and indirectly).

The president and an administrator of Tanganyika Concessions sit on the board of the Union Minière, while one of the two vice-governors and two directors of Société Générale (who are also vice-president and one of the two delegate-administrators of the Union Minière) are also on the board of Tanganyika Concessions. This shows the ties between Tanganyika Concessions on the one hand, the Société Générale and the Union Minière on the other.

Tanganyika Concessions owns, in effect, 14 percent of the capital of the Union Minière and collects "royalties" to boot. Because of the contribution made by its intermediary to the discovery of the copper-bearing deposits when the Union Minière was constituted, founders' shares were allotted to Tanganyika Concessions; the royalty was instituted after the discontinuation of founders' shares in 1937. Until 1960, this royalty consisted in an extra dividend paid to CSK which retroceded two-fifths of it to Tanganyika Concessions, Ltd.

TABLE 10
Establishment of Institutions in June, 1960

Date	Theoretical timetable (set by administration)	Effective timetable Katanga	Effective timetable Leopoldville (province)
June 1, 1960	—1st meeting of Prov. Asm. —Designation of Provisional President. —Transmission of candidacies for posts of coopted members.	—Assembly meeting. —Designation of provisional president. —Cartel withdraws.	—Assembly meeting. —Designation of provisional president. —Transmission of candidacies for coopted councilors (56 candidates).
June 2, 1960		—Assembly meeting. —Cartel withdraws.	
June 5, 1960	—2nd Assembly meeting and election of coopted members in afternoon, with complete Assembly (elected and coopted) elect officers; fix number of traditional senators and of provincial ministers.	—Assembly meeting in absence of Cartel, 37 present; no decision possible.	—Election of coopted members. —Designation of officers of assembly. —4 traditional senators and 10 provincial ministers are numbers fixed.

Date	Theoretical timetable (set by administration)	Effective timetable Katanga	Effective timetable Leopoldville (province)
June 7, 1960	—Drawing up the double list of nominations for traditional senatorial candidates. —Assembly session to receive all lists of candidacies (senators, provincial ministers).	—same as above.	
June 8, 1960		—Election of coopted councilors and Assembly officers. —Number of traditional senators fixed at 4; provincial ministers at 10.	—plan for an autonomous Bakongo government is announced.
June 11, 1960	—Election by Assembly of senators (traditional and nontraditional) and of members of provincial govt.		—Effective constitution of Bakongo government; Bakongo Assembly meets on June 9 and 10.
June 12, 1960		—Election of 10 nontraditional senators.	
June 13, 1960		—No vote; Cartel leaves session.	—Abako announces its government will take over only after June 30. —Full provincial Assembly elects senators.
June 14, 1960		—Election of 4 traditional senators. —"State of exception" decreed.	
June 16, 1960		—3 sessions at 10 A.M. 3 P.M. and 8 P.M. —Election of 10 members of government and of provincial president.	

Date	Theoretical timetable (set by administration)	Effective timetable Katanga	Effective timetable Leopoldville (province)
June 18, 1960			—Election of president and of 7 of 10 members of provincial government (without Abako).
June 21, 1960		—Balubakat Cartel announces constitution of its Baluba-Tshokwe government to take effect after June 30.	
June 29, 1960			—At 6 P.M. Assembly elects Diomi (Abako) vice-president of government and 3 Abako members provincial ministers.

The Katangan government was set up, therefore, five days later than planned in the administration timetable; non-traditional senators were elected with a delay of one day, and traditional senators after a delay of three days. In contrast to the province of Leopoldville, the delay in Katanga was only 24 hours for the senators. The planned schedule projected the first Chamber of Representatives meeting for June 15 in Leopoldville; it took place on June 17. As for the provincial government, Katanga elected its ministers before the province of Leopoldville, where a partial government was elected on June 18 and the complete government on June 29. The coordination planned in the theoretical timetable was then scarcely affected by the events in Katanga.

I. TEXT OF THE PROCLAMATION OF INDEPENDENCE
OF KATANGA (JULY 11, 1960)

Belgium has granted independence to the Congo.

It has done so according to its promise of January 13, 1959.

This promise and the royal message which accompanied it were intended to endow us with democratic institutions, and, in keeping with the stipulations of the Charter of the United Nations, which pledges to respect the right of all peoples to self-determination, it was intended to endow us, not with a slavish copy of Western democratic institutions, but with a regime which the various regions composing the Congo would choose according to their own conceptions and the traditions which they hold dear.

The independence of the Congo is an established fact since June 30, 1960.

What do we behold at present?

Throughout the Congo and particularly in Katanga and in Leopoldville province, we see a tactic of disorganization and terror at work, a tactic which we have seen applied in numerous instances and in how many countries now under Communist dictatorship.

After improper elections in certain provinces, which gave the majority to a single party, a number of electors being unable to cast their votes, a central government with an extremist majority was constituted.

Hardly was it constituted, before this government, setting at naught the stipulations of the *Loi Fondamentale*, attempted to meddle in affairs which properly belonged solely within the competent jurisdiction of the provincial governments.

It is thus that the Prime Minister of the Congo ex officio and on his authority alone designated the Commissioners of State delegated for the individual provinces; only the intervention of the Senate succeeded in annulling this maneuver.

Incidents have erupted everywhere.

The tactic of disruption and subversion of authority is the very same that was ever employed by the propagandists and sectaries of the Communist Party.

The result was not long in coming.

Since July 5, soldiers knowing no discipline have given themselves over to acts of insubordination, of threats, to brutalities aimed principally against the European population, to searches and illegal arrests, to pillages, and finally, to murders.

The goal of these maneuvers and their premeditation were amply proven by the repeated protests of the Prime Minister of the Congo against the dispatch of Belgian troops from Belgium to protect property and human lives.

We declare that what the current central Congolese government wants is nothing less than the disintegration of the whole military and administrative apparatus, the installation of a regime of terror which ousts our Belgian colleagues.

It desires, by this method, to replace the destroyed cadres as rapidly as possible by an administration which it seems already to have recruited amongst nationals of countries under Communist rule.

Katanga cannot bow to such proceedings. The Katangan government was elected by a provincial assembly, itself elected on the basis of a program for order and peace.

Under these circumstances, and before the dangers we would bring down upon us by prolonging our submission to the arbitrary will and Communistic intentions of the central government, the Katangan government has decided to proclaim the independence of Katanga.

This INDEPENDENCE is TOTAL. However, aware of the imperative necessity for economic cooperation with Belgium, the Katangan government, to which Belgium has just granted the assistance of its own troops to protect human life, calls upon Belgium to join with Katanga in close economic community.

Katanga calls upon Belgium to continue its technical, financial, and military support.

It calls upon her to assist in re-establishing order and public safety.

If Belgium refuses to fulfill this imperative duty and if she refuses to recognize Katanga as a country free and independent and its government as the only legal government, Katanga appeals to the ENTIRE FREE WORLD and calls upon ALL to recognize its right, which is that of all its people, to self-determination.

If it is to Belgium that we address ourselves in an offer of economic cooperation, it is, above all, as a sign of gratitude for the benefits which she has brought to us.

To all the inhabitants of KATANGA, without distinction of RACE or COLOR, we ask that you gather around us to lead our COUNTRY and all its inhabitants forward to political, social, and economic progress, to the betterment of all.

We are determined to receive with open arms all those from other regions of the Congo who are determined to work with us in the same spirit of order, fraternity, and progress.

May GOD protect INDEPENDENT KATANGA.

Elisabethville, July 11, 1960

The College of Ministers

II. U.N. RESOLUTIONS ON KATANGA

RESOLUTION ADOPTED BY THE SECURITY COUNCIL ON AUGUST 9, 1960
(886TH SESSION)

The Security Council,

Recalling its resolution of July 22, 1960 (S/4405), *inter alia,* calling upon the Government of Belgium to implement speedily the Security Council resolution of July 14 (S/4387) on the withdrawal of its troops and authorizing the Secretary-General to take all necessary action to this effect,

Having noted the second report of the Secretary-General [S/4417] on the implementation of the aforesaid two resolutions and his statement before the Council,

Having considered the statements made by the representatives of Belgium and the Republic of the Congo to this Council at this meeting,

Noting with satisfaction the progress made by the United Nations in carrying out the Security Council resolutions in respect of the territory of the Republic of the Congo other than the province of Katanga,

Noting, however, that the United Nations had been prevented from implementing the aforesaid resolutions in the province of Katanga although it was ready, and in fact attempted, to do so,

Recognizing that the withdrawal of Belgian troops from the province of Katanga will be a positive contribution to and essential for the proper implementation of the Council resolutions,

1. *Confirms* the authority given to the Secretary-General by the Security Council resolutions of July 14th and July 22nd, 1960, and requests him to continue to carry out the responsibility placed on him thereby;

2. *Calls upon* the Government of Belgium to withdraw immediately its troops from the province of Katanga under speedy modalities determined by the Secretary-General and to assist in every possible way the implementation of the Council's resolutions;

3. *Declares* that the entry of the United Nations Force into the province of Katanga is necessary for the full implementation of this resolution;

4. *Reaffirms* that the United Nations Force in the Congo will not be a party to or in any way intervene in or be used to influence the outcome of any internal conflict, constitutional or otherwise;

5. *Calls upon* all Member States, in accordance with Articles 25 and 49 of the Charter of the United Nations, to accept and carry out the decisions of the Security Council and to afford mutual assistance in carrying out measures decided upon by the Security Council;

6. *Requests* the Secretary-General to implement this resolution and to report further to the Security Council as appropriate.

(Security Council, S/4426)

RESOLUTION ADOPTED BY THE SECURITY COUNCIL ON FEBRUARY 21–22, 1961
(942ND SESSION)

A

The Security Council,

Having considered the situation in the Congo,

Having learned with deep regret the annnouncement of the killing of the Congolese leaders, Mr. Patrice Lumumba, Mr. Maurice Mpolo, and Mr. Joseph Okito,

Deeply concerned at the grave repercussions of these crimes and the danger of widespread civil war and bloodshed in the Congo and the threat to international peace and security,

Noting the report of the Secretary-General's Special Representative (S/4691) dated February 12, 1961, bringing to light the development of a serious civil war situation and preparations therefor,

1. *Urges* that the United Nations take immediately all appropriate measures to prevent the occurrence of civil war in the Congo, including arrangements for cease-fires, the halting of all military operations, the prevention of clashes, and the use of force, if necessary, in the last resort;

2. *Urges* that measures be taken for the immediate withdrawal and evacuation from the Congo of all Belgian and other foreign military and paramilitary personnel and political advisers not under United Nations Command, and mercenaries;

3. *Calls upon* all States to take immediate and energetic measures to prevent the departure of such personnel for the Congo from their territories, and for the denial of transit and other facilities to them;

4. *Decides* that an immediate and impartial investigation be held in order to ascertain the circumstances of the death of Mr. Lumumba and his colleagues and that the perpetrators of these crimes be punished;

5. *Reaffirms* the Security Council resolutions of July 14, July 22, and August 9, 1960, and the General Assembly resolution 1474 (ES-IV) of September 20, 1960, and reminds all States of their obligation under these resolutions.

B

The Security Council,

Gravely concerned at the continuing deterioration in the Congo, and the prevalence of conditions which seriously imperil peace and order, and the unity and territorial integrity of the Congo, and threaten international peace and security,

Noting with deep regret and concern the systematic violations of human rights and fundamental freedoms and the general absence of rule of law in the Congo,

Recognizing the imperative necessity of the restoration of parliamentary institutions in the Congo in accordance with the fundamental law of the country, so that the will of the people should be reflected through the freely elected Parliament,

Convinced that the solution of the problem of the Congo lies in the hands of the Congolese people themselves without any interference from outside and that there can be no solution without conciliation,

Convinced further that the imposition of any solution, including the formation of any government not based on genuine conciliation would, far from settling any issues greatly enhance the dangers of conflict within the Congo and threat to international peace and security,

1. *Urges* the convening of the Parliament and the taking of necessary protective measures in that connection;

2. *Urges* that Congolese armed units and personnel should be reorganized

and brought under discipline and control, and arrangements be made on impartial and equitable bases to that end and with a view to the elimination of any possibility of interference by such units and personnel in the political life of the Congo;

3. *Calls upon* all States to extend their full cooperation and assistance and take such measures as may be necessary on their part, for the implementation of this resolution.   (Security Council, S/4722)

RESOLUTION ADOPTED BY THE SECURITY COUNCIL ON NOVEMBER 24, 1961
(982ND SESSION)

The Security Council,

Recalling its resolutions S/4387, S/4405, S/4426 and S/4741,

Recalling further General Assembly resolutions 1474 (SE-IV), 1592 (XV), 1599 (XV), 1600(XV) and 1601 (XV),

Reaffirming the policies and purposes of the United Nations with respect to the Congo (Leopoldville) as set out in the aforesaid resolutions, namely:

(a) To maintain the territorial integrity and the political independence of the Republic of the Congo,

(b) To assist the Central Government of the Congo in the restoration and maintenance of law and order,

(c) To prevent the occurrence of civil war in the Congo,

(d) To secure the immediate withdrawal and evacuation from the Congo of all foreign military, paramilitary and advisory personnel not under the United Nations Command, and all mercenaries, and

(e) To render technical assistance,

Welcoming the restoration of the national Parliament of the Congo in accordance with the *Loi fondamentale* and the consequent formation of a Central Government on August 2, 1961,

Deploring all armed action in opposition to the authority of the Government of the Republic of the Congo, specifically secessionist activities and armed action now being carried on by the provincial administration of Katanga with the aid of external resources and foreign mercenaries, and completely rejecting the claim that Katanga is a "sovereign independent nation,"

Noting with deep regret the recent and past actions of violence against United Nations personnel,

Recognizing the Government of the Republic of the Congo as exclusively responsible for the conduct of the external affairs of the Congo,

Bearing in mind the imperative necessity of speedy and effective action to implement fully the policies and purposes of the United Nations in the Congo to end the unfortunate plight of the Congolese people, necessary both in the interests of world peace and international cooperation, and stability and progress of Africa as a whole,

1. *Strongly deprecates* the secessionist activities illegally carried out by the provincial administration of Katanga, with the aid of external resources and manned by foreign mercenaries;

2. *Further deprecates* the armed action against United Nations forces and personnel in the pursuit of such activities;

3. *Insists* that such activities shall cease forthwith, and *calls upon* all concerned to desist therefrom;

4. *Authorizes* the Secretary-General to take vigorous action, including the use of a requisite measure of force, if necessary, for the immediate apprehension, detention pending legal action and/or deportation of all foreign military and paramilitary personnel and political advisers not under the United Nations Command, and mercenaries as laid down in part A, operative paragraph 2, of the Security Council resolution of February 21, 1961;

5. *Further requests* the Secretary-General to take all necessary measures to prevent the entry or return of such elements under whatever guise and also of arms, equipment or other material in support of such activities;

6. *Requests* all States to refrain from the supply of arms, equipment or other material which could be used for warlike purposes, and to take the necessary measures to prevent their nationals from doing the same, and also to deny transportation and transit facilities for such supplies across their territories, except in accordance with the decisions, policies and purposes of the United Nations;

7. *Calls upon* all Member States to refrain from promoting, condoning, or giving support by acts of omission or commission, directly or indirectly, to activities against the United Nations often resulting in armed hostilities against the United Nations forces and personnel;

8. *Declares* that all secessionist activities against the Republic of the Congo are contrary to the *Loi fondamentale* and Security Council decisions and specifically *demands* that such activities which are now taking place in Katanga shall cease forthwith;

9. *Declares* full and firm support for the Central Government of the Congo, and the determination to assist that Government, in accordance with the decisions of the United Nations, to maintain law and order and national integrity, to provide technical assistance, and to implement those decisions;

10. *Urges* all Member States to lend their support, according to their national procedures, to the Central Government of the Republic of the Congo, in conformity with the Charter and the decisions of the United Nations;

11. *Requests* all Member States to refrain from any action which may, directly or indirectly, impede the policies and purposes of the United Nations in the Congo and is contrary to its decisions and the general purpose of the Charter. (Security Council, S/5002)

III. UNPUBLISHED DECLARATION OF TSHOMBE AT THE TIME OF THE KASAVUBU-LUMUMBA RUPTURE (SEPTEMBER 6, 1960)

In the constitution that Katanga gave itself and that was voted by our Assembly on August 4, it says, in the first article:

"The State of Katanga adheres to the principle of association with other regions of the former Belgian Congo, provided that they are themselves organized politically in respect for order and law.

"It will open negotiations to constitute with them a confederation founded on equality of partners."

It seems to me the time has come to retrace the political line which I have drawn. As you know, from the month of January, 1960, at the political Round Table in Brussels, I have been a strenuous defender of a confederation grouping together the territories which formed the Belgian Congo. This formula alone permitted local particularisms to find their real expression [1] while safeguarding the unity of a whole which would have made the Congo one of the major powers in Africa. Unfortunately, in spite of the friends who supported me, namely, Presidents Kasavubu, Ileo, and Albert Kalonji, a strongly centralizing formula has been adopted and artificially imposed after pressure from Belgian ministers.

I do not have to dwell on the shortcomings of the *Loi Fondamentale*; events which we have lived through have proved in bloody fashion that it did not answer to the fundamental and legitimate aspirations of the Congolese peoples.

After the events of the month of July, I was obliged to be loyal to this policy that I had set for myself and to the program on which I had been elected, to refuse, in accord with the Katangan people, to collaborate with a regime which was setting up a self-centered, malignant dictatorship, supported by international Communism. And I broke my ties with this detestable regime which brought shame to all of Africa and proclaimed independence for Katanga, in the hope of bringing about one day a confederation of the regions of the former Congo.

Perhaps you will ask me what I mean by confederation.

It is a regime which, while respecting the independence of the member States, calls [*nine lines illegible here*] on the powers which have been expressly given to it, to the exclusion of all others. The examples of the United States and Switzerland prove on this factual level that such a system permits the harmonious development of diversity and of interests particular to each region. We shall be inspired by these examples to find original solutions adapted to local requirements, in order, as we all hope, that this confederation can have the place it deserves in Africa.

It is essential that certain powers be exercised, for the good of all, by the central authority. I am thinking primarily of foreign affairs, a confederal army, communications, certain scientific institutions, and so forth.

It is equally necessary for the central government to have a budget at its disposal to carry out the tasks which devolve upon it. To supply the budget, would not the solution be for each State to contribute to it a share proportional to its resources?

I weigh, as I speak these words, all the import of such a proposal. It shows clearly that Katanga does not practise a self-seeking policy; on the contrary, it is ready to participate in the common task. It is of little importance if the

[1] Author's note: At a time when the ANC threatened North Katanga and when the rupture was taking place between the Congolese Chief of State and Prime Minister Lumumba, this declaration of financial and political solidarity with Kasavubu and Ileo was made in Elisabethville by Tshombe and sent to Brussels by telex on September 6, 1960. It never reached those for whom it was intended in Leopoldville.

amounts differ; suffice it that each citizen makes a similar effort toward the goal of common interest.

At this point, I do not wish to develop my views on these questions at greater length. In fact, we have had too much to complain of in the past to wish to impose a solution ourselves.

It is indispensable that all those who share these views in general meet and agree to discuss together the future structures of the confederation, in the course of frank and loyal conversations. It is in this spirit that I gladly welcome the resolution that the Senate in Leopoldville has courageously voted.

I rally wholeheartedly to it, and I am today launching a solemn appeal to all the friends of the former Congo to accept, as soon as possible, the idea of a conference which will meet to seek together, in serenity, and in harmony, the constitutional rules of a freely chosen regime, which would be suited, finally, to the legitimate aspirations of the Congolese people. I have the profound conviction that this policy alone will enable us to bring to a conclusion, immediately, the dramatic differences which separate so many ethnic groups.

On this point I stand with the resolutions of the last Pan-African Conference in Leopoldville, where the independent States of Africa expressed the hope of seeing present conflicts dissolve peacefully in new-found brotherhood.

I have always striven to make union and peace reign, whether it be within each State or among States. I appeal, with all my hopes, for an end to conflicts which bring certain of our brothers into opposition. At a time when Africa is acquiring, on the international level, the place it deserves, African States cannot themselves allow the world to believe that our continent could still be torn asunder by tribal struggles.

The African States which have preceded us on the road to independence have a duty to contribute to this work. That is why I address to their Heads of State a message which summarizes the proposals which I have just expounded to you. Katanga, the only Congolese State in which justice and order reign, must also contribute mightily to the effort that the Congolese peoples have undertaken — to give themselves original African political structures which suit them. I salute with feeling the courage of all those who at this moment are fighting in Leopoldville or in South Kasai to rid themselves once and for all of the tyrant Lumumba. Katanga is with them and will aid them. Together, we will make the cause of Congolese honor triumph. The task is still rugged, but I know that I can count on the cooperation of all so that Katanga will continue to play the primary role which it has had until the present. I am proud of having been chosen by the Katangans as Chief of the model African State.

IV. KATANGAN DECREE ON THE STATE OF ENMITY WITH THE U.N.

The president of Katanga,

In view of the constitution, particularly in its Articles 4 and 11;

In view of the law of November 19 conferring the power of issuing ordinances of a transitional nature dealing with measures urgently needed for building the nation;

Considering that, in a resolution of March 14, addressed to the United Nations, the Council of States under the signature of the President of the Republic of the Congo denied all legality to the February 21 resolution of the Security Council of the United Nations and had asked the latter to request in this regard the consultative opinion of the International Court of Justice;

Considering that by another resolution, the authorities of the confederation of the States of the Congo have protested to the Secretary-General of the United Nations against the dispatch to their territory of United Nations troops belonging to countries who came to pursue in the heart of Africa their own national policy;

Considering that despite these unanimous protests, several times repeated since then, the United Nations are dispatching to Katangan territory troops from India, under the pretext of reacting against operations for pacification and the re-establishment of public order regularly executed by the government of Katanga;

Considering that this hostile and highly offensive attitude constitutes an interference in the internal affairs of a State and infringes its sovereignty;

Having advised the President of the National Assembly and having informed him of the reasons for immediate action;

Orders:

Article 1:

It is forbidden for anyone to enter into relations of any nature whatsoever with the United Nations or with its agents, in all zones and during periods which will be determined by an ordinance of the President of the State declaring the state of enmity.

Public officials expressly mandated by decision of the President are excepted.

Article 2:

In zones determined in conformity with the first article, the execution of contracts between residents of Katanga and the United Nations or its agents is subject to authorization by the Minister of the Interior.

The same holds for the execution of all other obligations undertaken previous to or after the ordinance provided for in Article 1.

Article 3:

Any infraction of Articles 1 and 2 is punishable with a week to five years of penal servitude or a fine of 100 to 100,000 francs, or both.

Article 4:

Without prejudice to the penal sanctions of Article 3, the Minister of the Interior can decide, for periods of three days to three months, to close establishments of any nature which have contravened the provisions of Articles 1 or 2, in particular by furnishing merchandise or offering services.

Article 5:

The present ordinance becomes effective on the day of its signing.

It is ordered that the present ordinance be published in the *Moniteur Katangais*.

Done at Elisabethville, April 3, 1961.

> Minister of the Interior
> Godefroid Munongo
> President of Katanga
> Moise Tshombe

V. PLAN OF NATIONAL RECONCILIATION (THANT PLAN)
AUGUST 10, 1962

1. *Constitutional arrangements*

The Central Government will by September present and support in Parliament, until it is placed in effect, a draft Constitution that will establish a federal Government for the Congo. To this end, the Central Government has requested the United Nations to make available to it the services of international experts in federal constitutional law. The Central Government calls attention to its *communiqué* of 28 July 1962 and invites all State governments and interested political groups in the Congo to submit to it their views on the dispositions to be made in this Constitution. Their views, in so far as they are consistent with the federal character of this Constitution, will be taken into account to the greatest extent possible. Subject to such views as it may receive from the States and the interested political groups, the Central Government will give the experts supplied by the United Nations the necessary instructions for the final preparation, by September, of a draft Constitution containing the following division of powers between the Central Government and the States:

A. The powers listed below will be reserved exclusively to the Central Government:
  a) Foreign affairs;
  b) National defence (other than local police functions);
  c) Customs;
  d) Currency, exchange control, and fiscal policy;
  e) Interstate and foreign commerce;
  f) Taxing powers sufficient for Central Government needs;
  g) Nationality and immigration;
  h) Post and telecommunications.

B. The State governments will, of course, have control over their own administration and will be given all powers not expressly reserved to the Central Government, including local police powers and taxing powers sufficient to meet the costs of local government activities.

2. *Revenue and foreign exchange*

The Central Government will prepare, with the assistance of experts supplied by the United Nations, and will present and support in Parliament a draft finance act which will determine arrangements for the division of revenue between the Central and State governments as well as the rules and procedures for the utilization of foreign exchange. All State governments and interested political groups will be invited to submit their views on the laws to be proposed. In the drafting of these laws, account will be taken of the views expressed by State governments and interested political groups, of the economic and financial needs of the several States, and of the division of powers to be established in the new federal constitution as set forth above, which will particularly affect the future financial needs of each State and of the Central Government. The financial arrangements should so far as possible secure to the individual States the maximum of the revenue originating in their region and give the Central Government as well as the State governments their own sources of taxation. With regard to the utilization of foreign exchange, the arrangements should take into account the essential needs of each State, in particular those connected with the operation of industries which produce foreign exchange.

The Central Government will commit itself to supporting in Parliament such legislation as may be needed to implement these definitive arrangements. Until the definitive arrangements have been implemented, the Central Government and Katanga agree (1) to share equally the revenue from all taxes or duties on exports and imports and from all royalties from mining concessions in accordance with the division proposed at the Round Table conference held at Brussels in 1960, and (2) to pay all foreign exchange earned by any part of the Congo to the Monetary Council or to an institution designated by it which is acceptable to the parties concerned; the Monetary Council will control the utilization of all foreign exchange and will allocate to Katanga, for its essential needs, at least 50 percent of the foreign exchange originating in that State.

3. *Currency*

The Central Government will invite the United Nations to request that the International Monetary Fund instruct its experts to work out a phased plan for currency unification. The unification will take effect in all parts of the Congo ten days after it is approved by the Central Government.

4. *Military arrangements*

The commanders of all military, paramilitary, or *gendarmerie* units who have not already done so will take the usual oath of allegiance to the President of the Republic. A commission composed of one representative from the Central Government and one representative from the State government of Katanga, with the assistance of the experts supplied by the United Nations, will develop within thirty days a plan for the rapid integration and unification of all military, paramilitary, or *gendarmerie* units into a national armed forces and *gendarmerie* structure. This plan will be implemented within the ensuing sixty days. All central, State and local authorities will ensure complete freedom of movement throughout the territory of the Congo for the aforesaid Military Commission and for the United Nations experts assisting it.

5. *Foreign affairs*

Since the conduct of foreign affairs is reserved to the Central Government there will be no need for any State authority to maintain abroad any official in charge of foreign affairs or any diplomatic or consular mission. States desiring to maintain other types of representation abroad may do so with the concurrence of the Central Government.

6. *Amnesty*

Consistent with the settlement of differences effected by this agreement, the Central Government will immediately decree, and if necessary present and support in Parliament, legislation declaring a general amnesty.

7. *Co-operation with the United Nations*

All central, State, and local authorities will cooperate fully with ONUC [U.N. Operation in the Congo] in the application and execution of United Nations resolutions.

8. *Reconstitution of the Central Government*

The Central Government will be reconstituted so as to provide equitable representation for all political and provincial groups. The Prime Minister, Mr. Adoula, will renew his offer to fill [. . .] ministries with members of the Conakat party; in addition he will announce that these be the Ministries of [. . .].

COURSE OF ACTION

The representative of the Secretary-General will adhere to the following course of action and will receive an assurance that Governments are prepared to take actions mentioned below in order to support the adoption of the proposal for national reconciliation and to achieve the reintegration of Katanga.

Phase 1

A. The proposal for national reconciliation and the course of action set forth in this memorandum will be presented immediately to the Secretary-General of the United Nations.

B. If this proposal for the course of action is approved by the Secretary-General, the Governments' final agreement to presentation of these texts will be conveyed by their Ambassadors at Leopoldville to the representative of the Secretary-General, who will then present them to the Prime Minister, Mr. Adoula.

At the same time, he will outline orally, in general terms, the course of action. The Prime Minister will be urged to accept the proposal and to carry out immediately all actions by the Central Government called for in the proposal. If the proposal is accepted by the Prime Minister, it will be presented to the Katangan authorities by the representative of the Secretary-General.

C. The Katangan authorities will be requested to indicate their agreement to these proposals within ten days after they are presented to them. The proposals will be explained to the Katangan authorities in detail and their attention will be called to the fact that, if accepted by the Katangan authorities, the United Nations and Governments will use all means available to them to ensure that the proposal is fairly carried out. The representative of the Secretary-General will explain to the Katangan authorities that the United Nations resolutions give the United Nations a right to free movement of its military force through the territory of the Congo. The Katangan authorities will be informed that the United Nations will exercise its right to freedom of movement should a need for it arise. For the time being the United Nations has no intention of establishing new garrisons in Katanga. Governments, in their contact with the Katangan authorities, will support the position thus taken by the representative of the Secretary-General.

D. Contemporaneously with the actions called for in Paragraph C above, the Prime Minister, Mr. Adoula, will be urged to enact or decree legislation (if it does not already exist) regulating exports and imports to and from the Congo and, in particular, forbidding exportation or importation from or to the Congo of any goods not authorized by the Central Government at Leopoldville.

E. As soon as the Secretary-General has indicated his approval of the course of action set forth in this memorandum, the following measures will be carried out in rapid succession:

1. Governments will issue public statements indicating their support of the Central Government of the Congo and making clear their determination to see an early end to Katanga's secession. These statements will also express these Governments' approval of Mr. Adoula's recently announced intention to submit a draft federal constitution to Parliament by September, 1962. The Governments will consult with each other and with the Secretary-General on the text, tactics, and timing of these statements.

2. The Government of the Congo will enter into negotiations with the Belgian Government to obtain its assistance in establishing arrangements for the collection in Belgium of duties on all goods exported from Belgium to the Congo, including Katanga.

3. In making reconnaissance flights over South Katanga, ONUC will avoid very low-level flights that might frighten the local population.

4. The United States will, through the United Nations, immediately consider giving the Government of the Congo a small and conspicuous shipment of military equipment.

5. The United Nations will promptly afford all possible assistance to the Central Government in an urgent modernization program for the Congolese Army.

6. As soon as there is agreement on controls over utilization of foreign exchange to be established by the Government of the Congo, the United

States will make additional aid available to that Government, and Belgium and other States are considering similar action.

7. The Government of the Congo will ask the Governments of neighbouring countries to co-operate with it in establishing arms control and antismuggling measures.

8. In accordance with the Security Council's resolutions, the United Nations will again urge all Member States to take necessary steps to prevent all movements to the Congo, which are not authorized by the national Governments, of mercenaries, arms, war material, or any kind of equipment capable of military use. Governments will engage in diplomatic efforts to support such action.

9. The Government of the Congo will invite representatives of the Union Minière du Haut-Katanga to enter into discussions on matters of mutual interest, including the future attitude of the Government of the Congo toward the activities of the Union Minière.

10. The United Nations will invite the Belgian government and the Union Minière du Haut-Katanga to discuss with it the problem of protecting Belgian nationals and Union Minière installations in Katanga.

11. At the request of the Government of the Congo, Governments will, to the fullest extent possible, refuse to grant visas to Katangese or to permit their entry if they are carrying travel documents other than Congolese passports. Similarly, Governments will indicate publicly their acceptance of the request of the Government of the Congo and will urge holders of their own passports to seek and receive the necessary authorization from the Government of the Congo before traveling to Katanga. Governments will urge the Government of the Congo to make convenient arrangements for the issue of passports to all Congolese nationals desiring to travel for purposes which are consistent with the Plan of National Reconciliation.

Phase 2

During the ten days immediately following the presentation of the Plan of National Reconciliation to the Katangan authorities, the following actions will be taken:

1. Governments will solemnly urge the Katangan authorities to accept that proposal. They will advise the Katangan authorities that the Governments consider it a reasonable one. Governments will also urge other Governments and private companies and individuals to support their efforts to gain acceptance by Katanga. If the Katangan authorities indicate that they will refuse or delay, the Governments will advise them that, if the proposal is not accepted within ten days, the Governments will, if so requested by the Government of the Congo, take all measures available to them to comply with the Central Government's laws and regulations on exports of copper anad cobalt from Katanga. The Katangan authorities will also be told that if, in spite of that boycott, Katanga's secession continues, more stringent measures will inevitably be applied.

These might include the withdrawal of Belgian technicians, the suspension of postal and telecommunications services, the cessation of all air traffic in and out of Elisabethville, and a blockade of Katangan exports and imports by the establishment of road blocks on the railway lines leading to Katanga. Governments will consult with each other and with the United Nations on the timing and tactics to be used in making their approaches to the Katangan authorities.

2. In connection with the action called for in Paragraph E(10) of Phase 1, the Union Minière will urge the Katangan authorities to accept the Plan of National Reconciliation.

Phase 3

If the Katangan authorities should fail to accept the Plan of National Reconciliation within the stated period of time, the following actions will be taken (subject to the review and further consultation in the light of the circumstances existing at that time):

1. The Government of the Congo will request all interested Governments to refuse to permit the importation into their territory of copper and cobalt exports from Katanga which are not authorized by the Central Government at Leopoldville.

2. Governments will take such actions as are available to them to comply with this request and to assist in achieving the intended results.

Phase 4

If the measures prescribed for Phase 3 do not induce the Katangan authorities to accept the Plan of National Reconciliation, Governments will consult with each other and with the United Nations on other measures that could be then taken in light of the circumstances existing at that time.

(U.N. Document, Security Council, S/5053/Add. 13, Annex I.)

VI. KATANGAN BUDGET FOR 1962

I. ORDINARY BUDGET

A. *Expenditures*

	Budgeted	Committed
Total	3,999.6 million	4,803.6 million

1. *Expenditures classed by agency account (in thousands of francs)*

i. Presidency

	Budgeted	Committed
a. *Cabinet* (personal staff)	51,350	56,713
b. SCCR (intelligence service)	8,330	10,021
c. Secretariat	8,780	10,048
Total	68,460	76,782

II. National Defense

	Budgeted	Committed
a. *Cabinet*	4,905	4,447
b. Gendarmery	1,290,600	2,252,783
Total	1,295,505	2,257,230

III. Civil Service

Total	11,520	12,579

IV. Ministry of Justice

Total	68,070	69,280

V. Ministry of the Interior

. . .

c. Local and regional administration	170,170	159,770
d. Police	301,180	107,355
e. *Sûreté*	27,690	27,926
. . .	. . .	. . .
Total	507,700	509,045

VI. Ministry of Labor

Total	41,620	36,422

VII. Ministry of Finance

Total	486,770	214,896

VIII. Public Works

Total	314,623	344,847

IX. Information

a. *Cabinet*	2,691	3,197
b. Written information	7,596	7,923
c. Spoken information	13,906	15,536
Total	24,193	26,656

X. Economic Affairs

Total	20,803	18,305

XI. Agriculture

Total	86,320	95,032

XII. Communications

Total	95,992	101,440

XIII. Public Health

Total	223,610	260,109

xiv. National Education

· · ·

	Budgeted	Committed
c. Elementary education	472,990	492,785
d. Secondary education	121,310	128,777
e. Technical education	37,210	32,587
· · ·	· · ·	· · ·
Total	652,900	676,400

xv. Foreign Affairs

	Budgeted	Committed
a. *Cabinet*	6,148	7,481
b. Foreign Affairs	15,559	18,823
Total	21,707	26,304

xvi. Foreign Trade

	Budgeted	Committed
Total	5,870	5,598

xvii. Parliament

	Budgeted	Committed
a. National Assembly	67,000	67,008
b. Great Council of Chiefs	7,000	5,721
Total	74,000	72,729
Total Ordinary Budget	3,999,663	4,803,654

2. *Expenditures classed by category* [*in thousands of francs*]

	Budgeted	Committed
0: Higher Katangan personnel	466,499	482,827
1: Lower Katangan personnel	155,871	219,374
2: Foreign advisers	247,772	242,606
3: Personnel under contract	1,296,012	1,735,139
4: Internal travel	44,794	36,689
5: Travel abroad	49,441	79,892
6: Miscellaneous indemnities	25,818	41,810
7: Supplies and equipment	440,131	949,188
8: Subsidies	652,315	688,833
9: Miscellaneous expenditures	621,010	327,296
Total	3,999,663	4,803,654

B. *Receipts*

	Budgeted	Received by Dec. 31,1962
	(in thousands of francs)	
Total	4,006,695	3,767,000

II. EXTRAORDINARY BUDGET

	Authorizations	Commitments
	(in thousands of francs)	
Total	223,200	160,339
Re-equipment; reconstruction	50,000	45,000
Housing	33,000	5,692
Roads	40,000	34,000
Air transport	30,000	27,114
Road maintenance and sanitation	31,500	20,090

VII. KATANGAN DECLARATION ON THE END OF THE SECESSION (JANUARY 14, 1963)

We are ready to proclaim before the world that the Katanga secession is ended. We are ready to allow the United Nations troops freedom of movement throughout Katanga. We are also ready to return to Elisabethville to arrange for the complete implementation of the Thant Plan.

We request that, at the same time as we make this declaration, the President of the Republic of the Congo and the Prime Minister may put the amnesty provided for in the Thant Plan into effect, in order to guarantee the safety and freedom of the President and the Government of Katanga, all their officials and agents, and all people who have worked under their authority.

We are resolved to establish loyal cooperation with the United Nations in the performance of its mission, and we ask that the day and hour for a meeting may be set.

In order to spare the people suffering, we hope that our proposal may be put into effect as rapidly as possible.

Index

Abako (Alliance des Bakongo): burgo-masters, 15; relations with the Fegeba-ceka, 15; mentioned, 35, 39, 46, 52*n*, 55*n*, 267, 280. *See also* Cartel Abako

Acmaf (Association des Classes Moyennes Africaines), 20, 29, 50

Adeuxien (mercenaries referred to in article A.2 of Feb. 21, 1961, Security Council Resolution), 211*n*, 214, *passim*

Adoula, Cyrille (Prime Minister of the Congo): government program of, 210; protests Katanga-UNF cease-fire, 222–24; and Kitona Accords, 231–35; asks Tshombe to meet, 240; Adoula-Tshombe talks, 241ff; denounces aims of Tshombe, 242, 242*n*; offers constitutional proposals on federal basis, 243–47; proposals for transitional period, 247–50; accepts Thant Plan, 258–59, 261–62; Tshombe tries to undermine, 267; Thant Plan "Course of Action" and, 270–71, 339; mentioned, 11, 133, 138, 144, 217, 221, 239, 273*n*, 292, *passim*

Advisers. *See* Belgium; Mercenaries in Katanga; United Nations

Afac (Association des Fonctionnaires et Agents de la Colonie), 113*n*, 178

Affreux, les. *See* Mercenaries in Katanga

Afridex (Société Africaine d'Explosifs), 324

Afrimeches (affiliate of Afridex), 324

Afro-Asian group (in United Nations): resolution of, 139, 196; importance of for U.S. policy, 192; mentioned, 195, 323. *See also* N'Krumah, Kwame; United Nations

Agence Belga-Congo (Belgian wire-service in Leopoldville), 31, 33*n*, 83, 84*n*, 95*n*, 97, 100*n*, 112*n*, 151, 190*n*, 200

Agence Congolaise de Presse (A.C.P.), 176*n*

Agence France-Presse (A.F.P.; French wire-service), 56, 57, 97*n*, 123, 163*n*, 240

Air-Katanga (Sabena-Sobelair), 228

Alain, Colonel (commander of Mouvement de l'Independance et de la Resistance), 228

Albertville (capital of district of Tanganika): anarchy in, 55; electoral results May, 1960, 66; during troubles in North Katanga, 126; A.N.C. offensive from Stanleyville against, 223; response of Katanga to attacks in region of, 228; agreement to allow U.N. contingents in, 236; Katanga objects to "illegal government" in, 241; political capital of North Katanga, 268. *See also* North Katanga

Alliance Rurale du Kivu, 43

Alliance Rural Progressiste, 38*n*

American Committee for Aid to the Katanga Freedom-Fighters, 181

American Friends of Katanga, 181

Amis de Présence Africaine (Belgian), 45

Amitiés Katangaises, 178–80

Anaconda (American copper-producing company), 322

Anany, Jérôme (senator from Kivu, Minister of National Defense in the second Adoula government), 268

A.N.C. *See* Armee Nationale Congolaise

Angola (*see map*, 117): contacts and communications with Katanga, 116*n*, 175 and *n*, 184, 283; mentioned, 13, 197 and *n*, 289

Armée Nationale Congolaise (A.N.C.): "Africanization" of cadres, 95; pacification mission, 100; threatens territory of Katanga, 115; military operation against Bakwanga and South Kasai, 120; withdrawal anticipated, 121; cease-fire between Katanga gendarmery and, 123*n*; threatens North Katanga, 130; Dayal criticizes, 132; set-back of at Bakuvu and mutiny at Thysville, 137; Belgian advisers in, 138; failure of attempt to reunify, 141; reorganizing of with U.N. assistance, 152; arrests Tshombe and Kimba at Coquilhatville, 154; threatens Katanga regime, 155ff; Tshombe-Mobutu agreement on Katanga gendarmery and, 188–89, 210; moves against Katanga, 223–26; attacks North Katanga, 232, 234, 242, 268; discussed at Adoula-Tshombe talks, 244, 251; takes Kongolo, 263; mentioned, 29, 53, 204n, 287, 289

Aspremont Lynden, d'. See D'Aspremont Lynden

Assembly, Katanga Provincial: setting up of Katanga government by, 68ff; majority in controlled by the Conakat, 70; first meetings of, 70ff; election of non-traditional senators to, 76; special provisions for meeting of, 78–79; secession attempt in, 88–89 and notes; Abstract of Proceedings of referred to, 94n, 98n, 107n, 229n, 230n; declares June 24, 1961 protocol invalid, 190–91; relations between Katanga cabinet and, 202ff; convoked by Kasavubu, 233; ratifies Kitona accords with reservations, 233–35; mentioned, 208, 220, 247, 252, 285

Associated Press (A.P.), 107, 175n, 240

Association de Baluba-Central Kasai au Katanga, 15 and n. See also Fegebaceka

Association of the Baluba: member association of the Balubakat, 25

Association of the Basonge: member association of the Balubakat, 25

Association of the Bena Marunga: member association of the Balubakat, 25

Associations des colons belges au Katanga, 18n

Association des entreprises de la province du Katanga (Assékat): declaration of, 59 and n

Association des Kanioka: joins the Cartel Katangais, 30n

Association of the Minungu: member association of the Balubakat, 25

Association of Bahenba Peoples (Allibakat): member association of the Balubakat, 25

Association France-Katanga, 180

Atcar (Association Sociale et Culturelle des Tshokwe du Congo, de l'Angola et de la Rhodésie), 11, 29, 37, 54, 65, 66. See Cartel Katangais

Attala (Lebanese businessman), 166n

Auximokat (Auxiliaire Immobilière du Katanga), 317

Azume: seeks financial aid in Elisabethville for campaign of the Abbé Youlou, 176

Babemba (ethnic group of the Kasenga region), 12

Bahemba (ethnic group of Manono and Kabalo regions), 25

Ba-Kasai (name for the Baluba of Kasai living in Katanga), 15, 29, 67

Bakongo (also "Mukongo"; ethnic group of the Bas-Congo): support Tshombe, 186; mentioned, 42, 100, 111n

Bakusu (ethnic group of Maniema, in the region of Kibombo), 15

Bakwanga (capital of territory of Bakwanga, district of Kabinda; capital of the State of South Kasai): massacre of Lumumbist figures at, 137, 142; military agreement including, 145–47, 172; mentioned, 120. See also South Kasai

Baluba (tribe of provinces of Kasai and Katanga): of Kasai in Katanga, 27–28; in the Fedeka, 29; influence in the M.N.C., 55; disturbances in North Katanga and, 123–27; used by Kasavubu against Tshombe, 152; massacre of, 154; A.N.C. and, 157; refugee camp of, 220, 264; mentioned, 12 and n, 13, 15, 67, 69, 188n. See also Balubakat; North Katanga

Balubakat (Association des Baluba du Katanga): founded, 25, 27; separates from the Conakat, 27; Makonga leads pro-Conakat faction, 27, 45; joins Cartel with Atcar and Fédéka, 28–30; in the communal elections, 33; on structure of Congo, 36; at the Round Table, 43; North Katanga and, 126–

27; U.N. pacification mission and, 132; Tshombe hostile to, 144; arms youths to defend Lualaba government, 170; role of in government of Katanga negotiated, 208–9; mentioned, 223, 233, 267. *See also* Parti Progressiste Katangais; Cartel Katangais; North Katanga; Lualaba

Bangala (tribe from Equateur), 16, 111*n*

Banque Centrale du Congo et du Ruanda-Urundi: dissolved, 128 and *n*; mentioned, 116, 118

Banque du Congo Belge (B.C.B.), 59

Banque Nationale de Belgique, 128*n*

Banque Nationale du Congo, 128*n*

Banque Nationale du Katanga (B.N.K.): created, 116; mentioned, 206*n*, 207, 260

Banza, Hubert (Balubakat deputy): spokesman of the Cartel in the first Provincial Assembly, 71, 208*n*

Banza, Ismaël, 208*n*

Banza, Thomas, 252

Bartelous (Tshombe's *chef de cabinet*): expelled, 214; mentioned, 183

Basanga (tribe of the territory of Jadotville), 12

Bas-Congo (district of the province of Leopoldville): rebellion against white officers of Force Publique in, 94; mentioned, 28. *See also* Boma Basonge (tribe in the territory of Kongolo): absorbed into the Fedeka, 29; in electoral results of May, 1960, 67; mentioned, 25

Bastin (Belgian adviser): expelled, 214

Batabwa (tribe of the territory of Baudouinville), 12, 70

Baudouinville (capital of territory of Baudouinville, district of Tanganika): electoral results of May, 1960, 66; mentioned, 126, 247

Bauxicongo (Société de Recherches et d'Exploitation des Bauxites du Congo; company for prospecting and mining bauxite in the Congo), 324

Bayeke (tribe living primarily at Bunkeya): leading element, with Lunda, in the Conakat, 28; mentioned, 11, 156

Baylot, Jean (president of Association France-Katanga), 180

B.C.K. (Compagnie du chemin de fer du Bas-Congo au Katanga), 59, 320

Beckers (U.M.H.K. agent): with Fréart, broadcasts over Radio-Ufac, 73

Beira (port of Mozambique), 5, 116*n*

Belga-Congo. *See* Agence Belga-Congo

BELGIUM

—Government of, in Brussels: minimizes secession threat, 58; intervenes militarily in Katanga, 95–97; attitude of towards Katanga independence, 100–101; aids Katanga, 102–6; sends gendarmes to Katanga, 114; withdraws aid, 120; credits funds to Banque Centrale du Congo, 128; dissolves Mistabel aid mission, 129; reacts to U.N. request to withdraw advisers, 132; exchanges notes with Leopoldville, 134 and *n*; sends memorandum to Tshombe, 135; policy of Lefèvre-Spaak government on Katanga, 152, 155, 197–99, 224–25; sends arms to Katanga, 156; limits military aid, 158; refuses to recognize Katanga diplomatically, 159; position of on structure of Congo, 314–15; hostile to Stevenson Plan, 195; discussions between Spaak and Hammarskjold, 213, 215; holds talks with other Western Powers, 253–54; summary, 282–84; mentioned, 17, 36, 54, 275, and *passim*

—King of: message of, on eve of Round Table, 34; Balubakat appeals to, 36; Conakat and, 43, 53; Katanga appeals to, 78; present at Lumumba tirade, 93; endorses policy of aiding Katanga, 103; receives Tshombe, 134; receives Kibwe delegation, 174–75; settlers approve Tshombe's loyalty to, 279; Cartel address to, against separatism, 306

—Cabinet of: divisions in, 100. *See also*, Eyskens, Gaston; Spaak, Paul-Henri

—Parliament: working group of the, 11; attitude toward Katanga, 100; mentioned, 81, 229

—Chamber: urged to amend quorum required in Provincial Assembly, 73; adopts amendment, 81

—Senate: on amendment of Provincial

quorum, 79, 81; Socialist group in, 107; mentioned, 281*n*

—Ministry of Foreign Affairs, 96, 134*n*

—Ministry of African Affairs: urges Leopoldville-Elisabethville-Bakwanga alliance, 130; policy of, on Belgian officers in Katanga, 158*n*; advises soldiers of jobs in Katanga, 163. *See also* Minaf

—Ministry of the Congo and Ruanda-Urundi: submits bill to amend *loi fondamentale*, at request of Political Commission, 72–73; mentioned, 81. *See also* Pétillon, Léon; Van Hemelrijk, Maurice

—Department of National Defense: orders occupation of Elisabethville, 96; publicizes jobs in Katanga, 162–63

—Sûreté: searches hotel room of Scheerlinck, 85; maintains communications net in Katanga, 114–15; Marissal Mission and the, 162; mentioned, 23*n*, 29*n*, 35, 72. *See also* Munongo, Godefroid

—Office Spécial d'Imposition de Bruxelles: acknowledges transfer of state revenues to Katanga, 115

—Institut Belge d'Emission: sends currency adviser to Katanga, 118

—Military forces in Katanga: reinforced, 95; intervene in Elisabethville, 96, 97; local initiatives in favor of secession, 102; attack Force Publique camp at Nzilo, 108; agreement to replace, with U.N. troops, 113–14; withdrawal of, 120; Kamina garrison crushes Force Publique mutiny, 155; efforts to circumvent withdrawal order, 155*n*; Brussels imposes withdrawal, 158

—Technical and military assistance to Katanga: forms of, 101–6; limitations on, 158–60; efforts to camouflage, 161–64; Spaak government reaches agreement with U.N. on, 197–98; problems of defining, 211–12; expulsion of advisers, 155, 213–14; list of Belgian advisers before independence, 307. *See* Crèvecoeur; Mistebel; mercenaries in Katanga; United Nations

—Belgians and other Europeans in Katanga: support autonomy for Katanga, 9–10; oppose the Fegebaceka, 15; ties with Conakat at Round Table, 43, 61; involvement in Katanga politics, 62; implicated in Scheerlinck affair, 86–87; attempt secession on eve of independence, 88; exodus to Rhodesia, 95; effects of departure, 98; "order" desired by, 102; attitude toward Mistebel, 105; *ultra* attitude toward Belgium, 111; attitude toward U.N. troops, 113; provide military volunteers, 114; affected by U.N. resolution, 211–13, 218ff, 237–38; relations with Conakat summarized, 277, 278; mentioned, 80, 118, 213, 225 and *passim*. *See also* Settlers

—Katanga Lobby in Belgium: 178–80, 182–83

—Belgian investment interests in Katanga: question of dividing the C.S.K., 48–49, 115; private sector aids Tshombe, 105; stock market (Brussels Bourse) rises after Tananarive, 150. *See also* Société Générale, Union Minière

Belina (adviser to Tshombe), 153, 169, 179, 201

Benguela (port of Angola): railroad from, 49*n*

Berendsen, Ian (New Zealander, U.N. representative in Elisabethville): Katangan authorities demand removal of, 132; reaches agreement with Katangan government, 172

Bintu, R. (Muluba from Kasai; resident minister of the State of South Kasai in Elisabethville), 220

Bistos (French official): sent on mission to Katanga by Debré in April, 1961, 184

Bisukiro, Marcel (minister in Gizenga government), 130

Bizala, Cléophas (Minister of Education in the Ileo government), 137

Blanche (U.S. ambassador at Brazzaville), 192*n*

Bocheley-Davidson, E. (deputy from M.N.C./L., extraordinary commissioner for Katanga), 221

Boerenbond (Flemish Catholic farmers' organization), 25

Bolikango, Jean (president of the Bangala federation, Deputy Prime Minister in the Ileo government): urges freeing Tshombe, 187; in Adoula-Tshombe talks, 241; mentioned, 55*n*, 111*n*, 267, 271*n*

Boma (capital of the district of Bas-Congo), 9

Bomboko, Justin (Minister of Foreign Affairs for Congo-Leopoldville): offers assurances to Tshombe, 144; rejects Tshombe proposal, 145; in the Adoula-Tshombe talks, 241–42; mentioned, 133, 185, 198

Bonte, Charles (spokesman of the settlers of Orientale province; president of Univol), 19

Bovagnet (French officer of Col. Trinquier's group), 168

Brabon, Mme. L. (adviser to Balubakat), 307

Brasseries du Katanga (breweries), 59*n*

Brazzaville (capital of Congo-Brazzaville): meeting of Kasavubu and Tshombe at, 134–35; conference of heads of state of French-speaking African countries at, 135; supports Katanga, 176; permanent liaison with Katanga, 184; Mobutu rebuffed at, 217; mentioned, 111, 115, 122, 129, 133, 152, 173, 282. *See also* Youlou, Abbé Fulbert

Brazzaville Group (Union Africaine et Malgache: Republic of Cameroun, Central African Republic, Congo-Brazzaville, Dahomey, Gabon, the Ivory Coast, Mauritania, Niger, Senegal, Chad, and Upper Volta): Brazzaville conference of December, 1960, 135; supports Katanga, 197; French support for recognition of Katanga by, 184; opposed to Stevenson Plan, 195; mentioned, 230

Brodur (Belgian; *chef de cabinet* under the minister of the civil service for Katanga): expelled, 214

Browne, Captain Richard (British mercenary), 171

Bruce, Donald C. (U.S. congressman from Indiana), 182

Brussels. *See* Belgium

Buisseret, Auguste (Belgian Minister for the Colonies), 21

Bukama (capital of territory of Bukama, district of Haut-Lomami): electoral results of 1960 in, 66; in zone of U.N.F. control, 127; mentioned, 294

Bukavu (capital of Kivu): Lumumbist, 130; defeat of A.N.C. at, 137; mentioned, 29

Bulawayo (city in Southern Rhodesia), 226*n*, 324

Bulletin de la Sûreté militaire au Katanga, 209

Bulletin interafricain belga, 57*n*

Bunche, Ralph (representative of U.N. Secretary-General in the Congo and Katanga): mission to Elisabethville, 112; and the Kitona accords, 231

Bunkeya (town in the territory of Lubudi), 11. *See* Bayeke

Burundi. *See* Ruanda-Urundi; Usumburu

CADBA (Comité d'Action et de Défense des Belges d'Afrique), 178

Calonne, Remy (member of Ucol and of the U.K.): biography, 300; mentioned, 61

Camp Massart (military camp near Elisabethville): mutiny at, 96; occupied by Belgian forces, 97

Cannup (U.S. consul at Elisabethville), 184

Cardoso, Mario-Philippe (representative of Ileo government at U.N.), 187

Cartel Abako-P.S.A.-M.N.C./Kalonji-Parti du Peuple, 29*n*, 31, 36, 38 and *n*, 40, 43 and *n*

Cartel Baluba-M.N.C./Lumumba: in the election of May, 1960, 66. *See also* Cartel Katangais

Cartel Katangais ("Cartel Balubakat"; alliance of Balubakat, Atcar, and Fédéka associations): formation, 30; and the Round Table, 37, 43; at economic conference, 46, 50; and the Jadotville riots, 54; efforts to meet with Conakat, 55*n*; influence of

M.N.C./L. and M.N.C./K. in, 55; anti-strike declarations, 60; Belgian advisers to, 62; in elections of May, 1960, 65–67; dispute with Conakat over election of provincial government, 68–83; collaboration with M.N.C./L., 69n; obstructs provincial assembly, 70–81; threatens to set up a government of Northeast Katanga, 79; accuses Conakat of planning secession, 80; announces coalition provincial government of "Baluba, Tshokwe and allies," 83; idea of separatist government abandoned, 88; alerts members to secession efforts, 94; receives offer to take part in government, 107–8; Ileo proposal on role of in Katanga government, 122; foundation of, leaders, program and European support, 301–308; mentioned, 93, 205, 208n, 209. *See also* Baluba; Balubakat; Atcar; Fédéka

Cartel of National Union: rallies to Conakat, 83–84

Casablanca Group (Ghana, Guinea, Mali, Morocco and the U.A.R.): ideological relation of to Congo conflicts, 161; withdrawal of contingents from U.N. Force by, 173, 176

Casques bleus (blue-hats; name given to U.N. troops), 105, 112, 113 and *passim*. *See also* United Nations, U.N. Force

Cassart (Belgian colonel), 266

C.C.C.I. *See* Compagnie du Congo pour le Commerce et l'Industrie

Centre Independant (Belgian party), 178

Centre National du Patronat Francais (national association of manufacturers), 180

Centre de Regroupement Africain (Ce. Re. A.), 39, 43 and n, 44n, 46, 52n, 144

C.E.P.S.I. (Centre d'Etude des Problemes Sociaux Indigènes): bulletin of, 12n, 13n; background of, 104n, article by Grosjean and Clemens in bulletin of, 205 and n

Cerea. *See* Centre de Regroupement Africain

C.F.L. (Compagnie des chemins de fer du Congo superieur aux grands lacs africains), 50, 269

C.G.L.S.C. (Centrale Générale des Syndicats Libéraux Congolais), 59n

Champion, Colonel (chief of Belgian forces in Katanga), 103

Change B.N.K.S.A. (Swiss corporation), 207. *See also* Banque Nationale du Katanga

Charbonnages de la Luena, 317, 324

Charbons de la Lukuga, Société des, 317

Chiefs of Katanga, traditional: agreement with the parties after the Round Table, 54; Grand Council of, in Katanga, 118, 203, 205; Jadotville meeting of, 234–35

C.I.A. (Central Intelligence Agency), 184

Cimental (Cimenteries d'Albertville), 317

Ciments Métallurgiques de Jadotville (C.M.), 317, 324

Cite, La (Christian syndicalist Belgian daily), 60

Clemens, R. (professor at the University of Liège, director of Mistebel): role in Mistebel, 104 and n; framer of Katangan constitution, 111, 203; directs technical assistance, 129; expulsion, 198 and n, 213 and n; analyzes Katanga finances, 205; role in university at Elisabethville, 213n; rejoins Tshombe at Kolwezi, 276; the "Clémens" *tendance*, 286; mentioned, 183, 201

Colbelkat (Société de Colonisation Belge au Katanga), 317, 324

Cocem (comité belge des chefs d'Etat-Major), 99

Collège Exécutif Général (transitional body set up by the Round Table): function, 45; and the disturbances of Elisabethville, Jadotville, Kolwezi, 54; mentioned, 71n, 72

College of Commissioners: set up by Mobutu, 123; Belgium supports, 129; relations with U.N., 132; stiffening of attitude toward Katanga and Belgian aid, 134; mentioned, 128n, 143. *See also* Congo, government of; Mobutu

Collège Saint François de Sales, 96

Comelco (Société Commerciale de matérièle Electrique; affiliate of Sogelec), 323

Cométro (Commandment Supérieur des forces métropolitaines d'Afrique), 114, 124, 155*n*

Comité d'Action et de Défense des Belges d'Afrique (C.A.D.B.A.): support in Katanga, 178

Committee for One Million, 181

Comité National du Kivu (C.N.Ki.), 50

Comité Spécial du Katanga (C.S.K.; commission created to administer joint assets of the State of the Congo and the Compagnie du Katanga): treatment of its status at Round Table, 46ff; dissolved, 49ff; background, charter, concessionary powers and administration, 316ff; independent Katanga appropriates revenues from, 115; chiefs demand share of rights in, 205; Belgian attitude toward, 281; mentioned, 9, 18*n*, 23*n*, 94, 104*n*

Compagnie Congolaise des Usines à Cuivre et à Zinc de Liège, 59*n*

Compagnie des diamants de l'Angola: relations with Société Générale, 320

Compagnie du Congo pour le commerce et l'industrie (C.C.C.I.), 48, 320

Compagnie du Katanga: future status of, discussed at Round Table Economic conference, 47–48, 50, 51, 52; placed in context of holding-companies, 320, 322, 323

Compagnie foncière du Katanga (Cofoka), 317, 323

Compagnie française de l'Afrique occidentale, 180

Conakat (Confédération des Associations tribales du Katanga): birth of, 11ff; the Cartel Katangais and, 24ff; in the communal elections, 31ff; and the Round Table, 37ff; documents of, 38–39 and *nn*, 61 and *n*, 63 and *n*, 297; at the economic conference, 46–52 *passim*; and the outbreaks at Jadotville, 53–54; and the troubles at Elisabethville, Jadotville and Kolwezi, 54; discussions and agreement between U.N.I.P. and, 57; relations of, with the Ucol and Union Katangaise, 60–62; seats won by, in elections of May, 1960, 63ff, 300–301; and election of Provincial President, 68ff; secret agreement with M.N.C./K. and struggle for majority in Provincial Assembly, 69–70; imposes its candidates for president and vice-presidents of Chamber, 74; threatens confederation with Northern Rhodesia, 76; dealings of, over composition of first national government, 84; the Scheerlinck affair and, 85; relations with central government, 93–94; offers to bring Cartel into Katanga government, 107; Ileo proposes role for, in central government, 122*n*; seen by U.N. and Leopoldville as balance to Gizengists, 187; unrepresented in Adoula government, 210; representatives sent to Leopoldville pursuant to Kitona accords, 232, 233; provisions of Thant Plan and, 255–56; joins opposition to Adoula in Leopoldville chamber, 267; summary of role of, 277ff; history, leaders, and program of, 293–99; advisers to, 299–300; mentioned, 208*n*, 242

Congo, central government of, at Leopoldville: formation of Lumumba's cabinet, 83ff; efforts of Conakat to gain posts in, 84, 85; relations of, with U.N. worsen, 112; Lumumba dismissed, 119; negotiations over balance of parties in Leopoldville and Katanga governments, 122; breaks diplomatic relations with Belgium, 126; relations with U.N. Forces, 132ff; Ileo government fails to restore authority, 137; shares pro-West sympathies with Katanga, 138; role of, in transferral of Lumumba to Katanga, 142; efforts to reach agreement with Katanga, 142ff; effect of Lumumba's death on bargaining position, 144; reaches military agreement with Katanga and South Kasai, 145; rejects U.N. cooperation, 147; at Tananarive conference, 148ff; realignment of, with Baluba and U.N., 152; military agreement between Katanga and, 169;

factors favoring Tshombe in, 186; agreement with Katanga, 188–89; Adoula government set up, 192*n*; U.N. agreement with, 199; rapprochement with Stanleyville and strong position at Lovanium, 210; criticizes U.N.-Katanga cease-fire, 223; notes failure of Tshombe to sign Kitona accords, 231; discussions with Tshombe March–April, 1962, 241ff; attempts offensive against Katanga, 243; Adoula proposals, 243–45; announces preparation of federal constitution and creation of North Katanga province, 254–55; attitude of to Thant Plan, 258, 261–62; implements Thant's Course of Action, 270; timetable for setting up institutions of, 325–27; *See also* Adoula, Cyrille; Lumumba, Patrice Emery; Ileo, Joseph; Kasavubu, Joseph; Mobutu, Colonel Joseph-Désiré

Congo, constitutional alternatives for the:
—Federal or "Confederal" Congo, conception of a: proposed by Abako Cartel, 36, 40; aims of Katanga government regarding, 109, 110; South Kasai separatism and, 120; as basis for "reconstruction" with anti-Lumumbist Congo leaders, 121, 122; proposed by Tshombe at Tananarive, 149; substance of, conceded by Adoula proposal, 244; Katangan counterproposal, 246
—United or "unitary" Congo, conception of: promoted by Cartel Katangais, 79; in the program of the Cartel Katangais, 303 *passim*; mentioned in summary, 280. *See also* Round Table of January, 1960; Round Table of January, 1961

Congo, Parliament of, at Leopoldville: sets up Lumumba government, 84–85; Kasavubu prorogues, 130; negotiations for meeting of, at Lovanium, 189–93, 210; mentioned, 143, 144, 187, 224

Conga Plan (to paralyze U.N. forces in the Congo), 174*n*, 193*n*

Congo-Brazzaville, Republic of: relations with Katanga, 176. *See* Youlou, Brazzaville, Brazzaville Group

Congochim (affiliate of Sogechim), 324

Congométaux (Compagnie Congolaise des Métaux), 323

Congovieilmont (Société congolaise de la Vieille-Montagne), 323

Congrès Scientifique d'Elisabethville (study by E. Toussaint), 12*n*

Copperbelt. *See* Rhodesias, Fed. of

Coquilhatville, conference of: 151ff; arrest of Tshombe at, 154; mentioned, 140, 141, 174, 186

Cornélis, Henri (Governor-General of Congo and Ruanda-Urundi), 73*n*

Costa Rica, Republic of: efforts to secure recognition of Katanga by, 175*n*, 286

Courrier Africain du C.R.I.S.P. (later renamed *Travaux africains*): 5, 162*n*, 181*nn*, 195*n*, 226*n*

Courrier d'Afrique, Le (Leopoldville daily), 12*n*, 14, 144*n*, 185*n*

Courrier Hebdomadaire du C.R.I.S.P., 18*n*, 178*n*, 226*n*

Cousin, Jules (president of Board of Directors of U.M.H.K.): founder of C.E.P.S.I., 104*n*

Couve de Murville, Maurice (French Minister of Foreign Affairs), 40*n*, 56*n*, 180

Crémer (Belgian mercenary in Katanga), 220 and *n*

Crener (Belgian consul in Elisabethville), 120*n*, 129, 198, 213, 219

Crèvecoeur (Belgian major): as new commander of Katangan army, 99; commander of Katangan gendarmerie, 114, 171; and Egge plan, 215

Croisettes et Casques Bleus (book by P. Davister and Ph. Toussaint), 215*n*, 218*n*

Cumont, General Charles P. (head of Cocem): favors secession, 99

Daily Express (London), 55, 57

Dannau, Wim (writer for Belgian weekly, *Pourquoi Pas?*), 114*n*

D'Aspremont Lynden, Harold (deputy *chef de cabinet* to Belgian Prime Minister): special mission to Katanga, 103; heads Mistabel, 104, 110, 113*n*;

named Minister for African Affairs, 120; on Katanga financial aid to Congo government, 121*n*; opposed to Stevenson plan, 195*n*; summary, 282

Davister, Pierre (Belgian writer for the weekly *Pourquoi Pas?*), 34, 113*n*, 124*n*, 125, 212*n*, 215*n*, 218*n*, 276*n*

Dayal, Rajeshwar (Indian, special representative of the U.N. Secretary-General to the Congo): reports Katangan reprisals, 131; reports key role of Belgians in Katanga, 131*n*; conflict with College of Commissioners, 132; second report of, 136, 137 and *n*; report of Feb. 20, 1961, 171–72*n*; departure of, 199; mentioned, 173. *See also* India; United Nations

Debré, Michel (French Prime Minister), 183*n*, 184. *See also* France

De Claem (Belgian mercenary in Katanga), 226

Decoster, A. (editor-publisher of *Echo du Katanga*, adviser to the Fedeka), 179, 214, 307

Defawe, O. (president of the Ucol-Katanga), 19

De Ferron, Vicomte Olivier (French financier, vice-president of the Imef-bank), 207

De Gaulle, General Charles (President of the French Republic), 168*n*, 228

De Hemptinne, Msgr. Jean (Apostolic Delegate to Katanga), 9

Delègue (French political adviser to M. Diur), 183

Delperkat (Permanent Delegation of Katanga to the Common Market), 182, 184

Delvaux, Albert (national secretary of the P.N.P., minister in Lumumba, Ileo, and Adoula governments), 133, 142, 144, 187

Denis, Jacques: study of Elisabethville by, 12*n*; as legal adviser of Kasavubu, 148

Dequae, André (Belgian Minister for the Colonies), 19

Dernière Heure, La (Brussels daily), 107, 110*n*, 163 and *n*

De Schrijver, Auguste (Belgian minister for Congo and Ruanda-Urundi): criticized in *Echo du Katanga*, 36; at Round Table, 41; in dealings over constitution of provincial government, 71, 77; urges principle of proportional representation in Katanga government, 81–82

De Smet, P. (senator of Christian Social Party of Belgium), 100

"De Voghel Commission" (preparatory mixed commission preceding Round Table), 50

De Vos (assistant to Professor Clémens at University of Elisabethville), 213*n*

Dilolo (capital of territory of Dilolo, district of Lualaba): and Atcar, 28; and electoral results of May, 1960, 66; Belgian forces ordered to occupy, 102 and *n*

Diomi, Gaston, 11

Dirksen, Everett M. (United States senator), 181

Diur, Dominique (Katangan representative in Paris), 183, 184

Dodd, Thomas J. (United States senator): and Katanga Lobby, 181; account of Struelens' visit to State Department given by, 192*n*; supports Tshombe, 221

Doucy, Arthur (director of the Institute of Sociology of the Université Libre de Bruxelles): views of, adapted by Katanga settlers, 19*n*; on Katanga national consciousness, 51*n*; as adviser to Cartel, 62, 307; Schoeller desires to influence Cartel via, 72; telegram of, to Cartel members, 73*n*; accused of plotting Tshombe's arrest, 198; biography, 307

Dubuisson, Marcel (rector of the University of Liège), 271

Duchemin, J. (co-author of *Notre Guerre au Katanga*), 142 and *n*

Dumontet, Georges (French; new U.N. representative to Elisabethville), 236

Echo du Katanga, L' (Elisabethville daily), 28*n*, 36, 37*n*, 41*n*, 45*n*, 51*n*, 53*n*, 55*n*, 56*n*, 57*n*, 58, 60*n*, 61, 69*n*, 85*n*, 94*n*, 103*n*, 108*n*, 111*n*, 309

Egge, Bjorn (Norwegian officer of U.N.): Egge Plan for replacement of

foreign cadres in Katanga, 169, 215–
18; Egge Report, 171
Eisenberg, R. (Deputy Director of Bureau of Central African Affairs in
U.S. State Department), 192*n*
Electrorail, 323
Elisabethville (capital of Katanga): first
communal elections in, 14; electoral
results of December, 1959, 33, 34;
strikes of May, 1960, 59 and *n*, 60;
electoral results of May, 1960, 65ff;
European pro-Conakat activities, 73;
arrival of U.N. reinforcements in,
174; private visit of Abbé Youlou,
176–77; political prisoners in, 188*n*;
as military headquarters, 226; riots
protesting U.N. Forces, 229; application of Kitona accords and, 235, 236;
anti-American demonstrations in, 271
—communes: Albert (African), 15, 33,
229, 273; Elisabeth (European), 15*n*;
Kasapa, 273; Katuba (African), 15*n*,
33, 104*n*, 229; Kenia (African), 15*n*,
24, 33. *See also* Katanga
Elvaluilu (Société d'Elevage de la
Luilu), 324
Entrelco (Société d'Entreprises Elec-
triques au Congo; affiliate of Sogelec),
323
Equateur (province), 3, 4
Essor du Congo, L' (Elisabethville
daily), 9*n*, 22*n*, 24*n*, 43*n*, 45*n*, 51*n*,
78, 81*n*, 83*n*, 85*n*, 96, 97*n*, 99*n*, 103*n*,
112*n*, 296, 304, 312, 313. *See also*
Essor du Katanga, L'
Essor du Katanga, L' (Elisabethville
daily replacing *L'Essor du Congo* after
Jan. 1, 1961), 139*n*, 147*n*, 162*n*, 172*n*,
174*n*, 183*n*, 191*n*, 208*n*, 214*n*, 235*n*,
259*n*, 266*n*, 275*n*
Etoile Nyota (bi-monthly periodical in
Elisabethville), 27
Eurafrica (Fédacol review), 21*n*, 309
Eyskens, Gaston (Belgian Prime Minister): promises assistance to Katanga,
25*n*, 103 and *n*; mentioned, 106, 112,
152, 178*n*

Faulques, Colonel René (French officer), 169*n*, 226, 237

Fayat, Henri (Belgian Deputy-Minister
of Foreign Affairs), 198, 213
Fédacol (Fédération congolaise des
Classes moyennes), 18 and *n*, 19*n*, 20*n*
Fédéka (Fédération des Associations des
Ressortissants de la Province du
Kasai): joins the Cartel Katangais,
28–29; declaration of, 29; loses many
lulua, 29; in local elections of January,
1960, 37, 38. *See also* Cartel Katangais
Fédération des Groupements et Associa-
tions du Katanga, 18*n*
Fédération des Tribus du Haut-Katanga
(Fetrikat; member-association of the
Balubakat), 25
Fédération Générale du Congo (F.G.C.;
party belonging to Abako-P.S.A.-
M.N.C./K. Cartel): in the elections
of May, 1960, 65, 67; mentioned, 29*n*,
38, 55*n*
Fegebaceka (Federation, formerly Association, of Baluba-Central Kasai au
Katanga): history of, 15, 17; opposes
the Union Katangaise, 23; mentioned,
27, 29
F.G.T.K. (Fédération Générale des
Travailleurs du Kongo), 59*n*
Filtisaf (Filatures et Tissages Africains),
269
Financial Times (London daily), 49*n*
Fin de la souveraineté belge au Congo
(book by Ganshof van der Meersch):
on Scheerlinck, 86*n*, 87*n*; on the last
attempt at secession before independence, 88*n*; mentioned, 74*n*, 84*n*, 281*n*.
See also Ganshof van der Meersch,
W. J.
Floribert, R. P. (later became Msgr.
Cornélis; adviser to the Balubakat),
307
Force publique (F.P.): role in wildcat
strikes of Elisabethville, 60; and rebellion in the Bas-Congo, 94; incidents
involving F.P. of Kongolo, 95; Belgians attack camp of, at Nzilo, antisecessionist elements purged, 108;
mentioned, 35, 59, 102, 114, 156, 162,
163, 164
Forminière (Société Internationale For-
estiere et Minière du Congo), 320

Fortemps, Henry (deputy general-director of the U.M.H.K. in Africa), 206*n*

"Fouga affair," 163*n*, 166*n*, 167*n*

France: idea of Katanga joining French Community, 135*n*; military assistance to Katanga, 166–68; problem of recognizing Katanga, 184; intelligence services of, in Katanga, 184; *Journal Officiel* cited, 209*n*; mentioned, 40*n*, 56*n*, 97, 148–49, 163, 209, 221, 282. *See also* De Gaulle, General Charles; Trinquier, Colonel

Fréart (representative of the U.M.H.K.): broadcasts over Radio-Ufac, 73

Frenkiel (Rector of the State University of Elisabethville; professor at the University of Liège), 182, 213 and *n*

Frenney (Belgian; *chef de cabinet* to the Belgian Minister of Health): expelled, 214

Fulréac (Fondation de l'Université de Liège pour les recherches scientifiques au Congo Belge et au Ruanda-Urundi): activity in Katanga, 104*n*

Ganshof van der Meersch, W. J. (Belgian resident minister to the Congo): position on elections of May, 1960, 73; interpretation of Cartel motives, 74*n*; contacts with the Conakat, 87; mentioned, 16, 281

Gardiner, Robert (Ghanaian official in charge of U.N. operations in the Congo, 1962–63): agreement with Kasavubu, 199; letter to Tshombe, 250*n*; revises Adoula proposals, 251 and *n*

Gavage, Achille (president of political committee of the Ucol): founder and president of the Union Katangaise, 22; declares Katanga success at Round Table, 45; Conakat relies on, 60; biography, 299; mentioned, 41*n*

Gbenye, Christophe (M.N.C./L. Minister of the Interior of the Congo): contacts Conakat in Elisabethville, 88; mentioned, 223, 241

Gendarmerie of Katanga: armament of, 113, 114; cease-fire between A.N.C. and, 123*n*; operations of, in North Katanga, 124, 137; affected by U.N. resolution on mercenaries, 139; organization of, 155, 158; taking of Manono by, 157; dependence on Belgian aid, 158; counter-offensive of, 170ff; military agreement of Tshombe and Mobutu and, 188–89; Egge plan and, 215–18; U.N. operations against Belgian mercenaries in, 219–22; measure of forces in late 1961, 226–28; evacuation of Kongolo, 232; Kongolo operations resumed, 239; discussion of status at Leopoldville conference, 247–48; Gardiner's compromise efforts concerning, 251; clash between U.N. Force and, 272–75

General Assembly. *See* United Nations

Géomines (Compagnie Géologique et Minière des Ingénieurs et Industriels Belges), 269, 317

Gerard, Jo (reporter for *Europe-Magazine* and correspondent for *La Libre Belgique*), 179

Germany, Federal Republic of, 97

Ghana, 286. *See* Nkrumah, Kwame; Afro-Asian group; Casablanca Group

Gilson, Arthur (Belgian Minister of Defense), 102

Gizenga, Antoine (president of Parti Solidaire Africain; Vice-Prime Minister of Lumumba government): discussions of with Tshombe, 88*n*; relations with North Katanga, 127, 170; heads Lumumbist regime at Stanleyville, 130, 139; urged by U.N. to attend Tananarive meeting, 148; effects of, on Tshombe-Leopoldville relations, 186, 189; Lovanium parliament and, 191-92; U.S. attitude toward, 194, 224; Munongo and, 216–17; mentioned, 113, 142*n*

Goldwater, Barry (U.S. senator), 181

Gonze, Jean (deputy-director of UMHK in Africa), 239

Grand Council of Chiefs. *See* Chiefs of Katanga, traditional

Great Britain (U.K.): envisages Constituent Assembly, 35; on recognizing Katanga, 87; MacMillan statement, 97*n*; support for Tshombe in, 182;

official efforts on Tshombe's behalf, 188; pressure on Hammarskjold, 221; supports Kitona accords, 231–32; favors political pressure only on Katanga, 253–54; proposes cease-fire, 273–74; Labour opposition, 274; supports Thant, 275; relations with Africa and Belgium, 282. *See also* Tanganyika Concessions

Grelco (Compagnie des Grands Elevages Congolais), 317

Groupement des Associations mutuelles de l'empire Lunda (Gassomel; member association of Balubakat), 25

Gullion, Edmund (U.S. ambassador to Leopoldville): role in arranging Kitona meeting, 230–31

Hammarskjold, Dag (Secretary-General of the U.N.): denounces "Belgian factor" in Katanga, 129; demands withdrawal of Belgian troops, 131 and *n*, 132; attitude toward College of Commissioners, 136; discussions with Spaak December, 1961 on "advisers," 213, 215; British pressure on, 221; death of, 222; mentioned, 113, 162*n*, 188. *See also* United Nations

Hason, L. (Turkish, spokesman for Zionist association in Elisabethville, Conakat adviser), 185*n*

Haut-Katanga (district of Katanga): electoral results of May, 1960, 65ff; grievance in Katanga Assembly over representation for, 203

Haut-Lomami (district of Katanga): demography of, 4; electoral results of May, 1960, 65ff

Henniquiau (Belgian colonel; chief of advisers to A.N.C.), 95

Herman, Fernand (professor, member of the scientific committee of C.R.I.S.P.), 5

Héros sont affreux, Les (book by Christian Lanciney), 124*n*

Hoeschstatter, J. (Swiss jurist, director of Change B.N.K.), 207

Home, Lord Alexander Douglas (British Foreign Secretary): initiatives with Spaak, 225–26, 230

Hoover, Herbert, 181

Houart (Belgian consul at Salisbury, Rhodesia), 276

Hougardy, Norbert (Belgian senator of the P.L.P.), 230

Humblé, Jean (president of the Central Committee of Ucol-Katanga, vice-president of the Fédecol): biography of, 299–300; mentioned, 20, 61, 308

Huyghe (Belgian; *chef de cabinet* for the Katangan Minister of Defense), 214

Ileo, Joseph (Congolese Prime Minister): centralist speech at Round Table, 42; College of Commissioners sets up moderate government under, 119–20; offers cabinet post to Tshombe, 122 and *n*; at Brazzaville conference of December, 1960, 135; legitimacy and status of his government, 136–37, 194; reacts to U.N. Afro-Asian resolution, 139–40, 140*n*; signs military accord with Tshombe and Kalonji, 146; U.S. attitude to government of, 194; efforts to free Tshombe and, 208; arrives in Eilsabethville as resident minister from Leopoldville, 276; Tshombe mentions, 301; mentioned, 11, 55*n*, 150, 204*n*

Ilunga, Leon (Balubakat Cartel), 319

Ilunga, Valentin (member of the Conakat): Minister of Justice in first Katanga provincial government, 82–83

Ilunga. *See also* Mwamba-Ilunga, Prosper

Imefbank (Banque d'Investissements mobiliers et de Financement, in Geneva), 175*n*, 207

Independance du Congo, L' by A. A. J. van Bilsen, 68*n*

India: U.N. contingent maintained by, 148, 151, 153, 173, 196–97; Ghurkas, 220. *See also* Dayal, Rajeshwar

Inga: dam and power station at, 42

Institut de Sociologie de l'Université de Liège: activities of in Congo, 104*n*

Institut de Sociologie de l'Université libre de Bruxelles (founded by Ernest Solvay), 39, 107

Institut International (secondary school): discrimination in, 204*n*

International Monetary Fund (I.M.F.), 256

Investments in Katanga. *See* Société Générale, Union Minière

Ireland, U.N. battalion from, 221. *See* O'Brien, Conor Cruise

Italy as member of Security Council of U.N., 132

Jadotville (in territory of Jadotville, district of Haut-Katanga; formerly in district of Lualaba); population of, 3, 4; election of December, 1957 in, 21; growth of Union Katangaise in, 22; movement of Kasaians into Fédéka at, 29; clash over appointments to council of Jadotville-Kinkula, 53; Force Publique in, 60; elections of May, 1960 in, 65ff; pillaged, 98; re-occupied by Force Publique, 99; European staff in gendarmerie of, 226; Tshombe gathers meeting of chiefs in, 234–35; mentioned, 33, 54, 247, 274

Janssens, Emile (Lieutenant-General of the Force Publique), 60n, 87, 178

Jaspar (Belgian with Radio-Katanga): expelled, 214

Jeune Europe (Belgian nationalist movement), 178

J. K. (Jean-Marie Van der Dussen de Kestergat, writer for *La Libre Belgique*), 125, 212n

John Birch Society, 181

Kabalo (capital of the territory of Kabalo, district of Tanganika): electoral results of May, 1960, 66; Force Publique parachuted into, 99; left to U.N. control, 127; mercenaries taken at, 164–65, 174; A.N.C. reoccupies, 269; mentioned, 95, 126, 157. *See also* North Katanga

Kabangi, Alois (national deputy for the M.U.B.M.N.C./L. Cartel): Minister for Economic Coordination, 85

Kabinda (district of, in the province of Kasai), 41n, 264

Kabongo (city and territory of, district of Haut-Lomami): electoral results of May, 1960, 66ff; mentioned, 27, 269

Kabongo, Boniface (Muluba chief from the Kabongo chieftancy): rallies to Katanga in secession, 109 and n; assassinated, 125

Kabulo, Roger (vice-president of the M.N.C./L. in Katanga), 59n

Kadima, André (president of the Fegebaceka): arrested, 16; President of the Fédération Générale du Congo, 29n, 55n

Kahamba, Joseph (Secretary-General of the Balubakat), 302

Kalala, Joseph (Acmaf-Katanga), 319

Kalikoni, Albert (Treasurer of the Balubakat), 302

Kaloko (territory of Kabongo, district of Haut-Lomami): chief assassinated at, 109n

Kalonji, Albert (president of the M.N.C./K.; President of State of Kasai): at Round Table, 38; position in Katanga, 55; makes deal with Conakat, 69; sets up autonomous province of South Kasai, 94; accord with Katanga, 138 and n; military accord with Katanga and Leopoldville, 146 and n; mentioned, 135, 153, 204n, 334

Kalonji, Isaac (Director of the Fédéka, President of Congolese Senate): a director of the Acmaf, 20; role in regrouping forces of Fédékat and Balubakat, 29; house attacked by Conakat partisans, 37; in dealings of Cartel with M.N.C./K., 69; proposed as Commissioner of State for Kasai in Lumumba government, 85; in efforts to get Belgian mediation between Katanga and province of Lualaba, 209; biography of, 302; mentioned, 55n, 73n, 108

Kambola, Henri Ndala (member of the Central Committee of Conakat): declaration on U.M.H.K., 128; Katanga delegate at Leopoldville discussions, 241; biography of, 295; mentioned, 192n

Kambove, territory of (district of Haut-Katanga): elections of May, 1960, 66ff; mentioned, 53

Kamina (capital of the territory of Kamina, district of Haut-Lomami): elections of May, 1960, 66, 68*n*; *Force Publique* disarmed at, 99; U.N. reinforcements at, 174; Katanga request for "confederal" parliament at, 190; Kasavubu convokes Katanga Assembly at, 233; Tshombe insists on Elisabethville instead of, 234; incidents between U.N. and Katanga gendarmerie at, 240; occupied by U.N., 274; mentioned, 226, 269

Kamina, military base of: Belgian paracommando reinforcements sent to, 95; prepares to occupy Elisabethville, 96; Kasavubu and Lumumba at, 100; Belgian evacuation of, 113; materiel at, 114; arrival of Indian U.N. contingents at, 151, 173; boycotted by Katanga, 174; lifting of boycott on, 193*n*, 202; mentioned, 236, 274

Kamitatu, Cléophas (Minister of the Interior in central government, President of the provincial government of Leopoldville): breaks away from central government, 133; at Tananarive, 148; represents central government at Adoula-Tshombe talks, 241–42; proposes new Katangan Assembly, 252; visits Albertville, 268; mentioned, 241

Kaniama (capital of the territory of Kaniama, district of Haut-Lomami): elections of May, 1960, 66; European volunteer corps at, 114

Kanioka (tribe of South Kasai and of the territory of Kabongo), 30*n*, 208

Kapanga (capital of the territory of Kapanga, district of Lualaba): elections of May, 1960, 66

Kapwasa, André (Conakat spokesman): criticizes Tshombe government, 203–4, 206

Kasai, former province of: demography of, 4; emigration to Katanga from, 12–13; burgomasters in Katanga natives of, 14–15; claims on territory of, 23; colonial declaration on status of natives of, 28–29; mentioned, 53, 109. *See also* Luluabourg, Ba-Kasai, South Kasai

Kasavubu, Joseph (President of the Abako Cartel, President of the Republic of the Congo): withdraws from Round Table, 40; campaigns in Elisabethville, 55*n*; on Collège Exécutif Général, 72; agrees with Lumumba on status of Belgian forces in Kasai, 100; accuses Belgium of aiding secession, 101; dismisses Lumumba, 119; calls on Ileo to form government, 120–21; offers Tshombe pacification mission to North Katanga under Sendwe, 123; plans a Round Table with Lumumba and Tshombe, 133*n*; meets with Tshombe at Brazzaville, 134, 135; Tshombe makes personal appeal to, 145–46; arrives at Tananarive to meet Tshombe, 148; makes demands of Tshombe, 153; opening speech of, at Coquilhatville conference, 154; makes agreement with U.N., 199; receives U.N. assistance, 200; orders expulsion of non-Congolese mercenaries in Katanga, 218; orders trial procedure for mercenaries, 223; convokes Katanga Assembly, 233; warns Katanga on colonial influences, 263–64; Tshombe statement on breaking with, 333ff; mentioned, 156, 188, 190, 191, 210, 288

Kasenga (capital of the territory of Kasenga, district of Haut-Katanga): elections of May, 1960, 66

Kashamura, Anicet (minister in the Lumumba and Gizenga governments), 130

Kasongo, Henri (permanent secretary of the F.G.C.), 55*n*

Kasongo, Julien (Secretary-General to the Minister of Foreign Affairs in the Ileo government): in negotiations for Tshombe's release, 187

Kasongo, Nyembo (or Niembo; Muluba chief of territory of Kamina), 50, 68*n*, 227, 235, 319

KATANGA

—Province of: in communal elections, 31–34; electoral results of May, 1960, 63–68; provincial government set up, 68–83; Tshombe promises independence for, 68*n*; independence sought, 78; composition of government, 82–83; troubles of July, 1960, 95ff; state of exception proclaimed in, 98; Tshombe proclaims independence of, 98

—Independent State of: first "secession" attempt by, 34–35; Scheerlinck affair reveals secession plans in, 85–87; proclamation of independence by, 98–99; attitude of Belgian government toward secession of, 103ff; Cartel offered places in government of, 107; proposals for confederation with other provinces, 109; declares opposition to U.N. intervention, 112; requisitions air units of Force Publique, 114; political and administrative structure of, 115ff; constitution of, 118; intelligence services of S.C.C.R., 118, 184; convention of with South Kasai, 120*n*; represses rebellions in North, 123; recognizes zones controlled by U.N., 127; Belgian aid mission dissolved in, 129; relation of with College of Commissioners in Leopoldville, 132–33; requests admission to Equatorial Customs Union, 135; agreement with South Kasai, 138*n*; reacts to Security Council Resolution of Feb. 21, 1961, 139; cooperates with Leopoldville in dealing with Lumumba, 142–43; military agreement between Leopoldville, South Kasai and, 145ff; decree on "civil mobilization," 146*n*; offers command of army to Col. Trinquier, 166; military accord between Leopoldville and, 169; at the Tananarive conference, 169ff; attempts to maintain military potential, 182ff; decrees boycott of U.N., 174 and *n*, 335, 337; Kibwe mission fails to get Belgian recognition of, 175; delegation to France from, 180; Tshombe signs agreement on behalf of at Leopoldville, 188; political prisons of, 188*n*; open letter to U.N. Secretary-General from interim government of, 193; relations of with Spaak government, 197ff; internal structure of government, 200ff; relations between government and Assembly of, 202ff; relations between Balubakat and, 208–9; effect of anti-Belgian wave in, 212;

forms mixed commission with U.N. on advisers to expel, 214; accepts agreement on A.N.C. in Mobutu-Tshombe talks, 216; cease-fire negotiated between U.N. Forces and, 222; military forces of, 226–27; declaration by Tshombe at Kitona meeting, 231; Kitona accords ratified with reservations, 232, 234; continues to reject U.N. views on mercenaries, 236; U.N. protests inaction of, 237; position of in Adoula-Tshombe talks at Leopoldville, 242; makes counter-proposal to Adoula plan, 246; responds to Thant plan, 258; blames Adoula government for failure of Thant plan, 262; incidents involving U.N. troops in, 265; relations of with Leopoldville, 266ff; clash between U.N. force and gendarmerie of, 270–76; secession of ended, 276

—official sources for: Secretariat d'Etat à l'Information, 103*n*, 129*n*; cabinet minutes, 123, 140*n*; declaration of independence, 328–29; decree on state of enmity with U.N., 335–37; 1962 budget of, 342–45; declaration ending secession, 345. *See also* Assembly, Katanga Provincial; Tshombe Kapenda, Moise

Katanga (Katangan weekly); opposes the Union Katangaise, 23; mentioned, 62*n*

Katanga, enjeu du monde (book by P. Davister, published in Brussels), 34*n*, 112*n*, 126

Katanga, 50 ans décisifs, Le (book by J. Sauvy, published in Paris), 12*n*

"Katangalisation" (Rothschild plan to rebuild confederal Congo around Katanga), 286

Katangans: "authentic," 12–17 *passim*, 22, 28, 277–78

"Katangism" (refers to plan offered by Tshombe at Tananarive), 149

Katangakommit, 182

Katinfor (Katangan information service in New York), 183

Kayembe, Baudouin (secretary of Fegebaceka), 16

K. D. L. (Compagnie des Chemins de

fer Katanga-Dilolo-Leopoldville), 324

Kennedy, John F. (President of the United States), 177, 181, 182, 230, 263

Kenya, 3

Khiari, Mahmoud (Tunisian; head of civilian operations of United Nations in the Congo): negotiates Ndola cease-fire, 222

Khrushchev, Nikita (premier of the U.S.S.R.), 101

Kibwe, Jean-Baptiste (vice-president of the Conakat and Minister of Finance for Katanga): scheme attributed to by Ganshof, 69n; formation of provincial government and, 75; gives ultimatum to Cartel, 76; pressures Belgium to amend fundamental law, 77; asks Belgian recognition of Katanga, 106n; declaration of Congolese personnel, 108; statement of, on U.M.H.K. dividends, 115n; on pressure from Mistebel, 128n; attacks Belgium for trying to force plan of unity, 160; mission to Brussels, 174–75; on triumvirate during imprisonment of Tshombe, 186; considered leader of extremist faction, 201; opposition to handling of finances by (Kibwe affair), 203–4; mission to South-Africa and Rhodesia, 217; question of U.N. action against, 222; Adoula plan and, 251n; talks with Welensky, 271; biography, 294; mentioned, 34n, 40n, 44, 50, 82, 83, 93, 190, 221, 258, 319. See also Triumvirate

Kiela, Alphonse (member of the Conakat): Minister of Communications for Katanga, 83

Kilonda, Sylvestre (member of the Conakat; Minister of Agriculture for Katanga), 82

Kimba, Evariste (Minister of Foreign Affairs for Katanga): describes origins of Conakat, 16–17; fails to be elected Balubakat President, joins Conakat, 27 and n; on Tshombe's tactics at Round Table, 39; deputy *chef de cabinet* to Ganshof van der Meersch, 73; on Belgian attitude to

independence for Katanga, 98; sent by Tshombe on Brazzaville mission, 122; appointed Katanga Minister of Foreign Affairs, 123; protests inclusion in Kasavubu delegation at U.N., 134n; Leopoldville Round Table of 1961 and, 144; arrested with Tshombe at Coquilhatville, 154, 206; influence of, in Katanga government, 201; mission to France, Italy, and Germany, 217; charges U.N. paves way for A.N.C., 218; reacts against Kitona accords, 233; Sendwe appeals to, for unity, 269; biography, 294–95; mentioned, 79n, 82, 133, 183n, 203, 213n, 222, 224n, 229, 235n, 237, 258, and *passim*

Kimvay, Félicien (national deputy for the P.S.A.), 137

Kindelungu (plateaus of the, in district of Haut-Katanga): Ucol project for, 18n

Kindu (capital of Maniema, province of Kivu): A.N.C. violence at, 223

Kinkula (a commune of Jadotville): riots in, 53

Kipushi (capital of the territory of Kipushi, district of Haut-Katanga): in elections of May, 1960, 66, 67; mercenaries fall back toward, 236; U.N. forces advance upon, 273, 274; mentioned, 217

Kisantu (town of, district of les Cataractes, province of Leopoldville), 36, 40

Kishiba: on Katangan delegation to Leopoldville discussions, 241

Kitawala ("Watch-tower"; religious sect found among Baluba of North Katanga), 124

Kitenge, Gabriel (national president of the Union Congolaise): on mission with Kibwe, 217; Leopoldville talks of 1962 and, 241; mentioned, 54n, 62n, 78n, 251n

Kitona, agreements and discussions at: the meeting, 231; Katanga Assembly accepts as basis of discussion only, 234; efforts to implement, 237; mentioned, 182

Kivu (former province of), 4, 18, 109. *See also* Comité Nationale du Kivu

Kiwele, Joseph (member of the Conakat; Minister of Education for Katanga): member of triumvirate while Tshombe in prison, 186; dies, 200*n*; mentioned, 82. *See also* Triumvirate

Kokolo, Justin (A.N.C. *adjutant*), 100

Kolwezi (capital of the district of Lualaba): troubles in, 54; elections of May, 1960, 66; evacuation of Europeans from, 98; armed parade in, 99; U.N. occupies, 276; mentioned, 22, 26, 28, 102, 226, 247, 273

Kongolo (capital of the territory of Kongolo, district of Tanganika): elections of May, 1960, 66; incidents at, 95; receives ultimatum after pillage, 99; A.N.C. advance threatens, 115, 120; Katanga gendarmerie withdraws from, 232; gendarmerie renews operations in area of, 239; taken by the A.N.C., 263; massacre during A.N.C. control of, 268; mentioned, 226, 269

Kouilou (dam at, in Congo-Brazzaville), 176, 186*n*

Koumoriko (senior member of Leopoldville Senate): presides over commission of conciliation, 144

Labourdonnaie (French officer, mercenary in Katanga), 238

Laloy, Paul (Belgian student, president of the Amitiés Katangaises), 179

Lambert, A. (editor-in-chief of *L'Echo du Katanga*, adviser to Balubakat), 307

Lanciney, Christian (pseud. of Christian Souris), 124*n*

Landsdowne, Lord: puts pressure on Hammarskjold, 221

Lasimone (French officer), 204 and *n*, 226

Lefèvre-Spaak, government of, in Belgium (Social Christian and Socialist), 152

LEOPOLDVILLE
—city of (capital of the province of Leopoldville and of the Congo): Camp Nkokolo mutiny in, 137; imprisonment of Tshombe heightens divisions in, 186

—government of: *See* Congo, central government of at Leopoldville

—province of: population, 4; attitude toward federalist regime, 28; boycott of elections for communal and territorial councils, 31. *See also* Kamitatu, Cléophas

Liberté (bi-weekly of the Amitiés Katangaises), 179

Libre Belgique, La (conservative Brussels daily), 34*n*, 59, 79*n*, 98*n*, 106*n*, 107, 110*n*, 119*n*, 124*n*, 125, 126*n*, 128*n*, 150, 188*n*, 190*n*, 191 and *n*, 212*n*, 219*n*, 230*n*, 239*n*, 240, 271*n*, 285

Lihau, Marcel (Commissioner-General of Justice), 133*n*

Linner, Dr. Sture (Swedish chief of U.N. civilian operations in the Congo), 197, 237, 238

Lobbies, 174–84, 198, 263, and *passim*

Lobito (port in Angola), 116*n*, 153

Longerstay (official Belgian chargé d'affaires in Leopoldville), 197

Loridan, Walter (Belgian representative at the U.N.), 120*n*, 162*n*

Lovanium (University of Leopoldville at Lovanium): parliamentary conference at, 191–92; conference mentioned, 210, 217

Lualaba (district of Katanga): population of, 3, 4; elections of May, 1960, 66ff

Lualaba, Government of the Province of: set up as Balubakat regime under Ilunga with support from Stanleyville regime, 127, 320; Lumumbist troops occupy Manono, 127*n*, 145, 170; excluded from Tananarive conference, 150 and *n*; Gizenga fails to aid, 170; Katanga retakes Manono, 171, 172–73; relations between Katanga and, 208–9, 269; Adoula offers to abandon, 245, 248, 251; offers place to Evariste Kimba, 269; offers place to Muhunga, 302. *See also* North Katanga

Lualaba (river): bridge over, blown up, 269; mentioned, 263

Luanda (capital of Angola): liaison with Katanga, 184; mentioned, 217

Luano (Elisabethville airfield): Belgian companies disembark at, 97

Luapula-Moero (former district of Katanga): population of, 3, 4

Luba. *See* Baluba

Lubilash (water-course on frontier of Haut-Lomami and Kasai): bridge on the, 262*n*, 263, 268

Lubudi (capital of territory of Lubudi, district of Lualaba): incidents at, 60; elections of May, 1960, 66; rail-line between Luena and, 171; U.N. forces attack, 240; mentioned, 70

Lubumbashi (mining center of Haut-Katanga, in territory of Elisabethville): U.N. force occupies U.M.H.K. plant at, 238–39; mentioned, 12*n*, 236*n*

Luena (territory of Bukama, district of Haut-Lomami): outbreaks and repression, 125; in U.N. zone of control, 127; U.N. intervention at, 157; mentioned, 269

Lufira (tributary of Lualaba River): Ucol plans for, 18*n*

Lulua (tribe of Kasai): brought into the Fédéka, 28–29; relation with M.N.C./ Lumumba, 55, 69; mentioned, 12

Lulua-Frères: in communal elections, 33

Luluabourg (capital of province of Kasai): mutiny in, 96; Kasavubu and Lumumba visit, 100, 101; attacked by Gizengist soldiers from Stanleyville, 137, 145, 172; seeks defensive ties with Elisabethville, 138 and *n*; mentioned, 223

Lumumba, Patrice Emery (President of the M.N.C., Prime Minister of first Congolese govt.): protests advisers' influence at Round Table, 42; Conakat position unfavorable toward, 44; political activity in Katanga, 55; ties with Lulua of Kasai, 69; forms first Congolese govt., 83–84; speech at independence ceremony, 93; deals with status of Belgian soldiers, 100; breaks relations with Belgium and appeals to Khrushchev, 101; accuses Belgium in telegram to U.N., 101; angry at Hammarskjold, 113; Kasavubu dismisses, 119; strength of, after dismissal, 130 and *n*; arrest of, mentioned, 132;

ideological significance of, 138, 139; transferred to Elisabethville, 142–43; death of, 144; significance of, for U.S. policy, 193, 194, 195; death of, affects U.N. stance, 195, 196, 330 (Security Council resolution); Tshombe declaration on dismissal of, 333–35; mentioned, 122, 133, 154, 167, 188*n*, 200, 283, 286–88 *passim*

Lunda (tribe of the territory of Sandoa): dominant role in Conakat, opposition to Tshokwe in Atcar, 28; in Katanga gendarmerie, 156; mentioned, 12, 13

Lundula, Victor (general of the A.N.C.): role in forming Fédéka, 29; confirmed as burgomaster of Kinkula/Jadotville, 54; general at head of A.N.C., 95; efforts to save Europeans in Jadotville, 98; attitude of Belgian commandant Weber toward, 99; expelled from Katanga, 108

Luputa (in territory of Mwene-Ditu, district of Kabinda, Kasai), 223

M.A.C. (Mouvement d'Action Civique): Belgian support for Katanga from, 178

MacColl, R. (writer for the *Daily Express*): interviews Welensky, March, 1960, 56

McGhee, George (U.S. Under-Secretary of State), 263

MacKeown, General Sean (commander of U.N. forces in Congo), 214

MacMillan, Harold (British Prime Minister), 97*n*

Mahamba (minister in Lumumba government), 85

Makonga, Bonaventure: candidate for presidency of the Balubakat, later rallies to the Conakat, 27; represents pro-Conakat wing of Balubakat at Round Table, 46; president of Conakat *ad interim*, 61; mentions tie with Brazzaville, 180*n*; biography, 294

Malenbu-Nkulu (capital of the territory of Malemba-Nkulu, district of Haut-Lomami): elections of May, 1960, 66, 67; ambush at, 124; in zone of U.N. control, 127

Maniema (district in the province of Kivu), 12*n*

Mangombo (chefferie of): experimental center for rural settlement at, 104n

Manono (capital of the territory of Manono, district of Tanganika): elections of May, 1960, 66; disorders at, 123, 125; included in zone of U.N. control, 127; occupied by A.N.C. from Stanleyville, 127n, 169, 170, 172; Lualaba government established at, 145, 170; taken by Katangan gendarmerie March, 1961, 157, 172–73; summary of military operations in, 170–73; Balubakat meeting at, 209; mentioned, 236, 269

Marissal (Colonel; president of Fraternelle des Agents Parachutistes): mission to provide military aid to Katanga, 162, 164

M.A.S. (Messageries Automobiles du Sankuru), 269

Masangu, Jacques (vice-president of the Senate of the Congo): rallies to Tshombe, 108n; note to Belgian minister on payment of officials, 146n; head of delegation to Common Market at Brussels, 182; in dealings to free Tshombe, 187

Massa, Jacques (Congolese Minister of Economic Affairs), 133, 187

Matadi (port, district of Les Cataractes, province of Leopoldville), 42, 116n, 153, 187

Matterne (colonel on Katangan General Staff), 96

Matthys, Major (Belgian): commands Katangan Task Group, 171

Maurice, A. (secretary of the University of Elisabethville, adviser to the Balubakat), 307

Mayele (leader in the Cartel Katangais), 69

Mbako Ditende (son of Lunda grand chief Mwata Yamvo), 25n

M'Bamba, Emmanuel (Kimbanguist delegate; Minister of Finance in Adoula govt.), 15n

M'Beka, Joseph (Congo representative to Common Market), 134n

Mekki Abbas (Tunisian, representative of U.N. Secretary-General in Congo,

successor to Dayal): report of, 173 and n

Meli, Justin (secretary-general of the Conakat): on special mission from Tshombe, 153; on delegation of Katanga at Adoula-Tshombe talks, 241; mentioned, 39n

Mendiaux, Edouard (Belgian magistrate; member of the Amitiés Katangaises), 179

Mercenaries in Katanga: Afro-Asian draft resolution on, 139; U.N. resolution of Feb. 21, 1961 on, 139, 145, 148, 158, 195–96; known as "affreux," 156; attempts to camouflage, 161–64, 227; recruitment of "internationalized," 164–69; application of U.N. resolution on, 211–18; U.N. operations against, August-September, 1961, 218–22; evacuation of, by U.N., 219; negotiations between U.N. and Katanga on, 235–40; remnant of, flee to Angola, 276. *See also* Belgium, Egge, Bjorn; Katanga; Marissal; Mistebel; Trinquier; United Nations

Messmer (French Minister of the Army), 166

Metalkat (Société Métallurgique du Katanga), 317, 324

Mikolzjczak (editor-in-chief of *L'Essor du Katanga*), 146

Milan, Italy: meeting in, to negotiate conditions for freeing Tshombe, 187

Minaf (Ministère Belge des Affaires Africaines): "Minaf status," 215; mentioned, 217, 219 *passim*, 287

Minière du Bécéka (Société de Bécéka; Mibéka), 320, 322, 323

Mining. *See* Union Minière du Haut Katanga

Mining State. *See* South Kasai

Minoteries du Katanga, les, 324

Minsudkat (Société d'Exploitation des Mines du Sud-Katanga), 317, 324

Misakabo, Pierre (Provincial President of M.N.C.-K. for Katanga), 69

Mistebel (Mission Technique Belge): foundation of as technical assistance mission to Katanga, 103, 104; tries to rally Cartel to Katangan govt., 108; warns Belgian officials against anti-

U.N. strike, 113; gets Belgian manpower for Katanga gendarmerie, 114; urges West support Tshombe, 122*n*; explains reprisals on U.N. forces, 124; moderating influence of on Tshombe, 127 and *n*; leaves Elisabethville at request of Katanga, 128; concluding observations, 320

Mitwaba (capital of territory of Mitwaba, district of Haut-Katanga): elections of May, 1960, 66; encircled, 125

M.N.C. *See* Mouvement Nationale Congolais

Mobutu, Colonel Joseph-Désiré: named Chief of Staff of A.N.C., 95; coup d'état by, mentioned, 115; setting up College of Commissioners, 122–23; Belgium supports, 129; visits Elisabethville, 133; weakness of, 137; tries to reunify A.N.C., 141; promoted general, 145; strategy of, 147–48; military agreement of July 18, 1960, with Tshombe, 169, 209–10, 216; prepares for Lovanium Parliament, 192; effect of coup on U.S. policy, 194; in talks on freeing Tshombe, 208; mentioned, 139, 142, 204*n*, 211

Monde, Le (Parisian daily), 146*n*, 151, 154*n*, 169*n*, 229*n*, 273*n*

Monetary Council of the Congo: role of discussed between Adoula and Tshombe, 248, 249; role attributed to under Thant plan, 260, 261; Tshombe poses conditions to monetary control by, 271; relations of U.M.H.K. with, 285

Moniteur Congolais, 136*n*, 255*n*

Moniteur Katangais, 98*n*, 114*n*, 188*n*

Morphologie des Groupes Financiers (C.R.I.S.P., Brussels), 48*n*

Morton, Thruston B. (U.S. Senator), 181

Moscow. *See* U.S.S.R.

Mouvement National Congolais (M.N.C.): first public manifestation of, 11; two wings of, 55

—/Kalonji (M.N.C./K.): activity in Katanga, 55; elections of May, 1960, 66ff; elections for provincial president,

68–69; agreements with Cartel and with Conakat, 69; mentioned, 29, 33*n*, 39, 46, 51, 55*n*, 267. *See also* Kalonji, Albert

—/Lumumba (M.N.C./L.): activity in Katanga, 55; elections of May, 1960, 66ff; offers to work with Cartel, 69*n*; mentioned, 39, 42, 43, 46, 52*n*, 144, 267. *See also* Lumumba, Patrice Emery

Mouvement Solidaire Muluba (M.S.M.): in communal elections, 33*n*; mentioned, 55*n*

Mozambique, 141*n*. *See also* Beira; Portugal; Angola

Mpolo, Maurice (President of M.N.C./L. at Leopoldville; Minister of Youth and Sports in Lumumba govt.), 142*n*, 143*n*, 330

Mpweto, Jean-Marie (Vice-President of Katangan Provincial Assembly), 74

M'Siri (King of Katanga): ancestor of G. Munongo, 293

Muhona, Paul (Tshokwe; Christian syndicalist): urges Cartel not to boycott Assembly, 81; elected Minister of Labor and Social Affairs for Katanga, 82; mentioned, 54*n*, 78*n*, 252*n*

Muhunga, Ambroise (President of the Atcar): warns Conakat against Rhodesian ties, 94; opposes secession, 108; biography of, 302; mentioned, 28, 37

Muké, General (Commander of Katangan Gendarmerie), 224, 226, 237, 275 and *n*

Mukeba, Cléophas (Vice-President of M.N.C./K.): agreements with Cartel and Conakat involving, 69; elected Minister of Public Health, 83

Mukenge, Barthélemey (President of the government of Luluabourg), 137–38

Mukongo. *See* Bakongo

Mukulakulu (in the territory of Bukama, district of Haut-Lomami): taken by Katangan forces, 171

Mukulu (*chefferie* of, in the territory of Kaniama), 27

Mukwidi, Thomas (nationalist deputy of P.S.A.), 137

Muller (special envoy of M. Fayat to

Katanga; asst. to Professor Clémens at University of Elisabethville): expelled, 213 and *n*

Muluba. *See* Baluba

Munich, Germany: Katanga liaison in, 184

Munongo, Godefroid (president of Conakat; Minister of Interior for Katanga): brother of chief of the Bayeke, 11; letter to Governor Schoeller, 13–14, 14*n*; resigns presidency of Conakat, 26*n*; member of Provincial Executive College, 54*n*, 78; positions of, during formation of provincial government, 75, 76; elected Minister of Interior, 82; involved in Scheerlinck affair, 85, 86; accused of secession attempt, 89; refuses to allow Kasavubu and Lumumba to land in Katanga, 99, 100; radio remarks of, 108; the Sureté under, 118, 126, 198, 233; decides for total independence, 123; member of triumvirate during Tshombe's imprisonment, 186, 202, 233; approves Tshombe's agreement, 188 and *n*; conciliates U.N., 193; considered an ultra in government factions, 201; U.N. operation of August, 1961 and, 218ff; blames and threatens U.N. troops, 228, 229; Baluba refugees and, 264; signs official Katangan declaration of enmity to U.N., 336–37; general observations, 277, 285; biography, 293; mentioned, 26, 93, 106, 190, 237, 240, 258

Munongo Mwenda (chief of the Bayeke; brother of Godefroid Munongo): contact with Scheerlinck, 85; makes demands on Assembly as spokesman for chiefs, 205; Tshombe meets, 235; mentioned, 11

Munukamawa, Sipalo (leader of Rhodesian United National Independence Party), 57

Mushidi, Jean (Secretary-General of A.T.C.A.R.), 304

Mutaka-wa-Dilomba, Charles (President of Conakat in Jadotville): burgomaster candidate for Kinkula, 53; Provincial Assembly member from Kambove, 70; elected president of Assembly, 74; opposes Sendwe, 85; critical of Tshombe government, 203–4; Assembly censures and curtails power of, 204; efforts on behalf of Cartel members in prison, 205*n*, 208*n*; countersigned acts of triumvirate, 207*n*; discussions with Leopoldville delegation, 252; refuses invitation to Leopoldville, 259*n*; biography of, 295; mentioned, 89, 222, 229*n*, 230*n*

Mutombo (*chefferie* of, territory of Kaniama), 27, 70

Mutuelle Immobilière du Katanga (M.I.K.), 317

Mutabwa. *See* Batabwa

Muyeke. *See* Bayeke

Muyumba, Prosper (provincial deputy from South Katanga), 204

Mwamba-Ilunga, Prosper (leader of Cartel Katangais): spokesman for Cartel in Provincial Assembly, 74, 76, 79–80; states Cartel protest at secession, 107; demands release of Cartel prisoners, 108; setting up of government "of the province of Lualaba" by, 127, 170; joins appeal for Conakat-Balubakat meeting, 209; biography of, 302; mentioned, 73*n*, 88*n*, 208, 223*n*. *See* Lualaba, Government of the Province of

Mwamba, Remy (general vice-president of Balubakat and member of Collège Exécutif Général): as president of the P.P.K., 30*n*; as Katangan representative on the Collège Exécutif Général, 54, 71, 73 and *n*; named Minister of Justice in Lumumba government, 85; biography, 301–2; mentioned, 27*n*

Mwata Yamvo (Lunda grand chief), 13, 25*n*, 235

Mwenda, Odilon (Minister Resident in Katanga; president of the Ocekat in Brussels), 183

Mwewa, Jean-Chrysostome (Minister of Public Health for Katanga), 203*n*

N.A.T.O. (North Atlantic Treaty Organization): French and British positions on Congo in, 177; Council of, supports

Spaak, 229; pleads for conciliation, 270; mentioned, 195 and *n*, 253

Ndjili (Leopoldville airport), 250*n*

Ndjoku, Eugene (A.N.C. colonel): plans to integrate Katangan army into A.N.C. under, 188, 189, 216

Ndola (city in Northern Rhodesia): cease-fire negotiations at, 222, 230

Netherlands, The, 97

New England Committee for Aid to the Katanga Freedom Fighters, 181

New York: official Katangan representation in, 183, 192 and *n*

New York Herald Tribune, 175*n*

New York Times: Committee of One Million ad in, 181; mentioned, 175*n*

Newsweek (U.S. weekly): on Katanga lobby, 183

Ngalula, Joseph (Congolese Minister of National Education): signs 1958 M.N.C. petition, 11; delegate to mixed commissions for applying Thant Plan, 259–60; mentioned, 268

Ngoy Luongwe, 252

Ngoye, Hubert (Balubakat deputy), 208*n*

Ngule (airport in territory of Lubudi, district of Lualaba): U.N. action at, 263

Nguvulu, Alphonse, 11, 85

Nixon, Richard (former U.S. Vice-President), 181

Nkokolo (military camp at Leopoldville): mutiny at, 137

Nkokolo, Justin. *See* Kokolo, Justin

Nkrumah, Kwame (Premier of Ghana): proposes plan for U.N. intervention in Congo, 196. *See also* Casablanca Group; Afro-Asian group

North Katanga (*see map*, p. 64): rebellion in, 119, 123–24; repression in, 124–26; balance of forces by end of 1960 in, 127; Tshombe resents Leopoldville ties with, 141; Leopoldville gives *de facto* recognition to, 152; Kasavubu demands Tshombe halt operations in, 153; Tshombe charged with Baluba massacre in, 154; U.N. Operation Rumpunch in, 218–19; refugees from, 220, 264; A.N.C. offensive in, 232, 234, 238; Katanga objects to "illegal" government in Albertville, 241; questions of in Adoula-Tshombe talks, 251, 245–51 *passim*; Congo promulgates Province of, by law of July 11, 1962, 254–55, 266–67, 269; military and political situation in, 268–69; estimate of violence in, 285. *See also* Albertville; Baluba; Lualaba; Sendwe, Jason; South Katanga

Northeast Katanga: aborted plan to create a government of, 88

Notre Guerre au Katanga (by Trinquier, Duchemin, and Le Bailly), 142 and *n*, 166*n*, 168*n*

Notre Opinion (Katangan bi-monthly): opposes Union Katangaise, 23

Nyangwile, Pierre: as member of Collège Exécutif Général, 72

Nyasaland. *See* Rhodesias, Federation of the

Nyembo, Albert (Conakat deputy, Katangan Minister of the Civil Service): Lumumba offers post in Defense secretariat to, 85; idealizes mercenaries, 230*n*; mentioned, 202

Nyunzu (capital of territory of Nyunzu, district of Tanganika): elections of May, 1960, in, 66

Nzilo (Force Publique camp in territory of Kolwezi, district of Haut-Lomami): Belgian attack on, 108

Nzimbe, Mathias (Vice-President of the Provincial Assembly), 74

O'Brien, Conor Cruise (U.N. representative in Katanga): Belgian consul asks to halt arrests, 219; expels mercenaries, 219; clash with Munongo, 220; blamed for distorting refugee problem, 264; mentioned, 198 and *n*, 212 and *n*, 213 and *n*, 214*n*

Ocekat (Office Culturel et Economique du Katanga), 183

Office Central du Travail au Katanga (O.C.T.K.): subsidizes C.E.P.S.I., 104*n*

Okito, Joseph (senator from Province of Kasai, second Vice-President of the Senate), 143*n*

Onckelinx, Joseph (vice-president of the Ucol-Katanga, member of the Fede-

col): Commission du Colonat and, 20; Conakat, the Round Table and, 38–39; asked to raise funds for Conakat, 61; becomes Conakat adviser, 62; U.N. expels, 214; biography of, 299

Orientale (province): population, 4, 5; Gizengist foothold in, 133

Pan-African Freedom Movement of Eastern, Central, and Southern Africa (PAFMECSA), 270, 274

Parti Indépendant (Belgian), 178

Parti de la Liberté et du Progrès (Belgian political party; formerly the Liberal Party): supports Katanga, 178

Parti National Belge, 178

Parti National du Progrès (P.N.P.; coalition of moderate local political parties in Coqhuilhatville), 31, 38*n*, 40, 43, 51

Parti du Peuple (P.P.; Congolese nationalist party), 39

Parti Progressiste Katangais (P.P.K.; alternative election label for Balubakat): program of, 304–6; mentioned, 28, 30

Parti Social Chrétien (Belgian): supports Katanga, 178

Parti Social Independent (Belgian), 178

Parti Solidaire Africain (P.S.A.): delegation of from province of Leopoldville at Tananarive conference, 148; mentioned, 39, 51, 52*n*, 144, 267

Parti de l'Unité Basonge: joins Cartel Katangais, 30*n*

Pastorale du Looami, Compagnie, 317

Perin, Francois, 149*n*

Perin-Hockers, Mme. Maryse (with Solvay Institute): Cartel adviser, 72, 307; residence of, searched, 73

Persian Airlines, 163

Pétillon, Léon (Governor-General of Congo, then Minister for the Congo): attitude of, toward the Union Katangaise, 23–24, 24*n*; replaced as Minister by Hemelrijck, 25

Pierkat (Pierres et Materiaux du Katanga), 317

Phare du Katanga, Le (weekly published in Kolwezi): Conakat declaration published in, 26, 296

Pholien, Joseph (former Belgian Prime Minister): member of Amitiés Katangaises, 179

Pinzi, Arthur, 11

Pirard, Albert (on Radio-Katanga): member of Amitiés Katangaises, 179

Pittsburgh Courier, 181

Pongo, Gilbert-Pierre (official of the *Sûreté* of Léopoldville), 142*n*

Port-Franqui (capital of territory of Port-Franqui, district of Kasai), 116*n*

Portugal: common interest with Katanga, 175 and *n*, 282; mentioned, 87

Potez (French aviation firm): contract with Belgium for delivery to Katanga, 166*n*

Pourquoi Pas? (Belgian weekly), 114*n*, 212*n*, 294*n*. *See also* Davister, Pierre

P.P.K. *See* Parti Progressiste Katangais

Pradier (French officer in Trinquier's outfit), 168

Problèmes Sociaux Congolais (C.E.P.S.I. bulletin), 104*n*

Protestant Council of the Congo, 25

Protin (Belgian captain), 171*n*

Provincial Assembly of Katanga. *See* Assembly, Katanga Provincial

Puna (Parti de l'Unité Nationale, 267

Pwati, J. (A.N.C. commander): heads delegation to Elisabethville, 142

Pweto (capital of territory of Pweto, district of Haut-Katanga): elections of May, 1960, in, 66

Pweto (member of Katangan delegation to U.S.), 192*n*

Radio-Katanga, 273

Radio Ufac (private broadcasting station of Elisabethville), 45, 62, 73

Railroads. *See* B.C.K., C.F.L., K.D.L., *and maps,* 32, 117

Rassemblement Katangais (political party of Conakat), 18, 26

Rassemblement National (Belgian independent party), 178

Rassemblement pour la défense de l'oevre belge au Congo, 178

Reko (Rassemblement de l'Est du Kongo), 85

Renkin, Jules (Belgian Minister of the Colonies), 9

République du Kongo Central: proposed by the Abako, 35–36

Reuters (British press agency), 56, 123

Revue Nouvelle, La (Belgian monthly), 18n, 23n

Revue de l'Université de Bruxelles, 19n, 51n

Rhodesias, Federation of the: Welensky declaration on ties with Katanga, 56–59; Conakat disclaims collusion with, 75; Europeans flee to, 95; transport links of Katanga with, 116n; pressures Katanga to shun Leopoldville ties, 141; interest of in Katanga secession, 175 and n, 176; the Copperbelt interest, 182; Kibwe and Kitenge visit, 217; mentioned, 3, 13, 15, 47, 86, 198n and *passim*

Rijckaert, G. (secretary of the Cartel; adviser), 307

Rolin, Henri (Belgian Socialist senator; Minister of State): opposes recognizing Katanga, 100 and n; insists on Cartel role in Katanga, 107 and n; mentioned, 41

Romaniuk, A.: on demography, 3

Ropagnol (French officer; mercenary in Katanga), 226n

Rothschild, R. (envoy of Belgian Minister of Foreign Affairs to Elisabethville): becomes chief of Mistebel, urges fiscal confederation, 121, 286; leaves with Mistebel, 128

Rouleau, Eric (French newspaperman on Le Monde): reports Tshombe's anti-U.M.H.K. statements, 229 and n

Round Table of January, 1960, on Belgian Congo: the conference of, 37–45; Congolese Common Front at, 39, 42, 44 *passim*; transitional organs set up by, 45–46; economic conference following, 46–52; Katangan Common Front at economic conference of the, 47; general remarks on, 280; mentioned, 34, 36, 54, 61, 62, 63 *passim*. *See also* Collège Exécutif général

Round Table of January, 1961: Tshombe appeals to Kasavubu for, 110; Katangan attitude toward, 133; plans laid for, at Brazzaville meeting, 134–35; Katanga boycotts, 143–46; mentioned, 141

Ruanda-Urundi (Rwanda and Burundi), 18, 109, 155n

Rubbens, Antoine: political analysis, 15n, 21n, 23

Rudahindwa, Edmond (member of Rassemblement de l'Est du Kongo): Katangan Minister of Mines, 85

Sabena (Belgian airline): airlift of Europeans, 95; delivers arms to Katanga, 114; monopoly of, 180; works with Katanga authorities, 228 and n; mentioned, 227

Sahbani, Taieb (Tunisian; special envoy of U.N. Secretary-General to Brussels), 198, 212

Sakania (capital of territory of Sakania, district of Haut-Katanga): elections of May, 1960, in, 66; mentioned, 102, 247, 275

Salisbury (capital of Southern Rhodesia): liaison with Katanga, 184; mentioned, 56, 168. *See also* Rhodesias, Federation of the; Welensky, Sir Roy

Samalenge, Lucas (Katangan Secretary of State for Information), 200n

Sandoa (capital of territory of Sandoa, district of Lualaba): Atcar center in, 28; elections of May, 1960, in, 66; mentioned, 25n

Saruc (Société Auxiliaire de la Royale Union Coloniale Belge), 317

Sauvy, Jacques, 12n

Scheerlinck, Francois (former agent of Belgian Sûreté in Katanga): role of, in secession plot, 85–87; significance of, 280; biography, 300; mentioned, 93

Scheyven, Raymond (Belgian Minister in charge of economic affairs for Belgian Congo and Ruanda-Urundi), 33

Schoeller, André (governor of Katanga, Vice-Governor-General of Belgian Congo and Ruanda-Urundi): welcomed at Elisabethville, 24–25; on problem of minorities, 28; discounts secession threat, 58; criticizes European political activity in Katanga, 59;

urges amendment of quorum provision for Katanga Assembly, 70–72, 74, 76–79 *passim*; vain efforts to guarantee Cartel-Conakat compromise, 77, 80–81, 83; calls for Belgian armed intervention, 96; mentioned, 14*n*, 104*n*

Schuyler, Georges (writer, editor-in-chief of the *Pittsburgh Courier*), 181

Security Council. *See* United Nations

Sékou Touré (President of Guinea): Conakat cites example of, 39; telegram to U.N. relating to College of Commissioners, 136 and *n*. *See also* Casablanca Group

Selkibara (Société d'Elevage aux Kibara), 317

Selwyn Lloyd (British Chancellor of the Exchequer), 56

Sendwe, Jason (president of Balubakat; Vice-Prime Minister in Adoula government): founds Balubakat, 25; first President of Balubakat, 27; voted burgomaster by Albert commune, 37; at Round Table, 46; disclaims ties with M.N.C./L., 55; opposes Elisabethville strikes, 60; electoral alliance with M.N.C./K., 68–69; protests provincial quorum amendment as national deputy, 80; Lumumba names Commissioner of State for Katanga, 84, 85, 94; Tshombe tries to contact, 107; Tshombe rejects pacification mission by, 123; on U.N. pacification mission, 132; Tshombe resents Leopoldville ties with, 141; Tshombe hostile to, 144; absent from Tananarive, 150, 209; mission to Brussels, 209; Katanga Assembly demands removal of, as Commissioner, 234; at Adoula-Tshombe talks, 241, 242; promotes North Katanga province, 269; biography of, 301; mentioned, 13*n*, 30*n*, 55*n*, 73 and *n*, 208, 235. *See also* Balubakat; Cartel Katangais; North Katanga; Lualaba, Government of the Province of

Senga, Raphaël (Union Congolaise, Katanga), 319

Senghor, Léopold (President of Senegal): suggested as mediator, 226, 287; criticizes U.N. actions, 230

Sépulchre, Jean (of *L'Essor du Katanga*), 9

Sermikat (Société d'Exploitation et de Recherches Minières au Katanga), 317

Settlers: nature of as group, 3; attitude of toward Conakat, 17, 277; organizations of, 18–22; send note to Minister for the Colonies, 20; disappointed by Pétillon declaration, 24; pressure on Katanga government, 141. *See also* Ucol, Union Katangais; Mercenaries in Katanga

Seven-Seas Airlines, 227*n*

Shabani, André (Balubakat deputy), 209

Shinkolobwe (Mining center and military camp for gendarmerie, in territory of Kambove, district of Haut-Katanga): troubles in, 98, 99

Société Générale de Belgique, La (Belgian financial group): controls U.M.H.K. before 1960, 48; influence in U.M.H.K. after 1960, 52; statistics on role of, in Katanga economy, 320–25; changes in management of, 225*n*

Société Métallurgique Hoboken, 323

Sogechim (Société Générale Industrielle et Chimique du Katanga), 324

Sogefor (Société Générale des Forces Hydro-Electriques du Katanga), 317, 323

Sogelec (Société Générale Africaine d'électricité), 317, 323

Sohier (U.M.H.K. representative; director of Ufac, a veterans organization), 73*n*

Soir, Le (Belgian daily), 33*n*, 49*n*, 101

Solvay Institute. *See* Institut de Sociologie de l'Université de Liège

Souris, Christian. *See* Lanciney, Christian

South Africa, Republic of (formerly Union of): supports Katanga, 175–76; contacts with Katanga, 184, 217, 282; mentioned, 86

South Kasai, Mining State of (capital at Bakwanga): poses military threat to Katanga, 115; resists A.N.C. attacks with aid from Katanga, 120 and *n*; military agreement with Leopoldville and Katanga, 145–48, 172; mentioned, 111*n*, 204*n*. *See also* Bakwanga; Baluba; Kalonji, Albert

South Katanga, 47, 259*n*, 263, 268. *See also* North Katanga

Soviet Union. *See* U.S.S.R.

Spaak, Paul-Henri (Secretary-General of N.A.T.O., Belgian Minister of Foreign Affairs, then Prime Minister): Katangans accuse, 198; talks with Hammarskjold, 213, 215; policy of Spaak-Lefevre government on secession, 224–25 and 225*n*; criticizes U.N. and presses for cease-fire, 229–30; position on financial aid to Congo, 253; meeting of with Thant and Stevenson, 254; talks with Gardiner, Thant, Kennedy, and Stevenson, 263; warns Katanga, 264; calls Tshombe rebel, 271*n*, 287; urges talks, 274; declaration on end of secession addressed to, 276; nature of solution desired by, 287–88; mentioned, 132, 152

Spandre, Mario (adviser of Tshombe), 287

Stanleyville (capital of Orientale Province): tie with Lualaba regime, 127; Lumumbist regime under Gizenga at, 130; military offensive from, against Luluabourg, 137, 172; military offensive against North Katanga, 148, 157, 169–70, 172; plan to liquidate attributed to Col. Trinquier, 167; U.N. contacts with, 187; Katanga fears role of in Parliament, 189–90; realigns with Leopoldville, 210

Stavropoulos, Constantin (Greek jurist, adviser to U.N. Secretary-General), 235

Stevenson, Adlai (U.S. representative to U.N.): "Stevenson" or American Plan, 163, 195; talks with Thant and Spaak, 254; mentioned, 181

Struelens, Michel (head of Katinfor): lobbies in U.S., 183, 213 and *n*, 217

Struye, Paul (president of Belgian Senate): writes in *Libre Belgique*, 150–51; hostile to U.N. Force in Congo, 180, 182

Sud-Kat (Société de Recherche Minière du Sud-Katanga), 324

Sûreté (Belgian, Katangan). *See* Belgium; Munongo, Godefroid

Sweden: Katanga-Lobby in, 182

Tananarive (capital of Malagasy Republic): conference of, 148–51; conference mentioned, 140, 190

Tanganika (district of Katanga): population of, 3, 4; elections of May, 1960, 65, 66, 67

Tanganyika Concessions Ltd.: relations with the Comité Spécial du Katanga (C.S.K.), 48, 52, 317, 318; relations with the Société Générale, 320, 323; structure and management of, 324–25

T.C.K. (Transport Communs du Katanga), strike against, 59

Thant. *See* U Thant

Thyssens, Georges (permanent secretary of the Ucol): liaison between Conakat and European interests, 61, 62, 63; relation to Scheerlinck, 87; on mission to recruit mercenaries, 125; expelled, 198 and *n*, 213; biography of, 299; mentioned, 106, 166

Thysville (capital of territory of Thysville, district of les Cataractes): mutiny at camp of, 137, 142

Tignée: adviser to Tshombe, 131 and *n*; expelled, 214

Times, The London, 56

To Katanga and Back, A U.N. Case History (Conor Cruise O'Brien), 212*n*, 214*n*, 215*n*, 218*n*, 222*n*

Tombelaine, Michel (French; U.N. representative in Katanga, deputy to O'Brien), 218, 220, 264

Toussaint, E., 12*n*

Toussaint, Philippe (Belgian editor of *Pourquoi Pas?*), 215*n*, 218*n*

Transport strike in Elisabethville, 59

Transport routes (*see* map, 117), 116*n*. *See also* Railroads

Travaux Africains. See Courrier Africain du C.R.I.S.P.

Trinquier, Colonel (French): visits Katanga in response to Thyssens proposal, 166; in charge of reorganizing gendarmerie, 167; Belgian attitude toward and refusal of Tshombe to hire, 168 and *n*; mentioned, 172*n*, 173, 201

Triumvirate (Katangan Ministers exercising power during Tshombe's imprisonment: Munongo, Kibwe, Kiwele): moves to negotiate with U.N., 193, 202, 211; bad relations with Belgium, 198, 213; mentioned, 186

Truman mission, 177

Tshangalele, Lake: incident involving Baluba fishermen, 55

Tshiteya, Dominique (Director of executive committee of M.N.C./L.): activity of in Katanga, 55

Tshizand, Salomon: elected Minister of Economic Affairs in Katanga government, 82; mission to France, 180; dies, 200n; mentioned, 202

Tshokwe (tribe of territory of Dilolo): hostility to Lunda, 13, 28; form the Atcar, 28; squatters expelled from Elisabethville, 236; mentioned, 12, 54n. *See also* Atcar

Tshombe, Daniel (brother of Moise Tshombe), 217

Tshombe Kabwita, Th. (Katangan provincial deputy), 204

Tshombe Kapenda, Moise (President of the Conakat; head of secessionist Katanga): statement on Conakat origins, 11–12, 12n, 14; leader of Acmaf, 20; succeeds Munongo as Conakat President, 26n; 1959 view on Katanga future, 31, 33; at the Round Table, 41, 44, 45, 47, 51; relations of with Rhodesia, 57–58; relations with Europeans in Katanga, 61; supports independence for Katanga before Congo government set up, 68n; alliance with M.N.C./K., 69; complains of Cartel advisers, 73; constitution of Katanga provincial government by, 75–83 *passim*; voted President of provincial government, 82; objects to composition of central government at Leopoldville, 84–85; tie with Scheerlinck, 85, 86, 88; weak in central government, 93; visits Leopoldville, 94; asks Belgian military intervention and appeals to Rhodesia, 96, 97; proclaims Katanga independent, 98; tries to broaden his government, 107; fails to rally Cartel, 108–9; proposes Round Table to Leopoldville, 110; demands U.N. guarantees of non-interference in Katanga affairs, 113; urges anti-Lumumbist coalition, 121; rejects offer of place in central government, 122; rejects Sendwe mission, 123; letter to Eyskens, 151n; Brazzaville meetings with Kasavubu, 133, 135; received by King of Belgians, 134; response to U.N. Resolution of February 21, 139; demands *de facto* recognition and military accord with Congo and Kasai, 145; signs military accord, 146 and n; opening speech at Tananarive, 149–50; letter to Kasavubu, 153; at Coquilhatville, 154–55; imprisoned, 154, 185; relation with Belgium, 160; gets Lumumba transferred to Katanga, 164–65; letter to De Gaulle, 168n; accord with Mobutu on gendarmerie, 169, 216; relations with U.N. and military operations to North, 171–73; release from prison negotiated, 185–88; negotiations before Lovanium Parliament, 189–93; visits Brazzaville, 192; attacks Kasavubu for U.N. accord, 200; relations with Balubakat opposition, 208–9; U.N. urges meeting with Adoula, 220–21; U.N. tries to capture, 221; negotiates cease-fire with U.N., 222; predicts new clash, 228; hostile to U.M.H.K., 229; agrees to meet Adoula with U.S. safe-conduct, 230; at Kitona, 231–32; calls for new talks with Adoula, 235; tries to placate U.N. on mercenary question, 237–38; talks with Adoula at Leopoldville, 240–52, 266; accepts Thant Plan for reconciliation, 258; repeats endorsement of Thant Plan, 262; U.N. ultimatum to, 263; U.N. carries out "Course of Action" against, 270–71; urges resistance to U.N., 273; flees to Kolwezi, 276; general conclusions concerning, 277–88 *passim*; biography of, 293–94; declaration on split between Kasavubu and Lumumba, 333–35; mentioned, 11, 60, 146n, 152, 154, 198, 207, 227, 233, 234, 266, 267, 272, and *passim*

Tshombe, Thomas (brother of Moise

Tshombe): elected at Sandoa, 70; mentioned, 183, 192*n*

Tsiranana, Philibert (President of Malagasy Republic), 195, 230

Tumba, Ferdinand (Balubakat director): emissary from Leopoldville Round Table Conference, 141; arrested by Tshombe, 144

Tungwe (paramount chief of Albertville), 70

U.A.T. (Union Aéro-maritime de Transports): French competitor of Sabena, 201, 227

Ucol-Katanga (Union pour la Colonisation): organization of, 18–22; gives impetus to founding of the Union Katangaise, 22–23; relation to the Conakat, 25–26, 278; abjures political activity, 61; political program of, 308–9; mentioned, 17*n*, 113*n*

Ufac (Union des Fraternelles des Anciens Combattants; veterans organization), 73*n*

Ugeux (Belgian; *chef de cabinet* to Katangan Minister of Information): expelled, 214

Umba, Pierre (deputy secretary-general of the Balubakat), 302

U.M.H.K. *See* Union Minière du Haut-Katanga

Union Africaine et Malgache (U.A.M.). *See* Brazzaville Group

Union Congolaise (African political party): hostile to Union Katangaise, 23; in elections of May, 1960, 66; mentioned, 14, 34, 38, 50, 54*n*

Union des Republiques d'Afrique Centrale (U.R.A.C.): constitution of, proposed by Abako, 36–37

Union Douanière Equatoriale (Equatorial Customs Union): Katanga asks admission to, 135, 176*n*

Union Katangaise (U.K.; political offshoot of the Ucol-Katanga): founded, 22–23; ties with the Conakat, 26–27, 278; poses secession alternative in questionnaire, 35–36; aids the Conakat and dissolves itself, 61; historical summary, leaders, program of, 309–14; mentioned, 24

Union Minière du Haut-Katanga (U.M.H.K.): recruits "strangers," 12, 17*n*; criticized by Conakat and Fegebaceka, 14, 15; interests of discussed at economic conference, 48 and *n*, 49; private interests retain majority in by convention on C.S.K., 52; relations with Rhodesia, 56–58; attitude toward Conakat, 61, 279; security of, 102*n*; Katanga receives revenues from, 115, 206*n*, 207–8; threat of nationalizing, 128; American policy and, 195; U.N. occupation of plant at Lubumbashi, 238–39; Thant Plan and, 254, 257, 289, 341 and *n*; agreement on foreign exchange with Leopoldville, 276 and *n*; role of, in secession, 279, 283–85; ties with the Société Générale charted, 321; organization and operations of, 322–24; mentioned, 42*n*, 104*n*, 183, 210, 271, 281, 317, and *passim*. *See also* United Nations, policy of on U.M.H.K.

Union Mongo (Unimo; political party), 39

Union Professionnelle des Cheminots Congolais (UPROCO; railroad workers), 59*n*

United National Independence Party (U.N.I.P.; political party in Northern Rhodesia), 57

United Nations: Katanga appeals to, 78; Kasavubu and Lumumba appeal to for military aid, 101; Security Council resolution on Belgian withdrawal, 101–2; Leopoldville impatient with, 112–13; demands Belgium withdraw Katanga troops, 113; Belgium and Allies pressure to protect Katanga, 115; reacts against A.N.C. violence, 120; Consultative Committee of for the Congo, 120, 132, 254, 264; protests Tshombist repression, 125; Kasavubu delegation recognized at, 128; policy toward College of Commissioners, 136 and *nn*; Belgian military aid policy justified before, 161–62; non-admission of Katanga to, 175; British, French, and U.S. Congo policies in, 177, 187; policy of, on U.M.H.K., 208, 238, 239, 254, 270,

272, 284, 341 and *n*, 342; Spaak-Hammarskjold talks, 213; ratifies Ndola cease-fire, 222; obtains cease-fire and Kitona meeting, 230–32; talks with Tshombe on mercenaries, 235–36; Thant Plan, 253ff, 337–42; compromise attempts by Western Powers, 263; general summary, 282–89 *passim*; U.N. mentioned, 107, 129, 134, 147, 159, 162*n*, 165 and *n*, 191 *passim*, 275*n*

—Security Council Resolution of February 21, 1961: Afro-Asian draft resolutions of (Nkrumah Plan), 139, 195–96; denounced at Tananarive Conference, 149, 150; Leopoldville agrees to accept, 151–52, 157, 199; Tshombe denounces Kasavubu for accepting, 154, 200; Belgium constrained by, 158; Tshombe's initial response to, 172ff; Katanga triumvirate states willingness to discuss, 193; adoption of, 195–96; Spaak interpretation of, 197; clause A.2 of concerning advisers and mercenaries, 211; Egge Plan to implement, 215ff; purposes of strengthened by November 24 Resolution, 228, 332–33; U.N. Force complains Katanga flouting, 237; text of, 330–32; mentioned, 139, 145, 146, 148 *passim*. *See also* Mercenaries in Katanga

—U.N. Force in the Congo: Congo government requests, 101; role of defined and first units sent, 112–13, 329–30; relieves Belgian forces in Katanga, 112ff, 119; closes airfields, 120*n*, 130; arranges A.N.C.-Katanga gendarmerie cease-fire, 123*n*; controls large parts of North Katanga by agreement with Katanga, 127, 131; relations with Katanga, 130ff; pacification mission by, 132; relations with College of Commissioners and Ileo government, 136; arrival of Indian contingents and agreement with Leopoldville, 151–52; expels Tshombe advisers, 155; Katanga fears North Katanga operations of, 157; Berendsen agrees with Tshombe to avoid incidents involving, 172; powerless to halt Manono counter-offensive, 172–73; captures merce-

naries at Kabalo, 174; "American (or Stevenson) Plan" urges strengthening, 195; agreement of new Spaak government with, 197; decides to expel advisers from Katanga, 213; mixed commission with Katanga on advisers, 214; role of in Egge plan, 215–18; operation Rumpunch, August 28, 1960, and expulsion of mercenaries, 218–19; open hostilities between Katanga and, 220–22; cease-fire, 222–24; officials of arrested, 228; press campaign against and Spaak protest, 229; relations of, with Katanga after Kitona, 235ff; discussions with Tshombe over mercenaries, 237–40; role in mediating Adoula-Tshombe talks, 244, 246, 250–52; demands cooperation of Katanga in Thant Plan, 262–63; refugee camp of, 264; ends secession by force, 290–94; U.N. Force mentioned, 106*n*, 124, 211, 226, 243, 247, 249, 261, 265, 266, 268 *passim*

United States of America: influence of, on Belgium, 159; position toward Katanga, 177; Katanga Lobby and spokesmen in, 181–84; Kennedy policies, 182 and *n*, 193–95; encourages freeing Tshombe, 187, 192; Stevenson Plan, 195; helps mediate Kitona meeting, 230; Tshombe blames, for troubles in Katanga, 234; aids Leopoldville, 253; favors economic sanctions against Katanga, 254; tries to get compromise on Thant Plan, 263; demonstrations at Elisabethville against, 271; supports U.N. operations, 272; mentioned, 97, 134*n*, 183, 224, 225, 288. *See* Kennedy, Stevenson

UNIVERSITIES

—Université d'Etat d'Elisabethville, set up with Mistebel, 213*n*, mentioned, 16*n*

—Université Libre de Bruxelles (U.L.B.), 270*n*

—*See also* Institut de Sociologie de l'Université de Liège; Institut de Sociologie de l'Université libre de Bruxelles

Upak (Union des Planteurs et Agriculteurs du Katanga): opposes U.N., 113*n*; mentioned, 18

U.S.S.R. (Union of Soviet Socialist Republics): Lumumba denounced as agent of, 54, 99; Lumumba and Kasavubu appeal to, 101; provides aircraft to Lumumba, 130n; opposes Stevenson Plan, 195; attacks Hammarskjold, 196; demands Security Council meeting on "sabotage" of Resolutions, 237; aid to Leopoldville, 288

Usumbura (capital of Burundi): liaison with Katanga, 184

U.T.C. (Union des Travailleurs Congolais; Congolese *syndicat*), 59n

U Thant (Secretary-General of the U.N.: successor to Hammarskjold): view of on U.M.H.K. revenues, 208, 254; Spaak and Lord Home urge cease-fire upon, 230; Plan for National Reconciliation, 253–58, 337–42; meets with Spaak and Stevenson, 254; writes to Adoula and Tshombe on application of plan, 258; blames Katanga for failure to implement plan, 260–61; replies of Adoula and Tshombe to demands formulated by, 262; meets with Spaak, Gardiner, Kennedy and Stevenson, 263; agrees with Leopoldville to implement "Course of Action," 270; London asks for cease-fire, 273; announces halt to military operations, 274–75. *See also* United Nations

Val Duchesse (castle in Belgium): Kibwe delegation stays in, 174–75

Van Acker, Achille (Belgian Prime Minister), 23

Vanaudenhove, Omer (Liberal Belgian minister), 100

Van Bilsen, A. A. J. (Profesor at Institut Universitaire des Territoires d'Outre-Mer; Abako adviser): Tshombe consults, 63; tells of Tshombe's early intent to secede, 68n

Vance, Sheldon B. (director of the Office of Central African Affairs in U.S. State Department), 192n

Vanden Blook (Belgian political observer at the Elisabethville consulate), 129

Vanden Boeynants, Paul (Belgian minister, Christian-Social Party), 100

Vanderbeken, Hector: Conakat asks to raise funds, 61

Van der Scheuren, Jacques (Belgian minister; Liberal), 100

Vandewalle (Colonel; former administrator of Leopoldville Sûreté): sent to Elisabethville as plenipotentiary, 163; present at Katanga cabinet meeting, 201; consul, 275n

Van Eeckhout, Dr. (first official Conakat adviser, professor at Université d'Etat d'Elisabethville), 16n

Van Gysel Marungu (Société Jean Van Gysel pour l'Elevage et la Culture aux Marungu), 317

Van Hemelrijk, Maurice (Belgian Minister for the Colonies), 25, 43n

Van Roey, André (Director of Banque Nationale du Katanga): expelled, 214; mentioned, 116, 260

Verhaegen, Benoit (Professor at Lovanium, member of scientific committee of C.R.I.S.P.), 204

Verhulpen, Edmond, 12n

Wachuku, Jaja (Nigerian Minister of Foreign Affairs; U.N. official), 287

Wankie Colliery Company, Ltd. (Rhodesian coal-mining company), 324

Washington, D.C., 86, 182, 192, 194. *See* United States of America

Watch-Tower. *See* Kitawala

Weber, Commandant Guy (commander of Belgian para-commandos): arrives at Luano airport, 97; Tshombe gives command of all Katangan military forces to, 98; stresses anti-Communist theme, 99; as symbol of "order" to Europeans, 102; formally included in Mistebel, 104; recalled to Belgium, 159, 198; interprets status of soldiers in Katanga, 163; Congo Plan against U.N. offered by, 195n; extols Katanga strength, 185–86; mentioned, 107, 201

Welensky, Sir Roy (Prime Minister of Federation of the Rhodesias): declarations of on Katanga, 55–58, 281; urges Tshombe to return to Katanga, 229; discusses aid with Kibwe, 271;